ROME

The Virago Woman's Travel Guides

Series Editor: Ros Belford

New York
Paris
Rome

forthcoming:

Amsterdam
Barcelona
London
San Francisco

VIRAGO WOMAN'S GUIDE TO

ROME

ROS BELFORD

Published by VIRAGO PRESS Limited 1993
20–23 Mandela Street, Camden Town, London NW1 0HQ

A CIP catalogue record for this book is available from the
British Library

Printed in Great Britain by Cox & Wyman Ltd, Reading, Berkshire

CONTENTS

ACKNOWLEDGMENTS

This book is dedicated to:
Pat and Colin Belford, Mary Whittam, Heather Clough, Claire
Evans, Gwyneth Moss and Fiona Cochran.

Thanks for help with access and travel to:
Mr Magnani of ENIT, Marco Chelo of Viaggiare, John Bennett of
Osprey and Andrew Delgrosso of SkyBus Holidays.

Special thanks to:
Flaminia Allvin, Sam Cole and Grace Timmins for research and
fact-checking; to Jonathan Buckley, Martin Dunford, Mark
Ellingham and Tim Jepson of *Rough Guides* Ltd for support and
advice; to Miranda Davies for editing, to Lennie Goodings for
accepting the proposal, and to my agent, Vivienne Schuster and her
assistant, Claudia Hill-Norton, for guidance and moral support.

Thanks in Rome to:
Cristina Cilli of *Noi Donne*, and the women at Buon Pastore,
Differenza Donna, Telefono Rosa and Panico; to Fulvia and
Pierluigi of Enjoy Rome; to Signore Casertano of the EPT and
Vittorio Rappacioni of Ripartizione 10; to Corry at the *Navona*,
Lanfranco of *Il Piccolo*, Pilar of *Osiris* and the Reggio family from
the Vineria; and to James, Boudicca, Roy, Pinuccia, Bill, Enrico,
Enrichetta, Valentina, Earl, Lucy, Jessica, Angela, Bruno, Francesco,
Daniela, David Geddings, Anna Maria Benzoni, the Bagnall family,
Matt Cohen and Monica Levy.

And very special thanks in Rome to:
Rupert Small, Bettie Petith, Jen Zaid, Marco and Suzy Chelo,
Barbara Baxter, and (again) to Sam and Flaminia.

Last but not least, thanks in the UK to:
David Hopwood, John Worrall, Anna Fielder, Fiona Wild, Sue
Nelson, Jean Barclay, Jackie Holmes, Josie Barnard, Annie Galpin,
Alessandro Gradenigo, Giovanni Zoli, Mary Hill, the women at
Stanfords, Roland Castro, Devin Scobie and to Mike of Supersonic.

Disclaimer

The author and publisher have made every effort to ensure the accuracy of information contained in *The Woman's Guide to Rome*, but can accept no liability for any loss, injury or inconvenience sustained by any traveller as a result of information or advice contained in this guide.

INTRODUCTION

Y ou don't observe Rome, you collide with it. It's an exuberant, chaotic city in which layers of history are piled one atop the other. A place where cars screech and rattle across ancient cobbles; where designer-dressed youths stand in Renaissance doorways chattering into portable phones; where tiny shrines to the Madonna bear offerings of plastic roses; and where tramps sleep beneath the arcades of the Colosseum.

Rome is a city of encounters, some predictable, some strange. Within the space of a few hours you can be chatted up by a Latin Lover, quizzed about your faith by a Mancunian pilgrim or a North Carolinan nun, receive advice on your hairstyle from a bank clerk, and be embroiled in a broken-English conversation about world peace with a self-styled guru.

If you are not to be cowed by it, you have to *react*. Be impetuous and spontaneous. The Romans are – whether they're screaming at you because you've hogged a public phone for all of two minutes, rubbing up against you on a crowded bus, or trying to short-change you as you buy a bus ticket. Respond in kind: yell back, elbow them in the stomach or count the notes and glare if you've been fiddled. Get the hang of the more abrasive aspects of the city, and you can relax and enjoy its gentler side.

For in many ways Rome is an old-fashioned, very human city where the life of the community continues alongside the droves of tourists. Shopping is done in little groceries, delicatessens and daily food markets; leftover pasta is put out for the neighbourhood cats; and locals stop to chat – on the streets, in bars and out of windows. It's not difficult to become a part of it, especially if you speak a little Italian. You simply become a regular in a bar, shop or trattoria.

By way of contrast there's designer Rome: streets lined with famous-name boutiques, where you can sit in a pavement café and watch the beautiful people swan by. And though the days of *La Dolce Vita* are over, there's still a certain dark decadence to the city's nightlife if you know where to look: bars where you can drink with lonely gays, dishevelled punks and ageing transvestites. If you prefer to bypass the decadence, there are any number of bustling cafés and chic wine bars – many of them ideal for solo drinking – and Italy's liberal licensing hours mean that you can often breakfast, lunch and drink into the early hours at the same establishment.

The city's historical and cultural heritage is overwhelming, and needs to be taken slowly: ancient sites, medieval churches and Renaissance palaces, to say nothing of the museums and art galleries. But Rome, above all, is the city of Baroque, the lavish, voluptuous fountains, palaces and churches at once expressing its glamorous, megalomaniac vulgarity and the wealth and power of the Roman Catholic Church.

That power is undeniable, and in Rome you will see the effects, both positive and negative, which the Church through the ages has had on the lives of individuals ranging from saints to courtesans. You will also witness the potency of twentieth-century Catholicism. There are monks and nuns everywhere – riding the buses, leading groups of pilgrims, sightseeing, shopping or going about their business in the Vatican. Whenever there's a beatification (and under John Paul II these have become increasingly frequent) Catholics from all over the world flood the city. And since the collapse of Communism, Catholics from Eastern Europe have travelled to Rome on arduous coach journeys, to pray in churches which, a few years ago, they could only dream of seeing.

You'll never be stuck for something to see or do, and when you tire of culture, there are plenty of escapes – shops, markets, parks, clubs, opera and concerts in the city itself, and Lake Bracciano and the sea short bus rides away.

Whether you're attracted by streetlife, nightlife, shopping, art, architecture or the Church, Rome is an invigorating city for women. Follow our advice, master the technique of dealing with the Romans, be ready for new experiences and prepared for the unexpected, and you'll soon find that things happen. The city is open to *you*.

PRACTICALITIES

WHEN TO GO

Rome's weather is a force to be reckoned with. The temperature can hit 30 degrees centigrade in May and June, soar to 40 degrees in July and August, and spasmodically break into dramatic storms. September is the most clement month; from November through to Easter it's rarely cold and sometimes sunny, but it can rain non-stop for a whole week. After Easter wild flowers scatter the ancient sites, banks of azaleas grace Via Veneto and the Spanish Steps, and though you'll still need an umbrella, you can expect some sunny days.

The Easter period is extremely busy, as Catholics flood the city for the Pope's blessing on St Peter's Square. If you're not coming for religious reasons, try to come later. May, June and July are all pretty busy – so book a hotel room well in advance – but in August, as the temperature reaches barbecue point, virtually all Romans abandon the city, and restaurants, bars, and some of the shops close. Reserve a room a couple of months in advance for September, the most popular tourist month, and don't count on finding a room easily in October, when the weather can also be lovely and warm enough to swim, if you're planning on day trips. If you can cope with the odd rainstorm, consider coming in late autumn or winter, when hassle is minimal. Not only are you inconspicuous, dressed in city winter clothes, but the testosterone level in Roman men appears to be diminished by the cold.

FESTIVALS AND EVENTS

Opera season from November to June, with open-air performances in the Baths of Caracalla from late June to early September.

Classical concert season from October to June, with open-air performances in the summer.

Estate Romana – a classical, jazz, film and rock festival with many events in outdoor venues – runs from mid June to the end of August.

JANUARY
5 Last day of *La Befana* in Piazza Navona (see December).
17 Festa di Sant'Antonio Abate – animal blessing service at Sant'Eusebio all'Esquilino.
21 Festa di Sant'Agnese – blessing and shearing of two lambs at Sant'Agnese fuori le Mura. The wool is used to make *palliums* (cloaks) for the Pope.

FEBRUARY
During the Lenten Carnival clubs and bars have fancy-dress nights and children have fun chucking water-filled balloons.
3 Sore throats are blessed at San Biagio on Via Giulia.

MARCH
9 (Or the first Sunday afterwards) Feast of Santa Francesca Romana, the patron saint of motorists. Celebrations include blessing the city's trams and buses.

APRIL
Holy Week Scores of events, including a pilgrimage to the Scala Santa. The tourist office produces a special leaflet every year.

MAY
Mid-month Antique fair on Via dei Coronari.
Art show on Via Margutta (precise date changes every year).

JUNE
Mid-month *Estate Romana* begins.
24 Festa di San Giovanni. *Porchetta* (roast pork) and snail eating in the Lateran District.

JULY
Estate Romana in full swing. Jazz concerts at the Castel Sant'Angelo.
Late Festa de Noantri in Trastevere – a folksy festival with fireworks, processions, lots of food, drink and dancing. Viale Trastevere is lined with stalls selling kitsch and tack.

AUGUST
Estate Romana continues.
5 Festa della Madonna della Neve at Santa Maria Maggiore.
15 *Ferragosto*. VIRTUALLY EVERYTHING CLOSES. Most people left in Rome are tourists (though an increasing number of Romans are electing to stay behind to make the most of the relative peace).

SEPTEMBER
Early *Sagra di Uva* – grape festival in the Basilica of Maxentius with folksy entertainment. Trade fairs.

OCTOBER
Mid-month Antique fair in Via dei Coronari.
Late Art exhibition on Via Margutta.

NOVEMBER
1 All Saints' Day. Special services in all churches including St Peter's.
2 All Souls' Day. Candlelit prayers for the dead in cemeteries.

DECEMBER
8 Feast of the Immaculate Conception, celebrated with flowers by the Pope and the fire brigade at the column on Piazza di Spagna.
Mid-month *La Befana*, a toy, Christmas decoration and sweet fair on Piazza Navona. The Holy Bambino is displayed in a crib scene in Santa Maria in Aracoeli, and children recite poems to him.
24 Midnight Mass celebrated by the Pope in St Peter's, and before the relics of the holy crib in Santa Maria Maggiore.
25 High Mass celebrated by the Pope in St Peter's.
31 Te Deum at the Gesù in the presence of the Pope. Wild parties elsewhere in the city (with glasses hurled out of windows).

Getting There

The first thing you need is a good travel agent – if you don't have one already. Italia nel Mondo is an efficient Italian specialist. Supersonic Travel Ltd are conscientious, knowledgeable and reliable, and used by many people who travel for their profession. If you're a student or under twenty-six, companies like Campus Travel or STA specialise in youth fares.

Rome By Air

The cheapest way to get to Rome (from under £100) is on an air/coach package, valid for six nights only. You fly out on a charter and return by taking a train to Milan, and from there a bus home. Such deals are operated from May to October by – among others – Italy SkyBus and Itavia.

There are charter flights to Rome year round from Gatwick, and in summer from Luton, Manchester and Edinburgh on selected days of the week. These currently cost from £159 to £249, depending on the date of departure and home airport (fares are cheapest in May and peak from mid July to the end of August). You can make further savings (around £20) by getting SkyBus's Skypass fare – there are a limited number available on all charters and they're sold on a first-come-first-served basis. You have to pay the full amount at the time of booking, and cannot change or cancel.

There are scheduled flights daily to Rome from Heathrow and Gatwick. From Manchester and Birmingham the only direct flights are on Saturdays. At other times you fly via Zurich, Milan, Amsterdam or Paris. Fares start at around £170 (for an Apex, bookable 14 days in advance, on condition that you stay at least one Saturday night), but can rise to £300 in high season. Ask your travel agent about cheaper, consolidated fares.

When travelling with a baby, especially if you're breastfeeding, it's worth asking, when you check in, for a seat next to another woman. Certain children's car seats are approved by the Civil Aviation Authority, and can be attached to seats in aeroplanes; they can make your child not only safer, but more comfortable. Approved models include Two Way, Two Stage and Recliner seats by Mothercare and Britax. In this case you will, of course, need to book your baby or toddler a seat, and pay the standard child fare.

Fares for babies and children vary considerably. With SkyBus, babies (i.e. under-twos) not occupying their own seat on charter flights travel free, and children are charged 25% of the adult fare, whereas on a scheduled flight you can pay as much as 50% of the standard fare and 65% of the adult Apex fare for a child aged between two and twelve. Finally, if you are over twenty-eight weeks pregnant certain airlines will refuse to carry you. Check when you book.

Packages

Many package companies specialise in city breaks, which can be better value than travelling independently. Thomson are usually the cheapest, with seven-day holidays starting from £279. Osprey and Cresta are also worth considering, as they usually use small, family-run hotels, while Time Off's holidays are slightly more expensive, but high-quality, and tend to attract a discerning clientele. When selecting a package, don't be afraid to phone the companies' head offices for more details about their hotels and locations, and do try to avoid staying near Termini station.

Overland to Rome

Unless you hate flying, there's little point in taking a train to Rome. Fares for under twenty-sixes are £170, for over twenty-sixes £176, and the journey takes around 25 hours. Trains do make sense, however, if you're calling into Rome as part of a tour around Europe, in which case the Interrail card (for under twenty-sixes) and Interrail Plus (for over-twenty-sixes), which offer unlimited travel for a month, are good value. In Western Europe sleepers are generally allocated according to sex (unless, of course, you're part of a mixed-sex group) but it *can* happen that you end up with men in your carriage. Berths in couchettes are NOT allocated according to the sex of the travellers. The train companies assume that because passengers are supposed to sleep in their clothes, solo women will be safe.

National Express Eurolines run a coach service to Rome, which takes approximately 32 hours. Fares are not particularly cheap – around £150 return for over-twenty-fives and around £140 for under-twenty-fives. If you want to drive, expect a journey time of around 17 hours from Calais (slightly less from Zeebrugge or Ostend). The AA will provide tailor-made routes, either on or off motorways (£13.75 for members, £15.75 for non-members).

The Channel crossing you choose will, of course, depend largely on where you live. From the North of England an overnight crossing (14 hours) with North Sea Ferries from Hull to Zeebrugge is worth considering. Fares are currently £52 each way for foot passengers (with a reclining seat), £63 each way for a basic cabin, and £72 for a cabin with loo, shower and basin. Women travelling alone are not put in cabins with men, and women travelling with babies get a cabin to themselves for the price of a single berth. Cars cost around £66 each way.

From the South, the swiftest and most frequent Channel crossings are operated by Hoverspeed from Dover to Calais (35 min by hovercraft; 50 min by the Sea Cat catamaran). Fares are from £46 return for foot passengers and from £112 to £260 return for cars (including driver) depending on the season. There are also some special inclusive deals if you're travelling in a car with children. Only the Sea Cat has special mother-and-baby facilities.

USEFUL PHONE NUMBERS

Italy SkyBus tel. 071 373 6055
Itavia tel. 061 740 5095
Supersonic Travel Ltd tel. 071 839 6856
Italia nel Mondo Travel Services tel. 071 834 7651

Campus Travel tel. 071 730 3402
30 branches in the UK including:
Edinburgh tel. 031 225 611
Bristol tel. 0272 292494
Cambridge tel. 0223 324283
Oxford tel. 0865 242067
Manchester tel. 061 274 3105
Leeds tel. 0532 461155

STA Travel tel. 071 937 9921
Branches include:
Bristol tel. 0272 294399
Cambridge tel. 0223 300247
Oxford tel. 0865 792800
Manchester tel. 061 834 0668
Leeds tel. 0532 449212

Cresta tel. 061 929 0000
Osprey tel. 031 557 1555
Time Off Ltd tel. 071 235 8070
Thomson Citybreaks tel. 071 387 6534
Eurotrain tel. 071 730 3402
National Express Eurolines tel. 071 730 0202
AA European Routes tel. 0272 308242 (or call into your local AA shop, who will also book ferry crossings)
Hoverspeed tel. 0304 240241
P&O Ferries tel. 0304 223000 or 0304 203388
Sealink Stena tel. 0233 647047
North Sea Ferries tel. 0482 795141

Ferries take longer and are not always cheaper. P&O have crossings every two hours (journey time 1 hour 15 min) from Dover to Calais (£23 one way for foot passengers; between £135 and £195 return for a car plus £24 return for each adult depending on the time of travel). Prices are the same for the four-hour Dover–Ostend crossing. They also have a special deal for adults travelling with children. All ferries on the Dover–Calais route have mother-and-baby facilities, but one of the Dover–Ostend ferries, the *Reine Astrid*, does not. All Sealink Stena's ferries have mother-and-baby areas, and their fares are similar to P&O's. They operate up to twenty Dover–Calais crossings daily, depending on the season.

Regulations

Passports and Permits

At the time of writing you need a full passport or Visitor's passport to visit Italy, and you are supposed to carry ID with you at all times. In fact, in the unlikely event of your being stopped by the police, giving them your hotel telephone number is sufficient – they can then phone and check your details. Bear in mind, though, that you WILL need your passport for changing money.

Once you arrive, you are obliged to register with the police within three days, but if you are staying at a hotel, this will be done for you. For information phone 4686 ext 2858 or 2987. Once you are registered you are allowed to remain in the country for three months if you are not working, eight days if you are. After this period you need to get a residence permit [*permesso di soggiorno*] from the police (go to the Questura's Ufficio Stranieri, Via Genova 3, tel. 4686 2987, and prepare for a long wait). Many expats avoid the bureaucracy by not registering when they arrive – which means there's no record of how long they've been in the country.

If you want to work, in theory you need a work permit [*permesso di lavoro*], though a lot of employers give work only to people without permits – that way they don't need to declare them. If your employer *is* above-board, he or she should help you sort this out, but you'll still have to spend a long time queuing at the Ufficio Stranieri. EC members should have no problem; non-EC members can expect to have to wade through seas of bureaucracy.

Insurance

It's wise to take out private insurance to cover you for cancellation or delay of your holiday, and loss of or damage to luggage, money and valuables. Some policies allow you to claim up to £100 if your luggage is delayed. It's also important to be covered for personal liability and accidents, and to make sure your policy includes treatment and repatriation in the case of illness or injury. Relying on an

E111 (see Health) for medical treatment is not recommended.

If you intend to ride a Vespa, make sure you are covered, and if you hire a car, sign the collision damage waiver. A good travel agent should be able to advise you on policies. A week's cover should cost less than £20.

Money

There is just one unit of currency in Italy – the lira – and for some time the exchange rate has been around 2200 lire to the pound. (1390 to the US dollar and 960 to the Australian dollar). Once you've paid commission or the Eurocard transaction fee, however, you can end up with less than 2000 lire to the pound. At the time of writing both the lira and sterling have moved out of the EMS and devalued, so future shifts in exchange rates are difficult to predict.

It takes time to get used to all the noughts – something of which less scrupulous Romans are only too aware. Try to ensure that you arrive with some low-denomination notes – even better, ask around your friends who've been to Italy if they've any spare coins. Keeping track of the change from L100,000 when you've spent L700 on a metro ticket is not easy.

DENOMINATIONS

COINS	NOTES
L5	L 1000
L10 these two are very rare, and virtually worthless	L 2000
	L 5000
L50	L 10,000
L100	L 50,000
L200	L 100,000
L500	

Changing Money

No bank or exchange bureau [cambio] will allow you to change money without a passport. Traveller's cheques and Eurocheques are widely accepted, and you can get cash advances on Visa, Amex and Access (MasterCard). You'll always be charged commission on traveller's cheques – sometimes a percentage of the amount cashed, sometimes a fixed fee per transaction, and sometimes a charge per cheque (so avoid £20 traveller's cheques). Make sure that your Eurocheques are the new-style ones with an EC watermark. The old ones, abolished because they were too easy to forge, are defunct.

There are a number of automatic cash machines in which (in theory) you should be able to use your Eurocard or credit card if you have a PIN number. Don't depend on them because if *one* goes wrong they all do. More reliable, if you have cash, are the cash exchange machines, where you feed in your sterling in exchange for lire. Read the instructions carefully first, or you may end up with yen or dollars.

Italy is still basically a cash culture, and outside banks and larger hotels credit cards are looked on with suspicion. Even shops and restaurants which claim to accept credit cards can be very unwilling to do so when the time comes. If you're short of cash, it's worth informing the restaurant when you book that you'll be paying with plastic.

Banks and Exchange Offices

There are banks throughout the centre, most of them open Monday to Friday from between 8 a.m. and 9 a.m. to between 1 p.m. and 1.30 p.m. and again for an hour or so in the afternoon. Precise opening times of branches of the major banks are:

> Credito Italiano: 8.35 a.m.–1.35 p.m.; 2.50–4.50 p.m.
> Banco di Santo Spirito: 8.15 a.m.–1.30 p.m.; 2.45–3.30 p.m.
> Banco di Roma: 8.35 a.m.–1.35 p.m.; 3–4.30 p.m.
> BNL: 8.35 a.m.–1.35 p.m.; 2.45 p.m.–4.15 p.m.
> Monti dei Paschi di Siena; 8.35 a.m.–1.35 p.m.; 2.45–4.15 p.m.

Outside these hours you could go to Termini station, where the Banco Nazionale delle Comunicazione is open Mon–Sat 8.30 a.m.–7.30 p.m., or to one of the exchange offices. The following are central: *Cambio* Via San Vincenzo 20 (near the Trevi) (daily 9 a.m.–8 p.m.) *Cambio* Piazza San Lorenzo in Lucina 39 (Mon–Sat 9.30 a.m.–1 p.m.; 4–7.30 p.m.).

The Cost of Living

The cost of living in Italy is roughly the same as in Britain, though some things are cheaper and others are more expensive. Public transport and wine are very cheap; meals and beer are slightly more expensive. Prices of alcohol, soft drinks, tea and coffee can be very high in smart cafés. Museum entrance charges range from around L4000 to L10,000. Bearing in mind Italy's current financial crisis the inflation rate could soar over the next year. Keep an eye on developments in the newspapers, or contact the Italian State Tourist Office in London (see below) before you go. All prices in this book were correct in late 1992.

If you take a room without a bathroom, have a picnic breakfast and lunch, a cheap meal in the evening followed by a couple of drinks standing up (it's cheaper) in a basic bar, you can manage (just) on under L75,000 per day. As soon as you decide to stay somewhere more comfortable – say a room with a bathroom in a two-star hotel – you can expect to spend well over L100,000 per day on subsistence. Doing Rome in style – staying in a four-star hotel, and eating and drinking in classy cafés and restaurants – can't be done for much less than L350,000.

Information

The Italian State Tourist Office in London has a selection of free brochures. Most useful is the yearly *Traveller's Handbook*. Write or drop in to ENIT, 1 Princes Street, London W1 (tel. 071 408 1254) open Mon–Fri 9 a.m.–2.30 p.m.

When you arrive in Rome – especially if you have no accommodation booked – it's worth going straight away to Enjoy Rome, Via Varese 39 (tel 445.1843). This recently established company will find you a hotel room in a safe location, store your luggage, give you maps and information on the city and its sights – all for no charge. They also will help in an emergency, for example if you lose your passport. Phone line currently open until 10 p.m.

The tourist offices (EPTs) in Rome itself have free maps, free leaflets about various sights, and produce a monthly, multilingual 'What's On' [Carnet di Roma]. There's also a practical guide, *Here's Rome*, but some of the information (particularly opening times) is unreliable.

Though the staff can't book a hotel room for you, they will phone and make a reservation – very useful if you arrive on spec, and far better than traipsing around or phoning yourself. Relying on the tourist office for public transport information is not recommended – they can be hopelessly out of date!

Maps
The free maps supplied by the tourist office are really not adequate. Ours should be OK for most situations, but you will need a detailed map if you intend to spend much time in the outlying areas. If you want a comprehensive street map with a directory, look out for *Roma Facile (Easy Rome)* on newsstands. It's in book form, which makes it easy to consult as you're walking along. If you want to buy a map in Britain, the best is a sheet map published by Studio FMB, which includes public transport routes. This is available from good travel bookshops like Stanfords (12–14 Long Acre, London WC2E 9LP). The main problem with the FMB map, however, is that the directory is on the back, which makes it awkward to consult in the street.

What's On
The listings in the *Carnet di Roma* are not comprehensive, and for the full range of what's on in Rome, you should get hold of *Trova*

Roma – a listings magazine which comes free with *La Repubblica* newspaper on Thursdays. If you miss it, there are daily arts listings in *La Repubblica* and *Il Messagero*, and the town is plastered with posters advertising classical concerts, political meetings, gigs, theatre and ballet. For information about women's and lesbian events, ask the staff and look at the noticeboard in the feminist bookshop *Al Tempo Ritrovato*, Piazza Farnese 103, though the information is not always up to date. More reliable sources are the women who run and attend Panico's lesbian night (Via del Panico 17) on Sunday evenings, and the women at the feminist centre, Buon Pastore (Via San Francesco di Sales 1A).

EPT Offices in Rome:
Via Parigi 5 (tel. 488 3748/488 1851) Open Mon–Sat 8.15 a.m.–7.15 p.m.
Termini Station (tel. 487 1270/482 4078) Open daily 8.15 a.m.–7.15 p.m.
Fiumicino Airport (tel. 65010255) Open Mon–Sat 8.15 a.m.–7 p.m.

Access for Study   If, as a student or researcher, you need access to ancient sites which are usually closed to the public, you need to find out whether the site in question is administered by the state or the local council, and then in which area [*ripartizione*] it lies. Write to them first, by all means, but don't expect a reply. Be prepared to go in person. You'll make more progress if you can get hold of someone's name.

Most sites are administered by either:

Ripartizione 10 (Comune di Roma)
Via del Portico d'Ottavia 29
00186 ROMA
Tel. 6710 3819/6710 2075

or

Soprintendente Archeologico di Roma
Piazza Santa Maria Nova 53
00186 ROMA
Fax 678 7689

Communications

TELEPHONE NUMBERS IN ROME ARE IN THE PROCESS OF CHANGING. FOR APPROXIMATELY TWO MONTHS AFTER A NUMBER HAS CHANGED THERE WILL BE A MESSAGE (IN ITALIAN) INFORMING YOU OF THE NEW ONE. AFTER THAT, IF YOU DIAL A DEFUNCT NUMBER THERE WILL BE A MESSAGE TELLING YOU TO PHONE DIRECTORY INQUIRIES (TEL. 12). IF YOU DON'T SPEAK ITALIAN ASK IMMEDIATELY IF THE OPERATOR SPEAKS ENGLISH. IT IS POSSIBLE THAT SOMEONE ON DUTY WILL.

Mailing

A recent survey proved what anyone who has ever posted a letter in Italy knew already: the Italian postal service is the worst in Europe. Only 14% of first-class letters to destinations within Italy arrive the next day (in Britain 90% do) and postage rates are high. Expect postcards and letters to take at least a week (usually longer) to reach Britain. Not surprisingly, no Italian trusts the postal service and there are more fax machines per head in Italy than anywhere else in Europe. If you need something to arrive swiftly, you should use a courier service (see below).

The Vatican postal service is far more efficient. There's a branch of the Vatican post office inside the Vatican Museums, and most of the ecclesiastical souvenir shops in St Peter's sell stamps. Postcards sent via the Vatican can arrive in Britain in less than three days.

There's no need to use an Italian post office for sending letters or postcards, as all tobacconists sell stamps. Normal opening hours are Mon–Sat 8 a.m.–1 p.m.; 4–8 p.m. If you can't afford a courier, use a post office and hope. To increase your chances you could register [raccomandare], insure [assicurare] or send your letter or parcel express [espresso]. In fact, for some reason registering is often quicker than sending express. Either registering or sending mail express costs L3,000; insurance L6,000. You can also use the central post office as a poste restante address.

USEFUL ADDRESSES

Posta Centrale, Piazza San Silvestro, 000186 ROMA (tel. 6771). Open Mon–Fri 8.30 a.m.–7.40 p.m. (for parcels under 1 kg.) and 5.30 p.m. (for parcels over 1 kg.). Sat 8.30 a.m.–11.50 a.m.

DHL, Via Labicana 78B and Via Portonaccio 21C (tel. 794 191)

UPS ALIMONDO, Via della Magliana 329 (tel. 550 3371)

Phoning

Most public phone booths are on busy roads, making it impossible to hear yourself, never mind the person on the end of the line. Fortunately, hundreds of bars have public phones – though here, too, blasting music and loud voices can make communication difficult. An increasing number of public phones take only cards – these cost L5000 and L10,000 from tobacconists. Otherwise, you need a supply of L100, L200 and L500 coins, which are dropped in before you dial. Very rarely in a bar or hotel you'll come across a phone which takes only tokens [gettoni]. These are worth (and function as) L200 coins, and you should be able to buy them from the bar or reception desk.

If you have long-distance calls to make, it's far cheaper to use the booths at the central post office than to phone from your hotel, where you'll automatically be charged a supplement. It's also less bothersome than using a public callbox, as Romans made to wait more than two minutes for a phone can get very aggressive. At the public phone office on Piazza San Silvestro (open daily 8 a.m.– 11.30 p.m.) you pay afterwards for the number of units [*scatti*] you have used. The cheap rate for international calls operates between 10 p.m. and 8 a.m., and all day Sunday.

To dial Britain, the code is 0044 followed by the city or area code minus the 0 and the subscriber's phone number. The ringing tone in Italy is long, with very long gaps; the engaged tone is similar to that in Britain. If the person you are calling has had his or her phone cut off for not paying the bill, it will still sound to you as if it's ringing.

When Italians answer the phone, they say *Pronto* (which means 'Ready'). To ask to speak to someone you should say either *Posso parlare con X?* or – less formal – *c'e X?*. To tell them who you are, say *Sono Y*.

Faxing

Most hotels – even many of the smaller ones – have fax machines which residents can use to send and receive messages. Otherwise, there are faxing facilities at many stationers [*cartolerie*] and a number of tobacconists are beginning to install public fax machines. Rates can vary wildly.

Some centrally located fax offices are:

> Esperia Fides, Via di S Pantaleo 63–5
> tel. 654 1634, fax 654 2973
> Via della Scala 10 (tobacconist in Trastevere – open Thur–Tues 8 a.m.–1.30 p.m.; 4–11.30 p.m.)
> Corso Vittorio Emanuele 133 (tobacconist near Piazza Navona)
> Piazza del Biscione 99 (tobacconist just off Campo dei Fiori)
> Via Guglia 68 (photocopy and fax bureau open 9 a.m.–7 p.m.)

The Media

TELEVISION

It's not true that Italian television consists solely of housewives playing strip poker – there are scantily clad games-show hostesses and dollyish continuity girls as well. The profile of women on TV is pretty depressing, largely because of the number of channels (there are over a thousand nationwide, and every Italian can receive at least forty).

The theory is that Italian men are more likely to pause as they zap through the stations with their *telecommando* if they see a sexy girl.

Television was deregulated in 1976 after the Corte Costituzionale ruled that the monopoly of the state-run broadcasting corporation, RAI (Radiotelevisione Italiana), was unconstitutional. Though live broadcasts (essential for news and sport) remained an RAI monopoly, it was otherwise a free-for-all. Nowadays there is only one nationwide rival to RAI – Fininvest, run by media mogul Silvio Berlusconi, which currently has four downmarket channels (which screen ALL the big American soaps, most of the major American films, and pads its output with quizzes and games shows – including the notorious strip poker show *Colpo Grosso*, which is broadcast nightly on Italia 7). Daytime TV is appalling – games shows financed by cake manufacturers with long breaks between rounds while the camera alternatively caresses the contours of a curvaceous hostess and a fruit bun.

Each of the three RAI channels is supported by one of the major political parties, and the propaganda level of their news coverage resembles that of the pre-glasnost USSR. RAI Uno, run by the Christian Democrats, is the one to watch if you want to catch up on the latest doings at the Vatican; RAI Due, run by the Socialists, has Socialist MPs commenting on everything from film to finance; and RAI Tre is owned and dominated by the PDS, the former Communist Party. Most Italians flick between all three. Even if you don't understand Italian, the news on any channel can be highly entertaining – newsreaders (usually tieless and leather-jacketed on RAI Tre) looking at the wrong camera, and news footage being screened at the wrong time. If you stay in a four- or five-star hotel, you can usually get CNN.

Of the three state channels, RAI Tre is the most intellectual and up-market, with good documentaries, arts coverage and some experimental programmes. RAI Uno is more middlebrow and family-orientated; RAI Due is slightly more up-market. All try their utmost to get the screening rights to major US films in order to attract audiences away from the Berlusconi channels.

Radio

Radio was also deregulated in 1976, and Rome's airwaves are so packed with stations that you can end up listening to a Mozart symphony overlaid by a House beat. Radio Uno and Due are a bit like the UK's Radio Two, with a mixture of light music, comedy and chat shows. Radio Due broadcasts news every hour on the half-hour, Radio Uno's is less frequent. Radio Tre is the classical music station, with delightfully pedantic presenters who never mention a composer without a Christian name (listen out for Mozart . . . Wolfgang Amadeus and Tchaikovsky . . . Peter Ilyich). The other two RAI stations play pop and rock, and all five link up at night as the US-and-Euro-rock-and-pop station Stereonotte. Best of the independent stations are Radio Centro Suona (101.3 FM), which plays mostly black music (and has its own record label); and Radio Radicale, a mix of pop, rock and Radical Party propaganda. The women's radio station, Radio Donna, appeared to have folded at last check, but it's worth flicking through the stations to see if it's started up again.

Newspapers and magazines

Look at the average Italian newsstand and you may have difficulty telling the difference between the news weeklies and soft porn. The three main news magazines, *L'Espresso*, *Panorama* and *Europeo*, compete with one another to produce the most provocative, talked-about cover of the week. 1992's most notorious cover was a supine nude photographed as an undulating desertscape. No prizes for guessing which part of her anatomy figured (thanks to a toy palm tree and green filter) as the oasis. The editors know their market: a cheeky cover can mean 50,000 extra sales. The inside pages are full of naked women as well – illustrating po-faced articles about the fear of skin cancer.

The editor of the weekly satirical newspaper *Il Cuore* (who ridiculed the porno-trend with a cover of former CD chairman, Forlani, with his testicles hanging out of his pants) published the nudity ratings for the three magazines for the first half of 1992. *L'Espresso* came top, with 91 pairs of breasts and 49 pairs of buttocks.

In the 1960s and 1970s, as Italy rebelled against Catholicism, female nudity was considered to be an expression of freedom, even a political statement. Nowadays it sells magazines.

Newspapers

Italian newspapers are relatively free of nudity, which may have something to do with why less than 10% of Italians buy them. Of the Rome-based papers, *Il Messagero* is written in the most straightforward style and is a good source for stories about the city; *La Repubblica* is more gossipy, but it's 'knowing' style can pall after a while and the stories rarely live up to the promise of the exciting-sounding headlines. Buying it on Thursday is a must, however, for the What's On supplement, *Trova Roma*. The right-ish *Corriere della Sera* is serious and authoritative, and of the left-wing papers, *L'Unità* and *Il Manifesto* are the best. The recently launched *Indipendente* owes much to the UK's *Independent* – it remains to be seen how it fares.

Women's Magazines

For decades the bestselling magazine in Italy was the pious handbook for happy families, *Famiglia Cristiana*, Vatican-approved and on sale in church. It has now been ousted by a Berlusconi publication – *TV Sorrisi e Canzoni* – a TV listings magazine. Neither of these makes compelling reading, but the downmarket gossip magazines are great fun; their pages are largely filled with the doings and misdoings of European royals. As you might imagine, the Windsors are particular favourites, and the Italian magazines speculate even more wildly about their private lives than their British counterparts. There are also loads of glossies – including Italian versions of *Cosmopolitan, Elle* and *Vogue*.

Feminist Magazines

For feminist magazines you need to go to the women's bookshop *Al Tempo Ritrovato* (see p. 311). The long-established monthly *Noi Donne* is reliable, taking a sharp, intelligent look at current affairs at home and abroad; *Inoltre* (founded in 1991) is an energetic political and cultural monthly, well worth checking out; *Leggere Donne* is a bimonthly review of books, theatre and cinema by women; and there are a number of more esoteric and specialist publications, like *Fluttuaria* produced by the Milanese women's group Cicip & Ciciap.

Expat Magazines

Rome-based English-language magazines come and go, but *Wanted in Rome* is a long-standing biweekly, usually more interesting for its ads and What's On listings than for its editorials. This is the place to look or advertise for flats, flat-shares, holiday accommodation, English doctors and dentists, babysitters and jobs. It's also worth looking out for *Metropolitan*, a free biweekly launched in 1992, which has the occasional revealing article, along with perfunctory What's On listings.

Language

It goes without saying that the more Italian you speak, the better time you'll have. It's not a difficult language and the BBC course, *Buongiorno Italia*, is a superbly organised introduction, deftly combining practical vocabulary with teaching grammar. It's well worth buying the cassettes – all the conversations are taped on the street and in cafés, so you hear Italian as it is really spoken right from the start – and you should also look out for repeats of the back-up TV and radio broadcasts. Beware of courses which are studio-recorded, with false conversations at an unrealistically slow speed.

You will, however, have to get used to the Roman accent. They often leave the ends off words – *vabbé* instead of *va bene* (OK) and *vie' qua* instead of *viene qua* (come here) – and the sound 'ch' (as in *il centro*) is often softened to 'sh'.

Remember, too, that there are informal and formal versions of the second person: you use 'tu' to a friend (or, if you're under thirty, to a stranger of your own age or younger) and 'lei' to strangers. If a stranger/business colleague introduces themselves as, say, 'Vittorio', you are supposed to use the 'tu'. You could continue using 'lei' in the hope of signalling that you want to keep things formal, but unless your Italian is very strong, it will just be assumed that you are ignorant! Or they'll explicitly tell you to use the 'tu' – and refusing is not the done thing.

Women who appear to be over thirty are usually referred to as *Signora* (Mrs or Madame). If you are (or look as if you are) under thirty, expect to be referred to as *Signorina* (Miss).

Pronunciation

Once you know the basic rules of pronunciation, you should have no problems: every word is pronounced exactly as it appears, with the emphasis on the penultimate syllable, unless there is an accent on the last vowel (as in caffè, così, però).

Vowels

a open – almost like the posh English u as in pub (Italians refer to a pub as a pab)
e like the English, as in met
i like the English ea, as in meat
o short, as in got
u long, like the oo in pool

Consonants

c before e or i soft, as in chance (in Roman dialect 'sh')
c before a, o, u hard, as in cat
ch before e or i hard, as in cat
g before e or i soft, as in gesture
g before a, o, u hard, as in gut
gh before e or i hard, as in get
To soften a c or g before a, o, or u, an i is inserted. This is not pronounced. Giovanni is pronounced 'jovaani', not 'jeeohvarni'.
sci and sce are soft, like sh
sca, sco, scu, sche and schi are hard, like sk
gn is like ni in onion
gli is like lli in million (a mix between 1 and y)
h is silent
r is rolled
z tricky! sometimes like ts and sometimes dz

BASICS

Good morning	Buongiorno
Good afternoon/evening	Buona sera (after about 4 p.m.)
Good night	Buona notte
Hello/bye bye	Ciao (informal: not to be used in business situations)
Goodbye	Arrivederci
Yes	Sì
No	No
That's fine/OK	Va bene
That's great	Va benissimo
Please	Per favore or (if you're really trying to charm something out of someone) Per piacere
Thank you	Grazie
How are you?	Come sta? (formal) Come stai? (to a friend)
Fine	Bene
OK	Abbastanza bene
So-So	Così Così
Do you speak English?	Parla inglese?
I don't understand	Non capisco/non ho capito
I don't know	Non lo so
Excuse me	Scusi (polite); scusa (informal)
Excuse me (more assertive, but polite)	Permesso (as you attempt to elbow you way off a crowded bus)
May I?	Posso?
Sorry	Mi dispiace (if you mean it) Scusi/scusa (if you don't really)
Morning	La mattina
Afternoon	Il pomeriggio
Evening	La sera
This evening	Stasera
Night	La notte
Today	Oggi
Tomorrow	Domani
Day after tomorrow	Dopodomani
Next week	La settimana prossima
Last week	La settimana scorsa
Yesterday	Ieri
Now	Adesso (i.e. in ten or fifteen minutes)
Immediately	Subito (i.e. in five minutes)
Ready	Pronto
Are you ready?	Sei pronto/a?
Wait!	Aspetta!
Here	Qui or Qua
There	Lì or Là
Everywhere	Dappertutto
Good	Buono

Bad	Cattivo
Very good	Buonissimo/Ottimo
Terrible	Terribile
Big	Grande
Small	Piccolo
Cheap	Economico
Expensive	Caro
Early	Presto
Late	In ritardo
Near	Vicino
Near here	Qui vicino
Far	Lontano
Is it far from here?	È lontano da qui?
Free/vacant	Libero
Occupied/busy	Occupato
I'm busy	Sono molto occupata/impegnata
With	Con
Without	Senza
More	Più
A bit more	Un po di più
Less	Meno
Enough	Basta
Hot	Caldo
Cold	Freddo
Open	Aperto
Closed	Chiuso
Entrance	Ingresso
Exit	Uscita
Toilet	Toilette or Bagno
Push	Spingere
Pull	Tirare

QUESTION WORDS

Where?	Dove?
Where is?	Dov'è?
Where are?	Dove sono?
What?	Che?
Who?	Chi?
When?	Quando?
Why?	Perché?
How?	Come?
How much?	Quanto?

STREET DIRECTIONS

Left	Sinistra
Right	Destra
Straight ahead	Sempre dritto

| On the corner | All'angolo |
| Opposite | Di fronte |

HOTELS

Hotel	Albergo
Do you have a room?	Ha una camera?
for one/two	per una/due persona/e?
for one/two nights	per una/due notte/i
for one week	per una settimana
with a shower	con doccia
with a bathroom	con bagno
with a balcony	con balcone
Do you have a cot?	Ha una culla? (be careful . . . culo means bum)
Do you have a less noisy room?	Ha una camera meno rumorosa?
How much is it?	Quanto costa?
Can I see it?	Posso vederla?
I'll take it	La prendo
I have a reservation	Ho una prenotazione

USING PUBLIC TRANSPORT

Timetable	Orario
Monday–Saturday	Feriale
Daily	Giornaliero
Sundays and holidays	Festivi
A ticket please	Un biglietto per favore
Five tickets please	Cinque biglietti per favore
The bus stop	La fermata
Where is the bus stop?	Dov'è la fermata?
What time is the next bus for . . .?	A che ora parte il prossimo autobus per . . . ?
Do you go to the Colosseum?	Va al Colosseo?
Can you tell me when to get off?	Può dirmi quando devo scendere?
Thief	Ladro
Pickpocket	Borseggiatore

IN A CAFÉ OR RESTAURANT (SEE ALSO MENU BOX)

A cappuccino please	Un cappuccino per favore
Can I have the menu?	Posso avere il menu?
I'd like . . .	Vorrei . . . or Prendo . . .
A quarter-litre of house white	Un quarto di vino bianca della casa
Do you have?/Is there?	C'è l'ha? or C'è?
Could I have the bill please?	Mi fa il conto per favore?
Could you telephone for a taxi please?	Può chiamarmi un taxi, per favore?
Where's the toilet?	Dov'è la toilette?
Can I telephone from here?	Posso telefonare da qui?
Out of order	Guasto

PRACTICALITIES

LATIN LOVERS AND EXCUSES

Hello beautiful!	Ciao bella!
Do you have a light?	Hai da accendere?
I don't smoke	Non fumo
What are you doing here?	Che fai qui?

Best response is silence and a withering look. But if you want to pursue it . . .

I'm on holiday/I'm working	Sono qui in vacanza/per lavoro
What's your name?	Come si chiama?/Come ti chiami?
Where are you from?	Di dove sei?
I'm from . . .	Sono da . . .
I live in . . .	Abito a . . .
What beautiful eyes . . .	Che occhi belli!
Would you like a drink?	Vuoi bere qualcosa?
Are you married?	Sei sposata?
Do you have a boyfriend?	Hai un ragazzo?
What sort of music do you like?	Che tipo di musica ti piace?
D'you want to go dancing?	Vuoi andare ballare?
I'm tired	Sono stanca
I have to go home	Devo andare a casa
I have to meet a (male) friend	Devo andare a incontrare un amico
Leave me in peace, please	Lasciami in pace, per favore

NUMBERS

one	uno/una
two	due
three	tre
four	quattro
five	cinque
six	sei
seven	sette
eight	otto
nine	nove
ten	dieci
eleven	undici
twelve	dodici
thirteen	tredici
fourteen	quattordici
fifteen	quindici
sixteen	sedici
seventeen	diciassette
eighteen	diciotto
nineteen	diciannove
twenty	venti
twenty-one	ventuno
twenty-two	ventidue
twenty-three	ventitre
twenty-four	ventiquattro

twenty-five	venticinque
twenty-six	ventisei
twenty-seven	ventisette
twenty-eight	ventotto
twenty-nine	ventinove
thirty	trenta
thirty-one	trentuno
thirty-two	trentadue etc. . . .
forty	quaranta
fifty	cinquanta
sixty	sessanta
seventy	settanta
eighty	ottanta
ninety	novanta
hundred	cento
two hundred	duecento
three hundred	trecento
four hundred	quattrocento
five hundred	cinquecento
six hundred	seicento etc. . . .
thousand	mille
two thousand	duemila etc. . . .

NB: When prices are spoken they are often abbreviated:
L2500 is duemila cinquecento
        or duemila cinque
        or due cinque

Seasons, Months, Days and Time

year	anno
month	mese
week	settimana
day	giorno
next	prossimo/a
last	scorso/a
spring	primavera
summer	estate
autumn	autunno
winter	inverno
January	Gennaio
February	Febbraio
March	Marzo
April	Aprile
May	Maggio
June	Giugno
July	Luglio
August	Agosto
September	Settembre
October	Ottobre

PRACTICALITIES

November	Novembre
December	Dicembre
Monday	Lunedì
Tuesday	Martedì
Wednesday	Mercoledì
Thursday	Giovedì
Friday	Venerdì
Saturday	Sabato
Sunday	Domenica
What time is it?	Che ora sono?/Che ora è?
It's one o'clock	È l'una
It's noon	È mezzogiorno
It's midnight	È mezzanotte
It's three o'clock	Sono le tre
It's half-past one	È l'una e mezza
It's a quarter to two	Sono le due meno un quarto
It's a quarter past two	Sono le due e un quarto
Twenty past	e venti
Twenty to	meno venti

TERMS OF ABUSE

Shit!	Merda!
Cretin	Cretino
You shit/idiot	Stronzo
Fuck off	Vaffanculo
Dickhead	testa di cazzo
I don't care	non mi frega niente

Police and Crime

Italy has four police forces. Let's hope you won't have to deal with the Guardia di Finanza, responsible for smuggling, tax evasion and other financial offences; nor, unless you're driving or park in a prohibited zone, with the Vigili Urbani, traffic police. The two mainstream crime-fighting forces are the Carabinieri (a men-only branch of the military) and the Polizia Statale; the distinction between who is responsible for what is blurred, and there's much rivalry between the two.

The Carabinieri wear dark-blue uniforms with red leg stripes and white belts designed by Armani. They have a reputation for being stupid, but are better trained than the Polizia. The Polizia (5% women) wear pale-blue trousers with cerise leg stripes and navy jackets with brass buttons. They are based at the Questura and at local Commissariati, where you should report thefts or other crimes.

Italians think of themselves as individuals rather than members of an institution, and what will actually happen when you come into contact with the police is unpredictable. For a start, even if you live a totally crime-free existence, you may not be able to avoid them. It's quite common for a policeman to stop a foreign woman simply to ask her if she'll come out for a beer and pizza. If you happen to be caught riding a Vespa the wrong way down a one-way street you could either get a fine, or be invited for coffee. And it's even been known for police conveniently to 'forget' they ever searched a car and found it full of drugs, as long as they can share the goodies. In general, being apologetic can let you off the hook. Non-EC members, particularly if they're not white, can be given a hard time. Be very very polite, even if you're seething inside.

Italian drugs laws are, however, strict, and possession, even for personal use, is a crime. A new drug law is currently passing through Parliament. Laws against drink-driving and enforcing the wearing of seatbelts are recent additions to the statute book, and are widely considered to be outrageous infringements on the liberty of the individual. Drink-and-drugs driving is the norm among the clubbing set, as many of the best venues are outside town. An alarming number of young Italians are killed in late-night car crashes.

Opportunist crime in Rome is rarely violent, and despite sensationalising in the British press, you can spend weeks on the streets of Rome without witnessing a bag-snatch. Pickpocketing on crowded buses is fairly common, but also easy to avoid – thieves always look for easy targets. Don't carry a purse in your back pocket, wear your bag across your chest, and keep your hand on it throughout a bus journey, or when walking down a crowded street. Put your bag on the table in a pavement café or, failing that, slip the strap under your chair leg.

Gypsy children (and gypsy mums with babies) can be a pain. The children can suddenly cluster around you, flapping a newspaper or piece of cardboard to hide thieving fingers. Don't push them away unless you can do so without taking a hand off your bag or pocket containing a purse (which is not a safe way to carry money in Rome). If you do, the children will disappear, but so will your belongings. However, as long as you spot them in advance there's little problem. Grab hold of your bag or money and walk fast. You can always step into the nearest café or shop, or quickly change direction. And if you want to give them money – stealing, is of course, all they've been taught to do – don't do so unless you've got some cash easily to hand. They don't make a living by being sentimental.

The favourite ploy of the gypsy mums with babies is to approach a tourist (preferably one who is gazing at the Colosseum or some such sight) and proffer a begging hand. The other hand is not supporting the baby (he or she is in a papoose); it's wandering in the direction of your bag, pocket or bum-bag. Incidentally, bum-bags, worn outside your clothes at the back or front, are not as easy to keep an eye on as you'd think. Again, if you want to give money, make sure getting it doesn't involve you fumbling in a stuffed purse.

If you are unfortunate enough to be the victim of a crime, report it at the Questura or nearest Commissariato.

Sexual Crime

According to statistics, since 1987 reported sexual crime has been on the decrease in Italy. Of reported cases, most victims are of school age (around a third are under four-teen) and the rapist usually knows his victim. Italian law currently differentiates between rape which involves vaginal penetration [*violenza carnale*] and rape which involves partial or anal penetration [*atti di libidine violenti*]. The penalties for the latter are less severe, and women are currently campaigning to remove the distinction.
There is a 24-hour support service:

Centro Anti-Violenza (tel. 58 11 473 or 58 10 926)
Staff – there are some who speak English – will come to the immediate aid of victims, accompany them to hospital, and support them during the legal process. Alternatively a victim can go alone to the **Pronto Soccorso** section of a hospital, or to the police station (Questura).

There is currently a campaign to introduce a police code for dealing with women who have been the victims of sexual violence. At present, there is not, and in some cases there may not be a female police officer present. Phoning the Centro Anti-Violenza is without doubt the best thing to do.

Emergencies
Any emergency tel. 113
Carabinieri tel. 112
Fire brigade tel. 115
Road assistance tel. 116

Central Questura
Via San Vitale 15, tel. 4686 (off Via Quattro Fontane)
For information, tel. 481 9161

Commissariati
Piazza Collegio Romano 3, tel. 679 2679
Via San Francesco a Ripa 64, tel. 582 580
Piazza Esquilino 12, tel. 474 0907

Sexual Harassment

At home, we all avoid walking in certain areas of our town or city at night; we know that assumptions are made about us based on the kind of clothes we are wearing; and we know that certain kinds of behaviour are considered provocative. Once abroad we cannot rely on our instincts, and tend to feel more vulnerable and threatened, even if we are actually in no more danger than we are at home. This book aims to furnish you with the knowledge of a native, so that you are equipped to make your own choices.

Obviously women's reactions to sexual harassment, and to the fear of sexual harassment, are individual. One woman might walk home at midnight without thinking about it; another would weigh up the risks and decide to take a taxi. One woman would be quite happy to spend an evening drinking with a man she's just met; another would not even consider it. There is no right and wrong and you should do only what you feel comfortable and confident doing.

Like all Italians, Romans spend most of their time in large groups of friends or family. In the evenings especially, a solo woman is something of an oddity, and many people will feel sorry for you. Sometimes you'll just attract puzzled gazes, sometimes men will come to 'rescue' you, and occasionally, in a restaurant, may invite you to join them. Don't always assume that they have ulterior motives – be wary, yes, but remember this is a chance to get to know more about the city and its people.

The reputation of Italian men is, of course, notorious, and to an extent they deserve it. Flirting with a woman is obligatory, a ritual performed by men of all ages from every walk of life. Even a bank transaction or bus inquiry can develop into an appreciation of the colour of your eyes, hair, and skin, and queries about your marital status. Telling an Italian that you have an English husband, fiancé or boyfriend often makes little impact, and cockier men will gleefully respond: 'So you've never had an Italian lover'. If you're a reasonably adept liar, a fictional Italian partner can be very useful. Often, though, the flirting is simply light-hearted and affectionate, and if you speak Italian (or they speak English) it's not too difficult to switch the conversation away from your hairstyle and marital status to something more interesting. This is where, as a foreign woman in Rome, you have a great advantage over foreign men – you are far more likely to meet Italians – and as long as you can handle a mild sexual subtext, you can find out about aspects of life in the city you would never otherwise know about.

If you go to Rome in late autumn or winter, you'll receive very little attention. This is partly because you can dress much as you would on a cold day in a city at home; partly because once the weather is warm, life moves outside. Waiters, when work is slack, stand on café and restaurant terraces; craftsmen take a break from work for a cigarette in the street; and young men spend evenings hanging out on piazzas or slowly strolling the streets. If a pretty woman (foreign or Italian) passes by, the instinctive reaction is to greet her with a 'Ciao bella'. This is all pretty harmless, and if you let it annoy you, can ruin your holiday, as around the *centro storico* it virtually never stops. If you ignore the guys, you probably won't even notice after a while, and if you're in a good mood, you might even feel like smiling at them.

The *burrini* are another matter. These are guys who come into the centre, often from the outlying suburbs, with the aim of picking up a foreign woman. The Italians have a phrase for it: *rimorchiare una straniera* – trawling for a foreigner – and presumably they have some success, or they wouldn't continue. A proportion of Rome's policemen are simply *burrini* in uniform (coming to the assistance of a foreign woman poring over a map is a great excuse for striking up a conversation). *Burrini* proper, however, tend to hang out on the Spanish Steps, in the Piazza Navona, in pizzerias and around St Peter's. Some ride the buses, others drive slowly along Viale Vaticano, calling out to women on the way to the Vatican museums. Their opening lines are not subtle – *Che fai*? – 'What are you doing?' (when you're standing on a bus); *Posso* . . .? 'Can I . . . join you?' (when you're sitting alone at a café table); or the ubiquitous 'Do you speek Eengleesh?'. Treat all these with the contempt they deserve. Men rubbing their penises against you on buses is a particularly revolting Roman phenomenon. It's pretty hard to avoid completely – you can hold your bag against your front, but this leaves your bottom exposed – and if the bus is crowded, it's difficult to turn round to confront them. If there's room, elbow them sharply. If not, try to move away.

People may also stop you on the street to ask you the time or for a light or a cigarette (bumming cigarettes is socially acceptable in Italy). Such requests are often completely genuine, but you can always walk on if you don't want to find out whether there's an ulterior motive.

Dress

Although you can avoid a lot of harassment by not looking like a tourist, if you are black, Asian or have red or blonde hair, you are always going to look foreign (black, coloured and pale skins are all considered rather exotic). Basically you should wear what you feel comfortable and confident in – bearing in mind that less conventional clothes will attract far more attention than they do in London or New York.

Italians are obsessively style-conscious, and dressing scruffily is read as a sign that you don't respect yourself – ripped jeans never caught on in Italy, and if yours are, it will probably be assumed that you've either just fallen over and torn them, or are too poor to buy a new pair. It is, however, fine to look scruffy or alternative in Trastevere (the one place where you might spot an Italian woman wearing DMs) or if you're going to non-mainstream clubs or gigs.

Dressing for Rome in cool weather is easy – just wear what you would at home, and expect attention only if your clothes are strikingly unconventional. If you're not used to the heat, you'll find you need to wear light summer clothes long before the Italians do – while you are sweltering in shorts and T-shirt, there will still be Roman women looking cool as ice in tailored suits. In high summer, however, city shorts and miniskirts are widely worn by Italian women (immaculately tailored, with court shoes, blouse and jewellery).

However, looking smart when you're spending an entire day trekking round the city in the heat is easier said than done. You may end up resigning yourself to donning trainers, your favourite old shorts and T-shirt and looking like a tourist but feeling comfortable! As long as your shorts are knee-length, you won't be banned from going into churches (even when there's a no shorts sign).

How you dress in the evenings depends on where you're going and how much attention you want to attract. If you have to travel on public transport or have much walking to do, you may feel more relaxed if you've dressed down – stepping on to a bus to be greeted by male eyes sliding up and down your body is not a pleasant experience. You don't need to dress up for homely trattorias or pizzerias, and it's wiser to look smart rather than glamorous for solo dining in a classy restaurant.

Life for black women can be particularly problematic, as the majority of blacks in Rome are (or are thought to be) illegal immigrants who make their living from vending in the streets. Romans have virtually no first-hand encounters with professional or middle-class blacks, so US and UK black women who live and work in Rome advise dressing more conservatively and smartly than you would at home. Hostility is rare – Romans are more likely to consider you exotic – but you have to accept that you are going to be conspicuous. 'You get used to it,' says one black woman living in Rome, 'but I breathe a sigh of relief every time I go to London or New York, sit in a café, and realise that no one is looking at me.'

Danger Spots

There are enough respectable Italians and tourists around the *centro storico* for you to feel relatively relaxed, even at night, though avoiding empty, unlit alleyways is sensible. Harassment in the suburbs always feels more threatening than it does in the centre, largely because you are likely to be the only foreigner around. Walk purposefully and ignore any approaches. Trastevere can get quite rowdy at night, and some cafés there are extremely *demi-monde*-ish. Familiarise yourself with the neighbourhood by day first. The Termini station neighbourhood at night is dangerous – full of the dispossessed, junkies, gypsies and the occasional prostitute or transvestite. The clubbing area around Monte Testaccio is not recommended for solo women at night.

EC members have the right to the same medical care benefits as Italians as long as they have an E111 form (available from the Department of Social Security). The welfare service is, however, currently undergoing drastic cutbacks, with each region taking its own measures to save money, so it's difficult to predict what will happen. However, you can expect to have to buy a 'ticket' (different prices for different services, e.g. visiting a doctor or getting medicine on prescription) on top of which you may have to pay a percentage of the actual cost. For example, for medicines, a 'ticket' currently costs L3000 plus 50% of the actual price to a maximum of L70,000. If you need hospital treatment simply take your E111 with you. If you need to consult a doctor, take your E111 to the local health clinic (USL) where you will be given a temporary form, a list of doctors and can buy the relevant 'ticket'. All USLs are open from 8.30 a.m. to 12.30 p.m. Ask your hotel which 'circoscrizione' (district) you are in and look up the relevant USL in the phone book. It is not, however, advisable to rely solely on the E111, as the reimbursement of doctors through the system can be very slow, and many are unwilling to treat E111 patients. Get private medical insurance instead (see p.8).

What you do if you or your child is ill obviously depends on how serious it is. If it's not too serious, and you think you can make yourself understood, go to a *farmacia*. The pharmacists are usually knowledgeable, and many have a good range of homeopathic remedies. **If you need a doctor and don't speak Italian, the British Embassy (tel. 482 5651/482 5441) has an up-to-date list of English-speaking doctors. In an emergency, phone 113 or go to the nearest Pronto Soccorso (First Aid section) of a hospital.**

***Tampons* etc.** Tampons, Tampax and sanitary towels are all available in chemists and supermarkets. They're not always on display in the former, which means you have to ask the assistant. The Italian is, for once, literal [*assorbenti interni/assorbenti esterni*] and Sod's Law is that the assistant will be male and the shop full.

Contraception and STD

Italian men are not fond of condoms (and still smarting from the shame of a recent EC ruling, which stated that Italian condoms were too small to meet EC regulations) though AIDS awareness is increasing. Italy has more drug addicts with AIDS than anywhere else in the world, but one of the world's lowest rates of AIDS among homosexuals.

Condoms are available in most chemists and are usually on display. If you need a repeat prescription of the Pill or the morning-after Pill, go to a **consultorio**, Italy's equivalent to a family-planning clinic, where consultation is free, once you have paid L15,000 to become a member. Alternatively you could go to a private clinic like AIED (Associazione Italiano per l'Educazione Demografico). You should also go to AIED or a *consultorio* if you think you have contracted a sexually transmitted disease.

Pregnancy and Abortion

Until the abortion law was passed in 1978 there was a massive industry in backstreet abortions. Indeed, the reason many doctors opposed the legalisation was that it robbed them of valuable extra income. Abortion is now available to women over eighteen within the first three months of pregnancy for 'economic, medical, psychological, and social reasons', though hospital personnel are permitted to refuse to perform abortions on grounds of conscience. The hospitals which *will* perform abortions cannot cope with the demand for legal abortions, which is why there are still an estimated 120,000 backstreet abortions annually.

If you think you might be pregnant, or need an abortion, you should go to a *consultorio* or AIED. You can also get home pregnancy testing kits from pharmacies: *Predictor* will give you a result in four minutes; *Rivela Beiresdorf-Milano* in 24 hours. Both cost around L25,000.

USEFUL ADDRESSES
Ambulance
Tel. 113

Hospitals (Ospedali)

GO IN PERSON TO A HOSPITAL. GETTING THROUGH ON THE PHONE IS VERY DIFFICULT.

Fatebenefratelli
Isola Tiberina (Tiber Island)
tel. 68371

Santo Spirito
Lungotevere in Sassia 1 (near the Vatican)
tel. 650 901

Regina Margherita
Via E Morosini 30 (in Trastevere)
tel. 58441

Istituto Materno Regina Elena Ostetrico
Viale Angelico 28
tel. 372 4085/372 5598
A reliable maternity hospital

Policlinico A Gemelli
Largo A Gemelli 8
tel. 30151
A Catholic-run hospital used by the Pope

Salvator Mundi International Hospital
Viale della Mura Gianicolense
tel. 586 041
Private hospital with English-speaking staff

Rome American Hospital
Via Longoni 69
tel. 22551
Private American hospital

Homeopathic treatment

Omeopatia Ambulatorio Samo
Piazza Navona 49
tel. 683 0703/6830 8379/687 7743

Simoh
Via San Saba 22
tel. 574 7841

Omeopati Allinica USL RM 11
Via Sabotino 2
tel. 317 095

Dentist

English-speaking dentists advertise in the biweekly magazine *Wanted in Rome*.

G. J. Nussbacher
Piazza Viminale 14, tel. 488 2369
English/German-speaking dentist

G. Eastman
Viale Regina Elena 287, tel. 445 4851 or 491 949
American dental hospital with 24-hour service

Caritas
Via Tullio Levi Cività 5 (near S. Paolo fuori le Mura)
Free dental service

Pharmacies [*Farmacie*]
A pharmacy rota operates, with chemists taking it in turn to stay open all night.
Otherwise they're usually open 8.30 a.m.–1 p.m.; 4/4.30–7.30/8 p.m. If a pharmacy
is closed, there will be a list on the door stating which pharmacies are open. The
pharmacy rota also appears daily in *Il Messagero*.

Farmacia Farnese
Via Baullari 41 (corner Piazza Farnese)
Homeopathic and regular medicines

Farmacia della Scala
Piazza della Scala (Trastevere)
Old-fashioned pharmacy

Galleria di Testa
Termini Station
Daily 7.30 a.m.–10 p.m.

All-Night Pharmacies
Piram
Via Nazionale 228
tel. 488 0754
Centrally located all-night chemist

Spinedi
Via Arenula 73
tel. 654 3278
Centrally located all-night chemist

Tre Madonne
Via Bertolini 5
tel. 8073423
All-night chemist in Parioli

Contraception, Pregnancy Tests and Abortion

AIED
Central Office
Via Piave 41
tel. 481 4646/484 559
Open Mon–Sat 10 a.m.–12.30 p.m.; 3–6.30 p.m.

CONSULTORI
There are consultori all over the city. These are the most central. All open Mon–Fri 9 a.m.–1 p.m.; 2–7 p.m. and most close in August!

Via Toscana 30A
tel. 482 7711
Open in August

Via Arco del Monte 99A
tel. 6830 7159/654 3545
(Near Campo dei Fiori)

Piazza Adriana 9
tel. 654 1528
(Behind Castel Sant'Angelo)

Via Canova 23 (in the Ospedale San Giacomo)
tel. 321 0203
(Off Via di Ripetta)

The best-known hospitals for abortions are:

Ospedale San Camillo
Centro Interruzione Gravidanza
tel. 332 6814

Ospedale San Filippo Neri
Via G Martinotti 20
tel. 330 6424

Useful Vocabulary

Tampons	Assorbenti interni
Tampax	Tampax
Sanitary towels	Assorbenti esterni
Condom/s	Preservativo/i or profilattico/i
The Pill	La pillola
Morning-after Pill	La pillola del dopogiorno
I think I'm pregnant	Penso che sono incinta
Laxative	Il lassativo
Diarrhoea	La diarrea
Stomach ache	Mal di stomaco
Headache	Mal di testa

Women and Feminism

Vestiges of ancient Roman laws affecting women persisted into this century – until the 1960s adultery was considered a crime only if committed by women, and punished more severely than rape. The social and legal position of Italian women has improved immeasurably over the past couple of decades, largely thanks to the feminist movement. Divorce became legal in 1974 and abortion in 1978. Forty-two per cent of mothers work, 87% of children aged between three and five are in pre-primary school, and women are entitled to maternity leave of 20 weeks (including 8 weeks before the birth) at 80% of earnings. Though it's no surprise that Italy's divorce rate is the lowest in Europe, the fact that the average number of children per family is also Europe's lowest is, to say the least, unexpected.

However, though the equality of men and women is enshrined in the Constitution, there is still some way to go before it becomes a reality. Women's earnings are on average 78% of men's (which is at least higher than in Britain) and, particularly in the south, women are still expected to be either virgins or mothers. Even in the more sophisticated cities most men live at home until they are married, when they expect their wives to do as *mamma* did and cook their meals, wash their clothes and clean the house. Macho attitudes are still prevalent in law and politics: the law against rape distinguishes between vaginal and anal intercourse (the latter is considered less grave); and so strong was the desire of the Christian Democrat

Party to preserve the sanctity of the family that they tried to exclude incest from the 1988 Sexual Violence Bill.

In this deeply conservative culture dominated by machismo and the Catholic Church, every victory for women has had to be fought for, long and hard. Although feminism was traditionally allied with the Communist Party – the feminist magazine, *Noi Donne*, began in 1940 as an organ of the Party – from the late 1960s onwards feminists began to realise that to get anywhere they would have to organise separately from men. In the 1970s old palazzi (like the Governo Vecchio) were occupied as women-only communes, and were visited by women from all over Europe. Massive (and occasionally violent) street demonstrations frightened the government sufficiently to change the labour laws and legalise abortion.

Nowadays things are considerably less dynamic, and much of Italian feminism is theoretical rather than practical. Rome's rape crisis centre, for example, was opened only in 1992, and there is little research on the aspects of society which impinge most on the lives of ordinary women. The separatists still exist, but it's the women who work within and with the PDS (former Communist Party) who appear to have most chance of changing things. Another hope is the National Commission for Equality (Commissione Nazionale per la Parità tra Uomo e Donna) set up in 1988 to analyse existing laws and provide a legal framework for changes.

WOMEN'S ORGANISATIONS IN ROME

Arcidonna, Via G Cesare 92, tel. 325 0921

Non-separatist women's movement allied with the PDS, running a babysitting service and financing (without much success) women's initiatives, like an association of artisans.

Centro Femminista Separatista, Via San Francesco Sales 1A, tel. 686 4201

A meeting-place (also in the Buon Pastore building on nearby Via della Lungara) for lesbian and separatist groups. There's a bar/restaurant, *Sette Streghe*, open Tues–Sat 5 p.m.–midnight.

Circolo della Rosa, Via dell'Orso 36, tel. 687 2961

Exclusive lesbian club. By invitation only.

Differenza Donna, Casa della Cultura, Largo Arenula 26, tel. 654 4909 (6880 4909)

A new organisation founded to establish support for women who are the victims of domestic and sexual violence. They run the Centro Anti Violenza (see p.26). Call in on Largo Arenula if you want more information about the centre.

Telefono Rosa, Via Tor di Nona, tel. 683 2820/6832690
Mon–Fri 10 a.m.–1 p.m.; 4–7 p.m.

Legal, psychological and gynaecological support, information and advice for victims of domestic violence and sexual crimes. Not somewhere to phone immediately after an incident (for that you need the Centro Anti-Violenza, see p.26).

REMEMBER ALL PHONE NUMBERS IN ROME ARE IN THE PROCESS OF CHANGING (DUE TO BE COMPLETED BY THE END OF 1993). PHONE DIRECTORY INQUIRIES (12) IF YOU HAVE PROBLEMS.

AIRLINE OFFICES
Air New Zealand, Via Bissolati 54, tel. 486 793
Alitalia, Via Bissolati 13, tel. 46881
Domestic flight booking, tel. 6564 1
International flight booking, tel. 6564 2
Flight info, tel. 6564 3
Fiumicino office, tel. 60101

American Airlines, Via Toscana 1, tel. 489 3949

British Airways, Via Bissolati 54, tel. 479 991

Quantas, Via Bissolati 35, tel. 486 451

AIRPORTS (see also p.43)
Fiumicino, tel. 65951
Flight info, tel. 6595 3640
Ciampino
tel. 794 941

BABYSITTING
Ask at hotel reception first. Otherwise:
Arcidonna, tel. 316 449
Or look at small ads in *Wanted in Rome* and the noticeboard at the Victoria pub (see p.290)

BIKE HIRE
Bicimania, Piazza Sonnino (in Trastevere)
Open Mon–Sat 9 a.m.–7 p.m.; Sat and Sun only in winter
From L5000 per hour

Pincio gardens (in octagonal wooden cabin)
Open all year and daily 10 a.m.–8 p.m. (Sat/Sun open from 9 a.m.)

Bikes from L5000 per hour. Baby seats free.
Leave passport as security.

Collati, Via del Pellegrino 82
Tues–Fri 8.30 a.m.–1 p.m.; 3–8 p.m.; Sat/Sun open till 7.30 p.m.
Bikes from L4000 per hour (L12,000 per day)

Largo dei Lombardi (outside San Carlo al Corso)
Open all day, daily May–Oct
Bikes from L5000 per hour

BUS, TRAM AND METRO INFORMATION
ATAC (bus and tram) tel. 4695
ACOTRAL (metro) tel. 591 5551

CAR BREAKDOWN
Tel. 116

CAR HIRE
See p.320

CAR PARKS
Via Ludovisi
Piazza San Bernardo
Villa Borghese (off Viale Porta Pinciana)

CHEMISTS
See p.32

CIGARETTES
There are moves afoot in Rome to ban smoking in restaurants. Cigarettes are available in tobacconists or bars with a T sign: there are no cigarette machines. Familiar brands like Marlboro and Silk Cut are fairly easy to get hold of, and cheaper than in the UK, but more expensive than Italian cigarettes. Low-tar Italian brands include MS Lights and Merit. *Al Castellino* café on Piazza Venezia has a tobacconist open 24 hours a day, seven days a week.

CONTRACEPTION
See p.30

DENTISTS
See p.32 and ads in *Wanted in Rome*

DOCTORS
See p.30

DRY CLEANING
See laundries

EMBASSIES AND CONSULATES
Australia, Via Alessandria 215, tel. 852721
Canada, Via G.B. de Rossi 27, tel. 4403028
Eire, Largo del Nazareno 3, tel. 678 2541
Great Britain, Via XX Settembre 80a, tel. 482 5441
New Zealand, Via Zara 28, tel. 440 2928
USA, Via Veneto 119a–121, tel. 46741

EMERGENCY SERVICES
Police/Ambulance/Fire tel. 113
Central Police Station tel. 4686
Fire (direct) tel. 115
Red Cross Ambulance tel. 5100
Carabinieri tel. 112/85291 (80981)
Gas leaks tel. 5107
Enjoy Rome tel. 445 1843 (see p.11)

EXPAT ROME
These organisations are very useful if you come to work in Rome and want to meet other women, or find out about various aspects of living in Italy. They should be able to advise you on schools, negotiating the Italian bureaucratic labyrinth, finding a flat, a plumber . . .
Professional Women's Association
Julie Bauer, tel. 324 91289
Cynthia Earlich, tel. 334 0457

American Women's Association
tel. 654 5298

Canadian Women's Organisation
tel. 521 5075/577 3485

FINDING A FLAT
Ads in *Wanted in Rome,*
Metropolitan, Porta Portese or
contact: International Services, tel.
684 0941/2 or 474 6439
(Short-term and long-term rents as
well as sales. Recommended.)

FINDING A JOB
Look at or place an ad in *Wanted in Rome*. Jobs for English-speakers with admin/secretarial/editing skills at FAO (UN Food and Agricultural Organisation), Via della Terme di Caracalla 0100, ROMA. Also English-teaching jobs and *au pairing* (look for ads in *The Lady* in the UK). Mainstream teaching at any British school where they follow the English National Curriculum, and lots of opportunities for TEFL teachers (look in the *Times Educational Supplement*).

FAXING
see p.14

FLOWERS
Tuesday morning market at Via Trionfale (nr Metro Ottaviano)
Italflora, Via dei Cappuccini 28, tel 488 5729. National and international deliveries. From L60,000 to UK.

LADIES' ROME
Sophisticated, customised tours of Rome (in English) run by a UN interpreter. You could see Rome with an art historian, attend cookery demonstrations, visit artisans' workshops, fashion houses and art and design galleries. Very popular with the wives of diplomats. Contact: Angela Ricci, Via Montegiordano 52, 00186 ROMA
tel. 686 9254; fax 854 3451

PRACTICALITIES

GYM
Navona Centre, Via dei Banchi Vecchi 39, tel. 689 6104
Small private gym. Recommended.

HELPLINES
ALL WILL OBVIOUSLY REPLY IN ITALIAN AND MAY NOT HAVE ENGLISH-SPEAKING STAFF.
Child line: 575 7113
Telefono Rosa (see p.35) tel. 683 2690/683 2820
Centro Antiviolenza, tel. 581 1473/581 0926 (see also p.26)
Drug dependency: tel. 6574 1188
Alcoholics Anonymous: tel. 475 5714

HOSPITALS AND FIRST AID
See p.31

KINDERGARTENS AND SCHOOLS
Tumble Tots, phone Lorenza, tel. 425 627
Rome International School, Via Morgagni 25, tel. 841 6994 (ages 3–15)

LAUNDRIES/DRY CLEANING
There are no coin-op laundries, but scores of tiny *lavanderie* and *tintorie*, which can usually have your clothes washed and pressed (and often dry cleaned – look for a sign saying *lavasecco*) within 24 hours. Most close on Saturday afternoons and Sundays.
Lavaservice, Via Montebello 11. The cheapest – 3 kg of clothes washed and dried for L12,000.
Lavanderia/Lavasecco, Piazza Nicosia
Lavanderia, Via di Ripetta 62
Tintoria, Via del Governo Vecchio 88
Tintoria/Lavasecco Mercanti, Via Gregoriana 6a

LEFT LUGGAGE
Termini Station
Fiumicino Airport

LESBIAN ORGANISATIONS
See p.35

LOST PROPERTY
On bus/tram: tel. 581 6040
On train: lost property office at Termini station

PACKING
Bring:
opera glasses or binoculars for seeing frescoes
Italian small change
tampons (more expensive in Italy)
a corkscrew (for picnics)
mosquito killer (in summer)
comfy shoes
passport-size photos (if you want a bus pass)
two-pin adapter (current is 220 volts)
umbrella (even in summer)
towel (if staying in a hostel or cheap hotel – if there *is* a towel it will probably be very rough, or more like a teatowel)

PHOTOCOPYING
See p.320

POLICE
tel. 113

SWIMMING POOLS
See p.318

TAMPONS
See p.30

TAXIS
Tel. 3570, 6645, 88177, 4994, 4517
Useful ranks:
Piazza Venezia
Largo Argentina
Largo Zanardelli
Piazza di Spagna
Piazza Barberini
Top of Via Veneto
Termini Station

Ostiense Station (difficult to find one after 9.30 p.m.)
Piazza Risorgimento (near the Vatican)

TOILETS
Clean loos in Rinascente department store on Via del Corso
Public loos outside Colosseum and on Piazza San Silvestro

TRAIN INFORMATION
Tel. 4775

VESPA AND MOTORINO HIRE
No licence necessary for the little chugging *motorinos* (mopeds). Helmet plus licence obligatory for a Vespa.

Scootalong, Via Cavour 302, tel. 678 0206
Open Mon–Sat 9 a.m.–7 p.m.

Scooters for Rent, Via della Purificazione 66, tel. 465 485
Daily 9 a.m.–9 p.m.

San Pietro Moto, Via di Porta Castello 43, tel. 687 4909
Open Mon–Sat 9 a.m.–1 p.m.;
3.30–7.30 p.m.

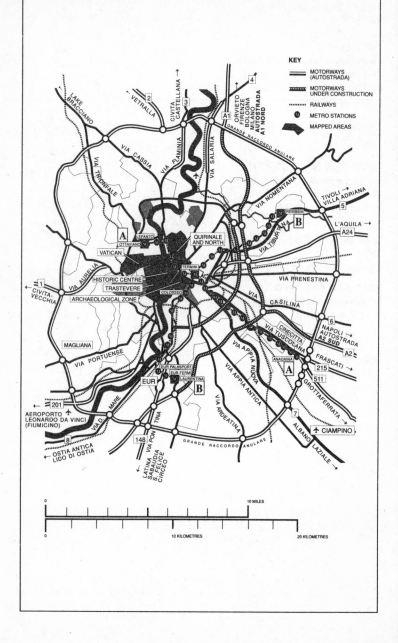

THE GUIDE

Rome can be an intimidating city, as anyone who has ever arrived at Termini will tell you. But if you plan your trip carefully, you can avoid the less savoury aspects of the city. In the Arrival and Getting Around sections you'll find ways of getting from the airports to your hotel on public transport which bypass Termini. And apart from a couple of fallbacks, the hotels we recommend are in the historic centre and other safe, attractive locations. It really is worth paying a little more and booking well in advance to secure a room in a pleasant neighbourhood. It can make all the difference to your experience of the city.

Once you've arrived, ease yourself into the city gently. Have breakfast on Piazza Navona; then wander the mazy streets of the *centro storico*, taking a look at Campo dei Fiori's bustling market, the antique shops of Via dei Coronari or a stunningly decorated church like Sant'Ignazio. Stroll up to the Spanish Steps for a spot of designer window-shopping, and have a drink at Vanni, whose outdoor tables are among the best in the city for people-watching. You could then either dine at the wonderful Edys, or head back to the area around Piazza Navona for a *prosecco* in an inviting wine bar like Il Piccolo, before dinner in a civilised but reasonable restaurant such as Tre Maghi or L'Insalata Ricca II.

It wouldn't be difficult to spend an entire week exploring the historic centre, Trastevere and the area around Piazza di Spagna, and you certainly shouldn't feel duty-bound to tackle the ancient sites or the Vatican and St Peter's. Getting to know certain neighbourhoods well, and keying into their shifts of mood through the day, can be far more rewarding.

The historic centre as defined in this book comprises the area of tangled cobbled streets around Piazza Navona and the Pantheon, Campo dei Fiori and the old Jewish Ghetto. On the other side of the main street, Via del Corso, are the Trevi Fountain, Piazza di Spagna, Via Veneto and the Villa Borghese. Directly across the Tiber from Campo dei Fiori and the Ghetto is Trastevere, focus of a trendy, alternative nightscene, and abutting it is the Vatican State. The archaeological zone is in the busy heart of the city, bounded by traffic-choked roads, and the swiftest escapes from city bustle are the lush Aventine and Celian hills. The urbanised Esquiline Hill is worth tackling if you're keen on mosaic-decorated churches, while for catacombs you could head to either the Via Appia Antica or the Villa Ada.

OPENING HOURS

Virtually all museums in Rome are closed every afternoon and all day Monday. In addition, some close without warning for lack of personnel. Many of the lesser-known ancient sites are closed to the public – see p.12 for how to get access if you are studying them.

Churches are usually open daily, from around 8 a.m. to noon and again from between 3.30 and 4.30 p.m. to about 7 p.m. If a church has unusual opening hours, we've tried to indicate this in the text. Bear in mind, though, that punctuality is not a common Roman virtue, and that even when opening hours are posted on the doors of churches, they are theoretical. It is acceptable to enter a church during a service, but though no one ever seems to object if you wander around, it's more sensitive not to. If a church has special treasures or an underground crypt, you usually have to search out the sacristan to open it up for you. This can take some time! If you're going to a church with famous paintings or mosaics, always take plenty of small change with you, as the lights are almost inevitably coin-operated.

Highlights

Piazza Navona (p.54)
The Pantheon (p.64)
Sant'Ivo (p.66)
Sant'Ignazio (p.83)
Ara Pacis (p.74)
Via dei Coronari (p.59)
Bernini's Elephant (p.79)
Campo dei Fiori (p.89)
Piazza Farnese (p.92)
The Ghetto (p.97)
Spanish Steps (p.120)
Trevi Fountain (p.109)
Galleria Barberini (p.115)
Galleria Colonna (p.110)
Galleria Borghese and park (p.133)
Santa Maria della Concezione (p.131)
Piazza and Santa Maria del Popolo (p.127–130)
Santa Maria della Vittoria (p.113)
Trastevere's Sunday flea market (p.305)
Santa Maria in Trastevere (p.144)
Villa Farnesina (p.142)
Colosseum (p.201)

Arrival

Rome is served by two airports: Fiumicino (also known as Leonardo da Vinci), 36 kilometres south-west of the city, is used by scheduled flights; Ciampino, 16 kilometres to the south-east, by charters. Ciampino is also a military airport and occasionally closes for 'repair' without warning. If you're on a package, and Ciampino closes while you're in Rome, the company should inform you; if you've simply bought a flight, phone to check that the airport is open the day before you are due to depart. Otherwise you could end up trekking to Ciampino, only to find that your flight is leaving from Fiumicino.

Getting from either airport to the centre is not particularly easy. A train link was set up between Fiumicino and Ostiense station for the 1990 World Cup. It all looks very slick, but unfortunately Ostiense is not in a particularly safe area, and if you're arriving at night, especially with heavy luggage, try to avoid hanging around for a bus or taxi. The idea of the link was that travellers could take a metro from the Piramide station at Ostiense to Termini (see p. 46). Termini is gross – unsavoury by day and dangerous at night, with endless passages and stairways to negotiate. At night, unless you're extremely confident, know exactly what you are doing, and have very little luggage, it is better avoided. We suggest alternative points of arrival by public transport for those who can't afford a taxi.

Ciampino is also linked by bus and metro with Termini, and though it's closer to the centre than Fiumicino, the journey takes longer. Again, we suggest points of arrival which omit Termini.

Fiumicino

Trains shuttle between Fiumicino and Ostiense station every 20 or 30 minutes from 5.40 a.m. to midnight. Most flights arrive within these hours, but if yours is delayed there's a night bus service from 2.15 to 6 a.m. Alternatively, you could take a taxi (approx. L65,000) to the centre. At the time of writing, train tickets cost L6000. Rather than tussle with the temperamental automatic ticket machines (surrounded by frustrated travellers folding, straightening and even licking their banknotes in an effort to get the machine to accept them) join the queue at the ticket office. You can also buy metro and bus tickets here.

All trains from Fiumicino stop at Trastevere station as well as Ostiense. As Ostiense is not a pleasant place to be at night unless you know exactly what you are doing, consider using Trastevere instead – it's actually slightly closer to the centre. Finding a taxi at either station can be a problem, and you may have to phone for one (see directory). [*Un taxi a stazione di Trastevere/Ostiense per favore.*]

If you want to use public transport from Ostiense and avoid Termini, you could take:

Bus 95 or night bus 91 to Piazza Venezia, where there are lots of taxis.

Metro to Colosseo. Then, from directly outside, bus 81 or 87 to the Centro Storico via Piazza Venezia, Largo Argentina, and Corso Rinascimento. If you're staying around Campo dei Fiori, get off at the stop after Largo Argentina; for Piazza Navona or the Pantheon, get off at the first stop on Corso Rinascimento. There's also a taxi rank on Largo Argentina.

And from Trastevere:

Bus 170 (cross over to the junction of Viale Trastevere and Via Orti di Cesare) to Largo Argentina or Piazza Venezia.

AIRPORT FACTS

FIUMICINO

Tourist Office
EPT (Airside)
Mon–Sat 8.15 a.m.–7 p.m.
Helpful. Will reserve a hotel room, and advise on public transport. Free maps and brochures.

Bank
Banco di Santo Spirito
Daily 7.30 a.m.–11 p.m. (Airside)
Daily 7 a.m.–midnight (Arrivals Hall)
Daily 7 a.m.–8 p.m. (Departures)
Astronomical commission rates (particularly in the airside branch).
There's also an automatic change machine if you want to avoid the queues.

Car Hire
Offices linked by a shuttle bus with Arrivals Hall.

Taxis
Clearly signposted.
Can also go to booth in Arrivals.
L65,000 to centre.

CIAMPINO
DON'T COME TO CIAMPINO WITHOUT CASH

Bank
Banco di Santo Spirito (Arrivals only)
Mon–Fri 8.15 a.m.–1.30 p.m. 2.45–3.30 p.m.
These opening hours are theoretical, owing to unofficial coffee breaks.

Exchange Office (In Departures and Arrivals)
Utterly unreliable opening times

Car Hire
In Arrivals Hall

Taxis
On the forecourt

Ciampino

Arriving at Ciampino is a pain, especially if you have heavy luggage. If you can afford a taxi (approx. L75,000), treat yourself. A bus runs to Anagnina metro station from the forecourt approximately every half-hour from 6 a.m. to 9.30 p.m., after which there is one further bus at 10.45. Brilliant Italian organisation means that you can get a bus ticket only from the newsstand in the departure lounge. Try to get some change as well for a metro ticket. Once you arrive at Anagnina, you have to join a queue of new arrivals with L100,000 notes at the ticket booth. Watch out – the staff make a fortune from short-changing tourists. From Anagnina it's approximately 45 minutes to Termini. If you want to avoid arriving at Termini, stay on the metro until Barberini. There are *usually* taxis on the piazza outside, or you could take bus 56 or 60 to Largo Argentina.

Arriving by Train or Bus

If you come to Rome by bus or train from elsewhere in Italy, there are a number of places you could arrive. By train, you'll probably have to pass through Termini, so try to avoid arriving at night. If you do arrive late, walk swiftly, following the signs to the taxi rank, and ignore any beggar or hotel tout who approaches you.

All the major bus stations are linked with metro stations. Find out where you're arriving, and you may be able to avoid using Termini by changing on to a bus at Barberini (Line A) or Colosseo (Line B).

Getting Around

The best way to see Rome is to walk, and there's little need to use public transport in and around the historic centre. It is, however, well worth using a bus, especially in hot weather, if getting from A to B involves walking along a busy, polluted road. Hiring a push-bike, *motorino* (scooter) or (if you have a driving licence) a Vespa is not a bad way to get around, though two-wheel travelling on Rome's busy roads is not for the inexperienced, and checking the daily air-pollution table in *La Repubblica* might put you off. It is, however, worthwhile hiring a Vespa for short day trips – but make sure you're insured.

Buses and Trams

Rome's bus and tram service (run by ATAC) is cheap, reliable, frequent and pretty comprehensive, although progress along the clogged streets can be very slow. Routes are listed on stops, but they won't mean much until you know the city well. If you are going to be using public transport a lot, it's worth buying a route map. These currently cost L6000 and are available from the information booth on Piazza dei Cinquecento outside Termini. Included with the map is a booklet with comprehensive information on metros, buses and trams. Every route is listed, and you can also look up a street or piazza and find out which bus or tram goes there.

Tickets cost L800 and must be bought in advance. They are sold in bars, newsagents and tobacconists with an ATAC sticker in the window, or from booths at Largo Argentina, Piazza dei Cinquecento, Piazza San Silvestro and other major bus termini. They are valid for 90 minutes of travel, and when you get on the bus you have to cancel the ticket in the machine by the rear doors. Most of the ticket-selling outlets close at around 8 p.m. and if you get caught at night without a ticket, ask people at the bus stop if they can sell you one. Failing that, you may consider it worth catching a bus and risking a fine. Travelling without a ticket used to be a popular Roman pastime, though the fine has now been raised to L50,000 and the number of inspectors increased, so fare-dodging is far less common. Avoid the necessity by buying a few tickets at a time.

Multiple-journey tickets and passes are an even better deal. You can get a one-day pass, valid on the metro as well as trams and buses, for L2800, and a one-week pass (valid on buses and trams only) for L10,000. If you are staying in the city for more than three weeks, consider getting a monthly bus pass for L22,000.

For both the weekly and monthly passes you need two passport-sized photos.

The buses are crowded, and pickpockets and fondlers are fairly common, especially on the number 64 from Termini to the Vatican. However, when buses are sardine-packed it's not easy to tell whether the object pressed against your backside is an erect penis or an umbrella, so don't be too hasty to kick or thump the person directly behind you: it might be a nun. If you're in no doubt, try to shuffle away, or if you speak good Italian, complain very loudly, preferably without swearing.

Buses run from around 5 a.m. to midnight, after which night buses cover certain routes. Travelling at night is not too worrisome – largely because there are far fewer drunk men than you get in Britain.

The Metro

Rome's two-line metro system is not particularly useful, as it was designed mainly to ferry commuters in and out of the city centre. The two lines cross at Termini station and there are convenient stops at the Colosseum, Piazza Barberini and the Spanish Steps. Tickets currently cost L700 and are on sale at tobacconists, bars and metro station newsagents, though as on the buses, these places close before the metro shuts down. Line A closes at around midnight; Line B at 9 p.m. on weekdays and 11.30 p.m. on Saturdays and Sundays. Some stations have automatic ticket machines, although only the newer machines give change. If you get stranded without a ticket, a used ticket will usually get you through the automatic ticket barrier, although if you're caught, pleading a foreigner's ignorance won't cut much ice, and you can expect a fine. Some metros have doors which open automatically at every station; others open only if you press the button alongside.

THE METRO

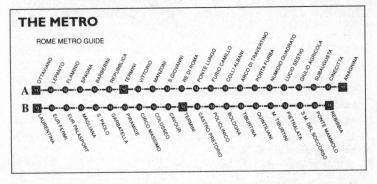

ROME METRO GUIDE

Taxis

Taxis are yellow and can be picked up either from a rank, or by phoning (see directory for phone numbers and ranks). Flagging one down is difficult. The one-way system means that routes can be very circuitous, and as the streets are congested it is rarely worth getting one unless you have a long way to go, are in a dodgy area, or it is very late at night. The minimum fare is L6400, which is good for nine minutes or three kilometres (whichever is shortest) and can easily be used up as you sit in a traffic jam. You then pay L300 for every 300 metres. There's a supplement between 10 p.m. and 7 a.m., on Sundays and holidays, and for pieces of luggage.

If a taxi is coming to pick you up, the drivers prefer to come to a bar, rather than a street corner.

There are sometimes unofficial taxi touts at Termini station – don't even dream of accepting a lift.

Driving Driving in Rome cannot be recommended, but if you do, make sure you don't park anywhere in the *centro storico* – it's residents' parking only, and you're more than likely to end up being clamped (and incur an L140,000 fine). Official car parks are listed in the directory.

USEFUL BUS AND TRAM ROUTES

Apart from Termini itself, there are major bus termini at Largo Argentina (close to Campo dei Fiori) and Piazza San Silvestro (off Via del Corso).
The most useful bus stops and sections of routes are listed.
Unless otherwise stated, return routes are reversed.

119: Circular minibus route around the *centro storico*
Piazza Augusto Imperatore–Via di Ripetta–Via Dogana Vecchia–Pantheon–Via del Seminario–Piazza Colonna–Via del Tritone–Via Due Macelli–Piazza di Spagna–Via del Babuino–Piazza del Popolo–Via di Ripetta–Piazza Augusto Imperatore

110: Special tourist bus around the main sights. From Termini daily in summer and on Saturdays and Sundays in winter at 3.30 p.m. L6000

4: From Santa Maria Maggiore via Termini to Piazza delle Muse (Parioli)

26: From Viale Trastevere to Largo Argentina and Corso Rinascimento

27: From Stazione Trastevere via Viale Aventino and the Colosseum to Termini

30b: Tram from the Colosseum via Porta San Giovanni, Scalo San Lorenzo and Viale Regina Margherita to Viale Belle Arte and Villa Giulia

44: From Viale Trastevere via Largo Argentina to Piazza Venezia

56: From Via Veneto via Via del Corso, Piazza Venezia and Largo Argentina to Piazza Sonnino (in Trastevere)

57: From Termini to Ostiense station (until 10 p.m.)

60: From Via XX Settembre via Piazza Barberini, Via del Corso, Piazza Venezia and Largo Argentina to Piazza Sonnino

64: From Termini via Piazza Venezia, Largo Argentina and Corso Vittorio Emanuele to Via dei Corridori (THE MAIN BUS TO ST PETER'S AND THE VATICAN, WATCH OUT FOR PICKPOCKETS AND FROTTEURS)

75: From Viale Trastevere via Largo Argentina, Piazza Venezia and Via Nazionale to Termini

81: From San Giovanni via the Colosseum, Piazza Venezia and Largo Argentina to Corso Rinascimento. RETURN ROUTE FROM PASSEGIATA DI RIPETTA

85: From Piazza San Silvestro via Via del Corso, Piazza Venezia, Via dei Fori Imperiali and Colosseum to Piazza San Giovanni

90: From Baths of Caracalla via Via Teatro Marcello, Piazza Venezia, Largo Argentina and Corso Vittorio Emanuele to Corso Rinascimento

95: From Ostiense station via Piazza Bocca della Verità, Piazza Venezia, Via del Corso and Via del Tritone to Via Veneto

97: From Viale Trastevere to EUR

118: From Piazza San Giovanni in Laterano via the Colosseum and Baths of Caracalla to the Via Appia Antica

218: From Piazza San Giovanni in Laterano via Via Appia Antica to Via Ardeatina

492: From Tiburtina station via Termini, Piazza Barberini, Piazza Venezia, Largo Argentina and Corso Rinascimento to Piazza Risorgimento (near the Vatican)

707: From San Paolo fuori le Mura via Via delle Tre Fontane to Piazza Marconi (in EUR)

Night Trams and Buses
20/21 From Metro Piramide to the Colosseum

29/30 From Metro Piramide via the Colosseum to Via Scalo San Lorenzo

45 From Corso Vittorio Emanuele via Largo Argentina, Piazza Venezia and Via del Corso to Piazza San Silvestro

75 From Viale Trastevere via Largo Argentina to Piazza Venezia

THE HISTORIC CENTRE
[CENTRO STORICO]

Rome's *centro storico*, cradled within a great loop of the Tiber, is a maze of cobbled streets and piazzas studded with fountains, palaces and churches. Layers of history are haphazardly superimposed, as Romans continue to do what they have always done, adapting old buildings for modern uses. Ancient columns are embedded in the walls of palaces, Egyptian obelisks are reused in Baroque fountains, and hotels, restaurants and bars have lounges, dining-rooms and wine cellars vaulted by arches two thousand years old. Opulent palazzi built for aristocrats and cardinals have become seats of government, and though a few are still privately owned, most have been divided up into apartments – ranging from basic basement studios to sumptuously frescoed suites owned by the rich and sometimes famous.

Although the area, originally known as the Campus Martius, was developed by Augustus as a religious and leisure centre (with temples, baths, gardens, a gigantic sundial, and an artificial lake), most of the ancient city has long disappeared. The main reason is human habitation. The area has been inhabited without a break since the sixth century, when an invading Goth cut all the city's aqueducts and forced the people to leave their homes on the hills to live near the only surviving source of water – the Tiber. They set up shacks among the ruins and, although the river was choked with animal corpses, were forced to drink the water. Hundreds died from starvation and disease.

During the medieval period the life of ordinary Romans continued, while nobles ferociously fought one another, appropriating the best of the ruins (including the Pantheon and the Mausoleum of Augustus) for fortresses, while the popes upped and went to Avignon. But in the fifteenth century, Catherine of Siena persuaded the Pope to return to Rome, and it wasn't long before the old quarter by the Tiber emerged as the wild, wealthy, raunchy heart of Renaissance Rome.

Popes, princes and cardinals moved in, or at least poured their money into the area; courtesans (high-class prostitutes) did a roaring trade; and artists and artisans were kept busy adorning the

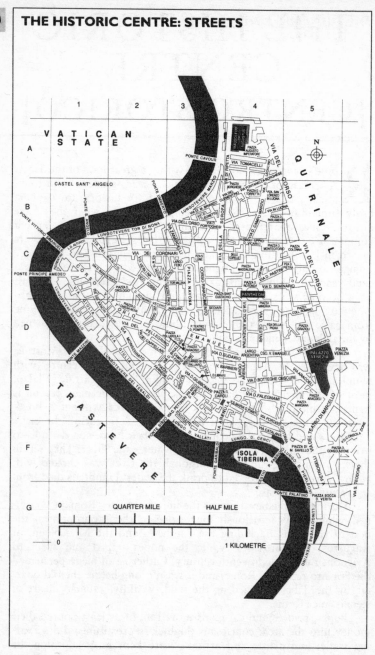

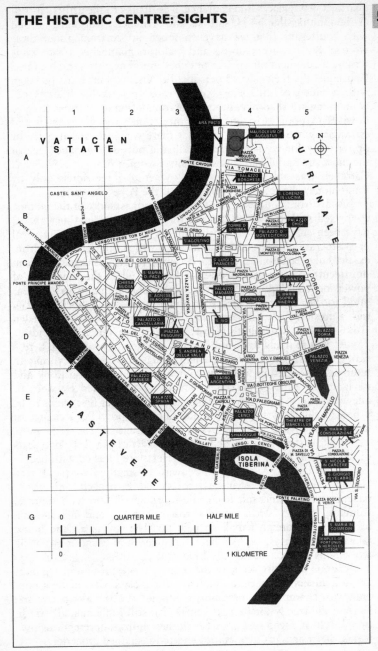

quarter's new palaces and churches. It is thanks to the artists, as well as the innumerable poets, satirists and scribblers, who hung around with courtesans that we have so much information about these women. But beware: painters and sculptors glamorised them, while writers made them the subject of either moral or pornographic tales. Consequently, their alleged personalities and exploits must be taken with a pinch of salt. The lives of more respectable Renaissance women remain shadowy, though the foundation of charities (to give dowries to poor girls, and accommodation to single women and estranged wives) is a clear sign that there was little social space or opportunity for women to make a living outside marriage. One of the most successful and shrewd businesswomen of the era, Vanozza Cattanei, was able to become the owner of three hotels only by using money she received while she was the Pope's mistress.

Apart from courtesans and lovers of popes, most of the women connected with the area (at least, those we know anything about) have been either saints, or the members of powerful (usually royal or aristocratic) families. The saints are a varied bunch, ranging from ex-alcoholic St Monica (fourth century) to St Catherine of Siena (fourteenth century), who died of fasting; while the inheritors of power include Napoleon's outrageous sister, Pauline (who compensated for her dull marriage by dreaming up ways to shock society), the refreshingly unconventional Queen Christina of Sweden (1626–89) and Mussolini's Neo-Fascist granddaughter, Alessandra.

As you're likely to spend the vast majority of your time here – eating and drinking as well as sightseeing – it's worth devoting an hour or so to getting to know your way around. If you think and navigate in terms of piazzas – which are interlinked by webs of alleyways – it's quite easy to make sense of what at first seems to be a bewildering labyrinth, and wandering also provides a chance to key into the diverse atmospheres of the different areas.

In the district around the Pantheon, sentries guard the two seats of Parliament; in the evenings whole streets are blocked with people eating ice cream. A short walk away is stagily Baroque Piazza Navona, the city's conventional social centre, fringed with pricey pavement cafés, and full from mid-morning till late with tourists, Romans, buskers, street vendors, rose-sellers . . . and men looking for a gullible foreign female to pick up. The streets around house takeaway pizzerias, stylish bars, antique shops, and restoration workshops where artisans regild Baroque cherubs.

Campo dei Fiori, scene of the centre's biggest fruit and veg market, is a gutsier neighbourhood; its working-class roots make it popular with champagne Communists, hippies and the alternative set. Despite the trendy-intellectual veneer, it's still fundamentally traditional, full of cheap and cheerful clothes shops, unpretentious trattorias, dusty artisans' workshops and old-fashioned groceries.

The Jewish Ghetto is the centre's most homely, old-fashioned quarter, its streets of ochre-washed palaces and tenements tangling around a decaying ancient Roman theatre. There are kosher groceries and Jewish restaurants, Hebrew graffiti and Stars of David, though the Gentile gentry are making inroads here too – the most coveted apartments are in a medieval fortress fused to the ruined theatre. Beyond is Tiber Island, occupied by the centre's main hospital, and Piazza Bocca della Verità, at the foot of Monte Caprino. The piazza itself is besieged by traffic, but the streets above are quiet except on sunny evenings, when they're jammed with gay men driving up the hill to the park of Monte Caprino.

PIAZZA NAVONA AND AROUND

Piazza Navona is somewhere virtually every visitor to the city spends time, but far fewer explore the labyrinthine streets around it. These are packed with trendy restaurants and bars, cheap and cheerful pizzerias, refined antique shops and restoration studios in which artisans repair, regild (and sometimes reproduce) elaborate Baroque cornices, cherubs and picture frames. Although it's a small area, it is one in which you're likely to spend a good deal of time, especially in the evenings. But it's also well worth coming by day to browse in the antique shops and trace the lives of courtesans, cardinals, bankers and artists along narrow cobbled streets lined with forbidding Renaissance palaces.

The neighbourhood really developed in the late fifteenth century, when Pope Sixtus IV (ruled 1471–84) drove two roads through it leading to the Vatican. One, the Via Recta, was designed to ferry pilgrims from the city's main street, the Corso; the other, the Via Papale, was a processional route starting at the Lateran. Bankers from Florence, Siena and Genoa flooded into the neighbourhood, keen to finance the wars and building schemes of popes and cardinals; rosary-bead and ecclesiastical souvenir-makers set up shops to tempt the pilgrims; hotels and inns were opened; and courtesans moved in to profit from the pleasure-seeking cardinals and the bright young poets, artisans and artists who made their livings from the commissions of churchmen and bankers.

Most of the Via Papale has disappeared under the modern city, but the final stretch – now consisting of Via del Governo Vecchio, Via dei Banchi Nuovi and Via del Banco di Santo Spirito – survives. Renaissance roisterer, braggart and goldsmith Benvenuto Cellini lived here, as did raffish man-about-town, satirist and pornographer Pietro Aretino. Cellini's autobiography is packed with flattering episodes about his street brawls and conquests of women; Aretino was kicked out of Rome for writing sonnets to accompany a set of engravings of sexual positions by Giulio Romano. A frequenter of courtesans (he once paid double to sleep with one on Good Friday to compensate for the grave risk to her soul), he also wrote satirical – at times sadistic – accounts of the lives of courtesans. In one play, *La Cortegiana*, he mocks their intellectual pretensions through a mother who advises her daughter that the way to advance in cultured society is to employ a poet to ghost-write verses for her, and to leave books like *Orlando Furioso*, the *Decameron* and the sonnets of Petrarch lying around.

Aretino was briefly a member of the circle of artists, writers and courtesans who clustered around the millionaire banker (and long-time lover of the courtesan Imperia, see p.224) Agostino Chigi. As their names suggest, Via dei Banchi Nuovi (Street of the New Banks) and Via del Banco di Santo Spirito (Street of the Bank of the Holy Spirit) formed the banking centre of Renaissance Rome. Bookies also operated here, pandering to the dreams of the less wealthy, and willing to take bets on anything from the election of a pope to the sex of a forthcoming baby. Nowadays the streets are pretty quiet, and the headquarters of the Chigi bank (where the papal tiara was kept for years as a loan security) in Via Arco dei Banchi is dank, neglected and cheered up only by a plastic bucket of flowers below a shrine to the Madonna. The Banco di Santo Spirito, founded in 1605 by Pope Paul V – capitalist Catholicism is an old tradition – is, however, still running.

Piazza Navona

Piazza Navona is the historic centre's main square, a tremendous cobbled arena surrounded by pavement cafés and dominated by the obelisk, cascades and gleaming marble gods of Bernini's Fontana dei Quattro Fiumi. It's lively from mid-morning till late, and there's no more entertaining place to stroll around or sit in a pavement café watching people.

They lean on the rims of its fountains; embrace, sleep or busk on its benches; and wander around with dogs, children, a camera or a triple-scoop ice cream. Gypsy children and Bangladeshis sell single cellophane-wrapped roses; caricature, portrait and cityscape artists try to interest you in their work; street vendors flog football banners, postcards, furry toys and friendship bracelets; bag-ladies and tramps beg; and groups of lads greet every passing female with a grin and *Ciao bella*!. On hot spring and summer nights it's like one big open-air party, swinging to an accompaniment of busked Seventies hits and multilingual conversations.

The piazza occupies the space of a first-century stadium built by Emperor Domitian for athletics, chariot races – and the occasional martyrdom, notably that of St Agatha (see below). During the Renaissance a market was established, and at the annual Lenten carnival there were jousting tournaments, races and processions; to add a touch of intrigue, people disguised themselves in masks, and courtesans, so as not to be recognised when off duty, often donned men's clothes.

In the seventeenth century Pope Innocent X, whose ancestral palace was in the piazza, decided to give it a facelift. He commissioned Carlo Rainaldi, his father Girolamo, and Borromini to build a church and a palace, and Bernini to create fountains, most notably the Fontana dei Fiumi, which he paid for by levying a tax on basic foods, including bread.

The market continued, run by peasants who would cook as well as sell their produce, as few Romans, especially the poorer ones, were prepared to cook at home. Mountebanks sold quack medicines, astrologers told fortunes, barbers and tooth-drawers set up stalls, and entertainment was provided by marionette shows, buskers and acrobats. Every Sunday in July and August the fountains were allowed to flood the square and the lower classes would swim, while the aristocrats held parties or looked on from their carriages.

The good-time spirit remains, but on summer evenings, especially at weekends, you may find yourself wishing you could follow the example of the courtesans and disguise yourself as a man. These are the peak times for *burrini* (see below) trawling the city for foreign girls, and Piazza Navona is one of the prime targets. It's worth having a book or newspaper (preferably Italian) to absorb yourself in as soon as you spot potential harassers: appearing to be oblivious of them is half the battle. If you don't have anything to read, developing a sudden fascination with a façade on the far side of the piazza, or deciding that now is the moment to strike up a conversation with other English-speakers in the café, can also be effective. If you actually want company, perch on a step, bench or rim of a fountain – you shouldn't have to wait long.

THE BURRINO

The original *burrini* were simply countryfolk who came to sell their butter (*burro*) at Rome's markets. They clearly got a bad name, for *burrino* is now Roman slang for a vain, cocky, and not particularly well-educated bloke from the suburbs and outlying villages. *Burrini* are best known for coming into town solely to pick up girls, and the fact that *burrino* is a term of abuse – in macho Italy, of all places – suggests that their namesakes may have cuckolded rather a lot of Romans.

Winter in Rome is largely *burrino*-free; like mosquitoes, they come out in hot weather. These are the men who hassle you on the Spanish Steps and Piazza Navona; who ask if they can share your café table even if every other one is free; and who, suddenly forgetting that they have a Crono or Scuba Swatch on their wrists, ask you the time. Their egos are unsquashable, and once you've made any contact, shaking them off can be time-consuming and occasionally dicey. Silence, pointedly ignoring them, or withering looks are the best strategies.

The Fountains

The fountains have recently been cleaned, and bleach has been added to their water to ensure that they stay that way. They look particularly splendid at night, when they're illuminated and water shadows flicker along the muscled contours of men and beasts. Bernini's Fontana dei Quattro Fiumi, in the centre, is the most striking of the three, with hefty male statues reclining on rocks spouting water at the foot of an obelisk. Innocent X invited any sculptor except Bernini (in disgrace after the collapse of a tower he had built on to St Peter's) to submit designs. Bernini took a chance, however, and presented the Pope's influential sister-in-law, Olimpia Maidalchini (see p.76), with a silver model of the fountain he wished to create. Olimpia showed this to Innocent, who was immediately enchanted, and gave the commission to Bernini. Work started in 1648.

It is little wonder that Innocent was won over by Bernini's design. The four statues represent the major rivers of the world – the Nile, the Plate, the Danube and the Ganges – and the obelisk (a symbol of paganism) is topped by a dove with an olive branch – not only a Christian symbol of peace, but the Pamphilj family emblem. Bernini's message is that the Church, under Innocent's guidance, has triumphed over heresy and brought peace to the world. Bernini was being somewhat economical with the truth, for although the 1648 Peace of Westphalia had put an end to the conflict between Catholics and Protestants, it had also severely limited the power of the papacy.

Bernini was also responsible for designing the Fontana del Moro at the south end of the piazza, in which a twisting Moor clamps a writhing fish between his thighs (the present sculpture is a copy). The third fountain, with Neptune struggling with a sea monster surrounded by sea nymphs and sea horses, is a nineteenth-century work.

Sant'Agnese in Agone

Opening hours unreliable. Supposedly Mon–Sat 5–7 p.m.; Sun 10 a.m.–1 p.m.

Tour guides inevitably tell their flocks that Bernini's river statues are recoiling in horror from the façade Borromini created for Sant'Agnese in Agone, and that the angels on the top of the church are turning their heads away from the fountain in disgust. The façade is in fact an extremely satisfying combination of curves and sharp angles, and there's no evidence to support the tale, though it's certainly true that Borromini and Bernini were arch-rivals.

The church stands on the site where in the fourth century, according to legend, Agnese, (see p. 243) a thirteen-year-old virgin, was exposed naked to the crowds for refusing to get married. Miraculously, her hair grew, cascading over her body and concealing it from the crowds. She was then thrown into a brothel (wherever there was a sports arena in ancient Rome, there were always brothels). After her ordeal in the brothel, an attempt was made to burn her at the stake, but the flames refused to touch her body, so she was killed by having her throat cut.

Innocent X commissioned the Rainaldis, architects of his Palazzo Pamphilj, to design the church. They began to build a centralised church on the plan of a Greek cross (with four equal arms), but soon realised that the west arm was going to jut too far out into the piazza. Borromini was called in to solve the problem, which he did by playing a few optical tricks inside and jettisoning the vestibule planned by the Rainaldis.

The ruins of the brothel remain below the church – musty rooms bearing traces of frescoes, with a coy relief by the Baroque sculptor Algardi, showing Agnese's hair wrapping itself around her body. In the church itself there are more representations of martyred females – St Emerantiana, Agnese's supposed foster sister, who was stoned to death; and St Cecilia, who was smothered to death in Trastevere (see p.147).

Pasquino

Just off Piazza Navona, on triangular Piazza Pasquino, is a battered stone statue with an eroded face and a speech bubble sprayed on the wall behind him. Sometimes – particularly during elections or political scandals – you'll find a satirical poem stuck on the pedestal. This is Pasquino, a third-century BC statue of Menelaus (cuckolded husband of Helen of Troy), who gave the Western world the word 'pasquinade' (a lampoon or abusive satire).

The statue was unearthed as nearby Via Leutari was being repaired in the fifteenth century, and it was in such a parlous state that no one wanted it. It was eventually dubbed Pasquino in dubious honour of a tailor who kept his ears open while working at the papal court, and became a famous source of salacious gossip. When the real Pasquino died in the mid sixteenth century the statue was erected near his old shop, and whenever anyone wanted to indulge anonymously in political satire, character assassination or rumour-mongering, while maintaining anonymity, he or she would attach a message, usually in verse, to Pasquino. The rich and famous – ranging from popes to courtesans – were the most frequent butts of pasquinades. One, from the mid sixteenth century, went:

Leave the courtesans alone
If you don't want to lose all you've got

They're prostitutes like the rest
But they cost more, for you know what.

There were three other 'talking statues' in Rome with whom
Pasquino would engage in 'dialogues' – Madame Lucrezia, who still
stands outside San Marco; Abate Luigi, by the wall of Sant'Andrea
della Valle; and Marforio, now in the courtyard of the Capitoline
Museum. Nowadays, however, you'll find far more pasquinades
graffitied around the city than on the statues.

Chiesa Nuova and Oratorio dei Filippini

Borromini's rippling façade of the Oratorio dei Filippini, and its
plainer neighbour, the Chiesa Nuova, stand on busy Corso Vittorio
Emanuele. Both buildings belonged to the Oratorians, a sixteenth-
century religious movement whose practicality, charity, and grass-
roots appeal, along with a charismatic founder, Philip Neri, were
just what the Catholic Church needed to regain credibility after the
hard knocks and violent criticism it suffered during the rise of
Protestantism.

Philip Neri (1515–95) was a Florentine businessman who had a
sudden conversion to Christianity, relinquished his old life and
came to live in Rome, paying the rent by giving lessons to his land-
lord's sons. At first he studied, but after a couple of years he sold his
books and went to work among the people, persuading bank clerks
and shop workers to abandon their evil ways and to begin caring
for the sick, the poor and pilgrims. The movement attracted people
from all strata of society, and eventually the Pope, Gregory XIII,
gave him a church, S. Maria in Vallicella. This was not overly generous, as the church was falling down – one of Philip's many visions
was of the Virgin supporting the collapsing roof over his head while
he said Mass. He soon decided he would have to build a new one.

The Chiesa Nuova (New Church), financed by donations from
rich and poor Oratorians alike, was a typically austere Counter-
Reformation church, with – on Philip's instructions – a pure white
interior. By the mid seventeenth century, however, the Church was
feeling far more confident, and the ceiling and dome were covered
with frescoes by Pietro da Cortona. Caked in gilt, its vaults and
dome aswirl with clouds, and its nave hung with red and gold brocade, this is now one of the city's most opulent churches.

Neri is depicted on the nave ceiling, with the church collapsing
around him while the Virgin plays Superwoman and holds up the
roof. In the apse is a frothy Assumption, and in the dome (unfortunately rather shadowy) you can just make out fluffy clouds, curly-
headed cherubs, and a God and Christ.

Rubens came to Rome in 1606, and two years later he was

commissioned to paint three canvases for the Chiesa Nuova. The
first versions were rejected, as they were too shiny, so he painted
them again on slate to reduce reflections. His visit was cut short by
the illness of his mother. He rushed back to Antwerp, but she was
already dead, and he placed the original versions of the paintings
over her tomb. The finest of the works here is *Domitilla, Achilleo e
Nereo* on the right, dominated by a regally dressed Domitilla.
There's no hint that the two men, as well as converting Domitilla to
Christianity, were her alleged eunuchs.

Oratorio and the Oratorians

The Oratorians' influence was not only religious. Philip can also be
credited with the invention of the oratorio, for one of the ways in
which he spread the Word to the people was in musical gatherings.
Biblical stories were retold in sung dialogue, and the congregation
would join in for the *laudi*, a kind of chorus.

These gatherings took place in the Oratorio dei Filippini next
door, largely rebuilt by Borromini, which is now used as a concert
hall. The oratory is actually just part of a complex which includes
accommodation for the Oratorians, a refectory and a library, but it
is open only for performances. Soon, however, you should be able
to see Borromini's other major contribution to the complex – a bell
tower at the back – which has been covered in scaffolding for the
past year or so.

The 'Antique' Streets

Of all the streets devoted to antique shops in the *centro storico*, Via
dei Coronari is the showpiece. It forms part of a long straight street
laid out in the late fifteenth century on the orders of Sixtus IV to
lead pilgrims from the Corso to St Peter's as quickly as possible. At
first it was imaginatively called the Via Recta (the straight street),
but it soon became known as Coronari after the rosary-makers
[*coronari*] who set up shops there to exploit passing trade.
Nowadays a stroll down Coronari is a must for anyone who is into
antiques – though it's wiser to browse rather than buy, as prices are
inflated. Although John Paul II has put a stop to priests selling off
church treasures (which they were frequently forced to do in order
to pay for repairs) you'll still find altarpieces, crucifixes and
cherubs, along with heavy Baroque furniture, chandeliers and copies
of antique statues.

Though it's diverting at any time of year, the street becomes
magical in late October and late May, when the shops stay open till
11 p.m., a carpet is laid over the cobbles, torches are lit above the
doorways, and pots of lemon and kumquat bushes are put out. The
shops are, however, rather chi-chi, and if you really want to find out

about antiques in Rome you'd be better off chatting to the artisans and dealers in the restoration workshops on Via del Panico, Via Monte Giordano, Via del Orso and Via del Parione.

Santa Maria della Pace

Enter through the cloisters
Open   Tues–Sat   10a.m.–noon;   4–6p.m.;   Sun 10a.m.–noon.
Closed Mon

Between Via dei Coronari and trendy Bar della Pace, at the head of a tiny cobbled piazza flanked by scabby walls and balconies lusciously curtained with ivy, is the little church of Santa Maria della Pace. The façade, with its jutting semicircular portico, is a seventeenth-century creation by Pietro da Cortona, but the church was built on the orders of Pope Sixtus IV in 1480. His obsessive nepotism had led to a violent clash with the Medicis, which plunged Rome into war with Florence. While war was still raging, a drunken soldier either stabbed or threw a stone at a painting of the Madonna, whose breast began to bleed. Sixtus came to witness the miracle, and vowed to dedicate a church to the Virgin if she ended the war. The war actually ended because the Turks invaded southern Italy and Sixtus had to redeploy his troops, but – apparently accepting that God works in mysterious ways – he built the church anyway.

Along with Sant'Agostino, Santa Maria was the most fashionable church in Renaissance Rome, frequented by artists, bankers and courtesans. Fiammetta (see below) left property to the church, and Agostino Chigi (see p.142 and box, p.224) commissioned a chapel from his protégé Raphael.

The church is usually entered through the cloisters, built in 1504 to a refined design by Bramante with arcades on the lower storey and colonnades above. It was his first work in Rome, and the city's first real taste of Renaissance architecture.

You can't get close enough to the high altar to see the Virgin icon properly, but – on a sunny afternoon, at least – Raphael's contribution is easily visible. He painted the four Sibyls above the arch of the Chigi chapel just to the right of the church's front (usually closed) door. Each of the Sibyls, ranging from a blonde beauty to an old veiled woman, is receiving a revelation from an angel. Though – as far as anyone knows – the blonde is not a portrait of a courtesan, Raphael himself wrote that in order to create a beautiful woman he had to see many beauties, so they no doubt made some contribution.

Opposite the Chigi chapel is an early-sixteenth-century memorial to the Ponzetti family, with delicately sculpted busts of father, mother and two almost identical daughters, Lavinia and Beatrice, who died in childhood of the plague. Equally exquisite are the stucco reliefs framing the Cesi chapel (second right) carved with rams' heads, twisting swans, cherubs, birds, and foliage. Inside, supported on sphinxes, are the tombs of Angelo Cesi (reclining with a pile of books) and his wife, Franciscina (reading). Above the chapel are frescoes of Adam and Eve by Rosso il Fiorentino, heavily influenced by Michelangelo's version of the same scene in the Sistine Chapel: he too made Satan a woman.

Casa di Fiammetta

On Piazza Fiammetta, overlooked by a military court, is a small mink-brown house with sloping walls, decked with ivy and roses. It was the fifteenth-century home of Fiammetta, a famous courtesan, mistress of Cesare Borgia and one of the few to die rich. The sources of her wealth are mysterious. In 1479, when she was probably only fourteen, a certain Cardinal Ammannati bequeathed her a house and *vigna* (a kind of garden). The rest of his will was disregarded by Pope Sixtus IV (the Church appropriated his estate), but Fiammetta received her portion. When Fiammetta died she left her estate to her 'brother' Andrea, stating that if he had no descendants it should be donated to the Sistine Chapel on condition that a Mass was said for her annually. The theory is that Andrea was probably Fiammetta's son, and, moreover, the son of a man who was powerful enough to ensure that his mistress received her bequest. Who the man was – Sixtus himself, or one of his relatives or colleagues – is a matter for speculation.

Via dell'Orso and the Courtesans

Now studded with restoration workshops and clothes boutiques, in the Renaissance this narrow cobbled street consisted almost solely of inns. One of them, the *Osteria dell'Orso*, still remains, a sturdy fifteenth-century building with a loggia and mighty overhanging eaves. Wealthy travellers were a major source of income for courtesans, and many of the most successful and fashionable (the only ones who could afford it) lived in or around this street. The doors of their houses were usually made of iron – to safeguard their considerable collections of jewels, precious objects and sumptuous clothes (most of them gifts) as well as to protect themselves. The revenge of rejected lovers could be vicious. Slashing a courtesan's face, and thereby ruining her beauty, was one popular measure; another was the *trentuno*, in which the woman was abducted and raped by thirty-one men; or the *trentuno reale*, in which the ordeal was tripled.

Among the courtesans who lived near Via dell'Orso was Beatrice Ferrarese, one of a handful of women suggested as the semi-naked subject of Raphael's *La Fornarina* (in the Barberini). She certainly posed nude for Giulio Romano (the painting, *Lady at her Toilet*, is now in Russia) and inspired two poems, *Il Vanto della Cortigiana Ferrarese* and *Il Lamento della Cortigiana Ferrarese*, probably by Giambattista Verini. In these monologues Beatrice (who ended up with syphilis) is made to embody the pride and fall of a courtesan. In *Il Vanto*, 'Beatrice' describes the luxuries of her house and wardrobe (dresses of gold, velvet and silk embroidered with pears and gems), her extravagant dinner parties (menus included quails, capons, partridges, pheasants, thrushes and pigeons, fruit preserved in liqueurs, and the finest wines), and a glitzy social life. In *Il Lamento*, Beatrice, by now old and suffering from syphilis, tells of her downfall: how she pawned her clothes and jewels, became a landlady, a procuress, a washerwoman and a cook, and went to work in the sordid brothels of Ponte Sisto before ending up in a hospital for venereal diseases. Beatrice's life was doubtless embroidered by her unofficial biographer, but few courtesans were astute enough to plan for the time when their beauty had faded.

A letter from Beatrice to Lorenzo de' Medici survives, and its disarming frankness gives a rare glimpse of the personality behind the façade, even if the letter is obviously designed to amuse and titillate Lorenzo.

First she apologises for not writing earlier (too busy doing 'you know very well what, night and day'), and tells him about her attempts to purify herself during Holy Week ('I confessed to our preacher at Sant'Agostino . . . Gambiera and Taddea confessed on the same day as me, all of us one after another. Just think, Your Excellency, what a lot of fine things he must have heard . . .'); she then describes how she suffered during a self-imposed eight-day abstinence ('It seemed like eight years, and I began to wonder if I was still capable') and finally confesses ('I've made up for it since').

Torre della Scimmia

At the point where Via dell'Orso becomes Via dei Portoghesi is a crumbling pale-brick tower draped with ivy known as the Torre della Scimmia. If you look closely, you can see a statue of the Virgin with a lamp at the top. According to legend, the family who lived there had a pet monkey, and one day the father came home to find his tower surrounded by distressed neighbours praying to the Virgin. He looked up, and saw at the top of the tower the monkey holding the family's baby. He muttered a prayer, then whistled to the monkey, who obediently climbed down, carefully holding the infant. Grateful for the miracle, the father placed a statue of the Virgin on top of the tower, and vowed that a lamp should burn in front of it for all eternity. In the days before electricity this was quite a job – in Nathaniel Hawthorne's *The Marble Faun* the highmoralled Hilda lives in the tower and looks after the lamp – but nowadays, the vagaries of Rome's electricity supply permitting, the lamp is perpetually on.

THE PANTHEON AND AROUND

The compact core of cobbled streets and piazzas around the Pantheon is crammed with enough churches and palaces, restaurants, cafés and ice-cream parlours to keep you busy for several days. The city's layers of history are obvious at almost every turn. Sentry boxes and entry-phones mark the doors of *palazzi* – depending on whether they're used as seats of government or apartments; tramps sleep outside the Pantheon, and the tombs of Italy's ex-royal family lie within; and embedded in the walls of the former Stock Exchange are the pollution-chewed columns of an ancient temple.

The bustle is constant. Businessmen remonstrate into portable phones; ice-cream eaters jam the streets between Giolitti and the Gelateria della Palma; chauffeurs leap into action as press photographers pounce on their politician; *burrini* (see box, p.55) walk round and round Piazza della Rotonda, trying to meet the eye of a female foreigner; and everywhere there are tourists, struggling with maps as they try to work out exactly where they are in the labyrinth of the *centro storico*.

Apart from the Pantheon and Mausoleum of Augustus, little of the ancient city has survived intact. Keep an eye out, though, and you will see fragments of the ancient city – such as a marble foot from a statue of Isis (on Via Pie' de Marmo) and a stone cat from her temple (on Via del Gatto). The lives of women are richly interwoven in the area's history.

The cult of Isis (see p.82), an Egyptian fertility goddess, was particularly popular with women, and though it was banned on numerous occasions (it gained a reputation for sexual licence) Caligula embraced the cult, and built a temple to the goddess. From the Renaissance onwards pregnant women and mothers began to go to the church of Sant'Agostino seeking help and solace from the Madonna of Childbirth and St Monica, the patron saint of mothers. They still go today, and the church is the focus for the annual celebrations in honour of St Rita, a saint whose patronage of unhappy marriages has earned her a popularity which outdoes even that of the Virgin Mary. It was hereabouts too (though the building has vanished) that St Ignatius Loyola founded a hostel for prostitutes and women who had left their husbands.

Powerful women have also been associated with the neighbourhood. Catherine de' Medici and Margaret of Parma lived in the Palazzo Madama before going off to rule France and the Netherlands as regents, persecuting Protestants and Huguenots. St Catherine of Siena, who shamed the Pope into returning to Rome from Avignon (see p.81), died of anorexia here; and St Monica's body was brought here after she died in Ostia (see p.71).

As for the aristocracy, Pauline Bonaparte, Napoleon's sister, reluctantly married to a Prince Borghese, cheered herself up by shocking polite society (see p.73); and Princess Doria (see p.77), the daughter of a Scottish doctor, shocked Mussolini by refusing to surrender her wedding ring to swell the nation's gold reserves. Nowadays more newspaper column inches are devoted to his granddaughter Alessandra than to any other woman in Italy. Voted in April 1992 into the Chamber of Deputies, the ex-actress and onetime pin-up girl is the pretty face of Italian Neo-Fascism.

As there is too much around the Pantheon to see comfortably in a single day, we have traced two routes through the district. One leads from the Pantheon, up Via della Scrofa to the Ara Pacis and Mausoleum of Augustus; the other snakes up from the Palazzo Doria to Piazza San Lorenzo in Lucina.

FIRST ROUTE

The Pantheon

Open Mon–Sat 9 a.m.–2 p.m.; Sun 9 a.m.–1 p.m.; free

Designed by a goddess – according to a credulous medieval guidebook writer – the Pantheon is the most remarkable and best preserved of Rome's ancient buildings. A dour brick cylinder fused to a shallow dome, it towers above the obelisk-fountain and pavement cafés on Piazza della Rotonda and dwarfs the bag-ladies, gypsies and down-and-outs who shelter beneath its immense portico.

The streetpeople's bundles heaped around the column bases may appear to be something of an eyesore, but finding practical uses for the Pantheon is nothing new. In medieval Rome the portico was packed with the booths of a poultry market (you can still see some of the scars left by poles which supported the tarpaulins) and a fish market flourished outside on Piazza della Rotonda until 1847. Wealthier folk abused the Pantheon even more – a Byzantine emperor stripped the gilded tiles from the roof, medieval barons used it as a fortress, and Pope Urban VIII removed the portico's bronze ceiling and had it melted down for Bernini's *baldacchino* (see p.156) in St Peter's.

It's not so surprising that the writer of the *Mirabilia*, a thirteenth-century pilgrims' guidebook to Rome, was so awed by the Pantheon that he credited its design and structure to Cybele, the mother of all gods (see p.200). According to the *Mirabilia*, on the eve of a battle against the Persians Cybele appeared in a vision to

Emperor Augustus's right-hand man, Agrippa and told him he could expect victory as long as he promised to build a temple. She even showed him what it should look like and exactly how to construct it. Being a dutiful kind of man, Agrippa, when he returned victorious to Rome, built the temple and dedicated it to Cybele, Neptune and all deities. (The word *pantheon*, incidentally, comes from the Greek *pan* [all] and *theos* [god].)

The current Pantheon, however, is not the one built by Agrippa, though its pediment, pocked with holes (into which a sculptured relief was pegged), still bears a Latin inscription proclaiming that it is. The writer of the *Mirabilia* had no way of knowing that Agrippa's Pantheon had been a small, straightforward rectangular temple with columns. This was damaged by fire in AD 80, and although Domitian restored it, Hadrian decided to rebuild it completely. Hadrian has been credited with designing the new Pantheon himself, allegedly inspired by contemplating a pumpkin.

In the seventh century Christians found themselves afflicted by demons as they walked past the Pantheon, so Pope Boniface IV obtained permission from the Emperor, Phocas, to turn it into a church. Though the demons may have been exorcised, the Pantheon's pagan past was not entirely forgotten. Boniface dedicated the new church to the Virgin and all martyred saints, just as the Pantheon had been dedicated to the mother goddess and all gods.

The Building   *Those less interested in technical details should perhaps skip the next paragraphs, wander inside the Pantheon, and just feel its incredible harmony. But if you want to know why it feels like it does, and how it was achieved, read on.*

From the outside the Pantheon looks pretty straightforward – a cylinder fused to a shallow dome with an immense pedimented porchway stuck on the front. Step inside, however, and you'll find that instead of the shallow roof you expected, there's a stunning hemispherical coffered dome with a hole in the middle – the outer dome is simply a lid. What's more, the radius of the hemisphere is exactly equal to the height of the cylinder – a ball (or, indeed, a pumpkin) with a diameter of 43.3 metres would fit perfectly inside it.

The technology involved in constructing and supporting the great dome was ingenious. The key to its success was concrete. Concrete (made of sand, lime and rubble) had been in use since the late third century BC, but by Augustus's time sand had been replaced with *pozzolana*, a reddish volcanic dust which reacted with lime to form a particularly hard, solid mass. The Pantheon's cylinder is made of two walls of brick with concrete sandwiched between, and in order that the walls could support the dome, the kind of rubble used in the concrete was graded. The rubble in the lower tier was heavy – travertine and tufa; in the second tier a slightly lighter mix of tufa and brick was used; and in the third tier, simply brick. The dome itself was also made of graded concrete – which was probably poured on to an immense mould. The rubble in the lower section is of brick and pumice, and in the top of pumice alone.

Inside the Pantheon An odd thing about the interior of the Pantheon is that it looks more Renaissance or Baroque than Roman. Its coffered dome, the inlaid marble floor and walls, and the alternating triangular and rounded pediments around its walls are familiar from scores of Renaissance and Baroque palaces and churches. But the decor is original, and its overfamiliarity is merely a result of the Pantheon's influence on later generations of architects.

Raphael is buried in the Pantheon, in an illuminated tomb decorated with a pair of eroded doves and a hefty Madonna and Child. According to his wishes the name of his fiancée, Maria Bibiena, was inscribed on a plaque to the right. Raphael protracted the engagement for six years – probably because of his affair with *La Fornarina* (see p.117 and 142).

The Pantheon also contains the bodies of some of Italy's short-lived royal family – the first king, Vittorio Emanuele II (who has probably given his name to more streets in Italy than any other individual, except perhaps Garibaldi); his successor, Umberto I, who was assassinated by an anarchist in 1900; and his wife, Margherita, who gave her name to a pizza. Their descendants are alive and living in Switzerland, occasionally make the pages of weekly magazines, and there are still rare calls to bring them back. Italian royalists still come to pay homage, placing chrysanthemums before their massy marble and porphyry tombs or signing their names on registers honouring the dead monarchs.

Sant'Ivo della Sapienza

Open Sun mornings only

To the west of the Pantheon, Sant'Ivo, Borromini's most ingenious church, is concealed within the sixteenth-century courtyard of the city's former university, La Sapienza. From a distance you can see its scalloped cupola and golden spiralling pinnacle peeking above the walls, but close up, it's possible to walk straight past without realising it. On weekdays you enter the courtyard along a tunnel just off Piazza Sant'Eustachio, passing the entrances to the national archives offices which now occupy the old university building. On Sunday mornings, the only time the church itself is open, you can enter through a door on Corso di Rinascimento.

WOMEN AND EDUCATION

Though the current building, by Giacomo della Porta, dates from the sixteenth century, Rome's university, the Sapienza, was founded by Pope Boniface VIII in 1303. The establishment of this and similar institutions throughout medieval Europe proved to be a massive blow to women. Up until then, joining a religious Order had provided their main access to education, and many convents and monasteries had become dynamic centres of learning and debate. The shift to the universities, which were open only to ordained priests, meant that women were automatically excluded from intellectual life. Boniface himself expressed a common fear of the malign effect the presence of women, even nuns, could have on men, and was in no doubt about what the proper place of religious women should be : 'All and sundry nuns, present and future, to whatever Order they belong . . . shall henceforth remain perpetually enclosed . . . so that no nun . . . shall henceforth have or be able to have the power of going out of those monasteries for whatever reason or excuse . . .'

It was at about this time that the story of Pope Joan evolved, an insidious cautionary tale about what happens when women are educated. Disguised as a man, Joan entered a religious Order, and because she was a brilliant student she went on to become a cardinal in Rome. She was eventually elected pope, but, 'being a woman', she could not control her baser instincts, and secretly slept with a man. On the day of her inauguration as pope, as she was riding from St Peter's to the Lateran, she collapsed in a narrow street between the Colosseum and San Clemente, and died giving birth in the gutter. The belief that there had been a female pope sometime in the ninth, tenth or eleventh century persisted until the seventeenth century.

During the Renaissance poor women (and men) received no education, while for the daughters of the middle and upper classes learning was largely restricted to domestic skills, and perhaps music and dancing. If they were taught to read and write, it was exclusively in Italian – at a time when Latin was the language of scholarship. They were encouraged to read about the lives of saints and other morally uplifting works, though vernacular romances were also avidly devoured. Boccaccio's often raunchy *Decameron* is addressed to an audience of 'dear ladies', though his *Concerning Famous Women* (a catalogue of the lives of 160 women written for a female patron) reinforced stereotypes of the ideal woman as demure, silent and chaste. The handful of active women portrayed get their comeuppance (imprisonment, martyrdom, etc.) for breaking the rules of 'normal' female behaviour. The cachet of culture can be gauged from the fact that courtesans were keen to advertise their literacy.

Without Latin, the intellectual world was closed. Most nuns were taught only enough Latin to understand prayers – many would have made no sense whatever of the Latin sermons they heard. Nevertheless, some determined women did manage to study to a high level – either within a convent, or because they were the daughters of enlightened men. It was not until 1678 that a woman – the Venetian aristocrat Elena Cornaro Piscopia – was granted a doctorate by an Italian university (Padua), and she had studied independently. A few years earlier, though, Queen Christina of Sweden had visited the Sapienza, and appears to have impressed the authorities with her formidable intellect and learning, for she was presented with a hundred books.

Borromini was commissioned to build the church in 1642. A restlessly inventive architect, fascinated with intricate geometry and the interplay of convex and concave curves, he was also a difficult man, smarting from the indignity of having worked for years in the shadow of his hugely popular contemporary, Bernini. It was Bernini, however, who recommended Borromini for this job.

The church took over twenty years to build, spanning the regimes of three popes, and Borromini deftly incorporated all their coats of arms in the decorations: Urban VIII's Barberini bees, Innocent X's Pamphilj dove with an olive branch in its beak, and Alexander VII's Chigi star and jelly mould. If you have binoculars you'll be able to make out some more bizarre details – like the bald heads beneath the cornice of the drum.

On Sunday mornings Sant'Ivo's hexagonal interior is packed with families singing jolly hymns and teenagers strumming guitars. Though the Italian version of 'Go Tell it on the Mountain' is hardly the most appropriate accompaniment for the most sophisticated church in Rome, no one seems to mind if you stand at the back. The shape of the church – basically a hexagonal star – resembles an exotic, geometric flower, with alternating scooped and sharply angled bays forming the 'petals'. The floor plan is echoed in the six segments of the pure cream dome, decorated with Chigi stars and angels with folded wings.

Palazzo Madama

Instantly recognisable by the stone doughnuts wrapped around its columns, the Palazzo Madama was built in the seventeenth century on the site of a palace which had been home to two women who became regents of foreign countries. Catherine de' Medici (1519–89) left the palazzo to marry Henri II of France; after his death (from a jousting wound) in 1559 she ruled France as regent for her sons. After Catherine had left, her sister-in-law Margaret of Parma moved in. As the illegitimate daughter of Emperor Charles V (who was also King of Spain) her only official title was 'Madama' – hence the palace's name. In 1559, after Charles had abdicated and retired to a monastery, his fanatically Catholic son Philip passed the Spanish-ruled Netherlands over to Margaret, leaving her to carry out his rigidly anti-Protestant policies. She performed her duties with relish, and instigated some of the bloodiest excesses of the religious wars.

Nowadays little columns of soldiers emerge at intervals from the grand gateway; sentries stand guard in wooden boxes; clusters of demonstrators regularly chant outside; and every so often a shiny black car arrives to pick up an elderly besuited man. This is Rome's Senate House, home to 315 elected elder statesmen and 10 honorary life members. After the 1992 elections, although the overall number of women in Parliament fell, the number of women in the Senate rose from 21 to 31, over half of them members of the PDS (the reformed Communist Party). Nilde Iotti, veteran member of the ex-Communist Party, got more votes than any other woman (72,000) and was nominated as a candidate for President of the Republic.

San Luigi dei Francesi

Open daily 7.30 a.m.–12.30 p.m.; 3.30–7 p.m. Closed Thur p.m.

Catherine de' Medici contributed a substantial proportion of the funds to build San Luigi, the church of Rome's French community. It had been founded by her relative, Giulio de' Medici (the future Pope Clement VII), in 1518, but work progressed slowly and it was only thanks to funding from Catherine, her husband and son that it was completed in 1589.

The interior is lavish, with exotic marble columns, fluid stuccoes, lashings of gilt, and a frescoed ceiling showing France's patron saint, Louis, being sucked up to heaven. Louis (1214–70) was also King of France, and when he tried to ban prostitution in Paris, the city's gentlemen were furious. Their excuse was that it was no longer safe for their wives and daughters to walk the streets.

The main reason for visiting the church is the Contarelli chapel at the foot of the left aisle, which holds three tremendous canvases by Caravaggio. In order to see them you'll need a generous supply of 200-lire coins to feed the slot-machine lights. Each painting depicts a scene from the life of St Matthew, and all three reveal Caravaggio's skill at using light as a dramatic device. The left-hand canvas shows the young Matthew being called by Christ from the tax office where he worked. The light glints on the rims of coins, glides along slim hosed thighs, and spotlights the faces of Christ and the main characters. In the sinister *Martyrdom* (right) the detail of every figure – from the the the sprawling saint and the muscled body of his executor to the screaming face of a young acolyte – is bathed in sickly light. The original version of the third scene, *St Matthew and the Angel*, was rejected by the priests of San Luigi, because Caravaggio had (irreverently, they considered) painted Matthew with dusty feet. In the second version, Caravaggio jettisoned dirty realism for the acrobatics of a swirling angel.

In 1614 Domenichino (who tried to engineer Lanfranco's death in Sant'Andrea della Valle; see p.88) frescoed five episodes from the life of St Cecilia (see p.146) in the second right-hand chapel. The pale lucid scenes include Cecilia distributing clothes to the poor, refusing to sacrifice to an idol, and fainting as she is suffocated to death in the hot steam bath of her house. On the altar is a copy of Raphael's sombre *St Cecilia* (in Bologna) by Guido Reni.

Now the most important church in the city for Roman mothers, as it holds the tomb of *St Monica* (long-suffering mother of Augustine) and a statue of the Madonna (devoted to helping pregnant women), Sant'Agostino used to be a favourite with courtesans. For well-heeled courtesans in Renaissance Rome, going to church, dressed in all one's finery, was a crucial publicity exercise. Crowds of young men would gather outside the severe façade of Sant'Agostino waiting for the courtesans to arrive with entourages of servants and pages.

The women looked magnificent, dripping with jewellery and dressed in the latest, most sumptuous and ostentatious styles, with their hair usually bleached blonde and elaborately curled. It was a priest from Sant'Agostino who, in Beatrice Ferrarese's hilarious account (see p.62), heard the confessions of courtesans in Holy Week, and many of them, including the courtesan-poet Tullia d'Aragona, were buried here. This was in fact against the law: prostitutes were supposed to be buried outside the walls near the Muro Torto.

The most sought-after courtesans were not only skilled in bed but, at the very least, had to be witty conversationalists and competent musicians or singers, while some even studied literature and wrote poetry. A famous courtesan was thus a highly desirable accessory to a dinner party. She was also a demonstration of the host's wealth – sticking with him only for as long as he was the richest man she could find. It would regularly happen that the courtesan had at one time been the lover of most of the men present. The most fashionable parties were thrown by a circle of artists and writers who gathered around one Giovanni Goritz, a wealthy patron. Goritz's acolytes included Raphael, the sculptor and architect Andrea Sansovino, and writers like Castiglione, author of *The Book of the Courtier*, the era's most sophisticated handbook of courtly behaviour, and the poet, literary theorist and eventual cardinal Pietro Bembo, who as a young man had a tender, passionate and probably Platonic affair with Lucrezia Borgia.

All were heavily into Neo-Platonism, a seductive and arcane fusion of paganism and Christianity which conveniently allowed them to believe that physical beauty was a manifestation of spiritual purity. At Goritz's parties guests would dazzle one another with their wit and erudition, ruminate over the meaning of love, and improvise verses in which the Virgin, saints and mistresses alike were addressed as if they were Classical goddesses such as Venus and Juno.

Something similar may have been in Jacopo (pupil of Andrea) Sansovino's mind in 1521 when he sculpted the so-called *Madonna*

ST MONICA AND ST AUGUSTINE

St Monica, best known as the mother of St Augustine, lived in North Africa in the fourth century with her unfaithful, debauched, hot-tempered husband and his difficult mother. Not surprisingly, she took refuge in alcohol, but managed to kick the habit and convert her husband and her mother-in-law to Christianity. Nor did she have an easy time with her son Augustine (she once got so fed up with his wild lifestyle that she threw him out), who rejected Christianity after studying philosophy, lived with a woman for fifteen years, and had an illegitimate son. She stopped arguing with him after a priest told her to be patient, and that the time for Augustine's conversion would eventually come, but when he sneaked off to Rome and Milan, she followed him.

In Milan, he sampled various religions before St Ambrose, then the city's bishop, convinced him to convert to Christianity. The squabbles were not quite over – Monica began to plan his marriage, whereupon Augustine opted for celibacy. As a born-again celibate and rabid misogynist he has arguably had a more pernicious effect on the lives of Catholic women than any other individual. He decided that sex was a culpable act which could be justified only by procreation – a theory which still lies at the heart of Catholic teaching and its belief that contraception is sinful. He also developed what can only be called a phobia about women, most probably because he knew he was easily tempted. His lodger reported: 'No woman ever set foot inside his house. He never spoke with a woman except in the presence of a third person or outside the parlour. He made no exceptions, not even for his elder sister and his nieces, all three of them nuns.' In time Augustine decided to return home, accompanied (presumably in the presence of a third party) by his mother, but Monica died at Ostia, blissfully happy to have seen her son turn into a good Catholic. She is now considered by the Church to be *the* model Catholic mother.

ST RITA OF CASCIA (1377–1447)

Because of its special associations for women, every year, from 18–22 May, Sant'Agostino hosts the festival of St Rita of Cascia. In a recent women's magazine survey asking readers to vote for their favourite saint, St Rita came out top, beating the Madonna. The reason is sobering. Married to a man who was not only unfaithful but violent towards her, she has been adopted as the patron saint of women with marital problems. As a young woman she wanted to become a nun, but married to keep her parents happy. She endured the marriage for eighteen years, until her husband was killed in a vendetta. Shortly afterwards her two sons died, and Rita became a nun. As she devoted herself to contemplating the Passion of Christ, wounds appeared on her forehead, as if it had been pierced by a crown of thorns. They remained for fifteen years – time which she mostly spent caring for sick nuns. She died in 1447 of tuberculosis, and though she was beatified in the seventeenth century she was canonised only in 1900.

del Parto (Madonna of Childbirth), which stands right at the back of the church. The Virgin's Classical features and heavy drapery look as if they should belong to a pagan goddess, and it has even been suggested that she may have been inspired by the mother-goddess Juno. For centuries she has been one of the most popular

Madonnas in Rome, visited by women who wish to conceive, or give thanks after the birth of a child. In ancient times women did exactly the same at the shrine of *Juno Lucina* on the Esquiline Hill.

The Madonna del Parto is surrounded by silver heart ex-votives, paintings of grateful suppliants (including, perplexingly, two of men falling off ladders) and bouquets of flowers. Her foot is covered with a bronze shoe, because the alabaster was being worn away by the hundreds of women who stroked it as they prayed. Presumably the baby Christ wears a bronze loincloth for a different reason.

Goritz commissioned two works of art for the church. Raphael's contribution is easy to miss: a macho, Michelangelesque fresco of the prophet Isaiah on the third left-hand pillar. Michelangelo liked it. When Goritz complained about what it had cost, he retorted that the knee (which is actually rather knobbly) alone was worth the price.

Below it is a caramel-coloured marble statue group by Andrea Sansovino of the Virgin, St Anne and Child. Like the Isaiah, it was commissioned by Goritz, who for some reason considered St Anne (the Virgin's aged mother) to be his patron saint. On 26 July, St Anne's feast day, Goritz and his followers would gather below the medallion and recite the pagan-Christian poems which they had written to the saint.

Also easy to overlook is the tomb of St Monica, the patron saint of mothers (see box), in the chapel to the left of the high altar. Finally, don't miss a canvas by Caravaggio, the *Madonna di Loreto* (a.k.a. Madonna dei Pellegrini) in the first left-hand chapel. It shows a peasant-like Virgin standing in her doorway with two pilgrims kneeling at the threshold. The priests of Sant'Agostino were clearly less fussy than those at neighbouring San Luigi: the soles of the pilgrims' feet are filthy, and even the Madonna has dirty toenails.

Palazzo Borghese and the Borghese Princesses

Former home of Napoleon's sister, Princess Pauline Borghese (1780–1825), and later to the pious Princess Gwendolen (died 1840), the Palazzo Borghese is known as *il cembalo* (the harpsichord). You'll see why if you walk from the narrow façade facing the Tiber (the 'keyboard' is a terraced garden) around the gracefully curving structure. The palace was probably designed by Vignola (who was responsible for the interior of the Gesù) in the mid sixteenth century, and bought in 1605 by Cardinal Camillo Borghese, just before he became Pope Paul V. For centuries it housed the paintings from the family collection which are now in the Villa Borghese.

In 1803, already a widow at the age of twenty-three, Pauline Bonaparte, Napoleon's favourite sister, married Prince Camillo Borghese, a fantastically wealthy, handsome, though rather stupid young man. They came to live in the Palazzo Borghese, where their arrival was celebrated by an invitation for an audience with the Pope (Pauline pleaded fatigue), a banquet for eight hundred guests, and a ball for one thousand six hundred. Pauline charmed the Romans, but was not happy with her new home. It was cold and damp, and the vast number of paintings made it look like an art gallery. Even worse, there was no bathroom. Nor was she happy with her husband, and claimed that she would rather have remained a widow than be married to a eunuch.

ELIZABETH PATTERSON BONAPARTE

After Napoleon's death, Pauline invited her ex-sister-in-law, Elizabeth Patterson Bonaparte, to Rome. An American woman from Baltimore, she had met Napoleon and Pauline's younger brother, Jerome, when she was nineteen and he was serving in the French navy. They fell in love, and despite the opposition of her father, who suspected that Napoleon would hardly consider a match with a Baltimore girl desirable, they married. When Napoleon found out, he was indeed livid and demanded that Jerome return to France. After two years Jerome eventually relented, and he and Elizabeth sailed across to France, only to discover that Napoleon had forbidden Elizabeth to enter French territory. While Jerome went to see Napoleon, Elizabeth sailed to England and gave birth to a son, Jerome, in Camberwell.

As the Pope (understandably, given the existence of Jerome Junior) refused to annul the marriage, a French Council of State issued a divorce decree, and Napoleon gave Elizabeth an annual pension on condition that she remained in America. Jerome was married off to a German princess, and Elizabeth went dutifully back home. She hated Baltimore, and loathed Americans so much that she even contemplated suicide.

Once Napoleon was dead, she jumped at the chance to return to Europe and stayed for twenty-five years, doing the High Society rounds and planning a splendid match for her son. To her utter horror and disbelief, he sloped back to America and married a girl from Baltimore. 'I always told him', she said, 'that he should never degrade himself by marrying an American.'

Some time later her father died, cutting her out of his will because 'Betsey has through life been so disobedient. . . . she has caused me more anxiety and trouble than all my other children put together, and her folly and misconduct have occasioned me a train of expense . . .'

She returned to America, aged forty-nine and adopted the lifestyle of a pauper, living in Baltimore boarding-houses in rooms piled high with trunks of old European party dresses. In fact, when she died in 1879 at the age of ninety-four, she left a fortune of one and half million dollars.

As soon as she could find an excuse (the death of her son and Napoleon's forthcoming coronation) she left Rome for France, delighting and shocking polite society with her numerous, very public affairs, and a penchant for being carried scantily clad in the arms of a black servant to her daily milk-bath. She returned to Rome only after Waterloo, presiding over *salons* and attempting to persuade influential English friends to secure Napoleon's release from

St Helena. By this time she was over forty and had given up her affairs, but she still delighted to shock, inviting guests to come and observe her daily foot manicure.

Gwendolen Talbot was a completely different type of woman. The daughter of the Earl of Shrewsbury, she married the hapless Camillo's nephew, Prince Marcantonio Borghese, in 1835. Her time was spent caring for the poor and the sick, and in 1837, when cholera raged through the city and anyone who could afford to left, Gwendolen remained to help. Three years later, she and Marcantonio put on a public fête in the grounds of the Villa Borghese. The princess spent the day chatting to mothers and playing with children. A few days later she developed a sore throat, and doctors, on examining her, realised that she would not recover. She died that night, followed shortly by three of her four children. She was twenty-three.

The palace – now looking extremely sumptuous – is not officially open to the public, though a suite of richly frescoed, mirrored rooms is sometimes used for carpet and antiques sales. The palace is also home to the most exclusive male club in Rome, the Circolo della Caccia, which is dedicated to hunting.

Mausoleum of Augustus
Closed to the public

A shabby brick cylinder, tufted with creepers and ringed with cypresses, the Mausoleum of Augustus is the burial place of most of the emperors, wives and children from Augustus's family (the Julio-Claudians). Augustus had it built in 28 BC, by which time he was sole ruler of the Empire and had decided to jettison the old (and admittedly dishevelled) democratic ways of the Republic in favour of inherited power. Thus the Julio-Claudian dynasty of emperors came into being, and the Ara Pacis and Mausoleum were designed to accredit them.

Originally the mausoleum, plated with marble, crowned with a gilded statue of Augustus and with its entrance flanked by two obelisks (one is now on Piazza del Quirinale; the other on Piazza dell'Esquilino) was magnificent. Now, inhabited by cats and surrounded by litter, it is – from the outside, at least – one of the city's most decrepit ancient sites. The interior, overgrown with wild grasses and flowers, is a strangely forlorn, though restful place. Unfortunately, however, it is closed to the general public.

Ara Pacis

Open Oct–Mar Tues–Sun 9 a.m.–1 p.m.
Apr–Sept Tues–Sun 9 a.m–1.30 p.m.; Tues, Thur, Sat also 4–7 p.m.

The reconstructed Ara Pacis, or Altar of Peace, is one of the most immediately appealing and artistically distinguished ancient monuments in the city. In 13 BC the Senate vowed to build the Altar to celebrate the wealth and security Augustus's victories in Spain and Gaul had brought to the Empire. Four years later, on 30 January, the birthday of Augustus's wife Livia, the Altar was dedicated.

IMPERIAL WOMEN: PAWNS IN A DYNASTIC GAME

The first person to be buried in the Mausoleum of Augustus was Augustus's nephew, Marcellus, the son of his sister, Octavia and her first husband, Gaius Marcellus. Octavia was the model Roman wife, sacrificing herself for the good of the state and her family. After Gaius's death Augustus handed her over to his co-ruler Mark Antony, and she accompanied him to Greece. Antony, by then involved with Cleopatra, sent her home. She then witnessed her husband and his lover fighting her brother for control of the Empire. Nevertheless, after Antony and Cleopatra committed suicide, Octavia took their children into her own family.

Marcellus was Augustus's favourite nephew – a pretty, light-hearted youth who had been married to Augustus's equally pretty and light-hearted daughter, Julia. Augustus was shaping Marcellus to be his successor – something which severely irritated his wife Livia, who felt that her sombre, taciturn son Tiberius (from her first marriage – she and Augustus had no children) was a more reliable candidate. When Marcellus died suddenly, it was rumoured that Livia had poisoned him (but then such accusations were almost always made of Imperial women after a convenient death) and as one scholar recently pointed out, it is probable that most food-related deaths were due to salmonella poisoning.

Julia was then reluctantly married off to her father's ageing, lower-class general, Agrippa, though she probably cheered herself up by having a brief fling with her step-brother, Tiberius. Agrippa died in 12 BC, leaving Julia with five children. Her sons Gaius and Lucius rapidly replaced Marcellus in the affections of Augustus, who planned that one of them should be his successor. Julia, however, was by then celebrating her freedom with wild affairs, and Augustus decided that a marriage to Tiberius was necessary to keep Gaius and Lucius on the straight and narrow. Tiberius was forced to divorce his wife, Vipsania. Julia, understandably weary of being used as a pawn in her father's dynastic chess game, rebelled. She was accused of having numerous extremely indiscreet affairs with Augustus's political enemies, and things apparently reached crisis point when she was observed copulating on the Rostra in the Forum (from which her father had promulgated his new morality laws). In fact, it is equally probable that Julia was involved in a political conspiracy against her father with these men, and that the accusations of immorality were a cover-up.

Julia was banished to the island of Pandataria and died in exile; Lucius and Gaius also died; and Tiberius became emperor.

Protected by a modern glass building, the Altar itself, painstakingly reassembled from ancient fragments, is mounted on a flight of steps in a small rectangular enclosure whose walls, inside and out, are carved with delicate, realistic reliefs. Running right round the exterior is a dado of furling acanthus leaves entwined with graceful swans, butterflies and snakes. The panels above are more political.

On the right of the main entrance is a relief of Aeneas sacrificing a white sow before arriving at the site of the future Rome, where he is treated to a vision of the glorious reign of Augustus. On the left panel are scant relics of a relief of Romulus and Remus. On the right of the opposite entrance is a helmeted woman in a short tunic sitting on a pile of weapons: she, of course, represents Rome. On the left is a woman with two babies playing on her lap, accompanied by two other women – one sitting on a bird; the other on a sea monster. These three women represent the bountiful, fecund earth, wind and water.

Most interesting, though, is the procession that occupies the two long sides of the Ara Pacis, which gives you a chance to put faces (albeit some of them rather eroded) to the names of the members of Augustus's family. No one is quite sure why they are in procession, though it has been suggested that it may have been to the inauguration of the Ara Pacis itself. If you want to identify the individual members of the family (including Livia, Octavia and Julia) it's worth buying the booklet on sale at the ticket desk, which has a diagram.

SECOND ROUTE

Galleria Doria Pamphilj

Open Tues, Fri, Sat and Sun only, 10 a.m.–1 p.m.
Book in advance for guided tours of the private rooms (tel. 679 4365)

The grimy, lumbering Palazzo Doria occupies a whole block of the Via del Corso. It is still owned by the Doria Pamphilj family, whose collection of art and sculpture – along with some sumptuous private rooms – is open to the public. The art works are displayed in four galleries (numbered braccios 1–4) surrounding a central courtyard, and in little rooms off it. Unfortunately, most of the paintings are crammed three high on walls directly facing windows, and on a sunny day the reflections can be so bad that all you can see when you look at a canvas is your own face. It's a pity that the works are not more sensibly displayed, for there are some real gems. The paintings are also labelled only with numbers, so if you want to know what anything is you have to buy a 5000-lire catalogue.

Some Doria and Pamphilj Women The collection was begun by Olimpia Maidalchini, who married Camillo Pamphilj, brother of Pope Innocent X. Commonly known as the 'Papessa' because of the influence she wielded over Innocent, she was an unpopular woman and the subject of numerous pasquinades. The rumours were that as the Pope was dying she earned herself half a million crowns by selling benefices, and that she visited him in his last hours only in order to steal two coffers of money from under his bed. After his death she pleaded poverty so that she could avoid paying for the funeral, and Innocent's body was dumped in a rat-infested storeroom until a monsignor agreed to pay for the burial.

Olimpia then attempted to ensure that the new Pope would be sympathetic to her interests, and gathered together a party of cardinals to block the election of anyone she didn't like. The cardinals squabbled for three months until, exhausted and frustrated, they settled on a neutral candidate, the harmless, honest Fabio Chigi, who became Pope Alexander VII. The Doria and Pamphilj families united when Pope Innocent X's great-niece, Anna, married a Doria.

Subsequent female members of the clan have been far more admirable. In the early nineteenth century Princess Teresa Doria founded two Orders of nuns – one devoted to nursing, the other to helping prostitutes and pilgrims; Princess Emily Doria (1863–1919), daughter of the Duke of Newcastle, founded Rome's first nursing school, the Regina Elena, attached to the Policlinico Hospital, which is still running; her successor, the daughter of a Scottish doctor who married Prince Doria before World War II, was (with her husband) a staunch opposer of Fascism. When, in order to boost the nation's gold reserves, Mussolini ordered all the women in Rome to surrender their wedding rings, Princess Doria refused. The Fascists stormed the palace, but they walked straight past Princess Doria because she looked too ordinary to be an aristocrat.

In 1940, when Italy entered the war, the prince was arrested and the family was sent into exile. During the German occupation – by which time they had returned – the palace was again stormed, this time by the Nazis, but its labyrinthine layout allowed the family to escape. When the Allies entered Rome in 1944 Prince Doria was made mayor, and his palace was frequently used by British soldiers who needed a bed for the night.

The Collection Along Braccio 1 you'll find Titian's *Salome con la testa di San Giovanni Battista* (Salome with the Head of John the Baptist), showing Salome as a quietly powerful, reflective and thus disturbing beauty. Salome was a popular subject with Renaissance artists – the archetypal *femme fatale* whose sensual dancing so enraptured King Herod that he granted her anything she wanted. She asked for, and was duly given, John the Baptist's head.

Equally arresting, though in a very different way, are two works by Caravaggio. In the bizarre *Riposo durante la fuga in Egitto* (Rest during the Flight to Egypt) Mary nuzzles the baby Christ while Joseph holds up a sheet of music for an erotic angel violinist with satiny thighs emerging from his fluttering drapery. His

Maddalena depicts Mary Magdalene as a penitent prostitute in a bleak room, grief-stricken among her perfumes and broken jewels. There's also a Caravaggio copy worth looking at – a *San Giovanni Battista* in which the young saint, curly-headed and with dimpled buttocks, sensuously embraces a lamb.

At the end of the corridor is a portrait bust by Algardi of a stout, sour, cantankerous and very masculine-looking Olimpia Maidalchini glaring out from beneath a large veil. British soldiers staying in the palace in 1944 called her The Matron.

Most of the gallery's statues are in the Aldobrandini room: beautiful heads of Roman women and a centaur comprising a polished red marble human torso, shiny black horse's body and red marble tail, but none is identified.

Braccio 2 has paintings by Guercino, Guido Reni, the Carraccis (and their school and imitators), and a bust by Algardi of Innocent X with a sunken bronze face and porphyry gown. The suite of rooms leading off it is worth more time – particularly Room 5, which contains *Caricatura di Quattro Uomini* (better known as the Usurers) by Quentin Metsys – a scathing portrait of four grotesque usurers, gloating over glittering golden coins. Also here are works by Jan Brueghel the Elder and his brother Pieter. There are more Flemish works in the little room known as Gabinetto 1, notably copies of Roman landscapes by Paul Bril, including two showing the Forum when it was a cowfield.

The gallery's most famous works are two portraits of Innocent X in the tiny Gabinetto 2. When the Spanish artist Velazquez visited Rome in 1648 to buy paintings for King Philip II, the Pope commissioned him to paint his portrait. The work is superb – not only for the way in which it captures the character of this sly yet diffident man, but for the glorious, almost impressionistic, technique Velazquez used to convey the textures of fabric and the fall of light. The other representation of Innocent is a bust by Bernini, in which the Pope looks altogether more austere and regal.

The Private Apartments Tours of the private apartments, beginning in the oldest (sixteenth-century) part of the palazzo, give a taste of aristocratic life through the ages. Rooms range from those hung with tapestries or paved with marcasite to an English-style wood-panelled smoking-room (created for homesick Emily) which looks like a set from a BBC costume drama. Some of the furniture is amazing – like the gilded boat-like crib and a folding ebony and ivory table – and there are also some good works of art worth looking out for. These range from an *Annunciation* by Filippo Lippi and a *Madonna* by Beccafumi to a bust of Emily Doria and a portrait of another English Doria Pamphilj wife, Mary Talbot, sister of Gwendolen (see p.72).

It's the opulence of the mid-eighteenth-century suite of rooms, however, which is most memorable. The ballroom, with rose-printed silk walls, frescoed ceiling and glittering candelabra; the 'Yellow Room' decorated with Greek deities and the signs of the zodiac; and the 'Green Room' lit by a multicoloured Murano glass chandelier suspended from a rope of gilded rosettes.

Piazza della Minerva

Were it not used as a car park, Piazza della Minerva would be one of Rome's most endearing squares. Poking up from the Fiats and Vespas is the weirdest statue in the city – a baby elephant with a miniature obelisk on its back – and enclosing the square are the walls of three fine buildings: the Pantheon, the apricot façade of Santa Maria sopra Minerva (currently being restored), and Rome's Holiday Inn, an eighteenth-century convent slickly refurbished by postmodern architect Paolo Portoghesi.

This cute obelisk-bearing elephant, with tail flicked across his rump, was designed by Bernini for Pope Alexander VII. The obelisk belonged to a temple to Isis (see box, p.82) founded by Caligula, which once stood in the vicinity and was discovered in the garden of Santa Maria sopra Minerva. Obelisks were understood to represent the sun (Sol) and Wisdom.

Elephants symbolised strength, intelligence and (particularly close to the hearts of the pleasure-hating Church authorities) sexual continence. The sex lives of elephants should, the Church felt, be a model for all Catholic marriages, because they took only one partner and mated for just five days every two years. Catholic couples were still being told to emulate elephants in the nineteenth century. Presumably, as Pope (and a devout and prudish one, who was frightfully annoyed when Queen Christina of Sweden removed fig leaves from the statues in the Palazzo Farnese) Alexander surpassed the elephants in his capacity for abstinence. He was, however, quite happy to have one representing the strength of his intelligence, and composed an inscription for the base to leave no one in any doubt of the meaning: 'A robust intelligence is required to support solid wisdom'. One can't help wondering whether Bernini, in creating such a cheeky elephant, wasn't subverting the message – not least because the inspiration for the monument came from an illustration in a Renaissance romance, in which a young man wanders through an enchanted garden full of bizarre statues (including an obelisk-carrying elephant) looking for his lover.

Santa Maria sopra Minerva

Built in 1280 on the ruins of a temple dedicated to Minerva, goddess of wisdom, Santa Maria sopra Minerva now holds the relics of

St Catherine of Siena. It's an odd place, its mood shifting with the weather. On a sunny evening it's a warm, welcoming church, and its frescoes glow richly; in winter it feels shadowy, mysterious and even slightly sinister. The latter impression is not entirely inapt, for it was the Roman headquarters of the Dominicans, an Order which provided the Church with some of its most skilled Inquisitors. Paul IV (ruled 1555–59), possibly the most loathed of all popes, is buried here, and Galileo (1564–1642) was tried for heresy in the adjoining monastery, though afterwards he was given a comfortable apartment to live in.

Refurbished in the nineteenth century in Gothic style – complete with midnight-blue star-sprinkled vaults – the church has a wonderful collection of art. One of the most interesting is an *Annunciation* in the fourth right-hand chapel, attributed to the Renaissance artist Antoniazzo Romano. As the Virgin listens to the angels, she hands over small bags to three young girls kneeling before her, accompanied by a cardinal. The cardinal is a Spaniard, Juan Torquemada, who founded the Confraternity of the Annunziata in 1460 to provide dowries for poor girls. For many families, scraping together a dowry could mean financial ruin, yet without a dowry it was virtually impossible for a girl to get married. Unless she decided to become a nun, she would have to resign herself to being a social oddity, accepting that she would be both pitied as a spinster and vulnerable to the approaches of philandering men. Until the nineteenth century the Confraternity's dowries were presented by the Pope on Annunciation Day, and girls who had decided to become nuns were given twice as much as the others. On a rather more different note, the fifth right-hand chapel has a statue of Saint Sebastian by Michelangelo, muscles and ribcage visible beneath the skin. It probably started out as a model for the Christ (which now stands on the high altar) and appears to have been finished by another sculptor.

At the end of the right transept is the Carafa Chapel, which is said to be wonderfully frescoed by Filippino Lippi, son of renegade monk Filippo Lippi and a nun. It has been closed for restoration for some time, but should look splendid when the work has been completed. The frescoes include an Assumption, an Annunciation and – a subject close to the heart of the Dominican Inquisitors – St Thomas confounding the heretics.

The chapel also contains a monument to the Carafa Pope, Paul IV, who excommunicated Elizabeth of England, suppressed Protestant 'heretics' in the Netherlands, burned sodomites alive, and confined the Roman Jews to a ghetto. He also banned them from certain jobs and made them wear an identifying badge. He wanted to destroy every pagan monument in the city, and referred to Michelangelo's *Last Judgement* as a 'stew of nudes' (stew as in brothel). When he died, the head of his statue on the Capitoline was struck off and thrown in the Tiber, and the monastery adjoining Santa Maria was stormed by a mob.

SAINT CATHERINE OF SIENA AND HOLY ANOREXIA (1333/1347–80)

Born (probably) in 1347, Catherine Benincasa was the youngest of twenty-five children. The family (her father was a dyer) was wealthy enough to send their infants to a wet-nurse in infancy, though Catherine was nursed by her mother (her twin sister was not, and died). Devout even as a child, she devoted herself to prayer and penance, and in adolescence mortified herself by wrapping a chain round her hips. She also put herself on a diet of bread, raw herbs and water. Giving up food was common among holy women – in Italy between the fourteenth and seventeenth centuries scholars have estimated that 30% of them subjected themselves to rigorous fasting regimes. This was not only a sign of discipline, but left the body in a pure state to receive the 'true food' of the Eucharist. In addition, as menstruation ceased, the women became essentially asexual. The Church (supported by the medical profession, which believed menses and afterbirth to be poisonous) hotly debated whether or not a menstruating woman could receive communion, or whether a woman who had died in childbirth could be buried in consecrated ground. The appeal of amenorrhoea is hardly surprising.

At eighteen Catherine refused to marry, and – with hair shorn, and skin wounded by the chains – insisted, despite severe family opposition, on becoming a Dominican nun. She joined a Tertiary Order, which meant that she took only simple vows and could continue to live at home. At first she spent her time praying in solitude and was rewarded by ecstatic raptures – most famously, a vision of being mystically married to Christ – and the pain of the stigmata. At the age of twenty-three, prompted by visions to go out into the world, she put her faith into action, nursing plague victims and gathering together a group of male and female disciples. As her visions became known, she gained the confidence to write letters (or rather dictate them, as she was illiterate) admonishing the rich and powerful. She chastised Queen Giovanna of Naples for her arrogance and persuaded the Pope, Gregory XI, to return from Avignon to Rome to reunite the Church.

After ten years on her frugal diet, she could stomach nothing – and eventually died of starvation in Rome at the age of thirty-three.

Having virtually erased her femininity through fasting, Catherine had as little sympathy as any of her celibate brothers for normal humans. Among the visions reported by her confessor and biographer, Raymond of Capua, is one in which she sees a group of couples in Hell 'who sinned in the married state' (which means they used methods of birth control). When Raymond asked her why such sins, which were no graver than any others, were punished so severely, she replied: 'Because the sinners are not so aware of them, and hence do not feel so much remorse as for other sins. Furthermore, they commit these sins more regularly and frequently than other sins.'

Illuminated below the high altar is the masked corpse of Saint Catherine of Siena who, as the patron saint of Italy, lies draped with ribbons striped with the red, green and white of the national flag and stamped with the SPQR (Senatus Populusque Romanus – the Senate and People of Rome) motto of the city. Catherine died in

Rome, in a room in nearby Via S. Chiara, which was dismantled and rebuilt behind Santa Maria's sacristy. If you can find the sacristan he'll show you a whitewashed room, next to a tiny chapel, with reproductions of paintings of the saint stuck on the walls.

Standing alongside the altar is a chunky, stocky *Christ Bearing the Crucifix* by Michelangelo. The bronze drapery is not original. Buried at the other side of the altar is the artist Fra Angelico, a devout Dominican monk and painter of exquisitely simple and contemplative works, often featuring astonishingly pure Madonnas, which were more than somewhat out of step with the ever-increasing secularisation and realism of the Renaissance. As a sign of how much he still means to people, his simple tomb usually bears at least one bouquet of flowers.

THE CULT OF ISIS

The Egyptian goddess, Isis, had been worshipped since at least 2500 BC. According to the myth, Isis and her brother Osiris were the children of the earth-god and the sky-goddess, and fell in love while still in the womb. Osiris brought peace to the world, but was killed by his jealous brother, Set, who tore his body into fourteen pieces and scattered them. Isis gathered the pieces together, gave him eternal life, and – although she failed to find his genitals – miraculously conceived a child, Horus, who was understood to be simultaneously an incarnation and a son of Osiris. Horus was sometimes represented by a phallus.

Isis's cult arrived in Italy in the second century BC, and rapidly became hugely popular. Isis was omnipotent, concerned with and open to the entreaties of the individual and, unlike the wrathful Roman gods and goddesses, merciful. Her cult appealed particularly to those who did not have a stake in the affairs of state, met with fierce opposition from the authorities, and gained a reputation for sexual licence. A later version of the Isis myth (written by a Christian) charged her with having been a prostitute for ten years, and indeed, many of her temples were close to brothels.

The temples of state-approved gods and goddesses were open only on their feast days – usually once a year. The temples of Isis were open every day. Every morning the statue of the goddess was 'woken' and dressed (in a special knotted gown); there were sacrifices, ceremonies, processions, and initiations; and astrologers, priests, lamplighters and basket-bearers bustled about in the service of the goddess. Worshippers would often dine together and even live in the sanctuary for a while.

Isis's temples and shrines were banned on numerous occasions, and in Tiberius's reign the cult was brought into further disrepute when the priests of Isis told an upper-class matron, Paulina, to come to the temple because the dog-god Anubis wanted to have sex with her. Paulina complied, only to discover that Anubis was in fact her earthly admirer, Decius Mundus, in disguise. Caligula was the first emperor to embrace the cult, ordering a temple to be built on the Campus Martius. Most of his successors followed suit, and by the second century BC scores of magistrates and other officials dedicated monuments to the goddess.

The angular façade of Sant'Ignazio looks far too august for its setting on a pretty, ochre-washed Rococo piazza. It was built in 1626 to celebrate the canonisation of Ignatius Loyola, Basque founder of the Jesuits, a highly intellectual, all-male Order that is still heavily involved in education and missionary work. As for the church, it was built on to the Collegio Romano, the city's Jesuit college, and though the initial designs were by Carlo Maderno they were carried out by a Jesuit mathematician, Orazio Grassi. The interior was decorated by a Jesuit artist, Andrea Pozzo.

When Sant'Ignazio was built, the Catholic Church was still reeling from the blow dealt by Protestantism, and wary of appearing too worldly or flamboyant – hence the austere façade. By the late seventeenth century, when the interior was decorated, the Church was far more confident and, largely through the influence of Ignatius's Spiritual Exercises (a four-week course in spiritual enlightenment which consists of imagining, in vivid physical and emotional detail, phenomena ranging from Sin to the Crucifixion and Resurrection), it had been realised that the direct appeal to worshippers' emotions was an extremely effective means of intensifying faith.

IGNATIUS LOYOLA AND THE JESUIT ATTITUDE TO WOMEN

Ignatius (like most Churchmen) was convinced that all women were sexual temptresses, and devoted considerable time to trying to save prostitutes. In 1547, largely financed by contributions from the city's do-gooding noblewomen, he set up a hostel for penitent prostitutes and women separated from their husbands. Unlike the Convertite, the convent for penitents, the regime was relatively lenient, and the women could live securely, but without the prison-like restrictions of a closed Order. The theory was that given the chance, the women would repent – the hostel was dedicated to St Martha, patron saint of housewives, implying that this was the condition to which the Jesuits hoped the women would aspire.

One particular housewife, Signora Cesare, certainly did not fit Ignatius's ideal. In 1553 her sixteen-year-old son Ottaviano ran away from home to join the Jesuits. Signora Cesare was furious and barraged Ignatius and his Order with letters demanding the release of her son. 'Concern yourself with your daughters,' was the Jesuits' reply, 'and allow your son to hear the call of God.' Eventually, however, in 1558 (by which time Ignatius was dead), thanks to the help of several well-placed men (including two popes), Ottaviano was released from his vows.

Entering Sant'Ignazio is like stepping into a divine ballroom. It looks particularly lovely in the evenings, when the marble columns and pavement gleam and the polished brass glints in the lamplight. For once you're unlikely to resent feeding 500-lire coins into a slot machine to illuminate the illusionistic frescoes in its vault and dome, for they are among the most brilliant in the city, with figures seeming to float, midair, below a hazy, almost translucent heaven of clouds.

To enjoy the full effect of the frescoes you need to stand on the star set into the nave. Figures are sucked, as if by a vacuum cleaner, into the dome: you'd never guess that it is nothing more than a skilfully painted canvas disc, seventeen metres in diameter. The fresco above the nave is an allegory of the missionary work of the Jesuits, with the four continents, Europe, Asia, America and Africa, represented by women perched on cornices. The prejudices of European Catholicism are clear: blonde Europa, in a Britannia-like pose, is by far the most regal, while Asia and Africa are all-too-familiar stereotypes of a toiling tea-planter and an exotic tribal queen. The space above them swims with leggy adolescents and angels, while illusionistic columns burst beyond the confines of the real church, to a heaven with a crucifix towards which Ignatius soars on a cloud.

If you're into ecclesiastical kitsch, take a look at the Capella di Sant Cuore, which features walls studded with ex-votives, a bronze crucifix surrounded by little glass reliquaries stuffed with bones, and a painting of Christ languidly pulling back his chest-skin to reveal a red love-heart radiating light.

Piazza di Pietra

Piazza di Pietra is a rather mournful square, one which people pass through rather than linger in. The most striking feature is the Borsa, Rome's defunct Stock Exchange (Milan is now Italy's financial centre), with eleven chewed Corinthian columns and a frieze engraved with lions embedded in its wall. They belonged to a temple dedicated to (the by then deified) Hadrian in AD 145 by his adopted son, Antoninus Pius. Hadrian and his era fascinated the Belgian-born writer Marguerite Yourcenar, and she made him the subject of a sombre, contemplative novel, *The Memoirs of Hadrian*. Asked why she had chosen to write about an historic man rather than a woman, she replied that it was 'virtually impossible to take a feminine character as a central figure... Women's lives are much too limited, or else too secret. If a woman does recount her own life she is promptly reproached for being no longer truly feminine.'

Piazza di Montecitorio

As you approach Piazza di Montecitorio along narrow Via Guglia, the first things you see are jagged lumps of rock jauntily protruding from the façade of a palace. This is the Palazzo di Montecitorio, designed by Bernini for the family of Pope Innocent X (ruled 1644–55) and now housing the Chamber of Deputies, one of Italy's two parliamentary houses. There's usually a heavy police presence and the space in front of the palazzo is often barricaded off. In the centre of the piazza is an obelisk brought from Heliopolis in Egypt by Augustus, to be used as the giant pointer of a huge sundial in the Campus Martius.

ALESSANDRA MUSSOLINI

After the 1992 elections, the number of women in the Chamber of Deputies fell from 82 to 51. As in the case of the women in the Senate, the majority (22) are members of the ex-Communist Party, the PDS. In the 1987 election it was ex-porn star La Cicciolina who hit the headlines. In 1992 attention was focused on Alessandra Mussolini, ex-actress, qualified doctor, niece of Sophia Loren and granddaughter of Benito. She stood in Naples (a traditional Fascist stronghold) for the MSI, Italy's Neo-Fascist party, and won with a 56,000 majority, second only in the number of votes she received to veteran Communist Nilde Iotti.

Born in 1962, she attended a convent school, basically unaware of the significance of her heritage: 'And then one day we were reading the history books and everyone started staring at me. I could not understand, and then I saw the name in the book and realised that it was my name and that I was a part of history too.' No one ribbed her about her grandfather: 'I would have slapped them if they tried.'

Alessandra was actually far more interested in having Sophia Loren as an aunt, and started her acting career aged nine in one of Loren's films. When she left school she enrolled at Rome university and continued to take minor TV roles. In 1983 she posed for *Playboy*, and – with astounding lack of sensitivity on the part of the casting directors – was asked to play the role of a Jewish woman in the film *Assisi Underground*. The Jewish community was understandably appalled, and the role was withdrawn, though in 1989 she did play an Israeli soldier in a film.

1989 was also the year in which she got married (to a soldier) in Mussolini's old villa. The date chosen – 28 October – marked the anniversary of Mussolini's march on Rome. While the wedding guests were partying, local Fascists gathered nearby at her grandfather's tomb and gave the Fascist salute.

When, bored with acting, she decided to stand for Parliament, the MSI couldn't believe their luck and tried to persuade her to stand in Rome and Bologna as well as Naples. Running on an anti-immigration ticket, she professes to abhor violence (despite the fact that the murderers of two North Africans in Rome in 1992 were self-confessed Fascists and her great admirers). When she was asked, in a recent interview, why her grandfather had aligned himself with Hitler, she replied: 'We all make mistakes'. But, like the rest of her party, she has done nothing to stop the party's youth wing, the Fronte della Gioventù (Youth Front), sporting swastikas.

Piazza di Colonna

Named for the Column of Marcus Aurelius in its centre, Piazza di Colonna is home to another heavily guarded palace – the pale-peach Baroque Palazzo Chigi, the Prime Minister's official residence. The column was erected to celebrate Marcus Aurelius's victory over tribes who had invaded the Roman Empire's border along the Danube in the late second century. It is basically a rather clumsy imitation of Trajan's Column, with a seemingly endless procession of soldiers, war machinery and horses, punctuated by the occasional city gate, spiralling up its 42-metre stem. There is also a spiral staircase inside, but it is closed to visitors.

Piazza and Chiesa San Lorenzo in Lucina

Located just off the Corso, and close to Rome's classiest clothes-shopping streets, Piazza San Lorenzo in Lucina is a scruffy little square, surrounded by chafed terracotta-washed houses. Its two pavement cafés, however, are great places to sit and watch people. Wealthy middle-aged women walk arm in arm as they return from shopping sprees, young couples perch on Vespas arguing, businessmen sweep past in trenchcoats with portable phones bulging from their pockets, and plainclothes policemen slip into the Carabinieri base across the piazza.

Take a look, too, at the church of San Lorenzo in Lucina, an oddly rustic-style church with a scuffed façade and a shadowy Ionic porch sheltering fragments of inscriptions, two eroded lions and a slice of a mosaic-covered Paschal candlestick. Christian worship began on the site in the fourth century, in the house of a woman named Lucina, but the first church was not built until the twelfth century. In the late seventeenth century a Roman aristocrat, Count Francheschini, married a young girl, Pompilia Comaparini. Shortly afterwards he murdered her on suspicion of committing adultery with a young priest. While Robert Browning was living in Florence he came across an account of the murder trial in a second-hand bookshop. The story inspired *The Ring and the Book*, his longest – and possibly greatest – work.

The church has been rebuilt several times, but still has the flat coffered ceiling of a traditional basilica. On the high altar is a Crucifixion by Guido Reni, and in the fourth right-hand chapel a portrait bust by Bernini of Innocent X's benign, mustachioed doctor, Gabriele Fonseca. The church's most precious relic, however, is in the first right-hand chapel – a portion of the rusty grill on which Saint Laurence was allegedly toasted to death, displayed in an illuminated glass-fronted altar.

CAMPO DEI FIORI

Campo dei Fiori, the quarter between the Tiber and Corso Vittorio Emanuele, was the bustling, raffish, and at times rough heart of Renaissance Rome. Most of the city's hotels were here, and most of the great courtesans lived close by, until they could afford to move to the more upmarket Via dell'Orso. Rodrigo Borgia also lived in the area – until he became Pope Alexander VI and moved across the Tiber – as did the two great loves of his life, Vanozza Cattanei and Giulia Farnese. Vanozza and Rodrigo's four children, including Lucrezia and Cesare, were born in Campo dei Fiori, and her eldest son, the Duke of Gandia, was murdered here. Murders were not uncommon: Caravaggio killed his opponent on the central square because he had beaten him in a game of tennis; and the goldsmith Cellini murdered a business rival on Vicolo della Moretta.

Campo dei Fiori, even more than the area around Piazza Navona, was full of artisans, each street being given over to a specific trade. Many still bear the names of the old trades – Via dei Giubonnari (Street of the Jerkin-makers), Via dei Capellari (Street of the Hat-makers), Via dei Chiavari (Street of the Locksmiths) and – a sign of the murdering times – Via dei Balestrari (Street of the Crossbow-makers).

Today, despite becoming fashionable, this is still a lively, earthy and occasionally dodgy neighbourhood. The main square, Campo dei Fiori itself, is the scene of a large food market, and the streets around are packed with the workshops of jewellers, carpenters and antique restorers. It's also host to an eclectic night scene. Tourists mingle with PDS (see p.335) leaders at the Carbonara; expats, bikers, young tourists and ageing hippies cram into the Vineria, then move on to Goldfinch, the resort of gays, local artisans, and the occasional transvestite. There are bars in which the entire staff are perpetually stoned; but there are also any number of conventional, respectable trattorias and a handful of exclusive and extremely expensive restaurants.

It's a fascinating and invigorating, rather than threatening, neighbourhood to be in at night, though to be on the safe side, try to stick to Campo dei Fiori itself and the busy, well-lit streets directly off it, rather than taking a short cut down a dark alleyway. You are unlikely to encounter any violence, but it's as well to be aware that the neighbourhood is worked by local gangs. These are mainly bag-snatchers on Vespas (a large proportion of them drug addicts), and the fruits of their robberies are handed over to the gang leader, who organises the sale and gives the robber a percentage of the proceeds. Such leaders often become local heroes – after the recent death of one of them, all the shutters on Via dei Capellari, where he lived, were lowered as a sign of respect.

As for sightseeing, there are three wonderful palaces, though the Farnese (once the home of Queen Christina of Sweden) and the Cancelleria (where Louise Stohlberg stayed after leaving her husband, the decaying alcoholic Bonnie Prince Charlie) are not open to the public. The Palazzo Spada *is* open, and has a small art gallery which includes a handful of paintings by women. Apart from this, you'll want to spend most of your time outside, exploring the maze of alleys, the nightlife, shops and markets.

Area Sacra di Largo Argentina

At some time you're bound to end up waiting for a bus on Largo Argentina, on the fringe of Campo dei Fiori. Fortunately, the bus stops are ideally placed for having a look at the ruins of four Republican Era temples. Sunk in the centre of the Largo, surrounded by banks, cafés, and an eighteenth-century theatre, the overgrown ruins are now populated solely by cats, which the locals keep well supplied with little heaps of leftover spaghetti.

Since they have not been identified, the temples are inspiringly known as A, B, C and D. There's little to see of C and D, and the best preserved is temple A (directly below the bus stop) which was protected by having a church built on top of it – you can still see the outline of the apse. It has a rectangular base, columns standing at various heights, and a little altar. Behind it is a trough which used to drain an ancient Roman public lavatory. Temple B is circular, with six columns surviving, and the podium behind it formed part of the Curia Pompei, where Caesar was assassinated. He had refused to listen to his wife, Calpurnia, who tried to persuade him to stay at home after dreaming that she was holding his dead body.

Teatro Argentina

Now threatened with closure, the Teatro Argentina was for a long time the most important theatre in Rome. In 1816 Rossini's *Barber of Seville* (which he claimed to have written in two weeks) was premiered here. It was an unmitigated disaster. Having lost the original overture, Rossini substituted one he had written for another opera, and at the last minute the tenor persuaded him to insert a Spanish song accompanied by guitar, to add a bit of local colour. Unbeknown to Rossini, Pauline Borghese had packed the audience with hecklers (she hated Rossini, probably because he was a more talented and successful composer than her ex-lover, Giovanni Pacini).

Events played right into Pauline's hands. The tenor, having forgotten to tune his guitar, stopped to tune it on-stage, broke a string, and had to replace it. The audience screamed with laughter. Then Figaro entered – with a guitar – and the audience's laughter completely drowned his singing. When the laughter had died down, Rosina appeared on a balcony and launched into her next line, 'Segui, o caro, segui cosi'. Unfortunately this means 'Continue, my dear, continue like that', and the audience, now unable to think of anything except guitars, collapsed into giggles once again.

Sant'Andrea della Valle

The stunningly rhythmic spotless cream façade of Sant'Andrea della Valle (designed by three architects called Carlo – Maderno, Rainaldi and Fontana) rears above the traffic-clogged Corso Vittorio Emanuele. It featured as the opening scene in Puccini's *Tosca*, a typically tragic tale of love, jealousy, murder and suicide involving a beautiful opera singer, an artist, a freedom fighter and an evil police chief.

First impressions of the church, with its stripy gilded pilasters and barely visible figures swarming around the second-largest dome in Rome, are of a splendid ballroom – until you notice an alarming number of collection boxes for souls in Purgatory, a recently canonised saint in an illuminated glass-sided tomb (the totally obscure Giuseppe Maria Tomasi), and a painting of St Andrew skewered to his X-shaped crucifix.

It was while praying in the Barberini Chapel that Puccini was inspired to write *Tosca*. The chapel is usually in darkness, but you may just be able to make out the figure of a woman in a red dress praying. In *Tosca*, the artist Cavaradossi is painting a Mary Magdalene, modelled, to the horror of the sacristan, on the Marchioness Attavanti. His lover, Tosca, its – not surprisingly – furious (though Cavaradossi is, in fact, faithful). Also in the chapel is a delicate sculpture of St Martha, patron saint of housewives, by Mochi, who also created the lovely St Veronica in St Peter's (see p.157).

Melodrama on the site did not happen only in Puccini arias. When the artist Domenichino lost the job of painting the dome to his contemporary Lanfranco, he was so bitter that he allegedly tampered with his rival's scaffolding, hoping that he would fall and break his neck. Lanfranco survived to fill the dome with rings of figures painted *sotto in su* (from the bottom up) in a showy extravaganza of illusionism that makes Domenichino's three scenes from the life of St Andrew look extremely dull.

Finally, take a look at the relief-decorated tombs of two Renaissance popes, Pius II and his nephew Pius III, embedded high up on the end of the nave's walls. Pius II was a cultured, rakish man of the world who wrote an erotic comedy and fathered several illegitimate children before relinquishing debauchery to become a priest. His nephew was elected as pope mainly because he was inoffensive and seriously ill, and the cardinals thought he would give them time to find a more dynamic candidate. In the event, Pius III died ten days after his election.

Campo dei Fiori

Home to central Rome's best food market, Campo dei Fiori (in Roman dialect: de' Fiori) is an amiable, down-to-earth piazza surrounded by chafed orange-ochre, buttery-yellow and grey houses with warped shutters and pigeons nestling on their sills. Stall-holders trundle around in three-wheeler trucks and tricycle trolleys; priests with briefcases step gingerly through piles of discarded cabbage leaves; teenagers sputter home from school on motorinos; and

Rome's foodies scrutinise mounds of green cauliflowers, artichokes and *fiori di zucchini*. It's a brilliant place to shop for a picnic, for as well as the fruit and veg stands there are delis, takeaway pizza shops, and a bakery.

The sombre hooded statue in the centre is Giordano Bruno, burnt at the stake on the piazza in 1600 on the orders of the Inquisition. An ex-priest, he dabbled with Calvinism and Lutheranism (before being excommunicated by both sects) and may briefly have worked as a spy at the English Court. He eventually concluded that philosophy and magic were superior to religion, beliefs which led to him being tried and found guilty of heresy, and condemned to death. Nowadays his pedestal is a popular place to picnic.

VANOZZA CATTANEI (14??–1518)

Vanozza Cattanei, for ten years the mistress of Pope Alexander VI, lived for most of her life in the streets around Campo dei Fiori. When the affair began, around 1473, she was married, quite poor and living in a modest house in Via del Pellegrino, close to the palazzo of the then Cardinal Rodrigo Borgia. She and her husband moved into a house next door to the palazzo (the Sforza Cesarini on Corso Vittorio Emanuele) and it was probably here that her four children, Juan, Cesare, Lucrezia and Jofré, were born. Her children, however, were not permitted to remain with her, and were taken to more sumptuous surroundings. She did see them often, though, and was still writing to Lucrezia in 1515. The only request she ever made of her daughter was that after her death she would care for Jofré's illegitimate son, whom he had sent to live with Vanozza.

Unlike many women in her position, she was discreet, undemanding and invested the money the Pope gave her wisely, buying three hotels just off Campo dei Fiori. She was married three times, and while the affair was in progress her husbands appear to have condoned the situation, aware of the financial benefits as well as the fact that Alexander was not a man to cross. She bought an inn – the Vacca (on Vicolo del Gallo, off Campo dei Fiori) – and when Alexander died in 1503 she faked the sale of this and her house on Via del Pellegrino, conscious of a time-honoured Roman tradition which involved ransacking the property and possessions of dead popes. By 1513, however, she was secure enough to advertise her papal connection to the world: the façade still bears an escutcheon comprising the coats of arms of Vanozza, her latest husband and the Borgias. By then she owned two more inns on the other side of the Campo – the Biscione and the Albergo del Sole, which is still running.

Towards the end of her life she devoted herself to good works, giving money to churches and hospitals, and having the jewels and ornaments Alexander had given her converted into religious objects. She had her own private chapel built in Santa Maria del Popolo, and left the church sufficient funds to ensure that Masses were said for her for two hundred years.

Palazzo della Cancelleria

The Palazzo della Cancelleria is the purest Renaissance palace in Rome. It's built of travertine, with a façade sectioned by slender pilasters, and decorated solely with exquisitely sculpted stylised roses. The architect is unknown, but it was built for Raffaele Riario, the nephew of Pope Sixtus IV (ruled 1471–84). Raffaele was made a cardinal by his uncle at the age of seventeen, though this had nothing to do with his suitability for the post – he paid for the palazzo with the proceeds of a single night's gambling. Raffaele was also the victim of one of Michelangelo's practical jokes: he bought what he thought was an antique statue of Cupid, but was in fact a fake which Michelangelo had carefully aged. Someone blew the whistle on Michelangelo: Riario tried to return the statue and get his money back. Mysteriously, however, the statue disappeared, never to be seen again.

In the fifteenth century the Riarios participated in the Pazzi Conspiracy, a plot designed to oust the Medicis from Florence. It failed, but resulted in a Medici being murdered, a Pazzi being lynched, Raffaele being kidnapped, and Pope Sixtus IV declaring war on Florence. The Medicis had long memories, and when Giovanni de' Medici became Pope Leo X in 1513 he confiscated the palace and turned it into the papal chancellery. In the late eighteenth century Cardinal Henry Stuart was Vice-Chancellor of the Roman Church, and in 1781 he allowed his sister-in-law, Louise Stohlberg, to live in the palace when she left her husband (and his brother) Charles Edward. Louise was nineteen when she was married to the former Bonnie Prince Charlie, who by then was fifty-two, fat, embittered, slightly mad, violent and an alcoholic.

Although the Vatican had long given up hope of restoring the Catholic monarchs, the couple were given a palazzo and a pension. The marriage, of course, was a disaster. While they were staying in Florence Louise met and fell in love with a poet, Alfieri, and with his help she escaped to a convent. Henry understood what Louise's life with his brother must have been like, and with no inkling of the affair he arranged for her to stay in a convent in Rome (on Via Vittoria) where other royal ladies, including her mother-in-law, had also taken refuge.

Convent life was not exactly what Louise wanted – her only contact with Alfieri was through a grille – so she soon managed to persuade Henry that she would be happier in his Palazzo della Cancelleria. He agreed, after getting the Pope's permission, and she moved in. She introduced Alfieri to Henry, who liked him so much that he arranged for him to have an audience with the Pope, despite the fact that in his youth he had been renowned for his diatribes against the papacy and the priesthood. The Pope assumed that he had reformed, and blessed him. The Pope and Henry were probably the only people in Rome not to know about the affair, for Louise and Alfieri went everywhere together. Eventually it was Charles Edward himself who spilt the beans. Henry was horrified, and persuaded the Pope to banish Alfieri from Rome, though he allowed Louise to stay in the Cancelleria. A year later Charles agreed to a separation. Louise and Alfieri stayed together until Alfieri died, aged fifty-three, in 1803.

Piazza and Palazzo Farnese

There are few greater contrasts in Rome than that between the colourful shabby hubbub of Campo dei Fiori and the refined magnificence of adjacent Piazza Farnese. As you approach the piazza down a narrow alleyway, the façade of the Palazzo Farnese is gradually revealed, a triple-storeyed Renaissance structure with Doric, Ionic and Corinthian tiers separated by finely chiselled decorative bands. The two lower storeys are by Antonio da Sangallo the Younger, but after he died in 1543 Michelangelo took over. Try to see the palace at least once at night when, if you're lucky, the façade will be illuminated and some of the chandeliers inside will be switched on, revealing sumptuously frescoed and richly coffered ceilings.

Palazzo Farnese was built for Cardinal Alessandro Farnese, who became Pope Paul III in 1523. The costs were so steep that they virtually bankrupted him, and an anonymous satirist attached a placard to the palace's scaffolding reading: 'Alms for the building of the Farnese'. Farnese's rise to power says much about how the Church of the time operated. Pope Alexander VI made him cardinal deacon in 1493 largely because he was having an affair with Farnese's sister Giulia (earning Alessandro the title 'petticoat cardinal'). Farnese himself was a father of four from a protracted affair with a Roman aristocrat, though unlike Alexander VI he had long renounced philandering when he became pope.

When Queen Christina of Sweden (see p.128) came to Rome in 1655 she was lent the Palazzo Farnese, which rapidly became the centre of a dazzling social set. Although she came from the north, she found Roman winters so cold that she ordered the servants to chop up some of the palace's doors for firewood. This apparently scandalised the authorities less than the fact that she had all the fig leaves removed from the Farnese's prodigious collection of marble statues. Sadly, unless you happen to be a diplomat or a certificated art history scholar, you are unlikely ever to see the inside of the palace, as it is now the French Embassy. The main thing you'll miss are the glowingly coloured frescoes by Annibale Carracci which fill the barrel vault of the Galleria, depicting the love lives of gods and goddesses inspired by Ovid's *Metamorphoses*. They set the trend for ceiling frescoes for years to come, but Carracci was apparently so disgusted with the pittance he was paid (he slaved over it for seven years) that he turned to drink.

GIULIA FARNESE

In 1489, when she was fifteen, Giulia Farnese married Orsino Orsini, great-nephew of Cardinal Rodrigo Borgia. She was so lovely that when she arrived in Rome she was dubbed 'Giulia Bella', and Borgia fell madly in love with her. With his niece (and Giulia's mother-in-law) Adriana acting as go-between, an affair started. Everyone knew about it – people wanting favours from Rodrigo (who became Pope Alexander VI in 1492) would ask Giulia to put a word in for them – and Giulia, Adriana and the young Lucrezia (Borgia) moved together into a splendid palace next to the Vatican.

Giulia and Lucrezia got on well, and in 1494, when fourteen-year-old Lucrezia left Rome with her husband for her new home in Pesaro, Giulia went with her. Both of them kept Alexander in touch with events, writing unflattering descriptions of other women and, in Giulia's case, telling him how much she missed him. Alexander missed the two women as well, and was furious when, having rushed to the family home in Capodimonte to be with her brother as he died, Giulia showed no sign of returning to Rome. He began sending letters ordering her to do so, but still Giulia made no move, so he threatened to excommunicate her. She still resisted. It is uncertain why Giulia delayed, but the fact that her husband was nearby – and toying with the idea of an insurrection – may have played some part. Eventually, however, Orsino gave Giulia permission to go.

On the way to Rome, Giulia and Adriana were kidnapped by a group of French soldiers (the French had just invaded Italy, and were planning to depose the Pope). When Alexander discovered what had happened he immediately dispatched the ransom, then set about dolling himself up to meet his lover. He chose an extremely un-papal outfit – a black-and-gold velvet cloak, Valencia boots, a Spanish scarf and a velvet cap. He also put on a sword to make him look especially virile (he was sixty-two).

A few weeks later the French invaded Rome, and Giulia disappeared, probably into a safe house. From about this time the affair became far more discreet, and by 1500 Giulia was being referred to as the Pope's former favourite. In fact, no one really replaced her, though Borgia hardly became celibate. The fact that her brother, Alessandro, remained at the fore of the papal court, and in a position to become pope himself some twenty years on, is possibly a sign that the Pope still had some affection for her.

Palazzo and Galleria Spada

Open Tues–Sat 9 a.m.–4 p.m.; Sun 9 a.m.–1 p.m.

After the Renaissance refinement of the Farnese and Cancelleria, the Palazzo Spada comes as something of a shock, for the façade is a stucco extravaganza studded with noble Romans, medallions, urns, ribbons and swags of flowers. It was built in 1540, but was bought in 1637 by the fabulously wealthy Cardinal Bernardino Spada, who was a keen collector of art. The exuberant decor continues in the courtyard, with a frieze of battling centaurs, fleeing women, Tritons and mermaids, and yet more flowers. The wittiest contribution, though, is the work of Spada's friend Borromini in the form of a long colonnaded tunnel visible to the right. Ask the porter to take you round to see it, and you discover that the gallery is about four times shorter than it appeared to be – an illusion created by having the columns gradually decrease in size between an upward-sloping floor and a downward-sloping ceiling.

The palazzo still houses Spada's collection of paintings – which, though not exactly stunning, does have one work apiece by Andrea del Sarto, Dürer, Rubens and Jan Brueghel. Women artists are fairly well represented – there are two works by Artemisia Gentileschi, and one each by Lavinia Fontana and Sofonisba Anguissola. The paintings are numbered, not labelled, but photocopied lists are available in each of the four rooms. These are not entirely accurate – a portrait of Salome with the head of John the Baptist is identified as Laura Dianti, mistress of Lucrezia Borgia's third husband, Alfonso d'Este!

First to greet you are two paintings of Cardinal Spada. He was for some years papal legate to Bologna, and had his portrait painted by two of the city's leading artists, Guercino and Reni, both of whom also worked in Rome. The artists loathed one another – Reni accused Guercino of filching all his ideas and techniques: here's a chance to make up your own mind about which is best. Look hard and you'll find a minutely detailed sixteenth-century French painting on glass of *Susanna and the Elders*, showing the lascivious Elders approaching Susanna as she takes a bath in her garden.

Lavinia Fontana's (see box, p.110) *Cleopatra* is in the next room. For once the Egyptian queen is depicted not as a *déshabillée* seductress but as a self-possessed, androgynous woman, wearing an almost military outfit. Most of the rest of the walls (apart from the mistitled Salome) are covered with formal portraits of gentlemen – a Titian School *Portrait of a Musician*, long-haired, baggily clothed, with haunted, slightly red eyes, is a bohemian exception.

Continuing, you reach a portrait of a young girl by Sofonisba Anguissola. She was born in Cremona in the 1530s; her father was a widowed nobleman who was determined that his six daughters and son should receive a broad, enlightened education. Sofonisba and her sister Elena studied painting with a local artist, Bernardino Campi, and passed on their knowledge to their sisters, who also became artists. Her father engaged the help of Michelangelo, asking him to send Sofonisba a drawing which she could colour in (Michelangelo helped a number of artists in this way). He also asked her to send him a drawing of a boy crying, which she did. Eventually Sofonisba's work attracted the attention of the Spanish Duke of Alba, then governor of nearby Milan. Sofonisba was taken to Spain, with great ceremony, as court painter and lady-in-waiting to the Queen. She stayed there for ten years, and as her fame spread, other fathers (most of them artists) began to think that perhaps art was not so unfeminine a profession after all, and began to allow their daughters to paint.

One such daughter of an artist was Artemisia Gentileschi (see box, p.118) who has two works in the gallery. Of the two works shown here, her *Virgin and Child* is a profound evocation of the intimacy of motherhood, with the Child reaching up to his mother, who sits with her eyes closed. The other painting, *The Lute Player*, is of a large, powerful woman, her eyes lost in thought as she plucks the strings. Like Lavinia Fontana, Artemisia shuns cliché – most men painted female lute players as courtesans.

Via Giulia

Via Giulia is a broad, perfectly straight cobbled street, lined with Renaissance palaces, churches and antique shops. It is particularly pleasant in the evenings, when its lamplit vista stretches out, fretted with the pediments, rusticated arches and cornerstones jutting from the façades of palazzi.

It was laid out in the early sixteenth century on the orders of Pope Julius II, to connect the city centre with the new St Peter's (which Julius had also commissioned). Funds ran out, and both Julius and its planner, Bramante, died before the link could be completed with a bridge. Nevertheless, it became one of the most fashionable streets in Rome. Raphael lived at numbers 84–86, in a palazzo whose façade looks like a slab of chocolate. He also designed the church of Sant'Eligio in Orefici, now standing on a drab alleyway just off the street. The sculptor and architect Antonio Sangallo the Younger lived at and probably designed number 66, a now grimy Renaissance palace with a gorgeous garden; and Pope Paul III (Farnese) built the palace at number 93 for his granddaughter.

Where there were wealthy, talented and well-connected men, there were courtesans, and Via Giulia, though a notch down from Via dell'Orso, was still considered a desirable address. Angela Greca lived on nearby Vicolo Cellini (then, rather rudely called Via Calabraga, meaning take-your-breeches-off-street) in the still prettily frescoed house at number 31. Cellini never lived there, but he was a regular courtesan client. Angela was a Cypriot woman who arrived in Rome in dire straits, having been robbed, raped and left with VD. She was, however, beautiful and Machiavellian enough to end up as one of the most successful early-sixteenth-century courtesans. She took a wealthy Spanish lover, who gave her the house on Via Calabraga, and subsequently had other lovers – all swiftly dropped whenever anyone more affluent came along. Eventually she was rich enough to move to the more fashionable Via dell'Orso, in company with other great courtesans. In 1536 she shocked the city and became a nun, much to the satisfaction of Vittoria Colonna (see p.112). At the time Angela's decision was unusual, and the only convent she could go to, the Convertite, was extremely strict.

The Farnese Viaduct

Paul III's Palazzo Farnese backs on to Via Giulia, and spanning the street behind is an arch dripping with vines. Michelangelo planned to link the Palazzo Farnese and the Villa Farnesina on the opposite bank of the Tiber with a viaduct, but this is as far as the project got. Just below the arch is a grotesque fountain, the Fontana Mascherone, with water dribbling from the miserable mouth of an ancient Roman mask resembling a wasted hippie. On one occasion the election of a new Grand Master of the Order of Malta was celebrated by making it flow with wine instead of water.

Santa Maria dell'Orazione e Morte

Grimacing skulls on either side of the church's door are the first clues to the *raison d'être* of this eighteenth-century church by Ferdinand Fuga. It belonged to a confraternity established in 1551 to collect the bodies of the anonymous dead and give them a Christian burial. The oval church is open only on Sunday evenings, when you can slip inside to see more skulls decorating the windows.

Sant'Eligio dei Orefici

Open 10.30 a.m. only. Closed Sat and Wed. Ring at porter's door round the corner

Standing in a dank, graffitied alleyway sunk between Via Giulia and the Tiber, this church was designed by Raphael (though it was actually executed, and somewhat modified, by his pupil Peruzzi). It doesn't look much from the outside, but the interior is pure and simple, built on a Greek cross-plan inspired by Bramante's Tempietto (see p.148), and crowned with a white dome.

Carceri Nuove

Built in 1655 for Pope Innocent X, this orange building with sturdy iron-grilled windows was for centuries considered to be one of the most 'solid and salubrious' prisons in Europe. It now houses a (closed) Museum of Criminology, a UN crime and justice research unit, the Ministry of Justice for Juveniles, and a Civil Penitentiary for Adults.

San Bjagio della Pagnotta

This small hall-shaped church is dedicated to Blaise, a fourth-century Armenian bishop who was martyred by being shredded with the combs used for untangling fleeces. Oddly, he became the patron of wool-combers (who worked on nearby Via Pettinari – the Street of the Combers). He is also credited with the power to heal throat diseases, for he once saved a young boy from choking to death by removing a fish bone from his throat. Sufferers from sore throats still go to the church to be healed – by holding two candles to the throat. 'Pagnotta', incidentally, means bread roll, and if you visit on 3 February you'll see why – after an Armenian Mass, bread is distributed to the congregation.

San Giovanni dei Fiorentini

Via Giulia ends with San Giovanni, a grubby white Baroque church ornamented with popes and saints raising their fists like football supporters. It was built on the orders of the Florentine Pope Leo X, who held a competition to find an architect. One of the contestants was Raphael, but the commission was granted to Jacopo Sansovino – perhaps an error of judgement on Leo's part.

THE JEWISH GHETTO AND AROUND

Rome's Jewish Ghetto has a village-like feel. Narrow cobbled streets knot together to form intimate piazzas; water dribbles from the rusty spouts of drinking fountains; little heaps of spaghetti are left for the neighbourhood cats; and fag ends and pumpkin seeds – the signs of a social life led mostly on the street – encrust the dusty cracks between cobbles. In the early evenings families queue at the bakery for slabs of glacé fruit-studded cake, and women sit outside their houses sewing, chatting or flicking through *Lubavitch News*.

Since AD 70, when Jerusalem fell to Titus and thousands of Jewish captives were transported to Rome to work as navvies on major building projects, there has been a substantial Jewish community in Rome. Originally they lived across the river in Trastevere, but in the Middle Ages they crossed over to what became the Ghetto. At that time their reputation for hard work, financial acumen and medical know-how made them invaluable to the popes, who allowed them to build a synagogue. They were first ghettoised in the thirteenth century, but the worst period was in the sixteenth, when Pope Paul IV, dreaded Inquisitor and notorious bigot, built around the Ghetto a wall whose five gates were opened at dawn and closed at sunset. He also forced the Jews to wear distinguishing hats. Future popes banned them from all trades except selling old clothes and scrap iron, though some had a surreptitious and highly profitable sideline concocting love potions, lending money and reading horoscopes. Until 1870, when Italy became one nation, Jews were not allowed to own land, practise any of the professions or take part in public life. Even today in the Ghetto, the majority of businesses are connected with the rag trade.

Although many Jewish people have moved out to the more monied suburbs, the Ghetto still provides a focus for the community. There are bookshops, a synagogue, kosher delicatessens and restaurants; walls are scrawled with Zionist graffiti; and Stars of David hang in mechanics' workshops. Much of the bigotry of Italy's resurgent Fascist movement is aimed at the Jews – and since a bomb exploded in 1982, outside the synagogue, killing a two-year-old boy, it has been guarded, and taking photographs inside its museum is forbidden. Things look set to get worse. Ten years later the old Nazi slogan 'Juden 'raus' (Jews out) was chanted at a Fascist demonstration on Piazza Venezia.

Apart from the synagogue and museum, most of the things to see in and around the Ghetto are not directly connected with the Jews. You'll pass the church of Santa Caterina ai Funari, where a hostel for poor women was established in the mid sixteenth century; the Roman Teatro di Marcello, now converted into yuppie flats, with the remains of a portico outside recommended by Ovid for men on the pick-up; and the Palazzo Cenci, home of Beatrice Cenci, who was condemned to death for murdering her abusive father. For the most part, though, the Ghetto is simply a relaxing place to wander – or to sample Jewish specialities, ranging from fruitcake to *carciofi alla giudea*, crispy fried artichokes.

Before you enter the Ghetto proper, however, it's worth pausing on Via del Plebiscito to visit a quintessentially Catholic monument: the Gesù.

Gesù

The Gesù is the principal church in Rome of the Jesuits, a religious Order founded in the 1530s by a Basque priest, Ignatius Loyola. All-male, highly intellectual, and heavily involved in missionary work and education, Jesuits were also active in war and politics.

From 1520 until 1648 (when the Thirty Years War ended) wars between Catholics and Protestants raged throughout Europe, and the Jesuits played their part. They organised an insurrection against Protestant Queen Elizabeth I in England and Ireland, organised to fight the Huguenots in France, and helped to enforce Bohemia's conversion to Catholicism.

The Gesù church was also influential. Its richly articulated façade, with superimposed columns, mighty scrolls and double pediment, was designed by Giacomo della Porta in 1568, and set the style for many Baroque churches to come. The interior, conceived by Giacomo Vignola, was also a trendsetter, with a single, broad and well-lit nave designed so that the congregation could see the priest and read their prayer books. This was a subtle ploy – the Jesuits hoped that if people felt involved in the proceedings they would be less likely to be attracted to Protestantism.

By the late seventeenth century the Jesuits and the Catholic

Church were riding on a wave of glory. It was in this confident mood that the Gesù was decorated – with triumphant paintings, and statues which either ridiculed or made a bogeyman of Protestants and 'heretics'.

Toffee-coloured pilasters and marble columns, glinting chandeliers and flickering candles make the Gesù almost gaudily opulent. The fresco in the nave ceiling, painted by G.B. Gaulli (better known as Baccicia) in 1672, features ecstatic hosts of naked cherubs and sumptuously draped women swimming in the light radiating from a hazy monogrammed mist. It's actually rather tacky (particularly once you notice the grubby pastel stuccoed figures in the squinches, which look like cardboard cutouts). If you disentangle the monogram, it reads IHS (in Greek the first three letters of Jesus's name) which, the Grand Duke of Tuscany joked, stood for 'Iesuiti habent satis' – the Jesuits have sufficient.

Equally melodramatic is the chapel of St Ignatius Loyola, who was canonised in 1622. It is designed to give the impression that the green serpentine pediment is splitting open to reveal God, Christ, a lapis lazuli globe and a glory topped with a dove. Below is a statue of Ignatius, the light glittering on his bald silver head, sunflower-like halo and jewel-studded gown. The lapis lazuli globe is the largest block of the gem in the world, though the statue of Ignatius is a copy, as the original was melted down during the French invasion. At either side are two risibly reductive marble statue groups. In the 'Triumph of Religion over Heresy' a female embodiment of Religion stamps on the fanged head of a wide-jawed serpent. In 'Barbarians Adoring the Faith', 'Religion' holds a torch aloft while a cute recording angel aims a sharp kick at a traumatised old couple embroiled with a snake.

Santa Caterina dei Funari

In 1543 Pope Paul III permitted a hostel for poor women to be established next to the church of Santa Caterina dei Funari, now with a splendidly ornate 1564 façade. The hostel was run, not by the Church, but by a committee of charitable men and women. Though such institutions made only the tiniest inroad into the problem of poor women whose families had no money for dowries, they were better than nothing – and a far more appealing option to many women than entering a convent.

Fontana delle Tartarughe

According to legend, the Fontana delle Tartarughe (Fountain of the Tortoises) was erected in a single night in 1585 on the orders of Duke Mattei, who lived in the Renaissance palace which overlooks the square. The story goes that after Mattei lost all his money gambling, his fiancée's father refused to let the wedding go ahead. To prove that he could work miracles – even when he was penniless – the beleaguered Duke called in one Taddeo Landini to build the fountain. Whether or not the story is true, it's a delightfully frivolous piece, with delicately poised naked youths astride squirming dolphins, holding up tiny tortoises so that they can 'drink' from the upper basin. The tortoises were actually added later, probably by Bernini.

Portico D'Ottavia and Sant'Angelo in Peschiera

At the foot of Via Portico d'Ottavia, just outside the Theatre of Marcellus, a row of gnawed Corinthian columns held together by rusty metal braces have been clumsily turned into a porch for the scruffy church of Sant'Angelo in Peschiera. The columns belonged to the Portico of Octavia, bordered by colonnades, adorned with statues, built around two temples and dedicated by Augustus to his sister Octavia (see p.75). It was a popular meeting-place, acted as a foyer for the theatre, and was one of many spots in the city recommended for men wanting to pick up women by the poet Ovid in his manual of sexual harassment, *The Art of Love*.

If she's taking a leisurely
Stroll down the colonnade, then you stroll there too –
Vary your pace to hers, march ahead, drop behind her,
Dawdling and brisk by turns. Be bold,
Dodge in round the columns between you, brush your person
Lingeringly past hers.

Sound familiar?

From the Middle Ages onwards the portico was used as a fish market, and there is still a peculiar plaque on the wall of the church, stating that the head and body (up to the first fin) of any fish longer than the plaque had to be given to the conservators (municipal authorities). Fish heads, incidentally, were considered a delicacy.

If the church is open, it's worth going inside – not because it is particularly beautiful, but because you may witness an extremely bizarre spectacle. If, as you enter, the church is packed, and the atmosphere is charged with the tension of a dentist's waiting-room, and if all eyes are surreptitiously fixed on a man in an anorak with his hand on someone's forehead, you've encountered the Catholic faith-healer.

The Theatre of Marcellus

Porticos were all right, but a theatre, reckoned Ovid, was an even better hunting-ground for a man on the prowl. Fashionable women, he wrote, flocked to the theatre as much to be seen as to watch the performance. Juvenal accused women of going to the theatre to swoon over actors and, when the theatre season was over, of hiring actors to put on plays in their homes in order to seduce them. The theatre was not considered a respectable profession, and actresses were sometimes expected to appear nude and even to perform sexual acts on-stage. Most actresses were young women who, having been abandoned as babies (see p.185), were picked up by pimps and Svengalis who trained them to be prostitutes or showgirls. There were, however, some actresses who performed in Greek plays – though the only one we know about is a young freedwoman called Eucharis, who died in the first century BC, just before the age of fourteen. The inscription on her tomb reads: 'I was educated and taught as if by the Muses' hands. I adorned the nobility's festivals with my dancing, and first appeared before the common people in a Greek play.'

Theatre in ancient Rome, however, was considerably less popular than blood sports and races. There were three theatres – Pompey, Marcellus and Balbus – which together could seat only around 50,000, about the same as the Colosseum and a third less than the Circus Maximus. The quality of the shows was usually pretty dire, and since no one could see or hear properly, the same plots were reiterated time and time again. All parts were played by men, and characters were identified by different-coloured masks and stock costumes.

The Theatre of Marcellus was begun by Julius Caesar but completed in 13 BC by Augustus, who dedicated it to his nephew Marcellus (the son of Octavia and Gaius Marcellus), who had died some ten years earlier at the age of twenty-five. It is currently undergoing much-needed restoration work, and is closed to the public, so you'll have to make do with looking at it from a distance (the best view is from the alleyway which begins at the back of Sant'Angelo in Peschiera). It is, however, occasionally used for open-air concerts in summer.

Two arcaded layers remain, one decorated with Doric and the other with Ionic columns. The top layer was Corinthian, and the combination of arcades and columns served as a model for the Colosseum. In the sixteenth century the ruins were incorporated into a palace for the Savelli family, which has now been converted into upmarket apartments. The three white Corinthian columns supporting a corner of architrave belonged to a temple to Apollo.

Palazzo Cenci

Now housing a minimalist architect's studio on the ground floor, the golden-brown Palazzo Cenci used to be the home of the Cenci family. In the late sixteenth century a noblewoman, Beatrice Cenci, her two brothers and mother, were tried and found guilty of murder. The victim was Beatrice's father, and the reason was incest. The Pope was so moved by the account of events given by Beatrice's lawyer that he almost pardoned her. Eventually, though, he decided that Beatrice, her mother and elder brother had to be executed, and granted a pardon only to her younger brother, Bernardino. Two hundred years later Shelley wrote a play, *The Cenci*, about the episode, which was banned in London until 1886 because incest was taboo.

Synagogue
Museum open Mon–Fri 9 a.m.–2 p.m.; Sun 9 a.m.–noon

Rome's chief synagogue is an exuberant and eclectic *fin-de-siècle* fantasy. Its dome is like that of a Riviera hotel, and its walls are adorned with classical pediments and columns, scrolly arches, Stars of David and Hebrew inscriptions. A plaque commemorating the 1982 bomb which killed two-year-old Stefano Tache Guy and wounded forty other Jews is a sobering reminder of what the community had – and still has – to endure.

The synagogue's museum, heavily guarded with electronic security doors, is well worth a visit, and is far more interesting than the synagogue itself. There is a collection of ornate silver crowns which had to be made for the Jews by Christians, as Jews were forbidden to work with precious metals. More mundane objects include a stamp used for marking kosher meat and Red Cross money issued in the Theresienstadt concentration camp (the only one to which the organisation was given access).

Perhaps the most startling exhibit, however, is a prayer book peppered with shrapnel holes and spotted with blood, which saved the owner from more serious wounds during the 1982 attack. There is also evidence of earlier persecutions, like an edict issued by Clement VIII (ruled 1592–1605) expelling Jews from every part of the Papal States except Rome and the Adriatic port of Ancona.

San Nicola in Carcere and the Forum Holitorium
This eleventh-century church was built within the ruins of three Republican temples – you can see some of the columns embedded in the walls – which overlooked the Forum Holitorium, the ancient city's fruit, vegetable and oil market. Within the market area there was a column, known as the *Columna Lactaria*, which was either a hiring place for wet-nurses or one of many places in the city where unwanted infants could be abandoned (see p.185).

Isola Tiberina (Tiber Island)

This boat-shaped island in the middle of the Tiber is linked by bridges with the Ghetto and Trastevere. Virtually all of it is taken up by a hospital, the **Fatebenefratelli**, which probably occupies the site of a medieval hospice. The island has been associated with cures ever since 291 BC. For several years Rome had been ravaged by the plague, and on the advice of the Sibylline Books it was decided to send an envoy to Epidauros in Greece, cult centre of Aesculapios, the god of healing. The envoy left in 292 and returned a year later with a sacred serpent, the symbol of Aesculapios. As they were sailing up the Tiber, the snake suddenly slid into the water and swam to the island. A temple was duly built, with porticos where the sick could sleep the night in the hope of being healed. In ancient Greece Aesculapian treatment included sleeping with snakes and dream therapy. There is no record of what the treatment methods on the Tiberina were, but some at least were successful – in the last century hundreds of clay models, mostly of hands and feet, were discovered on the island: thank-offerings for cures like the ex-votives still common today in Catholic churches.

The church of San Bartolomeo stands on the site of the old temple, dedicated to a first-century saint who was flayed alive in Armenia and then beheaded. His corpse was apparently brought to the island in the tenth century, though by the eleventh King Canute's wife, Emma, had got hold of an arm and presented it to Canterbury. Nowadays the church is full of refined semi-abstract sculptures by Padre Andrea Martini, a resident in San Bartolomeo's convent.

Piazza Bocca della Verità

The wedge-shaped 'Square of the Mouth of Truth', now disagreeably choked with traffic, occupies the site of the ancient cattle market or *Forum Boarium*. This was Rome's oldest market, and was not only a place for selling cows and hay, but an elegant arena overlooked by temples. Two of the prettiest and best-preserved temples in the city still stand here, and a wonderful medieval church, Santa Maria in Cosmedin, now occupies the site of the market inspector's office.

The square is named after an ancient drain cover in Santa Maria's portico carved with a bearded, slit-mouthed, piggy-eyed face. This is the so-called Bocca della Verità. In the Middle Ages anyone suspected of lying (particularly wives accused of being unfaithful) had to put their hand inside the mouth – if they didn't tell the truth, the mouth would supposedly snap shut.

In the eighth century the area was home to Rome's Greek community, who had fled to the west after the Byzantine emperor had banned the worship of icons. Icons of the Virgin were particularly popular, and worshipped with increasing fervour. Two of the churches in the area were built to house miraculous Madonna icons: Santa Maria della Consolazione at the foot of the Capitoline (founded to console condemned prisoners *en route* to execution on the hill) and the now demolished Santa Maria del Sole, which occupied one of Piazza Bocca della Verità's two surviving pagan temples.

Santa Maria in Cosmedin

Santa Maria in Cosmedin is a squat medieval church built of brick and dwarfed by a campanile pierced with arcades. In ancient Rome the market inspector's office, or Statio Annonae, stood here, next door to a temple dedicated to Ceres, the corn-goddess. Aptly enough, one of the market inspector's most important functions was to distribute supplies of free corn to the poorer citizens of Rome.

In the late sixth or seventh century, the old food distribution centre was taken over by the ecclesiastical authorities to provide aid for the poor, the sick, the aged and pilgrims. This was not an entirely altruistic move, but a tried and tested method (as the emperors had discovered centuries earlier) of buying popularity. In the eighth century a church was built on the site, and given to the community of Greek refugees.

The interior is cosy, particularly in the evenings when it is lit by candles. The slightly tottering columns, with intricately carved capitals, belonged to the Statio Annonae, but most of the decor dates from the twelfth century. Craftsmen, known as the Cosmati, created geometric burgundy, blue and green marble pavements, a *schola cantorum* (where the choir sit), and a twisting Paschal candlestick inlaid with mosaics. Most of the twelfth-century frescoes have been heavily restored, but in the sacristy there is a fragment of an eighth-century mosaic of the Adoration of the Magi which came from the original St Peter's. Greek services are still held in the church at 10.30 a.m. every day.

Temples of Portunus and Hercules Victor

The diminutive, rectangular Temple of Portunus is dedicated to the god of harbours (the main Tiber port was nearby), and dates from the second century BC. The circular temple next to it was known for centuries as the Temple of Vesta (logically enough, as Vestal temples were traditionally round), but excavations proved that it was dedicated to Hercules, a model of machismo. Both temples were preserved by being converted into churches.

In 872 the Temple of Portunus became the church of St Mary the Egyptian, a legendary fifth-century hermit who left home at the age of twelve, worked as a prostitute for seventeen years, and then decided to join a pilgrimage to Jerusalem (she paid for her passage by sleeping with the sailors). When she reached Jerusalem an icon of the Virgin Mary told her to go to Jordan, where she would find peace. She dutifully went to live in the desert, on a diet of dates and berries, and when her clothes wore out her hair grew to shield her body. Her cult (which has no historical foundation) was extremely popular with Eastern Christians, like the Greeks who lived in the area, because it hinged on the power of an icon (see above).

The Temple of Hercules Victor was dedicated to another miraculous Madonna icon, discovered in the Middle Ages floating down the Tiber in a coffer. When the coffer was opened a ray of light streamed out, and the icon and church were thence named Santa Maria del Sole (of the sun).

San Giorgio in Velabro

Like Santa Maria in Cosmedin, San Giorgio is a medieval church with a Romanesque campanile, built in the ninth century over an earlier church. The interior is one of the coolest, most tranquil in Rome, with antique columns, an aged wooden ceiling and soft grey walls. The altar contains part of St George's skull, which was discovered in the Lateran palace. Most people know George only as a dragon-slayer and patron saint of England, but he was also believed to have the power to protect against the plague, leprosy and syphilis.

Churches for the Condemned

In ancient Rome, condemned criminals were thrown to their death from the Tarpeian Rock, a spur of the Capitoline Hill, named after Tarpeia (see p.177), who opened the Roman gates to the Sabines. It continued to be used as a place of execution in the Middle Ages, and in the fourteenth century a condemned nobleman, Giordanello degli Alberini, was promised justice if he paid for an image of Mary to be painted. He did, and it was placed along the route taken by prisoners on their way to death. In the late fifteenth century the church of Santa Maria della Consolazione was built to house the icon of a sad Madonna holding the baby Christ.

In 1488 a confraternity, the Arciconfraternità della Misericordia, was founded to support condemned criminals through their last hours, and to give them a decent burial. The succour was not only spiritual – the brothers also soothed them with herbal medicines, aromatic vinegar (which performed the same function as smelling salts) and Dutch courage. The name of the confraternity's (now shabby) church is dourly appropriate: San Giovanni Decollato (St John the Beheaded).

If you go in the early evening, don't be surprised to find the roads around jammed with cars. They're all driven by men, but you're unlikely to be hassled – Monte Caprino (part of the Capitoline) is a favourite meeting-place for Rome's gays.

THE QUIRINAL HILL [QUIRINALE] AND THE NORTH

Northern Rome is a curious patchwork of neighbourhoods, stretching from the seedy fringes of the Termini district to the lush expanses of the Villa Borghese. In between are the dreary Quirinal Hill, home to the President, the city's best art gallery and some wonderful Baroque churches; at its foot are the Trevi Fountain, hidden among a maze of streets, and the sumptuous Palazzo Colonna. To the north is Via Veneto, raunchily glamorous after midnight but forlorn by day; and to the west the Piazza di Spagna quarter, swarming with foreigners, packed with swanky shops, and full of endless opportunities for people-watching and – if you're interested – acquiring a man (the Spanish Steps are prime hunting-ground for men wanting to *rimorchiare una straniera* – pick up a foreigner).

Though the Quirinal has most of the 'sights' and the Villa Borghese has some good museums and pleasant walks, it's in and around Piazza di Spagna that you'll probably want to spend most time. This neighbourhood became the centre of Rome's tourist trade in the eighteenth century, when a tour of Europe's historic cities was considered to be an essential part of a young male aristocrat's education. Hotels and lodging-houses in the neighbourhood were packed with the English, most of whom seem to have been less interested in culture than in gambling, whoring and collecting ancient statues to adorn the family home.

If young women travelled, they were usually heavily chaperoned – though romantic trysts in the Colosseum were not unknown. Several more independent-minded women did make it to Rome, particularly in the nineteenth century as women in America and Britain began to fight for their rights. The intrepid travel writer Mary Wortley Montagu passed through, as did the novelist Mrs Oliphant, who wrote a book about the city. Anna Maria Babington arrived in the 1890s with £100 and set up Babington's Tea Room, one of the city's most successful and enduring cafés and a group of American women sculptors, including Harriet Hosmer, came to study and work. Many, like Hosmer (who refused to marry), the poet Elizabeth Barrett Browning (who had eloped), the actress Fanny Kemble (who had divorced) and the artist Angelica

Kauffmann (accused of having painted live male models in London), found more freedom on the fringes of a foreign community than they did at home, and stayed for long periods – sometimes permanently. Most women, however, probably had more in common with the characters in Edith Wharton's marvellously malicious *Roman Fever*, spending afternoons gossiping or, like a certain American tourist at the turn of the century, searching out outlandish home accessories such as marble well-covers which could be converted into lavatory bowls.

The other women connected with the district are a mixed bunch, ranging from intellectuals like Vittoria Colonna and Queen Christina of Sweden to Lucrezia Borgia and Messalina. There are very few works by women in the art galleries, so prepare to meet the figments of male imaginations: vicious Venuses, beautiful murderesses, enigmatic courtesans, and demure – and not so demure – Madonnas and saints.

THE QUIRINAL HILL AND AROUND THE TREVI FOUNTAIN

The Quirinal Hill, bounded by Via del Corso, Via del Tritone and tawdry Via Nazionale, is the highest of Rome's seven hills. It is the legendary home of the Sabines, a tribe whose women were victims of a mass abduction by Romulus's tribesman, in what became known as the Rape of the Sabine Women (see p.182). A quiet residential neighbourhood in Classical Rome, it was abandoned during the Middle Ages and called the Monte Cavallo (Horse Mountain) for the heads of two ancient horses half buried in the ground. They were dug up in the 1580s by Sixtus V, and incorporated in a monument along with an obelisk, to liven up the view from the windows of the new papal summer palace. Sixtus was also responsible for crisscrossing the hill with two dead-straight narrow roads, which are now among the most grubby and oppressively traffic-choked in the city.

Via Nazionale has not changed essentially since the 1950s, when novelist Eleanor Clark described it as a 'hell of neon'. Full of hotels, restaurants and shops designed to trap bewildered tourists, it is rootless and anonymous, and there's no reason ever to set foot in it unless you want to visit the exhibitions or cafés in the Palazzo delle Esposizione. Trekking between the sights on the Quirinal proper is also a chore, while the maze of streets at its foot are off-puttingly packed with souvenir shops and takeaway pizzerias cashing in on the presence of the Trevi Fountain. That said, there are three wonderful art galleries on the fringes of the Quirinal, a couple of inspired Baroque churches, and the Trevi Fountain, however clichéd, is definitely not to be missed. There are brief historic encounters with a number of talented women – the Renaissance

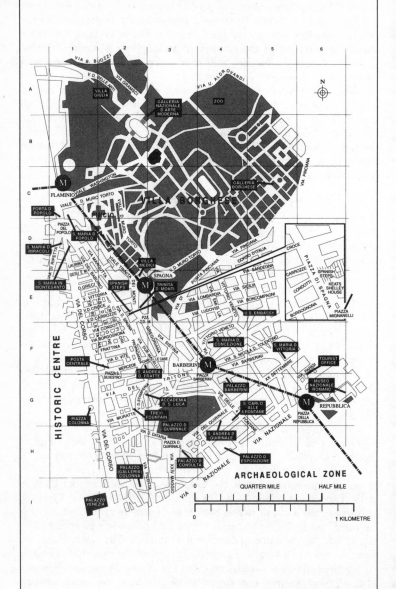

poet Vittoria Colonna, and artists ranging from Artemisia Gentileschi to Angelica Kauffmann.

The best and largest art collection is in the Palazzo Barberini, but the Accademia di San Luca is worth a visit if you want to see self-portraits by women artists, and the Galleria Colonna should be seen as much for its lavish decor as for its paintings. Bernini's Sant' Andrea al Quirinale and Borromini's San Carlo alle Quattro Fontane are both ingenious little Baroque churches, while Santa Maria della Vittoria contains a sculpture of St Teresa by Bernini which has shocked and titillated visitors for generations.

The Trevi Fountain [Fontana di Trevi]

Despite being tucked away on a tiny piazza, the Trevi Fountain is almost impossible to miss, as the narrow alleyways which approach it are glutted with tacky shops and takeaway pizzerias and filled with the sound of water. An eighteenth-century Rococo extravaganza of rearing sea horses, conch-blowing Tritons, craggy rocks and flimsy trees, the Trevi looks particularly magnificent at night. It has just been cleaned, and its creamy travertine gleams beneath powerful torrents of water sparkling in the light of the submerged lamps and constant camera flashes. 'Come and see the Trevi at midnight' is possibly the most clichéd *rimorchio* line in the city. If you take up the invitation, try to resist the temptation to leap in, like Anita Ekberg in the 1950s film *La Dolce Vita*. The police patrol are unlikely to be impressed.

The water comes from the Acqua Vergine, an aqueduct built by Agrippa in 19 BC to fill Rome's first complex of public baths. The aqueduct is fed by springs about 14 miles from the city which are said to have been shown to some thirsty Roman soldiers by a young girl named Trivia. Whether the Trevi is named after her, or the fact that the piazza stands at the junction of three streets [*tre vie*], is uncertain.

The water was reputed to be the sweetest in Rome (nineteenth-century English residents would keep supplies at home for making tea), though the superstition that drinking a mouthful of Trevi water would guarantee a return visit to the city has long since been replaced by throwing coins into its basin. Nowadays, in fact, a sip could be fatal, as bleach is added to keep algae at bay.

Accademia di San Luca

Open Mon, Wed and Fri 10 a.m.–1 p.m. Sometimes opens late

Founded in 1577 to train artists and keep them on the straight, narrow moral path prescribed by the Counter-Reformation, the

Accademia di San Luca is one of Rome's more itinerant institutions, and moved into this palazzo only in the 1930s. The academy may have seen itself as a moral watchdog, but nineteenth-century mothers were rather more sceptical. As the Pope was opening a new headquarters for the academy on Via Ripetta, he looked out of a side window and was confronted by a mother in a house across the narrow alleyway. Surrounded by her daughters, whose morals she felt to be seriously threatened by the presence of loose-living artists, she roared at the Pope: 'Holy Father, save my daughters!' The Pope responded by having all the windows on that side of the palazzo walled up to prevent virgin eyes falling on the shocking scene of an art class.

Women, however, were allowed to join the academy, and though its collection of art is small, women artists are represented there. Among them is a self-portrait by Lavinia Fontana, in which a small woman seated at a piano looks confidently out. There are also self-portraits of a shy, nervy Angelica Kauffmann holding a canvas, and the French artist Elisabeth Vigée Lebrun assuredly meeting the gaze of the viewer.

The rest of the gallery includes a detached fresco of a quizzical, rosy-skinned cherub by Raphael, and what is presumed to be a portrait bust of Michelangelo, along with the usual assortment of women portrayed as vamps, virgins and victims.

LAVINIA FONTANA

Fontana, daughter of a Bolognese artist, began painting around 1570, when she was about eighteen. By the late 1570s she was well known as a portrait artist, and though she was heavily influenced by the style of the Carraccis she was forbidden to enter their academy because life classes were a major part of the curriculum. Despite this, and a marriage in 1577 which resulted in eleven children, she continued to paint — religious pictures as well as portraits. In 1603, at the invitation of Pope Clement VIII, she moved to Rome. One major commission was a *Martyrdom of St Stephen* for the church of San Paolo fuori le Mura (destroyed when the church burnt down) which was so disliked by the general public that Fontana gave up official commissions and restricted herself to painting portraits. Nevertheless, she was elected to the academy, prices for her work shot up, and, a major accolade in the form of a portrait medal was cast in her honour shortly before her death in 1611.

Galleria Colonna

Open Sat only 9 a.m.–1 p.m.

Still occupied by the Colonnas, this gargantuan palazzo, built in the fifteenth century by the one member of the family to become pope, is the most sumptuous of Rome's palaces to be open to the public. It was almost completely rebuilt in the seventeenth century, by which time the Colonnas had given up power-struggling with Rome's other princely families in favour of *dolce vita* and art collecting. As you walk along Via della Pilotta to the back entrance, you can just see the private walled gardens, linked to the palazzo by a series of bridges. Somewhere around here, according to a not very reliable fourth-century author, a mock senate of women would meet during the reign of Elagabalus in order to discuss such crucial matters as social precedence and footwear. In the Renaissance, Vittoria Colonna (see below) and Michelangelo would have been able to look down on to the gardens as they engaged in rather more serious discussions in the garden of San Silvestro al Quirinale.

The Colonna collection of art treasures is displayed in a series of rooms known as the Galleria Colonna, purpose-built in the seventeenth century. Deliciously frescoed ceilings, lashings of gilt, pink and turquoise glass chandeliers, painted mirrors and dazzlingly polished marble floors (superb, according to one Colonna princess, for roller-skating parties) create a setting more appropriate for balls and banquets than for looking at art. However, unless you manage to infiltrate the princely party circuit, resign yourself to walking, rather than waltzing or skating, through the halls.

Arguably the best painting in the entire gallery is Bronzino's *Venus and Cupid*. Pale-blue and pink, revealing silky expanses of milky skin, this decadent evocation of languid sexuality depicts Venus flirting with a voluptuously bottomed Cupid. Across the hall is another *Venus and Cupid*, in which the goddess is gorgeously clad in light-catching strawberry pink, painted by Michele di Ridolfo del Ghirlandaio, while a Bosch-inspired *Temptation of St Anthony* provides an artistic cold shower with its warnings of the dangers of the flesh.

As you walk down into the Great Hall, there's a nasty *Martyrdom of St Catherine* by Il Salmeggia, showing the saint being strapped to a spiky wheel, and a *Madonna del Soccorso* (Madonna of Help) by Niccolo Alunno, featuring a cartoonish struggle between mother and hairy demon over a child.

The next room has two disagreeably opulent desks supported on the backs of ebony slaves wearing stripy loincloths, a chilling example of the terrible excesses of imperialism. One desk is decorated with a relief based on Michelangelo's *Last Judgement*; the other is studded with lapis lazuli, amethyst agate and mother-of-pearl.

The next room has the Colonna Pope, Martin V, being apotheosised on the ceiling, and paintings ranging from a *Rape of Europa* (Europa was raped by Jupiter in the form of a bull) to Madonnas by Bronzino and del Sarto (tennis-ball-breasted and crowned by cherubs). Beyond the throne room (all Roman palaces have a throne ready and waiting in case the Pope should drop by) is a small salon, designed to resemble an arbour, with marble foliage and flowers inlaid in its floor and garlands of oak leaves painted on the ceiling.

It is named after Maria Mancini, the first mistress of French King Louis XIV, who later married a Colonna. The lady's morals are not reflected in the paintings, most of which are of primitive Madonnas.

VITTORIA COLONNA

Just above the Palazzo Colonna, in the garden of San Silvestro al Quirinale, Vittoria Colonna used to meet Michelangelo. This was no torrid affair – he was gay and she was virtually a nun – but an intense Platonic friendship, the meeting of two sharp, sombre minds. Vittoria was widowed while she was still young, and though she was too much of an independent thinker and too unhappy with the state of the Catholic Church to become a nun, she spent much of her time in convents and took to wearing a Franciscan habit. She was the most famous woman poet of her day, at first writing 'only to relieve the inner pain' caused by the premature death of her husband, later turning to religious and abstruse Neo-Platonic themes. Her unease with contemporary Catholicism led her to become attracted to Protestantism. She was at the centre of a circle of radical evangelicals, and narrowly escaped the clutches of the Inquisition. She was also a dedicated soul-saver: one of her major triumphs was persuading an ageing courtesan, Angela Greca, to take the veil.

Piazza del Quirinale

Piazza del Quirinale lies on the south brink of the Quirinal hill, backed by the vast orange **Palazzo del Quirinale** – its right wing stretches the entire length of Via del Quirinale – and overlooked by the flamboyant Palazzo della Consulta. The piazza is usually lifeless, apart from the elaborately uniformed Carabinieri in wooden sentry boxes guarding the Palazzo del Quirinale (once the Pope's summer palace, now the official residence of the President) and their off-duty colleagues leaning out of the windows whistling at female tourists walking down Via Dataria to the Trevi.

The centrepiece is a fountain spilling into an ancient basin below an obelisk, one of a pair which originally flanked the entrance to the Mausoleum of Augustus. On either side, dug up on the Quirinal on the orders of Sixtus V, are statues of Castor and Pollux, each of them accompanied by a disproportionately small horse.

The Palazzo della Consulta, designed by Ferdinando Fuga in the 1730s, is one of Rome's more outrageous buildings. Above each door are dogs, reclining statues with scrolls instead of heads, and grimacing old women with dangling breasts. It is home to the Corte Costituzionale, the supreme court for dealing with constitutional matters which was set up because the wording of Italy's 1948 Constitution was so abstract that the ruling parties were able to interpret it as they wished. This is one reason why, despite the fact that the Constitution granted theoretical equality to women in 1948, the laws to back it up were introduced only in the 1970s.

The Corte decides whether or not laws passed by Parliament are legal. In the 1970s, its most influential judgement was probably that the state monopoly over TV and radio was unconstitutional. Consequently, Italians have the Corte to thank for the fact that they have more TV stations (and probably game shows) per head than any country in the world.

Sant' Andrea al Quirinale

This is one of Bernini's most theatrical churches, in which he deftly combined architecture, painting and sculpture to enact the assumption of a saint. The church is an oval, set on its short axis, and as soon as you enter your eyes hit the high altar niche in which angels seem to be positioning a painting of St Andrew being crucified on his diagonal cross. For a moment this seems to be all there is, but if you look up, you'll see a statue of the saint floating on a cloud, as if he had just slipped through the broken pediment behind him. He is, of course, leaving earth for Heaven (in the dome), where cherubs and the Holy Dove await him.

San Carlo alle Quattro Fontane

This small church, on the corner of the grimy, frantically trafficked Quattro Fontane crossroads, is Borromini at his most enchanting. The springily curved façade has two leaping angels carrying a medallion, angel wings framing a statue of Charles Borromeo, and column capitals licked by curling fronds and tongues of foliage. Inside, you step into a lovely octagonal arcaded courtyard, before passing through a vestibule into a delicately scalloped oval church. Soaring above is an oval dome, its coffering of cruciforms, hexagons and octagons getting smaller as they reach the oculus, to give the illusion that it is higher than it really is. Amazingly, the interior of the church was Borromini's first solo work, and the one that made his reputation. The Procurator General (who had commissioned it) reported: 'In the opinion of everybody, nothing similar with regard to artistic merit, caprice, excellence and singularity can be found anywhere in the world.' At the time he wasn't far wrong – he was plagued by requests for copies of the plans from visitors from as far afield as India.

Santa Maria della Vittoria

This modest-looking Baroque church, its interior cosily candlelit and lovingly adorned with marble, gilt and carvings, holds one of the most notorious statues in Rome – Bernini's *St Teresa*. The church itself, designed in the early seventeenth century by Carlo Maderno, is named after an icon of the Virgin found lying among the debris following the 1620 Battle of the White Mountain near Prague. The Catholics, having just wiped out the Calvinists, considered the discovery of the unscathed icon to be a sign that the Virgin was on their side, and brought it to Rome, where it was placed with great ceremony. The church, originally San Paolo, was promptly rededicated to Santa Maria della Vittoria (Mary of the Victory). However, the icon proved not to be infallible – it was destroyed in a nineteenth-century fire – and has been replaced by a copy.

But what everyone comes to see is the art world's most famous orgasm, a creamy marble St Teresa climaxing on a cloud. She is in the throes of a vision, and her entrails have just been pierced by an angel with a burning arrow. Bernini took his cue from her description of the experience in her autobiography: 'The pain was so severe that it made me utter several moans. The sweetness caused by this intense pain is so extreme that one cannot possibly wish it to cease . . .'

Bernini's conflation of spiritual with sexual ecstacy is understandable, though the angel's sweetly sadistic smile is suspiciously earthly. What is more, Teresa is watched by lifelike statues of Cornaro cardinals sitting in boxes like the audience at a theatre. Deeply shocked, an art critic friend of Elizabeth Barrett Browning, Mrs Jameson, thought that the group was vile, that St Teresa resembled a languishing nymph, and the angel looked like Eros. President de Brosses of France, visiting in 1740, was even blunter, quipping: 'If that is divine love, I know all about it'.

ST TERESA OF AVILA (1515–82)

Saint Teresa of Avila, the subject of Bernini's sculpture, is now best known as a sixteenth-century Spanish mystic whose relationship with God included cataleptic seizures, levitation and the sensation of having her heart pierced with a burning arrow – all of which she vividly described in her autobiography. But her relationship with God could also be blunt. After virtually drowning in a flooded river, she told him that if that was the way he treated his friends, it was no wonder he had so few.

The river incident occurred after Teresa had broken away from the Carmelite Order, whose ways, she felt, had become too lax. She trekked around Spain, sleeping in squalid inns as she founded convents where nuns could live the austere lives recommended by the original Carmelites. As a symbol of their austerity, she named the new Order the Discalced (shoeless) Carmelites. The Carmelite Establishment fiercely opposed her reforms, and tried to persuade Rome to suppress the new Order. But the Roman authorities recognised that her extraordinary visions and reforming zeal made her an ideal Counter-Reformation saint, and despite her own feeling that notions of her 'supposed sanctity' were 'nonsense', she was canonised in 1622, just 45 years after her death.

Piazza della Repubblica and the Museo Nazionale Romana

Most of the museum is closed at time of writing. Hours for the rooms which are open are usually Tues–Sat 9 a.m.–2 p.m.; Mon and Sun 9 a.m.–1 p.m.

Piazza della Repubblica is a busy roundabout at the head of Via Nazionale, with an exuberant nymph-studded fountain at its centre. The surrounding area is choked with the seedy overspill from Termini – greasy takeaways, a porn cinema, and unsavoury loiterers – but it was originally covered by the largest and most luxurious bath complex in the city, the Baths of Diocletian. The baths occupied a vast square, stretching from the fringes of Termini, across Piazza della Repubblica, almost as far as Via XX Settembre. Parts of its dull brick walls remain – one of the caldarium (hot baths) apses forms the façade of Santa Maria degli Angeli, and its vestibule occupies the tepidarium (lukewarm baths), while the church of San Bernardo is built within an ancient rotonda.

The **Museo Nazionale Romana** (also known as the Museo delle Terme) is housed in a former convent which was built within the ruins of the baths. Frustratingly, its stunning collection of Greek and Roman statues and ancient frescoes has been closed for years, and only one room is open. Even if the whole museum hasn't reopened by the time you visit, it's worth popping in to see the few selected exhibits on show. One of the loveliest is a delicate relief of Aphrodite on the back of a throne rising from the sea, behind filmy drapery held by two female assistants.

Once the museum reopens, leave plenty of time, as there are some memorable representations of women. The *Gaul and his Wife*, in which a Gaul supports the collapsing corpse of his wife as he slays himself; *Venus of Cyrene* twisting her hair up as she rises from the sea; the *Maiden of Anzio* carrying paraphernalia for a sacrifice; and a *Daughter of Niobe*, dying as she attempts to pull an arrow out of her back. There are also frescoes which came from a country villa belonging to Augustus's wife Livia decorated with fruit trees, flowers and birds.

Palazzo Barberini:
The Galleria Nazionale D'Arte Antica

Open Tues–Sat 9 a.m.–2 p.m.; Sun 9 a.m.–1 p.m.

Maffei Barberini, who became Pope Urban VIII in 1623, was one of the great patrons of Baroque Rome, and all over the city there are palaces, churches and fountains incorporating the chubby bees from his family coat of arms. He was an intelligent, cultured man, whose patronage enabled Bernini and Borromini to produce some of their finest works.

The Palazzo Barberini, which now rambles along a terrace above a row of shops and fast-food restaurants, was actually designed by Carlo Maderno. But he died a couple of months after the foundations had been laid, so Bernini, assisted by Borromini, took over.

In the mid nineteenth century the American sculptor William Wetmore Story, his wife and children lived in an apartment in the Palazzo Barberini. One Christmas there was a children's party, with entertainment provided by Hans Christian Andersen reading 'The Ugly Duckling'. Browning followed with 'The Pied Piper', while Story played the flute and led the children in a procession around the Grand Salon. The Grand Salon, extravagantly frescoed in the 1630s by Pietro da Cortona, should look magnificent when the current restoration has been completed, and the palazzo too is undergoing much-needed renovation. Fortunately, however, the art gallery inside is still open.

This is Rome's best gallery, comprising the private collections of princes bought by the state late last century. The only women artists shown are Artemisia Gentileschi, Angelica Kauffmann and Rosalba Carriera, but the representations of women by male artists are illuminating. The main collection here covers the thirteenth to the seventeenth centuries – most later works (and a handful of early ones) are to be found in the Palazzo Corsini (see p.143) – although some eighteenth-century works are displayed in the newly reorganised upper floor mostly devoted to the era's decorative arts.

The First Floor The collection opens with a series of thirteenth- and fourteenth-century works, most of them formally posed Madonnas and Christs on gold backgrounds. A refreshingly realistic exception is *The Birth of St John the Baptist* by the Master of the Coronation of Urbino, a late-fourteenth-century work in which the Virgin is shown spoonfeeding the aged Elizabeth, who has just given birth to John the Baptist. The next room showcases two works by the tearaway fifteenth-century monk Filippo Lippi (see also p.169). The *Madonna and Child* is unusual for an irreverently ugly, obese baby Christ, while in the *Annunciation* the ideal atmosphere created by a wistful Madonna, gilt-edged feathers on the angel's wings and exquisite detailing of hair, flowers, and fabrics is subtly disrupted by a couple talking anxiously as they leave the room.

Room 3 has a beautiful early-sixteenth-century *Magdalene* by Piero di Cosimo. Male artists often show Magdalene as a penitent prostitute, but Piero's is self-composed and dignified, absorbed in the book she is reading. Early-sixteenth-century works continue in Room 5 with a *Holy Family* by Andrea del Sarto, and a voyeuristic depiction of motherhood, *Madonna, Child and St John* by Beccafumi, in which a demure heavy-eyed Virgin, with fingers splayed around her erect nipple, prepares to feed a sugary golden-haired Christ. The pose of Beccafumi's Madonna is not so different from that of the courtesan in the Barberini's most famous painting, *La Fornarina* in Room 6. This is supposedly a portrait of Raphael's lover, a baker's daughter from Trastevere (baker in Italian is *fornaio*) and was probably begun by Raphael and completed by his raffish pupil Giulio Romano after his death. In fact, though this woman is quite obviously a courtesan, no one is quite sure who she is – it has been suggested that either Imperia (see p.224) or Beatrice Ferrarese (see p.61) may have been the model. That this portrait should have aroused so much speculation is hardly surprising, for the dark-haired woman is inscrutable. She sits, almost smiling, with an expression which is at the same time both diffident and powerful. One hand holds transparent drapery between her naked breasts, the fingers spread below her left nipple; the other rests between her thighs.

As Renaissance artists spent so much of their time painting religious commissions, many became adept at spicing up holy subjects. Girolamo Genga's *Mystical Marriage of St Catherine* is a case in point – an almost lascivious work, in which a young, naked Christ, looking as dissolute as a spoilt Arab prince, leans languidly over to Catherine (of Alexandria; see p.220) as he places a ring on her finger. Sodoma (so-called because, in the words of his biographer Vasari, he 'loved little boys more than was decent') opted for a more innocent interpretation of the mystical marriage, though he was also responsible for the room's most offensive work – *Rape of the Sabine Women* in which the women, far from being disturbed by their ordeal, appear to be dancing with delight.

Room 7 has distorted acid-hued works by El Greco, an embracing *Venus and Adonis* by Titian, and Tintoretto's *Christ and the Woman Taken in Adultery* in which the apostles tut-tut and Christ looks sympathetic. Then, apart from an elongated, sickly greenish Christ and plump pink Madonna in an hallucinatory *Deposition* by Mannerist Jacopino del Conte (Room 9), there is little worth stopping for until you reach the late-sixteenth- and early-seventeenth-century works of Room 15. Most interesting is an assured self-portrait by Artemisia Gentileschi, who chose to show herself painting against a dark, shadowy background. The confidence is not limited to the expression on her face – as a close look at the powerful brushwork on her dress will prove.

A story to which Artemisia returned time and time again (there are six surviving versions) is that of Judith, a beautiful Jewish widow who dolled herself up, inveigled her way into the camp of Israel's enemy, Holofernes, partied with him, got him drunk, then sliced off his head. Artemisia's versions of the episode are confrontational works, centring on violent, energetic, powerful women (none of these is in Rome). Male artists responded to the story in various ways.

In one of Caravaggio's versions (Room 13) Judith looks as though she can't quite believe what's happening, frowning as she slices through Holofernes' blood-gushing neck. The Dutch artist Jan Metsys working around a century earlier, interprets the episode completely differently. Judith, exquisitely beautiful, her breasts revealed by her transparent gown, stands holding her sword and Holofernes' head. Metsys was not the only artist to depict Judith as dangerous and erotic – by the sixteenth century it was common to find pictures of Judith and Holofernes in brothels. Freud may have had a point when he concluded that decapitation was symbolic castration!

Room 16 has a portrait of another murderess – the young Beatrice Cenci (see p.101: Palazzo Cenci), who alleged that she had been raped by her father, and hired assassins to kill him. The artist Guido Reni is supposed to have painted her haunted portrait on the night of her execution, but the attribution to Reni and the identity of the red-rimmed-eyed girl are disputed.

THE RAPE OF ARTEMISIA GENTILESCHI (c. 1597–1651/3)

Artemisia Gentileschi was born around 1597, the daughter of an artist, Orazio Gentileschi, who was a follower of Caravaggio. She entered her father's workshop, and by the age of eighteen, though already an accomplished artist, was taking lessons in perspective from a colleague of her father, Agostino Tassi. Not long afterwards Tassi raped her, and promised to marry her – the one way to keep her quiet and to carry on sleeping with her. Artemisia agreed, and though her complicity may sound odd, in seventeenth-century Italy (and in parts of southern Italy today) women who had been raped, or had otherwise lost their virginity, were considered to be second-hand property, and therefore undesirable wives.

Having realised that Tassi was not going to marry her, Artemisia told her father what had happened, and Tassi was put on trial. Here it emerged that Artemisia (who was tortured with thumbscrews in order to test the validity of her statement) had resisted Tassi so vigorously during the rape that she had wounded him. Tassi retaliated, and produced 'evidence' (all of it hearsay) that Artemisia had been raped on three previous occasions by three different men. Tassi's ploy is transparent. Unmarried women were considered to be the property of their fathers, and it was for reducing the value of a daughter, rather than traumatising and assaulting a woman, that rape was reckoned to be a crime. Hence Tassi's eagerness to prove that Artemisia was no longer a virgin by the time he raped her – it meant that he was not personally responsible for damaging a valuable asset. Tassi was convicted, but soon acquitted. Artemisia, who nevertheless did manage to get married, became a highly successful and prolific artist, creating some of the century's most challenging portraits of women. As well as the series of Judiths, she painted *Susanna and the Elders*, a deeply traumatic evocation of a woman's shame and horror at being the object of voyeuristic men. It is an unforgettable riposte to the female figments of male fantasies which grace the walls of most Classical art galleries, and though the original is in Germany, there are many reproductions in feminist art history books (see Recommended Books).

The Eighteenth-Century Collection In the eighteenth century Princess Cornelia Costanza Barberini, fed up with the grandiose – and by then dated – rooms of her family palace, decided to modernise the second storey. A series of more intimate apartments was created, decorated in a variety of styles ranging from scenes of jolly

Native Americans (then the focus of Jesuit proselytising) to miniature grotesques inspired by Roman frescoes just discovered at Pompeii. Many rooms retain their eighteenth-century decoration, along with period furniture, and collections of ceramics, costumes, chinoiserie and other oriental exotica.

There are also some good paintings – views of Rome by Vanvitelli, Venetian canal scenes by Canaletto, and a pensive *Portrait of a Young Girl Dressed as a Bacchante* by the Swiss artist Angelica Kauffmann. There are also two pastel portraits attributed to Rosalba Carriera (1675–1757), a Venetian artist who started out painting ivory snuffboxes for the tourist trade, but ended up as one of the most distinguished and innovative pastel portraitists of her time. She became a member of Rome's art academy, the Accademia di San Luca, created flattering portraits of the French and Austrian royal families, and in Paris was elected to the Académie Royale. She was also famous for her *demi-vierges*, portraits of semi-clad young girls which verged on the pornographic.

ANGELICA KAUFFMANN (1741–1807)

Angelica Kauffmann was the daughter of a minor Swiss artist, and as a girl she travelled around Italy with him, copying famous paintings she saw hanging in art galleries. At the time, Neoclassical art was all the rage. Italy was full of British and American artists studying antiquities, and Angelica got to know many of the most influential. In the mid 1760s she moved to London where, within a year, she had earned enough money from her portraits of aristocrats to buy a house. Portraiture was considered to be a reasonably ladylike form of art. History paintings, which were taken far more seriously, were not. Subjects tended to be taken from ancient Greece and Rome, and thus involved painting nudes, which was something a nice girl simply should not do. Angelica, however, had other ideas, and began to paint historical and mythological subjects – romantic, rather sentimental works which became so popular that copies even appeared on sets of china. As a woman working in a male world, her success made her the butt of many satires. One poet (not entirely without justification) wrote:

But were she married to such gentle males
As figured in her painted tales
I fear she'd find a stupid Wedding Night.

But as far as London Society went, the burning question was: had she or hadn't she painted real live naked men? She was certainly not allowed to join the male members of the Royal Academy (of which she was the sole female founder member) in life classes, but it appears that she may have made her own arrangements. Speculation continued even after her death – so much so that one art historian went to the trouble of tracking down a model, then aged eighty-two, who admitted that he had posed for Angelica, but that her father was always present, and that anyway, he exposed only his arms, shoulders and legs.

In the 1780s Angelica and her husband, a decorative artist, returned to Rome, living on Via Gregoriana, near the Spanish Steps, in the Palazzo Zuccari. She continued to paint, and it is from this period that the canvas in the Barberini comes. She died, aged sixty-six, in 1807, and was buried in the church of Sant' Andrea delle Fratte (see p.124).

PIAZZA DI SPAGNA TO PIAZZA DEL POPOLO

The triangle of streets below Piazza del Popolo, bordered by Via di Ripetta and Via del Babuino, are packed with designer boutiques, art galleries, antique shops and up-market delicatessens. It's an area in which to wander, window-shop, and sit in cafés watching people. At times the crowds can be overwhelming, as you'll see if you try elbowing your way up Via Condotti to Piazza di Spagna on a Saturday afternoon.

Piazza di Spagna has been the heart of tourist and expat Rome since the eighteenth century, when its community of British Grand Tourists earned it the title *ghetto d'Inglesi*. Nowadays the tourists come from all over the world, and are catered for by McDonald's and a sushi bar as well as the venerable Babington's Tea Room.

With the exception of Messalina (who murdered for a garden and met a sticky end) and the actress Eleonora Duse (who narrowly escaped being murdered by her lover), most of the women associated with the area are foreigners and expats. And for a change, they're remembered for their own achievements, rather than being the lover or sidekick of a man. As well as Angelica Kauffmann (see p.119), who lived and was buried in the area, George Eliot and Elizabeth Barrett Browning stayed here when they visited Rome, while the American sculptor Harriet Hosmer shocked the locals (and disapproving fellow Americans) by frequenting cafés with men and riding through the city alone.

If shopping is one of your aims, most designer shops are concentrated in the grid of cobbled streets directly below Piazza di Spagna. Via del Babuino is crammed with antique shops, and Via Margutta with art galleries – and in autumn with stands selling shamelessly commercial canvases aimed at the tourist market. If you can tear yourself away from the shops, there are a few 'sights' worth seeing. The house in which Keats died; Santa Maria del Popolo, Lucrezia Borgia's favourite church, with works by Caravaggio and Raphael; and Sant'Andrea delle Fratte, with the tomb of Angelica Kauffmann and Rome's only sculpture by Harriet Hosmer. If you want to escape the human maelstrom for a while, the Pincio Park (which is connected with the Villa Borghese) is five minutes' walk from the Spanish Steps.

Piazza di Spagna and the Spanish Steps

Overlooked by shuttered russet, cream and mustard-washed palazzi, bow-shaped Piazza di Spagna is the resort of tourists from all over the world. Approach it along Via Condotti, and for much of the day all you can see is a human cascade, as the crowds spill down the Spanish Steps and flow into the city's swankiest shopping street. On the square itself chic women clutching designer carrier bags and businessmen remonstrating into portable phones snake through throngs of tourists; carriage-pulling horses feed from nosebags as their drivers look around for custom; and police stand outside their mobile cabin waiting to help anyone who has had their pocket picked.

Climbing (and even more, descending) the steps calls for dextrous footwork if you are to avoid tripping over a tub of azaleas, busker, hippie hair-wrapper, or caricature artist – to say nothing of tourists or young Italians drinking, smoking, posing for photos and watching the world go by. If you join them, watch out for *burrini* (see box, p.55), young men who come in to town on the prowl from the suburbs and outlying villages.

Designed in the 1720s by an Italian, Francesco de Santis, in three voluptuous flights, the steps were originally built to link the French church, Trinità dei Monti, with the piazza below. They were soon used for more than simply going to church. In the nineteenth century artists' models, dressed up as emperors, saints and Madonnas, hung out on the steps, vying with one another for the attention of gullible foreign artists.

Despite its name (owing to the presence of the Spanish Embassy on the square), English voices were far more common than Spanish or Italian. Elizabeth Barrett Browning had eloped to Italy and settled in Florence with her husband Robert, and on trips to Rome she stayed in nearby Via Bocca di Leone, where she was visited by women like actress Fanny Kemble, divorced from her slave-owner husband, and tomboyish American sculptor Harriet Hosmer.

Babington's Tea Room

The square's most enduring enclave of Englishness owes its existence to Anna Maria Babington, who came to Rome in 1893 aged thirty, with a hundred pounds, to set up a small business. Rome was fuller than ever of the English, most of them members of High Society come for the silver wedding celebrations of King Umberto I and Queen Margherita. Anna Maria suspected that however much they all appeared to be having a wonderful time, they would enjoy themselves even more if they were able to relax with a nice cup of tea. If you've had the misfortune to drink tea in an Italian café (cup of hot water, teabag and jug of hot long-life milk on the side), you'll realise that she had a point.

With a friend from New Zealand, Isabel Cargill, she set up the first **Babington's Tea Room** on Via Due Macelli, which was so successful that she opened another branch on St Peter's Square. A year later, a house at the foot of the Spanish Steps fell vacant, and Babington's moved in. It's been there, with motherly waitresses serving good cups of tea (and lots more besides), ever since, and has proved so popular with Japanese visitors that a branch has been opened in Tokyo.

The Barcaccia Fountain

The least stagey of the city's Baroque fountains, the Barcaccia is usually impossible to see, as it's directly at the bottom of the Spanish Steps and surrounded by people sitting on its rim or taking photos. Designed by Bernini or his father, it consists of a boat which appears to be sinking – an ingenious solution for creating a fountain at the point in the city where the water pressure was low.

Keats–Shelley Memorial House

Open Mon–Fri 9 a.m.–1 p.m.; 2.30–5.30 p.m.

On 23 February 1821, John Keats died in this rose-pink house at the foot of the Spanish Steps. He was twenty-five, and had come to Rome with his friend, the artist Joseph Severn, in the vain hope that an Italian winter would cure his tuberculosis. Severely depressed, largely because of obsessive and unrequited love for his Hampstead neighbour, Fanny Brawne, he never truly rallied. He spent most of his time in Rome confined to a tiny bedroom overlooking the steps, fevered, delirious and haemorrhaging. Early this century the house (which was on the verge of being turned into a hotel) was bought by an Anglo-American association. It now holds a collection of manuscripts, paintings and other ephemera connected with Keats, Shelley (who was drowned in a boating accident off Viareggio) and other figures linked to the English Romantics.

In the corridor, along with portraits of Keats, Shelley and Byron, is one of Mary Wollstonecraft, pioneering feminist and author of *The Vindication of the Rights of Women*. She died giving birth to a daughter, Mary (also pictured), who eventually married Shelley and wrote the novel *Frankenstein*.

Among the manuscripts, paintings and memorabilia that cram the walls and display cabinets of the museum's tiny rooms are brief glimpses of other women connected with Shelley and Byron. Jane Williams, one of Shelley's many lovers; Teresa Guiccioli, a Venetian countess with whom Byron had a long affair; and Claire Clairmont, Mary Shelley's half-sister and mother of Byron's child, Allegra, whose relationship with her brother-in-law Shelley was rumoured to have been not entirely Platonic.

ELEONORA DUSE (1859–1924)

In the late nineteenth century the Swedish doctor and author Axel Munthe lived in the house. One night the actress Eleonora Duse, whose fame at the time was equalled only by that of Sarah Bernhardt, rushed in, begging to be allowed to hide on the terrace. She stood and watched a smartly dressed gentleman pass by, then asked Munthe if she could stay the night. Munthe, conscious of the rules of propriety, refused, but agreed to take her to the nursing home he ran near Tivoli, where she stayed for several days. The smartly dressed man was Duse's lover, Gabriele d'Annunzio, warped writer and Fascist sympathiser, who had just threatened to kill her. Their affair had begun in 1885, while Duse was appearing in *La Dame aux camélias*, and endured for ten destructive years. Born in 1859 into a family of actors, Duse created a stir at the age of fourteen, with her interpretation of Juliet. She rapidly became a star, famous for her passionate, inspirational acting, and appears to have been a woman who immersed herself, absolutely, in every part. 'I have a thousand women within me, and each one makes me suffer by turn.'

Column of the Immaculate Conception

This column was erected in 1857 to celebrate the declaration by Pope Pius IX in 1854 that belief in the Immaculate Conception of the Virgin was an essential part of Catholic doctrine. It does not, as is commonly thought, refer to the Virgin Birth, but to the fact that Mary was the only human being ever to have been born free from original sin. She was incapable of sin – indeed, could not even think of sin – for God had predestined her since time began to be the mother of his only son.

There is no reference to Mary's freedom from sin in the Bible, and the first mention of her birth comes in an apocryphal second-century Book of James. Here, St Anne, old and barren, is told by an angel that she is no longer infertile. Illustrators of the episode, though knowing that it wasn't *quite* a virgin birth, usually showed a magic spark passing between Anne and her equally ancient husband Joachim. In fact, the belief that Mary was absolutely pure really has its roots in popular Catholicism, and though theologians have wrangled over the issue for centuries, belief in it is a matter of faith, not logic. For the rest of womankind, already caught in the double-bind of having a virgin-mother as a role-model, it simply made Mary's act even more impossible to follow.

If you're in the piazza on 8 December – the feast of the Immaculate Conception – you can watch members of the Roman fire brigade climbing a ladder to place a wreath on the head of the Virgin. Twelfth-century Bernard of Clairvaux would have been appalled – he felt that celebrating the anniversary of Mary's conception was the equivalent to venerating the lovemaking of Anne and Joachim. 'Do you mean that the Holy Spirit was a partner in the sin of concupiscence?' he roared at canons who were planning to introduce the feast in their diocese.

In 1842 a Jewish businessman popped into Sant'Andrea to have a quick look at two statues by Bernini, and the Virgin Mary appeared in one of the chapels. The businessman fell to his knees, converted to Catholicism and became a missionary. In memory of the miracle an illuminated Ave Maria sign now graces the dull brick façade. Stepping inside, the first thing you see is a chapel surrounded by ex-votives, containing a nineteenth-century painting of the Virgin with a halo of gold stars and rays of light shooting from her hands. Of considerably greater artistic merit is a demure reclining statue of one Judith de Palezieux Falconett, carved by the Neoclassical American sculptor Harriet Hosmer. On the opposite side of the church, by the door, is a modest plaque to the artist Angelica Kauffmann (see p.119), who was buried here in 1807.

HARRIET HOSMER (1830–1908)

Hosmer was one of a number of American women sculptors working in Rome in the 1850s and 1860s. Born in 1830 into a liberal Massachusetts family, she decided early on to become a sculptor, and, having been refused permission to attend anatomy classes in Boston, persuaded the doctor father of a schoolfriend to give her private lessons. Encouraged by the actress and patron of the arts Charlotte Cushman to join her in Rome, she arrived in the city in 1852, and stayed rent-free with Charlotte for seven years. 'Here,' she wrote, 'every woman has a chance if she is bold enough to avail herself of it' – though she nevertheless had to contend with a good deal of prejudice. Recognising that it was impossible for a woman to be a wife and mother as well as an artist, she decided that marriage was out, and instead adopted a tomboyish lifestyle, defying convention by riding alone through the city and meeting male artists for breakfast. 'Hatty', wrote fellow sculptor and expat William Wetmore Story 'takes a high hand here with Rome, and would have the Romans know that a Yankee girl can do what she pleases, walk alone, ride her horse alone and laugh at their rules. The police interfered and countermanded the riding alone, on account of the row it made in the streets.'

The sculptor Thomas Crawford was less tolerant: 'Miss Hosmer's want of modesty is enough to disgust a dog. She has had casts for the ENTIRE FEMALE model made and exhibited them in a shockingly indecent manner to all the young artists who called upon her. This is going it *rather strong*.'

Most of Hosmer's works are now in America, the most interesting of them depictions of women – often, like her *Beatrice Cenci* (based in part on Maderno's *Saint Cecilia*), responding with quiet dignity to their suffering.

What most people come to see, however, are the two Bernini angels, designed for the Ponte Sant'Angelo and known – for reasons which become obvious as soon as you look at their insane expressions and wind-whipped drapery – as the breezy maniacs. When the Pope saw this pair he declared that they were far too beautiful to be exposed to the elements, so copies were substituted, and until 1729, when

they were moved to the church, the originals remained in the care of
Bernini's family.

Finally, take a look at the homely cloister, where locals pop in to chat with the priests among the orange trees and arcades, then walk up Via Capo le Case to see a curvaceous dome drum and fancy bell tower created for the church by Bernini's rival, *Borromini*.

Villa Medici

Guided tours of gardens 1 Mar–31 May and 6–25 Oct on Sun mornings. Half-hourly between 10 a.m. and 12.30 p.m.

The Villa Medici's public face is austere, its slightly sloping façade virtually unadorned. Built in 1540, it was bought in 1576 by a Medici cardinal, who used it as a prison for those who fell foul of the Inquisition, including Galileo. In the seventeenth century it narrowly escaped being decimated by a cannonball, shot for a lark by Queen Christina of Sweden while visiting the Castel Sant'Angelo. The ball landed in the centre of the small fountain in front, and is still there.

Since 1803 the villa has been the seat of the French Academy in Rome, and famous pupils and directors – all male – range from Debussy and Berlioz to Poussin and Ingres. The French Academy is still here, offering accommodation to a couple of dozen privileged students and their families, and the palace is frequently used for prestigious art exhibitions.

The grounds, covering part of the Gardens of Lucullus (see Pincio, below), are vast, four-fifths of them taken up by a great undulating wood. The rest are stately and formal, with hedge-lined avenues crisscrossing a grid of lawns. It is this part that is covered by the Sunday tours. There is a brief visit to a pavilion, whose gorgeous frescoes of birds, flowers, fruit and trees were rediscovered only in 1986 (they had been hidden behind a protective layer of green paint for over a century). More memorable, however, is an unsettling group of statues, the Niobidi, concealed behind hedges on one of the lawns. Niobe was so insanely proud of her fourteen children that she persuaded the people of her town to stop worshipping the goddess Leto, who, as mother of a mere two (Apollo and Diana), she considered vastly inferior. She was punished for her vanity by having all her children killed by arrows. Niobe stands at the centre, clutching her last surviving child and looking in horror at the corpses of her other children, scattered among the grass and acanthus. This is merely a recent replica of an ancient work discovered by Ferdinando Medici, yet its power to shock is undiminished.

There have been beautiful gardens on the Pincio Hill since ancient times. The most extravagant, the Gardens of Lucullus, were so coveted by Messalina, Claudius's third wife, that she succeeded in getting their owner, Decimus Valerius Asiaticus, condemned to death simply so that she could have them. She was also madly jealous of Asiaticus's reputed lover, a society beauty named Poppaea, and managed to orchestrate her suicide by having her threatened with imprisonment for adultery.

Not that Messalina was a model of propriety herself – her sexual exploits, though doubtless exaggerated by Juvenal, Tacitus, Suetonius *et al.*, were notorious. Her liaisons with actors and ballet dancers, and forays into the bordellos of Suburra, were tolerated, but once she got involved with – and bigamously married – a powerful politician and consul designate, Gaius Silius, it was a different matter altogether. Silius and half a dozen other nobles suspected of affairs with Messalina were executed, while Messalina herself fled to the Pincio, and having attempted – but chickened out of – suicide, was stabbed to death by an imperial officer.

The ghost of Messalina was well and truly exorcised in the early nineteenth century when Valadier, designer of the Piazza del Popolo, created a formal park lavishly planted with pines and chestnuts. A couple of curiosities were added – an obelisk erected by Hadrian on the tomb of his favourite, the beautiful Antinous, and in later years a water clock designed by a Dominican monk (now still dripping, but wildly inaccurate). It soon became *the* place for anyone who was anyone to come in the evenings, to flirt, show off their finery, listen to bands and watch the sunset. In Henry James's novel *Daisy Miller*, Daisy shocks polite society by strolling unchaperoned on the Pincio with two men. Mrs Walker, a respectable fellow American, travelling around the park in a carriage, tries to save her reputation:

'Do get in and drive with me,' said Mrs Walker.

'That would be charming, but it's so enchanting just as I am!' and Daisy gave a brilliant glance at the gentlemen on either side of her.

'It may be enchanting, dear child, but it is not the custom here,' urged Mrs Walker, leaning forward in her victoria with her hands devoutly clasped.

'Well it ought to be then!' said Daisy.

The best time to visit the Pincio is still in the evening for views of the late light glowing on roofs and domes stretching from Piazza del Popolo to St Peter's. There are sometimes band concerts in summer, and the avenues are once again studded with the august busts of famous and forgotten Italian men, after some destructive joker decapitated them all in the early 1980s. The Pincio is connected with the Villa Borghese grounds – and if you're heading to the Villa Giulia or the Galleria d'Arte Moderna on its far side, you could hire a bike from the cabin in the Pincio (see directory) for a few hours.

The Porta and Piazza del Popolo

The Via Flaminia, which has linked Rome with the Adriatic since 220 BC, enters the old city at the Porta del Popolo, a sixteenth-century arched gateway which stands on the site of the ancient Porta Flaminia. The outer face was designed by Michelangelo, and is decorated with bobbles from the coat of arms of the Medici Pope, Pius IV, who commissioned it. The inner face, decorated with stars and jelly-mould mountains (from the Chigi coat of arms) was created by Bernini in 1655 on the orders of the Chigi Pope, Alexander VII. He wanted to impress Queen Christina of Sweden, who had just renounced Protestantism, abdicated her throne, become a Catholic, and was coming to live in Rome. Christina's conversion was a great victory for the Catholics, and she was welcomed with much pomp and ceremony. The Pope threw a banquet, she was given the Palazzo Farnese to live in, a firework-spewing dragon was killed in her honour on Piazza Navona, and the year's Carnival was named after her.

During the eighteenth and nineteenth centuries hundreds of Grand Tourists also entered Rome through this gate, though their first hours in Rome would probably have been spent inside the Customs house while officers ransacked their belongings. Travelling light was unknown in those days – people often travelled with hundreds of trunks – and the search could go on almost indefinitely if things weren't speeded up with a bribe.

It could, however, be far worse. At carnival time public executions were held in Piazza del Popolo, and tourists might well find themselves witnessing condemned criminals being savagely executed. Alternatively, they might see the beginning of the riderless horse race down the Corso, in which the horses' speeds were enhanced by feeding them with stimulants, wrapping them in nail-studded ropes, and letting fireworks off to scare them.

Today, you pass through the gate from chaotic Piazzale Flaminio to the relative peace of the vast oval Piazza del Popolo. It looks perfectly symmetrical, standing at the apex of a triangle formed by three dead-straight streets, with an obelisk in the centre, twin churches at one end and the triple-arched porto at the other. The impression you get standing at the obelisk is that the three streets, known as Rome's trident, form a perfect triangle. They don't. It's a visual trick pulled off by Carlo Rainaldi, who made the twin churches between them look identical, despite the fact that they are different sizes. One has a circular dome, the other an oval.

Lucrezia Borgia, daughter of Pope Alexander VI (see box, p.165), celebrated the announcement of her third marriage in the church of Santa Maria del Popolo. Her second husband had recently been strangled (on the orders of her brother Cesare) but she was barely given time to mourn (her father was infuriated by her constant weeping) before being married off again. Nevertheless, she threw herself into the celebrations, emptying Rome's shops of velvets and brocades as the town speculated over what she would wear and how she would do her hair on the big day. Thousands turned out on Piazza del Popolo to celebrate the announcement of the engagement, but when she left Rome by the Popolo gate a couple of months later for her new home in Ferrara, the piazza was empty – perhaps because it was freezing cold; perhaps because, since the engagement, rumours had begun to circulate that she was the mother of one of her father's sons.

QUEEN CHRISTINA OF SWEDEN (1626–89)

Christina was no compliant convert but a highly intelligent, cultured and formidably educated woman, who had studied Stoicism, Neo-Platonism, Hermeticism and Pythagoras in her search for the meaning of life. She was also at home with contemporary philosophy, and her conversion to Catholicism took place only after discussions with Descartes convinced her that faith was compatible with a belief in the infinity of the cosmos.

Once in Rome she expanded her already vast art collection, was granted permission to excavate a Roman palace, and employed A. Scarlatti as her chapelmaster and Corelli to direct her orchestra. She also developed an interest in alchemy and astronomy, founded an intellectual academy, and became the patron of a theatre, a scientist and an oceanographer. She had no respect for petty dogma, whether Catholic or Protestant, and delighted in shocking the Church authorities by dressing provocatively, hanging erotic pictures on the walls of her palace and removing the fig leaves from its statues. Enlightened though she may have been in religious matters, she retained the rights of a monarch within her own household and was a firm believer in capital punishment. On one occasion she declared: 'I find it less inconvenient to have a subject garrotted than to live in fear of him'.

Santa Maria del Popolo

The travertine façade of Santa Maria del Popolo, delicately decorated with a frieze of babies balancing urns on their heads, stands just inside the Porta del Popolo. According to legend it occupies the site of a garden in which Nero's nurse and mistress secretly buried his corpse to prevent it from falling into the clutches of the people (who would have doubtless torn it to pieces). Over the grave they planted walnut trees, and centuries later the ravens nesting there were believed to be the spirits of demons fleeing from Nero's soul. In 1099, in order to exorcise the site, Pope Paschal II dug up the walnut trees and built a chapel.

Almost four hundred years later Sixtus IV (the creator of the Sistine Chapel) rebuilt it, financing the work by taxing foreign churches and selling ecclesiastical jobs. When Lucrezia Borgia celebrated the announcement of her third marriage here in 1501, along with bishops, ambassadors and a cortège of 500 knights and ladies, the church already had frescoes by Pinturicchio. Her mother, Vanozza Cattanei (see p.90), was initially buried here, and in later years popes and wealthy citizens commissioned many more famous works. Among them are a chapel designed and decorated by Raphael, two paintings by Caravaggio, and statues by Bernini. The church is so richly endowed that you could spend hours exploring it. Here are a few highlights.

The Chigi Chapel (second left) was designed by Raphael in 1513 for the banker Agostino Chigi (see pp.60, 142 and 224) and captures the intellectual mood of his circle, effortlessly fusing pagan and Christian symbols. Agostino and his brother, Sigismondo, are buried in tombs shaped like pyramids, and the mosaic of God in the dome is surrounded by angels holding arcs decorated with the symbols describing Chigi's horoscope. With opera glasses you can just about make out a crab, a bull, a lion and a pair of scales.

Both Raphael and Agostino died before the chapel was finished, and it was completed by Bernini on the orders of Agostino's descendant, Pope Alexander VII. Bernini probably designed the distorted winged skeleton, holding the Chigi coat of arms set into the chapel's pavement, but his most significant contribution was a pair of prophets based on the story of Daniel and Habakkuk. In this apocryphal version of Daniel in the lion's den, an angel lifts Habakkuk, who is about to take food to the workers in the field, by the hair and flies him and the food across to Daniel's prison. Bernini's angel looks at Habakkuk, holding a lock of his hair between two fingers, and points across the chapel to Daniel, who kneels on a rock with a lion licking his foot.

Caravaggio and Annibale Carracci were contemporaries, and their radically different styles are juxtaposed in the chapel immediately to the left of the choir. Nowadays Caravaggio gets the attention, but at the time Carracci was more popular. It's easy to see why, for Carracci's richly coloured, gracefully choreographed *Assumption of the Virgin* could hardly offend. Caravaggio's works, with their arresting use of light and shadow and peculiar perspectives, are a different matter. The *Conversion of St Paul* is dominated by the rump of a horse, under which Paul lies sprawled on the ground. In the *Crucifixion of St Peter*, the saint looks in horror at the nail which skewers his hand, and the veins in the limbs of his executors bulge with the effort of hauling the cross into position.

In the early sixteenth century, before Raphael arrived in Rome, one of the city's most influential painters was Pinturicchio. He was based in Perugia but worked in Rome for short periods, largely for the Borgia Pope Alexander VI, and his taste for antique grotesquery and architectural detail rapidly became fashionable. The fresco in the apse vault with earnest Apostles, elegantly reclining Sibyls, and an intricate tracery of freakish and fantastic beasts is a prime example.

There are also frescoes by Pinturicchio and his followers in the two Della Rovere chapels (first and third right). The first chapel has an appealing fresco of the Nativity, featuring a shed supported by a tree trunk and a Classical column. The third chapel was frescoed by Pinturicchio's pupils and followers with scenes from the life of the Virgin. They're quite hard to see but you might just be able to make out her birth, her studying, her marriage and her Assumption.

VIA VENETO TO VILLA BORGHESE

Thanks to film-maker Federico Fellini, this area of Rome is more closely associated with *La Dolce Vita* than any other in the city. In the early 1960s film stars partied on Via Veneto plagued by the paparazzi, while prostitutes worked the Viale de Muro Torto. The reputation for sex, scandal and glamour lingers on. Local nightclubs (and some luxury hotels) are worked by high-class call girls; late at night the cafés teem with men on the make; and a close look at some of the taller, more provocatively dressed women reveals them to be transvestites.

This is not to say that the area is particularly dangerous – if you are (and act and look like) an innocent female tourist, you're unlikely to suffer any more sexual hassle than elsewhere in the city. By day, in fact, the Via Veneto feels very tame – the decadent scene emerges after dark!

The area's reputation for dissipated high living is centuries old. In the sixteenth century Pope Julius III, and in the seventeenth Cardinal Scipione Borghese, each built himself a pleasure palace. Julius (who favoured young men) spent his free time dining and being entertained by dancers and musicians at the Villa Giulia. He would doubtless not entirely disapprove of the fact that the nearby Villa Borghese park is now a favourite resort of the city's gay community. Scipione, who created the lavish grounds, was an even more notorious sensualist who commissioned Bernini to create titillating sculptures of mythological rapes.

Positive images of women are pretty thin on the ground here, though the Villa Giulia's Etruscan museum does offer the occasional brief glimpse of the lives of the Romans' ancestresses. The Bernini sculptures in the Galleria Borghese are undeniably brilliant, the

Villa Borghese park is beautiful, and if you want a break from history, there's a reasonable collection of modern art in the Galleria d'Arte Moderna, though women artists are poorly represented.

Piazza Barberini

Piazza Barberini, at the foot of Via Veneto, is a chaotic roundabout overlooked by the dour façade of the luxurious Bernini Bristol Hotel. Over the past year the piazza has been cheered up by an exuberant madman sporting an antenna and psychedelic sunglasses, who dances like a crazed satyr for the entertainment of traffic-jammed drivers. If he's disappeared by the time you get there, you'll have to make do with Bernini's equally irreverent Triton, supported by four goggle-eyed dolphins and spitting a vertical spurt of water through a conch shell. The fountain was commissioned by the Barberini Pope Urban VIII and you'll notice, entwined with the dolphins' twisted tails, chunky papal keys, the papal tiara and an armorial shield, this time with chubby Barberini bees scuttling across it. On the corner of Via Veneto is another Bernini–Barberini production, the Fontana delle Api, with crab-like bees poised to sip the water.

Santa Maria della Concezione

Cemetery open daily 9 a.m.–noon; 3–6.30 p.m.

Founded by Urban VIII's older brother Cardinal Antonio, a Capuchin friar, this unassuming church at the bottom of Via Veneto contains one of the most bizarre sights in the city. When Antonio was buried, his body was placed below a simple tombstone on which was written (in Latin): 'Here lies dust, ashes and nothing' – a far cry from the lavish tombs cardinals usually selected for their corpses. This same determination to make people confront the facts of death drove the friars to use the bones of their departed brothers to cover the walls of its underground chapels. Over four thousand skeletons were dismantled to make intricate patterns; vertebrae are wired together to create sacred hearts and crowns of thorns; fully clothed skeletons lie in niches constructed from pelvic bones layered like slices of mushroom; and in one chapel you can see the splayed skeleton of a Barberini princess who died in childhood. The cemetery may have become a major tourist attraction, but the friars ensure that they get their message across. Stuck on the wall of one chapel, translated into four languages, is an anti-abortion poem called 'My Mother Killed Me'. At the exit the bones are given the final say: 'What you are now we used to be. What we are now you will be.'

If you're feeling depressed after all this, pop up to the church, and amuse yourself with Guido Reni's sexually ambiguous *St Michael* clad in body-hugging sky blue under a billowing pink cloak, having apparently effortlessly killed the Devil (an alleged portrait of Innocent X). In Nathaniel Hawthorne's *The Marble Faun*, the American artist Miriam, who knows what struggling with evil is really about, is unconvinced by Reni's 'dapper Archangel' delicately 'setting his prettily sandalled foot on the head of his prostrate foe'. 'A full third of the Archangel's feathers should have been torn from his wings;' she objected, 'the rest all ruffled . . . His sword should be streaming with blood . . . his armour crushed, his robes rent, his breast gory.' Shortly after looking at the painting, on a bier in the nave, Miriam discovers the corpse of an evil Capuchin monk killed in her honour by an infatuated young count.

Via Veneto

Despite a brief flurry of late-night activity, the cafés of Via Veneto are half-deserted most of the day and evening, and many are in danger of bankruptcy. There are plans afoot to ban traffic and revamp the shops, most of which now specialise in glittery shoes and gimmicky jumpers, but so far nothing has happened.

Meanwhile Via Veneto, ascending in a leisurely curve from Piazza Barberini to the turreted Pincio Gate, lined with plane trees, tubs of azaleas and elaborate *belle époque* hotels does retain a certain elegance. It was created in the late 1870s, on land belonging to the fabulously wealthy Ludovisi family, who thought they could make a killing when Rome became Italy's capital and land prices soared. Unfortunately they forgot about the taxman, and ended up having to sell the new palace they had built to meet the bill. The palace, now behind rigorously patrolled iron railings, is the American Embassy, though from 1900 to 1926 it was the home of Queen Margherita of Savoy, widowed after an Italo-American anarchist came across from the States and assassinated her husband, Umberto I.

Margherita is now best known for giving her name to a pizza. In 1889 she and Umberto spent their summer holiday near Naples, and the Queen, who had heard about but never eaten pizza, demanded to try it. Her chef prepared various versions, but the one she liked best was covered with the colours of the Italian flag – white mozzarella, red tomato and green basil. Since then it has been called Pizza alla Margherita.

Villa Borghese

The Villa Borghese is one of Rome's largest parks, laid out in the early seventeenth century by Cardinal Scipione Borghese, the pleasure-loving nephew of Pope Paul V. A lavish patron of the arts, he amassed one of Europe's finest collections of paintings, statues and antiquities. The young Bernini created some of his best sculptures for Scipione, many of which are still displayed in the Casino Borghese, built specifically to house the collection.

The park – open to the public – was a kind of seventeenth-century Roman version of EuroDisney, with ingenious fountains, enclosures of exotic birds and strange animals, and a grotto featuring artificial rain. There was also a trick chair which trapped anyone who sat down in it, and a toy satyr which, in the words of the English diarist John Evelyn, 'artificially express's an human Voice with the motion of eyes & head that it would easily affright one'. However, following a visitor's outrage at the erotic paintings displayed in a summer house, Paul V decided to ban the public. He would then come to the gardens to relax, while his nephew partied with his friends.

In the eighteenth century the grounds were redesigned by a Scottish landscape artist, Jacob More, and over the years they have acquired artificial lakes, mock-Classical temples, fake antique statues, and an imitation medieval castle. The park was finally bought by the state in 1902, and reopened to the public. There's a jogging track on Piazza Siena, and as long as you avoid the areas around Piazza Firdusi and directly behind Villa Giulia (focus of a heavy gay scene) it's an ideal place to bring children. There's a zoo, Shetland pony rides, boats and bikes to hire, and sometimes a small fair.

As well as the Galleria Borghese, there are two museums well worth visiting on the fringes of the park – the Galleria d'Arte Moderna, and the Villa Giulia, which specialises in Etruscan antiquities.

Galleria Borghese

Open Tues–Sat 9 a.m.–1.30 p.m.; Sun 9 a.m.–1 p.m.

The Casino Borghese, as it used to be known, was designed like a typical country villa, its three wings embracing the surrounding gardens. It was originally caked with statues and reliefs, but these were removed in the early nineteenth century. The interior decor dates from the eighteenth century; there are rooms plated with multi-coloured marbles; fussy friezes showing monkeys, exotic birds, dolphins and cherubs entangled in a web of stylised foliage; and ceilings frescoed with scenes from mythology and Classical history.

The collection, however, is stamped with Scipione Borghese's taste. The sculptures which he commissioned from the young Bernini reveal a preoccupation with yielding women, while some of the antique statues he collected suggest a fascination with exotic – even perverted – sexuality. The gallery is currently undergoing restoration, but although the collection of paintings on the upper floor (including works by Raphael, Giovanni Bellini, Titian and Veronese) is closed, the sculpture rooms on the ground floor remain open. Until the work is completed, the order in which the rooms are visited may change. Nevertheless, the following highlights do try to follow a logical progression, starting in Room 4, close to the current entrance.

The centrepiece here is Bernini's sculpture of Proserpine and Pluto. This major work shows Proserpine, daughter of the corn-goddess Ceres, being abducted by Pluto, King of the Underworld, with the three-headed dog, Cerberus, who guards the gates to Hades, snapping at her ankles. It's a virtuoso piece, in which Bernini makes much of the contrast between the tense, powerfully muscled Pluto and vulnerable Proserpine, whose thigh dimples beneath the vice-like grip of his hand.

In the short corridor linking Rooms 4 and 3 there is a six-teenth-century painting of Lucretia, whose rape and subsequent sui-cide marked, according to Roman legend, the fall of the Tarquin kings and the beginning of the Republic.

Room 3 is dominated by Bernini's *Apollo and Daphne*, which shows Daphne in the process of metamorphosing into a laurel tree in order to escape the amorous clutches of Apollo. Slender roots spring from Daphne's toes, bay leaves grow from her outstretched fingers, and bark begins to enfold her body. Inscriptions on the base (by Ovid and Scipione himself) warn somewhat ingenuously against the pursuit of pleasure.

The star attraction in Room 2 is Bernini's *David*, who is shown with brows furrowed, lips gripped, the catapult taut, and about to swing the full weight of his body behind the giant-killing throw. Pope Urban VIII is alleged to have helped by holding up a mirror so that Bernini could model David's face on his own grimace. In the same room there is a version of a *Venus Emerging from Her Bath*, modestly screening herself with her hands.

Modesty was not a quality associated with Pauline Borghese (see p.72), the sister of Napoleon who married Prince Camillo Borghese. When she commissioned Antonio Canova to sculpt her, he suggested representing her as Diana. Pauline, not the best-edu-cated of women, went to find out who Diana was, and returned to Canova with her mind made up. 'Diana asked her father to endow her with eternal virginity,' she said. 'If I were represented as that goddess, everyone would have fits of laughter.' It was decided to represent her as Venus Victrix (Venus the Conqueror) instead. The result, a semi-naked statue of Pauline posing reclined on a chaise longue, shocked polite society, and when she was asked how she could have done such a thing she is supposed to have replied that the room was well heated.

The hall beyond contains a selection of Scipione's collection of antiquities – grotesque fighting satyrs, statues and busts of emperors and empresses, and a Roman copy of a fleshy *Bacchus* by the ancient Greek sculptor Praxiteles. The most memorable exhibit, however, is a third-century mosaic discovered on one of the Borghese estates showing gladiators fighting wild animals. The gladiators who have been killed are marked with the letter theta, which stands for the Greek thanatos, meaning death.

Room 8 is most noted for the *Dancing Faun*, an ancient statue discovered in the late nineteenth century. More compelling, however, is a selection of paintings by Caravaggio including the *Madonna del Palafranieri*. Removed from St Peter's because it was felt to be excessively realistic, it shows mother and child stamping on a serpent's head, and includes an extremely peasant-like, wrinkled St Anne. There is also a feverish self-portrait of Caravaggio as a pallid, dissolute Bacchus, and a decadent *Boy with a Bowl of Fruit*, in which vine leaves flecked with brown, overripe grapes and a maggot hole in an apple exude decaying fecundity.

Giardino Zoologico
Open daily 8.30 a.m.–4 p.m. in winter; 8.30–5 p.m. in summer

As zoos go, this one, spread out over seventeen hilly, tree-shaded hectares, is not bad, though some of the cages are cramped. It has all the live animals you'd expect to find, as well as a museum of stuffed ones, an aquarium and a reptile house. Worth a visit if you or your children need a break from 'culture'.

Galleria Nazionale d'Arte Moderna

Open Tues–Sat 9 a.m.–2 p.m.; Sun 9 a.m.–1 p.m.

Rome's collection of nineteenth- and twentieth-century art, housed in a gigantic 1911 colonnaded wedding cake, makes a refreshing change from the ancient and Classical art which dominate the city's other galleries. At the time of writing the nineteenth-century collection on the upper floor is closed, and the date of its reopening is, as ever, unknown.

A couple of thin mournful women by Modigliani grace the first room, along with Klimt's *The Three Ages*, an exercise in misogyny featuring a curly-headed infant, a slender beauty and an emaciated old woman with sagging breasts and bulging stomach. Also worth a look is a Pointillist view of the Villa Borghese's gardens by the Futurist artist Balla. Room 2 has a vaguely Cubist portrait of a middle-aged woman by Balla's fellow Futurist, Boccioni, and an unsettling *Hector and Andromache* by the bleakly bizarre de Chirico. The protagonists here are dressmakers' dummies, a ruse also adopted by his contemporary, Carlo Carrà, in *Ovale delle Apparizioni*, with the mannequins this time placed in a chill townscape.

Room 4 contains sculptures by Marino Marini and Manzù – the latter's depiction of women as appealingly pensive and self-sufficient – and an *Annunciation* by Martini, a gymnastic composition with a virtually sexless Mary. Up a short flight of steps is a room devoted to Lucio Fontana, who called virtually everything he ever created *Concetto Spaziale* (Spatial Concept) and had a penchant for piercing or slitting his canvases in order to suggest the infinity of space beyond.

Leaving Fontana to stew in his own pretensions, take a look at the textures of *Tabula Rasa* by the Catalonian artist Antoni Tàpies, Giacometti's lumpy, elongated *Grande Donna 1942* and the scribbles, splashes and graffiti of Jackson Pollock and Cy Twombly. You now reach a couple of works by women artists, the violent *Sole sul cespuglio* (Sun on the Bush) by Mattia Moreni, and *Rossoverde 1963* (Red–Green 1963) by Carla Accardi, an acid-tripping repetition of letters and squiggles.

To see the rest of the gallery you have to retrace your steps back to the sculpture room, where a door leads into a large gallery divided into bays. There are still lifes by another Futurist, Severini, a raffish, dissipated self-portrait by de Chirico, and a haunting *Solitude* by their contemporary Sironi, showing a self-absorbed woman sitting alone in a dark vaulted room. Also interesting are works by husband and wife Mario and Antonietta Raphael Mafai: contrast Antonietta's devilishly handsome portrait of her husband painting her, from 1928, with Mario's portrait of himself as an unremarkable-looking middle-aged man, fourteen years later. Reclining in the centre of the gallery are more sculptures by Marini and Martini, including the latter's disturbing *Le Sorelle* (The Sisters), in which one of the figures is headless. The most grotesque sculpture, however, is yet to come: Leoncillo's tawdry *Arpia* (Harpy), a gaudy vamp with fluorescent orange nipples, lips and nails.

Villa Giulia

Open Tues–Sat 9 a.m.–2 p.m.; Sun 9 a.m.–1 p.m.;
Wed 9 a.m.–7.30 p.m.

Villa Giulia was built in the mid sixteenth century as a pleasure palace for Pope Julius III, who was so excited about the project that he used to float up the Tiber to the building site on a flower-decked barge to keep an eye on its progress and suggest improvements. He was a fairly useless pope, and after embroiling his country in an unsuccessful war with France he spent most of his time indulging himself at the Villa Giulia.

The gardens were planted with 36,000 trees and studded with statues, fountains, grottoes and pavilions, and though Julius never lived there (ornamental ponds and fountains might look pretty, but were usually malarial) after he died 160 boatloads of statues were taken back down to the Vatican. In later years it was used by the Vatican as a guesthouse, and among its short-term residents was Queen Christina of Sweden (see p.128).

The villa is now – not entirely inappropriately – a museum devoted to the Etruscans, whose upper classes at least shared Julius's love of luxury. Occupying an area bounded by the rivers Arno and Tiber, they ruled their less sophisticated Roman neighbours from the seventh century BC. Then in 509 BC an Etruscan prince, Sextus Tarquinius, raped Lucretia. She told her father, her husband and her husband's friend Brutus what had happened before killing herself, whereupon Brutus led a Roman uprising and ousted the Tarquins. Within a century Etruscan power had declined, Rome began to attack its cities, and in the first century BC Etruria became part of the Roman Empire.

In its heyday Etruria was less a nation than a federation of politically and economically independent cities. The Etruscans were energetic traders – most of their wealth came from their prodigious natural resources of metals – with a voracious appetite for the glamorous artefacts produced by their Greek and Phoenician trading partners. Most of what has survived of Etruscan culture comes from the tombs of the moneyed classes, so little is known about the lifestyles of its presumably vast community of miners and other workers. It does seem, however, that wealthy Etruscan women were considerably freer than those of Greece:

THEOPOMPOS (FOURTH CENTURY BC) ON ETRUSCAN WOMEN

Sharing wives is an established Etruscan custom. Etruscan women take particular care of their bodies and exercise often, sometimes along with the men, and sometimes by themselves. It is not a disgrace for them to be seen naked. They do not share their couches with their husbands but with other men who happen to be present . . . They are expert drinkers and very attractive.

The Etruscans raise all the children that are born, without knowing who their fathers are. The children live the way their parents live, often attending drinking parties and having sexual relations with all the women. It is no disgrace for them to do anything in the open or to be seen having it done to them . . . When they are having sexual relations either with courtesans or within their family, they do as follows: after they have stopped drinking and are about to go to bed, while the lamps are still lit, servants bring in courtesans, or boys, or sometimes even their wives. And when they have enjoyed these they bring in boys and make love to them. They sometimes make love and have intercourse while people are watching them, but most of the time they put screens of woven sticks around the beds . . .

From *Women's Life in Greece and Rome*, translated by Mary R. Lefkowitz and Maureen B. Fant. Duckworth, 1992

The Collection   The early Etruscans cremated their dead, and placed the ashes in clay or bronze urns along with a few mementoes. Room 2 has a number of items which women were given as a send-off – decorated belts, chunky amber necklaces, bracelets, spindles and bobbins. When you move on to Room 5, there's a ghoulish collection of ex-votives – swaddled babies, hands, feet, and intestines – which were doubtless offered to gods in the hope of a cure. One, however, is rather different: a toddler quietly playing with a bird.

Funeral objects – this time from near Lake Bolsena – continue in Room 6, with a pair of wood-and-metal sandals, a verdigrised cheese-grater and a ladle, as well as more refined objects like an incense-burner decorated with a rooster.

In the seventh century BC wealthy Etruscans began to bury their dead in tumuli, funeral chambers covered with mounds of earth. A flight of steps leads down into a reconstruction of one such chamber, which, if you're staying in one of Rome's cheaper hotels, may appear familiar.

Beyond, in Room 9, is the *Sarcofago dei Sposi*, the joy of the entire collection. Smiling archaic smiles, as if sharing a joke, a young couple recline on a banqueting couch, he with his arm across her shoulders.

Room 10 is crammed with the kinds of ceramics that graced Etruscan banqueting tables. Chalices, *oinochoe* (wine jugs) and *kraters* (for mixing wine and water) from Corinth; made-in-Etruria replicas: and shiny black indigenous Etruscan *bucchero* pottery. Upstairs you'll find the mirrors, jewellery and make-up pots which the women used to prepare for parties, along with more objects from the ideal Etruscan home – lion-pawed candelabra, a fish dish (with a dent in the centre for sauce), ornate wine strainers, and the exquisite Chigi Vase, painted with miniature hunting scenes, the Judgement of Paris and a double-bodied sphinx.

The museum's priceless Castellani collection of jewellery, ranging from Minoan to Pre-Columbian, is usually closed, so you'll have to make do with the opulent earrings, pendants, combs, bracelets, and a sexily decadent candelabra supported on the back of a naked man, displayed in Rooms 30–33.

ACROSS THE TIBER: TRASTEVERE AND THE VATICAN

T rastevere and the Vatican have little in common but the fact that they lie next to each other on the far bank of the Tiber. Trastevere is an ancient workers' quarter, lively and non-conformist, whose people have always been ready to fight authority. The Vatican, on the other hand, is the all-powerful home of one of the world's most rigidly authoritarian religions. What they do share is a fierce independence: the people of Trastevere never considered themselves part of Rome, and the Vatican, since 1929, has been an autonomous state. As far as visiting them goes, St Peter's and the Vatican should be tackled only when you're in the mood for undiluted culture; Trastevere's exuberant street – and nightlife, its Sunday-morning flea market and alternative shops and bars, are the perfect antidote to an intellectual overdose – although there are a handful of churches and palaces worth visiting. Both are easily accessible on foot from the *centro storico*: Trastevere via the hump-backed Ponte Sisto or Tiber Island; the Vatican by walking across the city's most beautiful bridge, the Ponte Sant'Angelo.

As with everywhere in Rome, the Church's impact on the lives of women is only too evident. Santa Francesca Romana, a fifteenth-century Trasteverina housewife, responded to Catholic disgust for the female body by mutilating herself so that she could feel no plea-sure when she fulfilled her wifely duties and slept with her husband. Yet in the Borgo, the residential quarter around the Vatican, 10% of the inhabitants were prostitutes, capitalising on the trade from cardinals.

TRASTEVERE

Despite gentrification, Trastevere remains central Rome's most bohemian quarter. It is almost at its best in the early morning, when there is little to display the fashionable onslaught save the debris of the night before littering its cobbles, and perhaps a glimpse of a designer interior behind a flaking façade, or a Eurocard sticker on a shutter signalling the existence of a restaurant. Piazza San Cosimato hosts a good daily food market; street corners and tiny piazzas are protected by shrines of the Madonna; and the weather-chafed walls of houses are slung with power cables and hung with washing. By lunchtime shutters open to reveal bars, art galleries and clothes boutiques, and students, trendies and tourists begin to take over from the dwindling and ageing population of born-and-bred Trasteverini.

At night things can get pretty raucous, with people spilling out of bars and lads with ghetto-blasters or car radios throbbing hanging out on Piazza della Scala. Until you're more familiar with the quarter, you may well feel more confident sticking with the more mainstream crowd in Piazza Santa Maria in Trastevere's restaurants and cafés, or selecting one of the more refined wine bars. It's not a bad idea to make your first night in Trastevere a Monday, when many of the bars and restaurants are closed, street life is less hectic and the staff in the few bars and restaurants that *are* open have time to chat.

Trastevere is bisected by a main road, Viale Trastevere, and most of the action is concentrated to the west, around Piazza Santa Maria in Trastevere. The east is far more run-down, with warehouses dating back to the days when this was the home of Tiber dockers, and a number of shabby modern apartment blocks. At night the streets here are crammed with the cars of Romans from across the river trying to find a space to park, but there's little else happening, and walking through the area alone at night can be slightly unsettling. On Sunday mornings, though, it's well worth visiting the streets at the far end which host the massive Porta Portese flea market. Stalls sell everything from old clothes and junk jewellery to Bakelite phones and 1950s hairdryers.

In the fourth century St Cecilia lived in eastern Trastevere, and parts of her house (and the bath-house in which she was smothered to death) remain below and alongside the church of Santa Cecilia in Trastevere. Better known is Santa Maria in Trastevere, thought to be the oldest church in the city. It was certainly the first to be dedicated to the Virgin, and still contains mosaics (and an eighth-century fresco) which say a great deal about how her cult developed over the years. Santa Maria was the favourite church of another Trastevere saint, Francesca Romana, who in the early fifteenth century devoted most of her time to relieving the quarter's poor and sick (see box, p.145).

It goes without saying that these saints were hardly typical Trastevere women, though the quarter did have a fairly high population of nuns. Raphael's mistress, Margherita Luti, the daughter of a baker who lived by the Porta Settimiana (the house is now a restaurant), ended up in one of their convents.

If you tire of Trastevere, you could either head up the Janiculum hill behind for an unbeatable view of Rome, or walk or take a bus up to one of the hill's parks – the little Villa Sciarra or the enormous Villa Pamphilj.

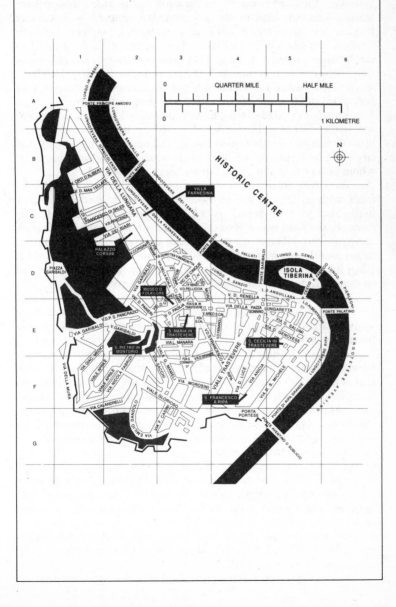

Open Mon–Sat 9 a.m.–1 p.m. Closed Sun

Standing in its own grounds on the bank of the Tiber, this apricot-washed villa was built in the early sixteenth century by Baldassare Peruzzi for Renaissance banking tycoon and playboy Agostino Chigi. Chigi's favourite courtesan, Imperia (see p. 224), was a frequent visitor, though if the ancient (and not always reliable) historian Suetonius is to be believed, they weren't the first lovers to have sequestered themselves on the site. He claimed that it was in a villa here that Caesar and Cleopatra sat up feasting until dawn.

Agostino's villa was a pleasure palace – his main home was across the river near his bank – designed for banquets, parties and brief holidays. The banquets were magnificent, attended by the city's greatest artists, writers, poets and philosophers, most of whom benefited at some time from Chigi's patronage.

Chigi was an ostentatious man – he paid more for two beds, inlaid with gold, ivory and precious stones, than he had for the land itself. And at one dinner party, in a riverside pavilion in the grounds, the food was served on gold and silver platters which were flung into the Tiber at the end of each course. This demonstration of his wealth was not quite as impetuous or reckless at it seemed – Chigi had taken the precaution of having nets laid on the river-bed so that his dinner service could be retrieved afterwards.

After Chigi died in 1520, his business collapsed – thanks to squabbling heirs. The villa's statues, paintings and furnishings were sold off, and the villa itself was abandoned until 1577, when it was bought by the Farnese family.

Fortunately, the best of the villa's art works – two gloriously frescoed *loggie* in part designed and painted by Raphael – were immovable. Both originally opened directly on to the garden, and though they have long been enclosed, exposure to Roman wind and rain has meant that they have had to be restored on numerous occasions. *Raphael* began work in 1510, but was apparently so distracted by an affair – presumably with La Fornarina (see p.116) – that he slacked off. He was also supposed to be frescoing the walls of the Vatican Stanze, and Pope Leo X, afraid that the work would never be finished, eventually asked Chigi to help. Chigi's solution was to kidnap La Fornarina, hide her, and tell Raphael that she had gone off with another man. Raphael was – not surprisingly – devastated, and at first tried to lose himself in his painting, but soon became so depressed that he was unable to concentrate. Chigi then miraculously 'found' the woman and allowed her to move into the villa while Raphael worked.

Nevertheless, the only painting Raphael completed here was the gorgeous *Triumph of Galatea*, for which the Sala di Galatea is named. The blonde beauty, with elegantly twisting body and hair streaming in the wind, is usually said to have been inspired by Imperia, though Raphael himself wrote that since there was a 'dearth of beautiful women I am using an idea which has come into my head'. Presumably he didn't show the letter to Imperia or La Fornarina. Galatea was painted to accompany a picture of the giant Polyphemus (who fell in love with her and killed her boyfriend Acis) by Sebastiano del Piombo. Until 1973 it was believed that his blue drapes had been painted on after a woman had been shocked by his nude body. In fact, restoration revealed that there was no body beneath the drapery.

If you've seen the chapel which Raphael designed for Chigi in Santa Maria del Popolo, you'll already be aware of Agostino's interest in astrology. His horoscope is represented here too – in hexagons around the top of the walls, the signs of planets and the zodiac are incorporated into mythological scenes. Hence Venus in the sign of Capricorn is represented by the goddess Venus and a goat, and the moon in the sign of Virgo is represented by Diana, virgin goddess of the moon.

The *Loggia di Psiche* was not only open to the garden, but designed to resemble a pergola. Scenes from the myth of Psyche and Cupid are painted against a sky framed by ribs garlanded with foliage, fruit and flowers, and 'suspended' from the centre are two fake tapestries showing the couple's marriage and wedding feast. It was designed by Raphael, but what with love traumas and work at the Vatican he got round to painting only one of the Three Graces. The rest was executed – not entirely successfully – by his pupils.

There are also a few rooms open upstairs, most strikingly the *Sala delle Prospettive* with *trompe-l'œil* views of Rome between dizzily disorientating fake columns. Next door was Chigi's bedroom, dominated by a prime example of art as aphrodisiac – the *Nozze di Alessandro e Rossana* (Wedding Night of Alexander the Great and Roxanne) by Sodoma – in which servants stand by watching as cherubs divest the newlyweds of their clothes.

Palazzo Corsini

Open Tues–Sat 9 a.m.–2 p.m.; Sun 9 a.m.–1 p.m.

Some remarkable women have been connected with the Palazzo Corsini and its Renaissance predecessor, the Palazzo Riario. Napoleon's mother, Letizia, who later went into (an admittedly comfortable) exile with him on Elba; Christina of Sweden, who filled it with her art collection and held *salons* for the city's wits and intellectuals; and, in the late fifteenth century, Caterina Sforza, who lived here after marrying Girolamo Riario. Both Girolamo and her second husband were assassinated and she twice defended her family's towns of Imola and Forlì, standing on the walls and directing the troops. On the second occasion, after managing to free her six children (who had been taken hostage), she was captured, carried back to Rome and imprisoned at the Vatican and the Castel Sant'Angelo before the Borgias' French allies, impressed by her courage, demanded her release.

The palace now contains the lesser half of the Galleria Nazionale d'Arte Antica's art collection. Among the better works are a triptych by Fra Angelico, a couple of Madonna and (giggling) Childs by Andrea del Sarto, and a sexually ambiguous *San Giovanni Battista* by Caravaggio. The most amusing painting of a woman is a portrait by J. Van Egmont of an Amazonian Queen Christina dressed up as the divine huntress Diana. It hangs in the room where she died in 1689. There are also clichéd representations of murderesses: two Judiths (one with her breast bared and Holofernes' head in her hand, the other *décolletée* and about to strike) and a sinister *Erodiade* (Salome's mother) by Vouet, carrying John the Baptist's head on a platter. Guido Reni, on the other hand, has a kind of empathy with his *Salome*, who appears almost as a victim of circumstance. His *Lucrezia* is a more conventional victim, pale, vacant and semi-naked with her hand ready on the knife with which she is about to kill herself.

Santa Maria in Trastevere

Piazza Santa Maria in Trastevere is the heart of the neighbourhood, a traffic-free cobbled square where tourists stroll or sit on café and restaurant terraces while hippies, old Trasteverini and the occasional dealer or down-and-out congregate round its central fountain. Overlooking it is the church of Santa Maria in Trastevere, at its loveliest at night, when the gold-backed mosaic along its curved cornice is illuminated.

This was the first church in Rome to be dedicated to the Virgin, and it is built on the site where – legend has it – a fountain of oil miraculously bubbled up on the day on which Christ was born. It is not entirely certain when the original church was built, but it may have been as early as the third century – which would make it the first church in Rome.

The church you see today dates largely from the twelfth century, and retains some of the city's most interesting mosaics. Those on the façade, probably dating from the thirteenth century, show a breastfeeding Madonna flanked by ten women holding lamps. Only five lamps are lit. This represents Jesus's story of the wise and foolish virgins (Matthew 25:1–13), a parable about the necessity of always being prepared (the wise ones took supplies of oil with them; the foolish ones didn't).

The interior is a basilica with a gilded coffered Baroque ceiling and a broad nave lined with granite columns filched from the Baths of Caracalla. The Cosmati-style trimmings – a Paschal candlestick, a tabernacle, a choir screen, and a burgundy-and-bottle-green pavement – date from the nineteenth century, when things medieval had become extremely modish.

SANTA FRANCESCA ROMANA

In the fourteenth century, a frequent worshipper in the church was *Francesca Bussi de' Ponziani.* Better known as Santa Francesca Romana, she was born in 1384 into a wealthy Trasteverino family, and though the family were devout Catholics, they ignored her wishes to become a nun, and made her marry at the age of thirteen. She moved into the house of her new husband, Lorenzo Ponziano, along with his brother and his wife, and the two young women devoted themselves to caring for the poor and sick. In 1400, aged sixteen, she had the first of her six children. Sex was a problem for devout married women, whose ideal of celibacy was clearly thwarted by a wife's 'duty' to sleep with her husband. Eventually she persuaded Lorenzo to agree to a chaste marriage, but not before she had mutilated herself with hot wax to remove any possibility of pleasure during intercourse.

Despite devoting herself to caring for the sick (she gave so much of the family's food away that her husband locked it up and kept the key), her utter conviction that Heaven was the best place to be resulted in a chilling detachment from her children. She reacted to the death of a seven-year-old son with complete equanimity, and when, shortly afterwards, she had a vision predicting the death of her five-year-old daughter, Agnese, she treated the child as a bride about to be married to Christ.

Francesca founded a society of devout women, called Oblates, who were committed to helping the poor and sick. They did not become fully fledged nuns, but continued to live with their families, though as soon as Lorenzo died Francesca took her vows.

Francesca is now best known for having a vision of her guardian angel which lasted for years. At some point it was decided that the people in most need of a constantly vigilant guardian angel were motorists, so Francesca was made their patron (see p.192).

The twelfth-century mosaic in the church's apse, however, is an original: the earliest known representation of Mary as the Bride of Christ. Specked with gold and gorgeously glinting, she sits, young, beautiful and sumptuously clad, next to her son, whose right arm lies across her shoulder. Each holds a scroll. Mary's is a quotation from the Song of Songs ('His left hand should be under my head; and his right hand should embrace me'); Christ's is a quotation from Gregory the Great's service for the feast of the Assumption ('Come, my chosen one, I shall place thee on my throne').

Below the depiction of Mary as Bride are other mosaic episodes from her life, most of which had to be invented because there is very little information about her in the Bible. Created by Pietro Cavallini in the thirteenth century, they are considerably more relaxed and realistic than the hieratic figures above. In the *Nativity*, the newborn baby's nurse checks the temperature of the water with her fingers, while other servants offer her mother food and drink.

In the Altemps chapel, to the left of the altar, visible through a securely locked gate is an ancient fresco of the Virgin as the Queen of Heaven, styled as a Byzantine Empress, wearing a pearly diadem, sitting on an imperial purple cushion and flanked by a guard of spear-bearing angels. Kneeling at her feet is the then Pope, John VII, the first living man to be painted in the Virgin's presence. At the time he was struggling with the Emperor in Constantinople to assert that Rome alone had the right to deal with ecclesiastical matters. The painting of himself with the Virgin was meant to show that he was in direct contact with the Divine Kingdom, and thus had a far better idea of what God wanted than a mere temporal emperor.

Museo del Folklore

Open Tues–Sat 9 a.m.–1 p.m.; Tues and Thur also open 5–7.30 p.m.; Sun 9 a.m.–12.30 p.m.

Housed in a seventeenth-century palazzo just off Piazza Santa Maria in Trastevere, the folklore museum brings to life the colourful chaos of popular Rome which so fascinated and frustrated the Grand Tourists of Northern Europe. Eighteenth-century paintings depict carnival scenes, horse races, street dancing and brawling watched from palace balconies by genteel masked ladies; later scenes show women washing clothes in the Acqua Vergine fountain, smoking on Piazza della Rotonda, and selling fish at the market which occupied the Portico d'Ottavia in the Ghetto.

There are also paintings of the major ancient sites before they were excavated, including a cattle-populated Forum, and casts of favourite Roman landmarks – the Bocca della Verità, Pasquino and Isis foot (the latter from Via Piè di Marmo).

This is a good museum for children, who particularly like the 3-D Nativity scene set in a chaotic Roman piazza and a series of tableaux featuring waxwork figures in a pharmacy, on a wine cart and dancing in a tavern.

Santa Cecilia in Trastevere

Open daily 10–noon; 4–6 p.m., but unreliable

On the other side of Viale Trastevere, close to a modern block of council offices and the old tobacco warehouse, stands the church of Santa Cecilia in Trastevere. Concealed behind a circuit of walls, its earthy red façade and pretty Ionic portico rise behind a rose garden.

Although the interior is eighteenth-century, the church stands above two Roman houses (one of which probably belonged to the saint). A corridor off the right aisle, painted with landscapes by Dughet, leads to the *caldarium* in which St Cecilia was suffocated to death. Since the *caldarium* has long been a place of worship, and is covered with frescoes (notably by Guido Reni, who – as you'll know if you've seen his Beatrice Cenci, Lucrezia and Cleopatra – was obsessed with female victims), there is little to indicate its original use.

Far more memorable is Stefano Maderna's statue of the saint in a niche below the high altar, lying on her side with her head turned away, her neck wounded, and the contours of her body visible beneath folds of diaphanous drapery. Though it hardly does justice to Cecilia's tenacity and determination, it is an exquisite work, and its portrayal of purity and vulnerability did much to popularise her cult.

Two thousand lire buys you access to the Roman houses below the church, a confusing labyrinth of vaulted rooms with patches of dusty mosaic pavement, early Christian sarcophagi and – perplexingly – an ancient Roman tannery, complete with vats.

ST CECILIA

Cecilia was a young Christian patrician, living in the third century, who married a pagan called Valerian, but, having vowed her virginity to God, she refused to consummate the marriage. Her single-mindedness so impressed Valerian and his brother that they converted to Christianity, an act which swiftly led to their arrest and martyrdom. Cecilia was caught by the authorities trying to bury their bodies, and was locked in the *caldarium*, or hot steam bath, of her house for three days, to suffocate to death. Miraculously she survived, and a soldier was sent to behead her. Roman law allowed official axemen to deliver only three strokes, and these proved insufficient to kill Cecilia outright. She hung on, half dead, for another three days.

In the ninth century her tomb was discovered in the catacombs of San Calisto, and brought to the church. The tomb was eventually opened in 1599 and her perfectly preserved body, dressed in a gown shot with gold and a green silk veil, was revealed. The corpse disintegrated on contact with the air, but sketches were made which Stefano Maderna later used to create a sculpture of the dead saint.

On Cecilia's feast day, 22 November, there are special musical services in the church, celebrating her role as the patron saint of music. Theories about why this is so vary wildly – one version credits her with the invention of the organ; another maintains that she sang hymns throughout her three days in the *caldarium*.

San Francesco a Ripa

Just north of Piazza Porta Portese, where the Sunday flea market begins, is the church of San Francesco a Ripa, one of the first Franciscan churches in Rome. It was built in the thirteenth century on the site of a hospice where St Francis stayed in 1219, but in the seventeenth century it received a Baroque façade and a statue by Bernini. The statue is the reason to visit.

Ludovica Albertini was a member of one of Rome's aristocratic families; she died of fever in 1533 after a life as a Franciscan nun. Bernini's statue shows Ludovica in the process of dying, and as in the more famous (and earlier) St Teresa in Santa Maria della Vittoria, he equates the sexual and the spiritual – despite the fact that Ludovica is not in ecstasy, but in agony (see also p.113).

The Janiculum and Beyond

The Janiculum is the highest of Rome's hills, but as it was on the wrong side of the Tiber it was not included in the original seven and did not even form part of the city. After the Etruscans were ousted from Rome in the early sixth century they retaliated by occupying the Janiculum. Eventually they agreed to withdraw in return for hostages. Among the hostages was a girl named Cloelia who, with a number of other girls, managed to escape and swim back across the Tiber to Rome. The Romans set up an equestrian statue of Cloelia on the Sacred Way – the first woman to be so honoured. Today the Janiculum is home to another statue of an equestrian woman, Anita Garibaldi. In 1849 the Janiculum was the front line in the battle between Garibaldi and the Republicans and the Pope's French supporters. The Republican volunteers won – the victory which is celebrated here – though it wasn't long before the French returned with reinforcements and the Roman Republic fell. Anita took part in the battle – as she always had done – though whether she actually fought in the manner shown in the statue, with a baby under one arm and a pistol raised in the other, is dubious.

It's a long, steepish climb up to the statue of Anita, and it's worth taking a break *en route* to see Bramante's Tempietto, in the courtyard of San Pietro in Montorio. Much of the rest of the hill is covered by parks and, to the south, the residential Monteverde district. There are, though, sensational views of the city from Piazza Gianicolo, which is full of lovers in parked cars at night, overlooked by a statue of Anita's husband, Giuseppe. The so-called Janiculum park is crisscrossed by roads. If you want peace and greenery, head instead for the gardens of Villa Sciarra or the vast Villa Pamphilj.

Bramante's Tempietto

Bramante's tiny, grubby ochre Tempietto, squeezed into the courtyard of San Pietro in Montorio, is reckoned by many to be the quintessential Renaissance building. Built in about 1501 on the site where St Peter was (wrongly) believed to have been crucified, it is a circular Doric temple whose design and proportions adhere precisely to those laid down by Vitruvius in ancient Rome. It is also a

perfect example of how pagan ideas were requisitioned for
Christian use. A Renaissance architect or thinker considered the circle *the* purest form for a building (a sphere would be purer, but impossible) because it reflected, in Palladio's words, 'the unity, the infinite essence, the uniformity and justice of God'.

CASTEL SANT'ANGELO TO ST PETER'S AND THE VATICAN

The Vatican State, the world's smallest independent sovereign state, was founded in 1929 under a treaty with Mussolini known as La Conciliazione. This was in effect the papacy's consolation prize for having lost all temporal power in 1870 when Italy united. As consolation prizes go, it wasn't bad. Italy gave the Vatican 750 million lire and the income from a thousand million lire worth of state bonds; exempted it from taxes and duty on imported goods; and agreed to adopt canon law in marriage and make Catholic teaching compulsory in all schools.

Over the past couple of decades the rise of feminism and the decline of Catholicism in Italy – coupled with a wave of Vatican scandals, ranging from Mafia connections and laundering drug money to the suspicious circumstances surrounding the death of John Paul I – have encouraged the state to backpedal a little. Divorce, contraception and abortion are legal, religious education is optional, and the Vatican is now taxed on its profits from the stock market (though its employees still aren't taxed on their earnings).

Though the Vatican State was founded only in 1929, St Peter's was built in the fourth century, and the popes moved into the Vatican in the fourteenth. At first there was simply a fortress, but over the centuries galleries, living quarters, chapels, and – most recently – a new audience hall and museums have been added. The walled complex now covers five hundred square metres, and in the public parts of the Vatican alone there are seven kilometres of galleries and corridors.

From the *centro storico* the most pleasant approach to the St Peter's and Vatican is to cross Ponte Sant'Angelo, past the Castel Sant'Angelo and up Via della Conciliazione, a dead-straight boulevard laid out by Mussolini. Otherwise it's a case of catching a 64 bus (watch out for pickpockets and fondlers) or taking the metro to Ottaviano. Either way, you enter an unreal world of tourists and ecclesiasts where the streets are lined with rip-off cafés, stalls piled with Sistine Chapel T-shirts, and shops selling benedictions, plaster pietàs and plates stamped with the portraits of the Pope.

The concentration of tourists means that the area around the Vatican is prime hunting-ground for men wanting to pick up foreign women. It's not unusual to be kerb-crawled as you walk from St Peter's to the Vatican entrance, to be invited for drinks by a policeman, or, in the Vatican's quieter museums (the Gregoriano Profano and Cristiano are the worst), to be pestered by staff. Ignoring, pretending not to understand, or – if you speak Italian – firm refusals are the most effective strategies.

Though women have not exactly been instrumental in the Vatican's history, they have been more closely associated with it than you might expect of an organisation run by ostensibly celibate men. In the fifteenth century 10% of the inhabitants of the Borgo, the area around the Vatican, were prostitutes and their dependants. Alexander VI set up his mistress, Giulia Farnese, in a palace nearby, and the first marriage of his daughter, Lucrezia, was celebrated by a wild wedding party inside the Vatican. Giulia, Lucrezia and La Fornarina all appear in paintings inside the Vatican, though perhaps the most startling depictions of women are those by Michelangelo on the Sistine Chapel ceiling. The recent restoration has made it clearer than ever that the women he painted are basically men with breasts.

Giulia also makes an appearance in St Peter's – as a model for Justice on her brother Paul III's tomb, though the other historic women you will encounter inside are either saints or those buried there for having served the Church's propagandist aims. It was largely Giulia's influence on the Pope which secured the promotion of her brother, though her power was nothing compared to that of Marozia in the tenth century, who controlled the papacy from the Castel Sant'Angelo. In later years it was the papal stronghold and prison, and women imprisoned there ranged from Alexander VI's daughter-in-law Sancha to parricide Beatrice Cenci.

The area covered by St Peter's, the Vatican and the Castel Sant'Angelo is small, and if all you want to see in the Vatican are the Sistine Chapel and the Raphael Stanze, it is possible to visit them all in a single day. However, if you want to see more of the Vatican's museums, set aside a whole morning for these alone, and don't expect to be up to much in the afternoon.

PAPAL AUDIENCES

To go to a papal audience you must apply in person (on Tuesday mornings) or in writing to the Prefettura della Casa Pontificà, 00120 Città del Vaticano, between one month and two days of the date you wish to attend. Audiences are held on Wednesday mornings, usually in the tent-roofed audience hall designed by Pier Luigi Nervi. You are unlikely to be able to meet the Pope yourself – there will be thousands of other Catholics present. In summer they are held at the Pope's country residence at Castel Gandolfo (accessible by train from Termini or by bus from Anagnin station).

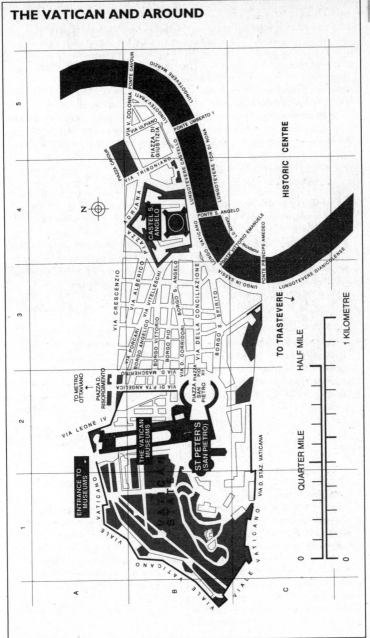

THE VATICAN AND AROUND

N

5

PONTE CAVOUR
LUNGOTEVERE MARZIO
VIA V. COLONNA
VIA ULPIANO
PIAZZA DI
GIUSTIZIA
PONTE UMBERTO 1
LUNGOTEVERE PRATI
LUNGOTEVERE TOR DI NONA

PIAZZA CAVOUR
VIA TRIBONIANO
LUNGOTEVERE CASTELLO

4
PIAZZA ADRIANA
CASTEL S.
ANGELO
PONTE S. ANGELO
LUNGOTEVERE VATICANO
L.GO IN SASSIA
L.GO TOR DI NONA
CORSO VITTORIO EMANUELE
PONTE PRINCIPE AMEDEO
FIORENTINI
LUNGOTEVERE GIANICOLENSE

HISTORIC CENTRE

3
VIA CRESCENZIO
VIA ALBERICO
VIA VITELLESCHI
VIA PORCARI
BORGO ANGELICO
BORGO S. ANGELO
BORGO PIO
BORGO VITTORIO
BORGO D. CORRIDOR
VIA DELLA CONCILIAZIONE
BORGO S. SPIRITO

TO TRASTEVERE

2
TO METRO
OTTAVIANO
VIA LEONE IV
PIAZZA D.
RISORGIMENTO
VIA DI PTA ANGELICA
VIA D. MASCHERINO
THE VATICAN
MUSEUMS
PIAZZA
PIAZZA
SAN
PIO
PIETRO)
XII
ST PETER'S
(SAN PIETRO)
VIA D. STAZ. VATICANA

ENTRANCE TO
MUSEUMS ►

1
VIALE
VATICANO
VIALE VATICANO

A

B

C

QUARTER MILE   HALF MILE

0   1 KILOMETRE

WOMEN AND THE CATHOLIC CHURCH

Catholics throughout the world look to the Vatican, rather than secular law, for guidance in moral matters. As far as the Catholic Church is concerned, tradition is a moral imperative, and it is a tradition of the Church that only men become priests and that priests take a vow of celibacy. This in effect means that an entirely male hierarchy governs a predominantly female congregation. Convents have, of course, made an important contribution to the education (and in some cases survival) of generations of young women, but nuns, convent girls and Catholic women alike operate within an organisation whose attitude to the female sex is deeply ambivalent.

Women were – and in some quarters still are – seen as temptresses who lure men into the sins of lust and fornication. Eve is the scapegoat for the Fall of Man, and at the opposite extreme is Mary, the Virgin Mother of Christ. Hers is the most seductive, powerful and impossible model for Catholic women: a mother without experience of sex; a mother who suffered; and a mother who was gathered up into the arms of God to save her from the ravages of death. Some popes, however, perhaps fearing that the cult of the Madonna would alienate women from the Church, perhaps showing a sensitivity towards the needs and aspirations of modern women, have gently remodelled the cult. In 1974 Pope Paul VI suggested that traditional images of Mary would not be appreciated by 'the modern woman anxious to participate in the decision-making processes of the affairs of the community . . . the modern woman will note that Mary of Nazareth, while completely devoted to the will of God, was far from being a timidly submissive woman . . . ' Catholic women may no longer be required to be timidly submissive, but the tension between the reality of modern life and the moral absolutes of the Church is great and can be painful, as was shown by the survey (see p.71) which revealed that Rita of Cascia, a battered wife, was the most popular saint among women in Italy.

In the early years of the Church, marriage was seen as a slightly lesser evil than casual sex for those who lacked the vocation for celibacy. Later it became a sacrament, an earthly reflection of the fidelity of humankind to God, and consequently the marriage vow became indissoluble. The only way out of a Catholic marriage is to prove that it was never truly a marriage. At first the only ground for annulment was non-consummation; now, if one of the partners does not wish to have children, or if it can be proved that one of the partners was immature, and did not really know what he or she was doing when the vows were taken, a marriage can be annulled.

But the Catholic conviction that the only justification for sex is procreation, and that experiencing pleasure during sex is sinful, remains. In 1968 the long-awaited document on sexual morality, *Humanae Vitae*, was published – to a vast outcry of disappointment. The use of artificial contraception 'is to be condemned as much as abortion', proclaimed Paul VI. Attitudes in the higher echelons of the Church have not changed, although some priests and bishops now attempt to interpret the rules liberally, deeming that artificial contraception is permissible as long as it is not used between confession and communion.

Despite – perhaps even because of – the demands Catholicism places on women, it continues to be a source of comfort and strength. It is estimated that around 25% of Romans attend Mass (though this does include a large proportions of clerics), and as you visit the city's churches you'll see a considerably greater proportion of teenage girls and women than men at prayer or waiting for confession. The familiar rituals of the Church are immensely soothing, and at the very least attending Mass gives women an hour's respite from the demands of everyday life; confession is therapy, with the added comfort of mercy and forgiveness; and suffering, patience, endurance and self-sacrifice are dignified and glorified through the examples of Mary and the martyrs.

Open Tues–Sat 9 a.m.–1 p.m.; Sun 9 a.m.–noon; Mon 2–6 p.m.

The Ponte Sant'Angelo is Rome's most dramatic bridge, built by Hadrian as an approach to his mausoleum. In the seventeenth century it was adorned with white marble statues of angels designed by Bernini, their fluid drapery streaming in an imaginary wind and revealing elegant silky legs. It is reserved for pedestrians and usually lined with street vendors selling sunglasses and fake Louis Vuitton.

In the sixth century, Pope Gregory the Great was leading a procession across the bridge to pray for the end of the plague then ravaging the city, when he looked up and saw the Archangel Michael standing on the roof of the Castel sheathing his sword – which is why it is called the Castel Sant'Angelo. The current rooftop angel is an eighteenth-century bronze – its Renaissance marble predecessor now stands in one of the Castel's courtyards.

Castel Sant'Angelo

This great brick cylinder on the banks of the Tiber started out as a family mausoleum, built by Hadrian and inaugurated in 134 AD. But within 150 years it had been converted into a fortress, and was used by bellicose nobles and warring popes as a stronghold and prison. One of its most notorious denizens was a noblewoman called Marozia who, in the early tenth century, had Rome and the papacy in her iron grip. Her exploits have undoubtedly been exaggerated, but she is reported to have used the popes as playthings and puppets, to be slept with, elected and eliminated as she saw fit. Eventually, however, she was herself deposed by one of her sons, Alberic, who ruled Rome for twenty years and, like his mother, was an arch-manipulator of pontiffs.

The Castel continued to be used as a fortress right up until the French occupation of Rome in the early nineteenth century. Whenever (and it was often) the popes felt themselves to be in danger, they retreated to the fortress. Clement VII cowered inside during the 1527 Sack of Rome, while (according to his not entirely honest autobiography) Cellini defended the Castel from the marauding Germans single-handed. In between firing cannons at the Lutherans he found time for a spot of needlework, helping Clement hide his jewels by removing them from his tiaras, rings and mitres, wrapping them in paper and sewing them into his clothes. A few months later he was accused of having pocketed some of the jewels himself, and ended up spending almost a year in prison before he managed to escape, shinning down a twenty-five-metre wall on a rope of sheets. He was, however, back again a few months later.

A number of women had the misfortune to be imprisoned in

the castle: Beatrice Cenci and her stepmother for murdering Beatrice's father, and Caterina Sforza (see p.143) captured by Cesare Borgia after commanding troops defending her family's town of Forlì.

Cesare also imprisoned his sister-in-law, Sancha of Aragon, in the Castel, after killing her brother Alfonso (who was married to Lucrezia). Sancha, a dark, sea-green-eyed beauty, was married to Jofré, the youngest Borgia, when she was sixteen and he was thirteen. She seems to have compensated for being married to a child by having affairs with his brothers, the foppish Duke of Gandia and the devilish Cesare. Sancha may have been permitted to live in the Castel's papal apartments under a kind of house arrest, for it seems that she was allowed to be visited by her current lover, Cardinal Ippolito d'Este, the brother of Lucrezia's third husband.

The papal apartments have changed a lot since Sancha's day. By the time of the Sack, Clement VII had a suite of frescoed rooms and a pretty little bathroom. Afterwards other popes commissioned even more sumptuous rooms – Paul III's new quarters included a bedroom frescoed with distinctly unholy scenes from the myth of Cupid and Psyche.

A tour around the Castel is unsettling. You pass from dark pits in which the urns of emperors were placed, gloomy dungeons and provision stores, through courtyards piled with pyramids of cannonballs, to lavish apartments and loggie with stunning views. The best views are from the terrace, immortalised by Puccini in the last act of his opera *Tosca*, which ends with the heroine leaping off the parapet. In 1992 a production of the opera was shot on location in Rome, at precisely the times specified in Puccini's score, and, with the help of five satellites, broadcast live to 107 countries. At 5 a.m. Rome time, opera lovers throughout the world were glued to their TV screens, waiting for the moment when Tosca jumps. It looked great – though the TV Tosca's fall was broken by a pile of cushions six feet below.

St Peter's

Open winter daily 7 a.m.–6 p.m.
Summer daily 7 a.m.–7 p.m.
Treasury open daily 9 a.m.–12.30 p.m.; 3–4.30 p.m. (6.30 p.m. in summer)

St Peter's was designed to impress the world with the awesome power of the Catholic Church, and from the piazza, walking through Bernini's pincer-like colonnades towards the Basilica, it takes time to realise just how huge it really is. It is the largest church in the world, a great Baroque barn of a place, created over almost two hundred years by – among others – Bramante, Raphael, Michelangelo and Bernini.

Given the Church's attitude to women, it's quite a surprise that any were deemed fit for burial in St Peter's hallowed precincts. The select few who did make it were either royal or aristocratic, and were accorded the honour because they served the Church's political purposes. The first woman to be buried in St Peter's was Countess Matilda of Canossa (or Tuscany) – though she had already been dead for over 500 years! Queen Christina of Sweden was also interred here, as was Maria Clementina Sobieska, wife of James Stuart and, in the eyes of the Roman Church, Queen of Great Britain, France and Ireland.

Other women made their presence felt in more outlandish ways. Paul III's sister Giulia Farnese, famous as the ex-lover of Pope Alexander VI, appears as a kiss-curled Justice on her brother's tomb, while the most famous monument in the entire church, Bernini's *baldacchino*, was – in part, at least – a thank-offering for the survival of one of Pope Urban VIII's nieces.

Besides the church itself, there's a treasury stacked with priceless objects ranging from rock-crystal crucifixes to a broken reliquary which once held St Veronica's handkerchief; and below the church, corridors lined with the tombs of popes, and the necropolis in which St Peter is supposed to have been buried. Far more fun is the lift to the roof, where you can stop for a Coke from a vending machine and browse in a shop of ecclesiastical souvenirs before climbing a vertical labyrinth of stairways up to the dome. From here you have not only a splendid view of Rome, but a chance to see something of the Vatican grounds. What follows is selective, focusing on the best art works along with monuments associated with women. If you want to see more, there are any number of illustrated guides on sale in the souvenir shops.

The most dramatic statue in the church occupies a vestibule to the right of the porch – a rearing equestrian statue of the church's founder, Constantine. The Emperor's shocked expression is a response to an apparition of a Cross and the words 'in this sign thou shalt conquer' midway through the Battle of the Milvian Bridge in 312 at which he defeated his co-Emperor Maxentius. It was this vision, followed by a victory, that decided him to convert to Christianity. If he hadn't, St Peter's might never have been built.

You enter the basilica to be confronted by two obese cherubs supporting holy-water stoups. Directly to the right is Michelangelo's *Pietà*, sealed behind a bullet-proof glass wall since a madman shot it in the 1970s. It's a wonderful piece, sculpted when Michelangelo was about twenty-five, with Christ's lifeless body seeming almost to melt into that of his exquisite young mother. It is the only work he ever signed (his name is on a band across the Virgin's breast), and he apparently did so because he overheard a group of Milanese saying it was by a sculptor from Milan.

Set into a nearby pier is a monument surmounted by a gracious statue of Queen Christina of Sweden (see box, p.000: Piazza del Popolo) sporting an elaborate beaded hairdo. She looked nothing like it. The year before she died (by which time she was referring to herself as one of the city's ancient monuments) the following description was written:

> She is exceeding fat . . . She has a double chin from which sprout a number of isolated tufts of beard . . . a smiling expression and a very amiable manner. Imagine, as regards her costume, a man's knee-length black satin skirted coat, buttoned all the way down . . . A very large bow of black ribbons instead of a cravat. A belt drawn tightly round the coat over the lower part of the stomach revealing its rotundity.

Christina was buried here because she was royal and because her conversion had been useful to the Catholic cause. Such propagandist considerations made it prudent to overlook the fact that she had hardly been a model Catholic. Alexander VII in particular had found Christina's unconventionality hard to swallow. Removing the fig leaves from statues in the Palazzo Farnese (see p.92) and dressing as a man had been bad enough, but after she had fallen in love with both a nun and one of his cardinals, and then made a bid for the Neapolitan throne, he lost his temper. She was, he ranted, 'a woman born a barbarian, barbarously brought up and having barbarous thoughts'.

A little further down the aisle is the tomb and statue Bernini and his pupils created for the 500-year-old corpse of Countess Matilda of Tuscany. A strong, highly intelligent woman who lived in the late eleventh and early twelfth centuries, she inherited her family's lands and title when her elder brother died. Her property, and the fact that her husband had died when she was still young, gave her the freedom to play a part on the centre stage of Church politics. She was a friend and staunch supporter of Pope Gregory VII, who was locked in a power struggle with the Holy Roman Emperor, Henry IV. Eventually Gregory excommunicated Henry, and so frightened was the Emperor by the sudden fall-off of support that he agreed to do as Gregory commanded. Gregory summoned him to one of Matilda's castles in midwinter, and made him stand outside the walls for three days, before agreeing to give him an absolution. The scene is carved on the tomb – a bare-shouldered Henry kissing Gregory's foot. A statue of Matilda stands on top: one of the few women ever to have been shown holding the papal keys and tiara.

Roped off beneath the dome is Bernini's *baldacchino*, loosely based on the lavish canopies which medieval artists used to paint above a particularly important place or person. As the *baldacchino* stands above the tomb of St Peter, the design is appropriate, though the decoration celebrates not Peter but Pope Urban VIII, who commissioned it. The *baldacchino* literally swarms with bees from Urban's coat of arms. But Urban also wanted to celebrate the survival of a niece and her baby after a dangerous pregnancy, and incorporated in the coats of arms on the column bases are a series of faces – seven women, suffering from increasingly severe labour pains, and finally, a smiling baby.

High up, in niches around the crossing, are four statues, all associated with holy relics which are displayed in Holy Week. Most precious of these is St Veronica's handkerchief – a piece of cloth with which she is supposed to have mopped Christ's brow when he collapsed on the way to Calvary. Like a miniature Turin Shroud (recently revealed to be a medieval fake) it holds an image of Christ's face. The fine, almost insubstantial statue of St Veronica is by Mochi. The puddingy woman is St Helena, who discovered the True Cross, and the two men are Longinus, a richly textured sculpture by Bernini of the soldier who pierced Christ with a spear, and St Andrew, whose head was presented by the Greeks to the Pope in 1462.

Occupying the apse (usually barricaded off), and positioned so that it appears to be framed by the *baldacchino*, is Bernini's *Cathedra*, with four saints effortlessly balancing a floating ornate throne on their fingertips. Toffee-coloured clouds billow from the chair and bubble around a yellow window, above which glinting cherubs clamber up the gilded rays of a glory. This bronze, gilt and stucco extravaganza was created to hold the relics of the chair from which Peter was supposed to have delivered his first sermon to the Romans. Bernini loved it so much that when he had to go to Paris, and leave his assistants to complete it without him, he wept.

The *Cathedra* is flanked by two papal tombs. The one on the left, by Bernini, is devoted to Urban VIII. Below the statue of Urban, happily waving from the afterlife, a behatted skeleton writes on the tomb, while two women lean against it. One is a motherly Charity, holding a baby and smiling at her toddler; the other is a dreamy Justice, with her mind on higher things and children forgotten at her feet. Bernini designed it to complement Guglielmo della Porta's earlier tomb of Paul III on the other side of the *Cathedra*. The beautiful figure of Justice here is a statue of Paul's sister, Giulia Farnese (see box, p.93), whose affair with a previous pope, Alexander VI, did much to further her brother's career. A student once became so obsessed with the voluptuous sculpture that he hid inside the basilica at night and died trying to make love to it.

Walking up the left aisle, past the tombs of other popes and boxes where multilingual confessions are heard, you come to the Stuart Monument, a white marble creation by Canova with busts of the three last Stuarts, James, Charles Edward and Henry. It was commissioned, surprisingly enough, by the foppish Prince Regent who, in the sarcastic words of Stendhal, 'in keeping with his reputation as the most accomplished gentleman in three kingdoms, wished to honour the ashes of the unhappy princes whom he would have sent to the scaffold had they fallen into his hands alive'. More recently the Queen Mother did her bit for her ancestor's enemies by paying to have the monument restored. Above it is a mosaic portrait of James Stuart's wife, Maria Clementina Sobieska. Like Louise Stohlberg, who later married her son, Charles Edward, she found life with a Stuart extremely difficult and at one point left her husband for a convent. She died of tuberculosis at the age of thirty-three.

The Vatican Museums
Open Mon–Sat 8.45 a.m.–1.45 p.m.
Easter period and 1 July–30 Sept open Mon–Fri 8.45 a.m.–4.45 p.m.; Sat 8.45 a.m.–1.45 p.m.
Also open (free) last Sun of the month
Closed 1 and 6 Jan, 11 Feb, 19 March, Easter Sun and Mon, 1 May, Ascension Day, Corpus Christi, 29 June, 15 and 16 Aug, 1 Nov, 8 Dec, Christmas and Boxing Days.
LAST ENTRANCE 45 MIN BEFORE CLOSING

The entrance to the Vatican is on Viale Vaticano, a ten-to-fifteen-minute walk around the State's walls from St Peter's. If you're feeling lazy, a special bus shuttles between the two every half-hour until the museums close. In certain parts of the Vatican, the crowds, even out of season, are horrific, and many people end up having a thoroughly miserable time. To avoid the worst of the congestion, get to the museum before it opens, and head straight for the Sistine Chapel and Raphael Stanze, which, from 10 a.m. onwards are packed and dizzyingly stuffy.

The only problem with this is that a one-way system operates throughout the Vatican, and if you go first to the Sistine, then want to return to rooms and museums bypassed earlier, this means backtracking. The guards don't usually object, but you can end up trying to climb a narrow staircase while a non-stop cascade of people pour down, proceeding in the correct direction. You will not be popular.

As there are at least a dozen museums, as well as frescoed chapels and galleries of tapestries and maps, first select what you want to see. Don't even consider trying to see everything – even our selection would keep you going for two or three visits – a couple of museums plus the Sistine Chapel, the Raphael Stanze and the Borgia Apartments are more than enough for one morning.

The best collections are in the Pinacoteca (an art gallery with a strong Renaissance bent) and the Pio Clementino Museum (which holds the most famous of the Vatican's ancient sculptures). Some of the less popular museums are also worth seeing – and are usually virtually empty.

Four colour-coded routes (all including the Sistine Chapel) are designed to channel the crowds through the labyrinth. Route A (purple) takes you directly to the Sistine; Route B (beige) includes the Etruscan Museum, the Pinacoteca, and the Gregorian Profane and Pio Christian museums; Route C (green) takes in virtually everything except these three; and Route D (purple) is a comprehensive five-hour, seven-kilometre trek. Select what you want to see first, work out, which route is most appropriate, and don't be afraid to skip anything you're not interested in.

Unless you're desperate, avoid coffee and food in the Vatican's café, and bring your own drink, because the vending machines are usually broken. The best place to rest is the Cortile della Pigna, a garden-courtyard dominated by a giant sculpted pine cone which started life as a weird fountain outside a temple of Isis.

The Egyptian Museum

As is evident from the number of obelisks in the city, things Egyptian were extremely voguish in ancient Rome. The cult of Isis (see p.82), which was particularly popular with women, had arrived in Italy in the third century BC, though as it gained a reputation for sexual licence it was banned several times before Caligula finally made it official. The collection in this museum consists largely of Egyptian antiquities brought to Rome – most of them once adorning the Temple of Isis, which Caligula founded, the Gardens of Sallust, and Hadrian's Villa at Tivoli. There are also a number of Egyptian-style artefacts made in Rome, and a few objects from Egypt itself.

Among the latter are gloriously painted mummy cases, a dark, wizened mummy (complete with toe- and fingernails) and a collection of *canopi*, vases decorated with the heads of birds, dogs and men into which the entrails of the deceased were placed before the body was mummified. There are also objects found in tombs – including mirrors, bowls and spoons for preparing cosmetics which were incarcerated with women.

Some of the decorations from the Canopos Serapeum, a temple from Hadrian's Villa, have been reconstructed. Among the statues is a bust of Isis and a statue of Hadrian's favourite, Antinous (who was drowned in the Nile) depicted as Osiris (see p.82). In the hemicycle, overlooking the giant pine cone which dominates the Cortile della Pigna, are more statues of Isis, lots of lion goddesses and a statue of Caligula's sister, Drusilla, in the guise of Ptolemy Philadelphus's sister Arsinoë II. Like Ptolemy (who ruled Egypt from 283 to 246 BC) Caligula married and later deified his sister.

When she died in AD 38 he instituted a period of public mourning during which it was a capital offence to – among other things – laugh or bathe.

The Braccio Nuovo

To get here, you have to walk through the Chiaramonti Gallery, a three-hundred-metre-long corridor lined with ancient busts, reliefs and statues. Save your energy for the more select collection in the Braccio Nuovo, which has probably the best surviving statue of Augustus, created for his widow Livia and discovered on the site of the couple's country villa (on the Via Flaminia). The cherub riding the dolphin at his feet is thought to be a portrait of Augustus's beloved grandson, Gaius Caesar. Beyond are Roman copies of ancient Greek works, notably *The Wounded Amazon*, a resting Satyr, a spear-bearer, the orator Demosthenes and the goddess Athena. Also worth a look is a bizarre statue of the Nile, crawling with miniature children, found near the temple of Isis (see p.79).

Pio Clementino

The Pio Clementino holds the best of the Vatican's Classical nudes, most of them Roman copies of famous, but lost, ancient Greek works. Most of the male statues have been given fig leaves, while the female statues are left naked.

Gabinetto dell'Apoxymenos   Leonardo da Vinci worked in this room until he was kicked out in disgrace for bringing in women to help him with his anatomical studies. In ancient Greece, after a woman, concealing her anatomy beneath her clothes, won a race at Olympia, athletes were obliged to train and compete in the nude so that there could be no doubt they were male. Women were, however, allowed to run (clothed) races in honour of the goddess Hera. The Gabinetto's current occupant is an ancient Greek male athlete languidly scraping the oil and sand (with which athletes were massaged) from his perfectly proportioned body. The statue, a Roman copy of a fourth-century BC work by Lysippos, was discovered in the nineteenth century in Trastevere.

Octagonal Belvedere Courtyard   The most famous of the Pio Clementino's statues are sheltered in alcoves around this pretty courtyard. Best known is the elegantly aloof Apollo Belvedere, long held to be a paragon of male perfection. Far more exciting is the Laocoön, a violently contorted Hellenistic work showing the Trojan priest Laocoön and his two sons struggling to escape from the writhing coils of a sea serpent. It was brought over from Rhodes in AD 69 to adorn – of all places – the Baths of Titus, and doubtless resulted in making any Roman of a nervous disposition think twice before plunging into the water. Pliny the Elder, however, reckoned that it was the world's best work of art. It was unearthed in a vineyard near Santa Maria Maggiore in January 1506, and Michelangelo and Giuliano da Sangallo immediately rushed off to see it. Giuliano, who knew his Pliny, immediately recognised it, and Julius rapidly snapped it up to adorn the Vatican, where it was carried with great ceremony. Michelangelo was heavily influenced by it, and it even became a fashion item. Isabella d'Este ordered a Laocoön hat badge!

In the fourth century BC the Classical Greek sculptor Praxiteles shocked the people of Kos by creating the first nude statue of the goddess Aphrodite (leaving her bath). They decided it was just *too* risqué for public display, so it was bought instead by the Cnidians. It became highly popular – so much so that it was indecently assaulted – and though the original is lost, there are numerous copies. There are two versions in the Pio Clementino – the one here, Venus Felix and Cupid (the Romans called Aphrodite Venus) has been given the head of an unknown second-century Roman woman.

Highlights of the rest of the museum include a Sleeping Ariadne – thought by Michelangelo to be Cleopatra – a Wounded Amazon and, in the Cabinet of the Masks, two bathing Venuses. One is another copy of Praxiteles' notorious Aphrodite of Cnidos; in the other the goddess crouches, not quite screening her breasts with her arms. The Room of the Muses is lined with statues of Muses and busts of the male Greek philosophers and writers they were supposed to have inspired. The most notable work, however, is the Belvedere Torso, whose bending, twisting form, rippling musculature and crinkling flesh were borrowed by Michelangelo for some of the male nudes on the Sistine ceiling.

The Etruscan Museum

The highlight of the Vatican's Etruscan collection are the finds from the Regolini-Galassi tomb, discovered in a necropolis near Caere. A man and a woman of high rank were buried here in the mid seventh century BC. The woman, who was possibly a princess or priestess, was buried with a bronze throne, a gold pectoral (a bib-shaped breastplate) embossed with winged women and animals, gold and amber necklaces, and, to while away the hours in the afterlife, five dice.

There are more objects buried with women in the next room. Among them are a casket for toiletries decorated with battling Amazons and mirrors delicately incised with scenes ranging from dancing girls to the goddess Aurora abducting the youthful hunter Cephalos. Beyond are more utilitarian objects – sieves and pans (including one with a naked woman as a handle) and in the final room, devoted to Roman artefacts, an ivory doll discovered in a sarcophagus belonging to a little girl.

Hall of the Greek Cross and the Room of the Biga

The small vestibule outside the Etruscan Museum is dominated by two huge porphyry sarcophagi; one belonging to St Helena (see p.222); the other to her granddaughter, Constantia (see p.244). Helena's is decorated with horsemen, prisoners and dead soldiers; Constantia's with vines, grapes, peacocks and cherubs.

Raphael Stanze

In 1508, the same year that Michelangelo began work on the Sistine ceiling, Pope Julius II decided to have a suite of rooms redecorated. The four rooms had already been frescoed by – among others – Piero della Francesca, but Julius was not the kind of man to live with second-hand decor. He asked his favourite architect, Bramante, to recommend some new artists to him. At first artists like Perugino, Lorenzo Lotto and Sodoma worked on the rooms, but Julius was not satisfied, so Bramante suggested he called in Raphael, the rising star of the art world. By 1509 Raphael was at work on what was to become one of his most famous creations, the Stanza della Segnatura. He worked on the rooms spasmodically until his death in 1520, though the later frescoes – notably the gung-ho scenes in the Sala di Constantino – were mostly painted by his pupils.

If the rooms are not too busy, the guards don't object if you nip back and forth, and see them in the order in which they were painted: Room 2 Stanza della Segnatura (1508–11); Room 3 Stanza di Eliodoro (1512–14); Room 1 Stanza dell'Incendio (1514–17); Room 4 Stanza di Costantino (post-1520).

Room 2: Stanza della Segnatura

The Stanza della Segnatura, a library where the Pope signed decrees, was the first to be painted by Raphael; it was finished about 1511. The frescoes unashamedly bring together Christian and pagan themes in order to celebrate a typically optimistic Renaissance theme: the ability of the intellect to discover the truth. Most famous is the *School of Athens*, in which Raphael painted contemporary artists and intellectuals as Greek philosophers standing, sitting, sprawling and squatting in a vaulted hall based, on Bramante's advice, on the Baths of Diocletian.

If you want to spot faces, the easiest to identify are the white-bearded Leonardo, standing in the centre of the steps playing the part of Plato; Michelangelo as Heraclitus, dark, bearded and melancholy in the foreground; and in the right-hand corner bald

Bramante (Euclid) surrounded by eager young pupils, among them a long-haired Raphael wearing a black cap. The fact that there are no women is not surprising. There were some female philosophers in ancient Greece (Plato is reported to have had two women students at his academy, who dressed as men) but none of their work has survived. Female philosophers do, however, appear in the occasional anecdote. Hipparchia, working in third-century Athens, is supposed to have responded to someone who criticised her lifestyle by saying that studying instead of weaving was hardly a waste of time. As for women living in Renaissance Italy, very few of them received a Classical education, and without Latin and Greek the intellectual world was largely closed to them.

Women were considered to be as little capable of theology as of philosophy, so apart from the Virgin they are completely absent from the fresco on the opposite wall representing the Truth of Religion. But women, ranging from Sappho and Corinna in ancient Greece to Michelangelo's mentor, Vittoria Colonna (see p.112: Palazzo Colonna), and courtesans like Tullia d'Aragona in Renaissance Italy, did write poetry. In the fresco of Parnassus above the window, Sappho and Corinna appear in the company of male poets ranging from Dante, Petrarch and Boccaccio to Homer and Ovid.

Sappho, the erotic lesbian poet, was highly esteemed in both ancient Greece and Renaissance Italy, though in the sixteenth century she was regarded as a kind of courtesan. Tellingly, the model for Sappho was long thought to be Imperia (see p.224). Corinna was renowned for beating Pindar in a poetry competition – though in later centuries she was accused of a victory based on her beauty rather than her poetic skills.

Significantly, however, Raphael gives a far more prominent position to a group of lovely, languid Muses, the traditional inspirers of men. As he used his own mistress, La Fornarina, as a model – even for Madonnas – this is no surprise. Imperia has been suggested as the inspiration for Calliope, though as ever, there is no evidence.

Room 3: Stanza di Eliodoro

Divine intervention is the theme of *The Expulsion of Heliodorus*, one of Raphael's most energetic works. Two flying angels and a rearing horseman are captured with photo-finish precision, propelling the king's treasurer Heliodorus out of a temple after an attempted robbery. Julius II watches from the back, and women huddle in a corner protecting their children.

The most striking of the room's other frescoes is the dazzlingly lit *Liberation of St Peter*, in which an angel is shown freeing Peter (a portrait of Julius) from behind the grille of a prison. The chains, incidentally, are now in San Pietro in Vincoli.

Room 1: Stanza dell'Incendio Julius was dead by the time work began on the Stanza dell'Incendio, and the subject matter was chosen by his successor, Leo X. The room is named for a fresco of a fire which raged through the Borgo (the quarter around the Vatican) in 847. The fire miraculously stopped when the then Pope, Leo IV, made the sign of the cross, which Leo X considered a neat parallel with his own success in extinguishing the flames of war which had ravaged Italy. Consequently, the pope standing with his hand raised in a loggia at the back of the painting was given Leo X's chubby face. The image of a baby being passed down from a wall behind which a fire rages made such an impression on Picasso that he incorporated it into *Guernica*, his semi-abstract rendering of a town bombed by the Nazis in the Spanish Civil War.

The Borgia Apartments

When Rodrigo Borgia became Pope Alexander VI in 1492, one of the first things he did was to call in Pinturicchio to decorate a suite of six rooms. They now form an incongruous setting for part of the Vatican's collection of modern art.

In 1493, when Pinturicchio had just started work, thirteen-year-old *Lucrezia* was married to her first husband, Giovanni Sforza, in the apartments. Crammed into the small rooms were cardinals and archbishops, barons and senators, glamorous women and Lucrezia's three brothers. Juan was at his dandiest in a Turkish robe of golden cloth, with 150,000 ducats' worth of rubies and pearls round his neck; Cesare was in his bishop's togs; and Lucrezia, with her blonde wavy hair snaking down to her waist, wore a sumptuous gown with a train held by a little black girl – considered a fashion accessory at the time.

In the evening there were comedies, music, dancing and a banquet which deteriorated into a debauched bun-fight, with chocolates being thrown down the fronts of the women's dresses. After all the excitement Lucrezia, still physically immature, went back to her palace to sleep alone.

In 1500 Lucrezia's second husband, Alfonso of Bisceglie, the illegitimate son of the King of Naples, was murdered in the first room, decorated with Sibyls and prophets. Cesare had by then allied himself with the French, who wanted the Neapolitan throne for themselves, so he decided that Alfonso had to be eliminated. Already wounded after one attempt on his life, Alfonso was laid up in the room. Afraid to leave him alone, Lucrezia and his sister Sancha slept there on improvised beds, and prepared all food for him themselves so that it could not be poisoned. Alfonso began to recover, and on 18 August, for some unknown reason, the women left him alone. On the orders of Cesare, he was murdered.

Lucrezia may have been the model for St Catherine of Siena, and Cesare for the Emperor Maximian with whom she is arguing. Above the door is a medallion of the Virgin and Child – the Virgin is probably a portrait of Alexander VI's mistress, Giulia Farnese (see p.93).

LUCREZIA BORGIA

Lucrezia Borgia, daughter of Rodrigo Borgia and his mistress, Vanozza Cattanei, was born in 1480, twelve years before her father became Pope Alexander VI. She was married at the age of thirteen to Giovanni Sforza of Pesaro, in order to further the dynastic ambitions of her father and her brother Cesare. She was forced to divorce four years later on the trumped-up charge that Sforza was impotent. Sforza claimed that the reason for the divorce was that Alexander wanted the blonde, beautiful Lucrezia for himself – a charge for which there is no evidence. She was almost immediately married again, to Alfonso d'Aragona, and after he had been murdered she was married again, this time to Alfonso d'Este of Ferrara. The announcement of her betrothal was celebrated by a month of partying, ending, on the eve of her departure for Ferrara, in a banquet at the Vatican attended by fifty top courtesans. According to the Papal Master of Ceremonies, Lucrezia and her father then moved on to party with Cesare; fifty lower-class courtesans entertained the guests by dancing naked and crawling on the floor picking up chestnuts. In her third marriage she gave birth to seven children, three of whom died in infancy, and although she was rumoured to have had an affair with the poet-cardinal Pietro Bembo and the Marquis of Mantua, there is no firm evidence. From the age of about twenty-eight she became devoutly religious, wearing a hair shirt and confessing daily. She died at the age of thirty-eight from an infection incurred during childbirth.

Museum of Modern Religious Art

The Vatican's vast collection of modern art is dreadful. Among the more interesting are an acid-yellow *Angelic Landscape* by Dalì, archaic-style horses and a buckled Fallen Angel by sculptor Marino Marini, and a bewildering Rodin featuring Pope Benedict XV, the hand of God and an entwined couple. Francis Bacon, who was notorious for paintings of popes screaming or contemplating raw sides of beef, is probably the last artist you'd expect to be shown in the Vatican. But Gianni Agnelli (owner of Fiat) donated an inoffensive version of *Study for a Velázquez Pope*, based on the Spanish artist's portrait of Innocent X. Other major artists are represented by minor works – two fish dishes by Picasso and a series of gaudy appliquéd copes by Matisse.

The Sistine Chapel

In 1508 Pope Julius II decided that the ceiling of the Sistine Chapel, the most important chapel in the Vatican, needed repainting. It had been built by his uncle, Pope Sixtus IV, and its upkeep, at least in part, had been financed by the bequest of a courtesan, *Fiammetta* (see p.61). The walls were decorated with scenes from the lives of Moses and Christ (by artists including Botticelli, Signorelli, Perugino and Michelangelo's old teacher, Ghirlandaio), but the ceiling was simply blue sprinkled with golden stars.

At the time Michelangelo was obsessed with creating a magnificent tomb for Julius, and furious because the Pope had lost interest in the project and frozen funds. When Julius approached him about painting the ceiling he was convinced that the plan had been cooked up by his rival, Bramante, in order to make him look a fool. Although Michelangelo had studied fresco-painting with Ghirlandaio, he had since concentrated mainly on sculpture. Reluctantly he accepted a commission to paint twelve apostles on the ceiling, but he soon realised that things were going badly. The Pope then gave him a free hand to paint whatever he liked. Instead of coming up with a simpler design, Michelangelo ended up painting not twelve, but 336 figures illustrating the story of the Creation of the world, the Fall of humanity and the foreshadowing of Christ, who was destined to save humankind. Contrary to popular opinion, largely fostered by the film *The Agony and the Ecstasy* (in which Charlton Heston played Michelangelo), Michelangelo did not paint the ceiling in solitude lying flat on his back. He stood up, though the position was far from comfortable. In a poem to a friend he writes: 'My belly is shoved up so far under my chin that it makes me look as though I've got a goitre . . . My beard faces skywards and the nape of my neck is wedged on my spine . . . My face is richly carpeted with a thick layer of paint.' To emphasise the point he drew a little distorted caricature of himself painting. Nor did he work alone – he had assistants to plaster sections of the ceiling every night, to grind the colours, and even to help him with the painting.

The ceiling took four years to paint, during which time Michelangelo was constantly being told to hurry up by an impatient Julius. He could hardly have worked any faster than he did. Adam was painted in three days, his Creator in four, and sometimes the artist was so rushed that he left hog's hair from his brushes embedded in the paint. Details are rendered with astonishing economy – the white of Adam's eye is simply unpainted plaster, and his penis consists of just two strokes of paint – and while some areas are lusciously rendered with layers of superimposed colour, in others hair, drapery, skies and clouds are almost impressionistically created with broad, swift brushstrokes.

The Restoration In recent years no work of art has aroused so much controversy as the ceiling of the Sistine Chapel. Over the 1980s a Japanese television company, NTV, spent three million dollars restoring the ceiling. Five hundred years of soot, candle smoke and glue – along with breadcrumbs and retsina, used by earlier ceiling cleaners – were removed. The familiar warmly glowing, faded and eggshell-cracked figures were discovered to have creamy rose-petal skins and vibrant lustrous hair, and to be wearing luscious strawberry-pink, lime-green, lemon and orange shot-silk robes. 'A Benetton Michelangelo', protested one critic; 'an artistic Chernobyl', said another, unable to believe that Michelangelo's palette could be as zingy as a packet of Opal Fruits. It was suggested that the restorers had ruined the fresco by removing the subtle veils of colour which Michelangelo had added as a final touch, and even that he himself had added a final layer of animal glues to darken the colours. The protesters were invited to examine the restoration process in detail, and discovered that the few 'final touches' added by Michelangelo had been preserved, and that a layer of dust had been discovered between the fresco and the glue, so it could not possibly have been added by Michelangelo. 'The new freshness of the colours and the clarity of the forms are totally in keeping with sixteenth-century painting and affirm the full majesty of Michelangelo's achievement', they reported. There are, however, two criticisms which are harder to refute – first that Michelangelo knew that his jazzy acidic colours would darken and mature in time, and second that the fresco, unprotected by grime and glue, is now exposed to an unprecedented degree of atmospheric pollution. The answer to the first can never be known, but the frescoes have indeed already begun to darken.

The Meaning of the Ceiling

Art historians have argued for centuries over what the Sistine ceiling means, struggling to explain the presence of the beautiful male nudes who frame the central panels, or why Michelangelo played about with the chronology in Genesis (in the Bible Noah sacrifices to God after, not before, the Flood). It has even been suggested that the central panels were designed to be read backwards, starting with the drunken Noah and progressing towards a state of pure spirituality!

This particular theory aside, it's pretty obvious that the pessimistic vision of the central panels, charting the creation of the world and humanity's downfall, is to be seen within the context of Christ's coming – an event foreseen by the Christian prophets and pagan Sibyls. To emphasise this the lunettes are devoted to the ancestors of Christ – ranging from David and Solomon to the unpronounceable Jehoshaphat and Aminadab. The corner spandrels are given over to Old Testament figures who saved their people – Judith, David, Esther and Moses.

THE WOMEN ON THE CEILING

Most of the women on the Sistine ceiling look like pentathletes pumped with male hormones, sporting muscled torsos, footballers' thighs, formidable biceps and improbably shaped breasts. Though it was not unusual for men to model as women, it is astonishing, given Michelangelo's obsession with anatomy – his research included the dissection of corpses – that his representations of women should be so unreal. Part of the answer lies in the fact that during the Renaissance the male body was reckoned to be a perfectly proportioned reflection of universal harmony (witness Leonardo's famous drawing of an outstretched man precisely framed by a square and circle). Part of it also lies in the fact that Michelangelo was gay, so his personal ideal of human beauty was male. The only typically 'feminine ' women on the ceiling are fully dressed mothers caring for babies in the lunettes. He had no problem in painting tender faces, but faltered as soon as he was confronted with the female body – as you can see if you look (preferably through opera glasses) at the breast poking out of Ruth's dress in the Boaz lunette. A more pernicious aspect of Michelangelo's attitude to women is revealed in the *Fall and Expulsion from Paradise*. Instead of being merely content to lay the blame for the fall of humanity on the shoulders of Eve, he also makes Satan a serpent with a woman's body.

THE LAYOUT OF THE CEILING

CENTRAL PANELS
1 Division of Light from Darkness
2 The Creation of the Sun and Moon
3 The Separation of the Sky and Water
4 The Creation of Adam
5 The Creation of Eve
6 The Fall and the Expulsion from Paradise
7 Noah's Sacrifice
8 The Flood
9 The Drunkenness of Noah
THE SPANDRELS
David and Goliath
Judith and Holofernes
The Punishment of Haman
The Brazen Serpent

PROPHETS AND SIBYLS
Zacchariah
Delphic Sibyl
Isaiah
Cumaean Sibyl
Daniel
Libyan Sibyl
Jonah
Jeremiah
Persian Sibyl
Ezekiel
Erithraean Sibyl
Joel
THE LUNETTES
The Ancestors of Christ

LAST JUDGEMENT

Restoration began on the fresco in the late Eighties, and was due to be completed in 1992. However, by late 1992 the work was still incomplete, and the finishing date is uncertain.

In 1536, twenty-four years after he had finished the Sistine's ceiling, Michelangelo began frescoing the *Last Judgement* on the altar wall of the chapel. It's a harrowing, pessimistic work, depicting the helplessness of humanity in the face of a pitiless Christ. The damned tumble towards and fester in a putrid hell, the saved are dragged up to heaven. Far from interceding on behalf of humanity, the saints clustering around Christ demand vengeance for their martyrdoms, and the only figure to show any pity is the Virgin. In his original sketches, Michelangelo showed the Virgin actively imploring her son to show mercy, but in the final version she sits, helpless, beside Christ, dwarfed by his mighty muscled torso and raised right arm. Michelangelo originally painted the figures nude, but in 1564 Pope Pius IV ordered Daniele da Volterra to add loin cloths. According to the latest reports from the current restorers, it has been decided to retain the loin cloths.

Pinacoteca

The Vatican's art collection is one of the best in Rome. It is also a manageable size, and has a particularly strong Renaissance section. Rooms 1 and 2 are devoted to fourteenth- and fifteenth-century works. Primitive representations of the Madonna include Bernardo Daddi's early fourteenth-century *Madonna del Magnificat*, a stylised Byzantine beauty with almond eyes. Somewhat more human are the massively pregnant *Madonna del Parto* by an anonymous Florentine and the *Madonna del Latte* by Francescuccio Ghissi, in which the Virgin sits on a rug breastfeeding Christ.

Perhaps the most engaging of the early works are four episodes from the life of St Nicholas of Bari by Gentile da Fabriano. In one the future saint throws three golden balls through the window of a room in which two sisters get ready for bed, while a third helps her father to remove a red stocking. The story goes that the father had no money for dowries, and saw no other option for his daughters than a life of prostitution. St Nicholas's three balls gave them the wherewithal to get married -- and, oddly, later evolved into the pawnbroker emblem. Another episode is even more bizarre – Nicholas raises back to life three boys who had been pickled to death in barrels by a butcher. Beyond are romantic Madonnas by two very different monks, Filippo Lippi, who was sent to join a monastery because he was an orphan, and ended up being expelled for fraud and impregnating a nun; and Fra Angelico, a devout Dominican preacher who felt that religious art should be didactic.

When you step into Room 6, you enter the claustrophobic world of the Crivelli brothers. Carlo, a Venetian who was imprisoned for adultery, worked mostly in a provincial town in the Marches, creating doll-like Madonnas, caged in a gilded, fruit-festooned space within the frame. His younger brother Vittore is represented by an equally exquisite, though rather petulant Madonna.

Room 8 is dominated by three canvases by Raphael: two Heaven-dwelling Madonnas and a Heaven-bound Christ. *L'Incoronazione della Vergine* covers two aspects of Marian dogma – her Assumption into heaven (signalled by the disciples gathered around her empty, flower-sprouting sarcophagus) and her coronation as Queen of Heaven (Christ places a crown on her head to an accompaniment of angel musicians). There is no basis in the Bible for either incident, but by Raphael's time these traditional beliefs were centuries old, and persist today. The *Madonna di Foligno* again places the Virgin in Heaven, bathed in light with her foot on a cloud, but this time she holds the baby Christ on her knee. It is a tender evocation of motherhood, though the heavenly setting clearly differentiates her from any mere mortal mother. Raphael did, however, manage to introduce an extremely mortal woman into his last work, the *Transfigurazione*. Dominating the foreground is a stunning woman, with lustrous red-gold hair and a bare shoulder, thought to be La Fornarina (see p.116). He died before finishing the painting, and four months later La Fornarina entered a convent for repentant women – on Piazza Sant'Apollonia, opposite the studio in which Raphael had worked on the *Transfigurazione*.

As you move on, there's an unfinished painting by Leonardo da Vinci of St Jerome (see box), shrivelled and emaciated among rocks, with only a lion for company. Beyond is a painting of Constantine's mother, St Helena (see p.222), by the Venetian artist Veronese. He virtually always set religious scenes in contemporary Venice, and this is no exception – Helena is represented as a weary Venetian contessa in a sumptuously decorated palace, gorgeously clad in brocade, resting on the True Cross she had discovered in the Holy Land.

Caravaggio can usually be relied on to introduce a note of realism; this he does uncompromisingly in the *Deposizione*, in which two men heave Christ's slumped body from the cross, as Magdalene weeps into a handkerchief and Mary watches with quiet, disbelieving pain. Magdalene appears again as the distressed subject of a painting by Guercino, created for Santa Maria Maddalena delle Convertite, a (now demolished) church and convent for penitent prostitutes which stood on Via del Corso.

ST JEROME, PAULA AND BLESILLA

Although artists inevitably show fourth-century St Jerome as an ancient man, he was actually quite young during his brief desert retreat, and was plagued by dreams of dancing girls. He left the desert for Rome in his mid thirties and under his guidance Paula, a wealthy aristocratic widow, became the first noblewoman in Rome to live as a 'consecrated ' virgin, and gave him the funds to set up a monastery, a pilgrim hostel and a school, running the monastery for women herself.

Her daughter Blesilla was also a devout Christian who ended up dying of starvation after rigorously adhering to Jerome's advice on fasting. Although he seems genuinely to have loved these women (chastely), he believed that the only good thing about marriage was that it produced virgins. Pleasure was taboo: 'Anyone who becomes too passionate a lover of his wife is an adulterer. . . the begetting of children is allowed in marriage, but feelings of sensual pleasure such as those had in the embraces of a harlot are damnable in a wife. ' Blesilla was his ideal wife. She was widowed after seven months, and Jerome wrote approvingly in a letter to Paula: 'the loss of her virginity caused her more pain than the death of her husband'.

This modern museum, opened in 1970, holds a collection of Greek sculptural fragments, and Roman portrait busts, tombs and funeral reliefs. Some of the finest, though, are Imperial Roman copies of Greek works. These include a relief of Medea and the Daughters of Pelias. Medea persuaded the girls that they could extend the life of their aged father, Pelias, by chopping him up and boiling him in a solution of magic herbs. Her motive was fair enough – Pelias had usurped the throne of her husband Jason. The relief shows Medea sprinkling herbs into a cauldron attended by two of the daughters. The story, incidentally, has a typically tragic ending. Jason ran off with another woman, and Medea went mad and killed her own children.

Niobe was another tragic Greek woman. A mother of fourteen children, she persuaded the people of her town that she was clearly far superior to the goddess Leto, who had only two children. Leto was livid, and sent her son and daughter, Apollo and Artemis, to kill all Niobe's children with arrows. One of the loveliest (though headless) statues of women in the entire Vatican collection is the Chiaromonti Niobid: one of Niobe's daughters running, with her drapery whipped by the wind and clinging to her legs.

The museum also has an intriguing collection of Roman funerary sculpture, many pieces tenderly carved with portraits of parents and children. The reliefs from the Tomb of the Haterii – probably the family of Haterius Tychicus, a first-century building contractor – are far more showy. As well as portraits of the family and scenes of a woman's funeral, there are reliefs of five ancient buildings, including the unfinished Colosseum, and a view of the ostentatious family sepulchre, complete with the crane used in its construction. Haterius was probably involved in constructing all these buildings, and appears to have seized the opportunity offered by the woman's (probably his wife's) death to advertise his business.

Other Romans preferred to have mythological scenes carved on their sarcophagi, among them an action-packed Massacre of the Niobids, a couple of Triumphs of Bacchus – one of them featuring castanet-clicking, cymbal-bashing dancing girls – and a Myth of Orestes which shows Orestes murdering his mother, Clytemnestra, and her subsequent descent (with her lover) to Hell. Orestes' murder was in revenge for the adulterous couple's murder of Clytemnestra's husband (and Orestes' father) Menelaus, which can only make one wonder about the circumstances of the family who commissioned it. Finally, don't miss the collection's most bizarre goddess, Diana of Ephesus, whose multiple breasts (coyly referred to as attributes in official Vatican literature) signify her life-enhancing powers.

PIAZZA VENEZIA & ARCHAEOLOGICAL ZONE

Although the relics of ancient Rome are strewn throughout the city, the most concentrated and fully excavated cluster lies in the area bounded by the Capitoline, Palatine, Esquiline and Quirinal hills. This was the official heart of the ancient city, where the fates of nations were decided, military triumphs were celebrated, and citizens were entertained by the death of gladiators and the mass slaughter of wild animals. There were also taverns, a dole centre, brothels and markets – including the world's first shopping mall – and the offices of usurers and tax farmers. Here too was the most desirable residential area in Rome, the Palatine Hill, where – if the ancient historians are to be believed – the sexual excesses of emperors, empresses, politicians and poets were matched by the passion with which they plotted against and poisoned one another.

Both the legends and the history of ancient Rome are dominated by men, while women (except for the occasional goddess) are characterised as virgins, victims, vamps or viragos. Men were immensely powerful. The male head of household had the right to kill a daughter who committed adultery or drank wine, and women had no vote and no official power. In addition, virtually the only surviving works of Roman history and literature are by male writers. The satirist Juvenal produced some of the most vicious attacks on women ever published, still read as fact by many historians; the poet Ovid devoted reams of verse advising men on how to pick up women, and even advocated rape; and the poet Catullus alternated between singing his mistress's praises and reviling her as a whore. The characters of empresses were also ridiculed and attacked, and as there are no objective accounts of their lives, discovering the truth is impossible. We shall never know if Augustus's wife Livia poisoned her nephews; if his daughter Julia made love in public; or whether Claudius's wife Messalina really got her kicks in brothels. Most evidence about ordinary women has to be inferred from art, legal records and funeral inscriptions, some of them deriving not from Rome but from better-preserved ancient towns like Pompeii and Herculaneum.

Visiting the Sites Many of the ruins are scanty and a good plan and reliable reconstructions (see Recommended Books) help no end in making sense of cracked pavements, lumps of stone and isolated columns. Unless you have a Classics background, or already know a lot about Roman architecture, it's worth taking the sights slowly, rather than trying to see the whole archaeological zone in a single day. The ancient core is bounded by thundering great multilaned roads and most of the cafés in the area are tourist traps, so you need to plan your breaks carefully if you want to avoid sitting on a roadside café with an overpriced drink. Ulderico and 313 Cavour (see pp.293–4) are notable exceptions, and in good weather you could always picnic on the Palatine.

It's not a bad idea to start with the Capitoline Museums, which have some of ancient Rome's finest statues, including busts of empresses, which help you to put faces to names. The best-preserved monuments are the Colosseum, and the markets and column erected by Trajan, one of the more socially benevolent of Rome's emperors. In the Roman Forum and Palatine colourful histories have to compensate for heavily ruined monuments, while the Imperial Fora are of limited, specialised interest.

LOWER-CLASS WOMEN AND WORK

Slave women were the property of their masters, and were obliged to be available for sex as well as more regular daytime duties. Women were usually given jobs as seamstresses, wet-nurses and general domestics, though in wealthier households they would be trained as midwives, ladies' maids, hairdressers, beauticians and masseuses. A few were taught to read and write so that they could work as clerks or secretaries, or entertain their mistresses by reading to them; others worked in their masters' business, particularly in textiles, finishing and dyeing new cloth and cleaning and rejuvenating old. Slaves were allowed to save money (tips and gifts were fairly frequent) with which they might eventually be able to buy their freedom. Sometimes, however, a master might feel that a slave deserved to be released for long service, or for producing a supply of baby slaves (children born to slaves were the property of the master). Freedwomen often continued to work for their ex-owners on a fee basis, but occasionally used the skills they had acquired to set up their own businesses or work independently as midwives or wet-nurses.

Poor freeborn women also had to work. If they had no skills they usually worked as wet-nurses or nannies; other options included becoming a barmaid, a dancer, a mime actress, a musician or a prostitute. None of these professions was considered respectable – indeed, actresses were usually little more than strippers – and they had as little redress as a prostitute when it came to sexual harassment.

Widows and daughters sometimes took over their husband's or father's business – there were twenty-one women just outside Rome who owned clay pits which produced bricks, tiles, and pottery – though they may have left the day-to-day management to men. As for women in professional jobs, most seem to have been midwives, though there were a fair number of female doctors.

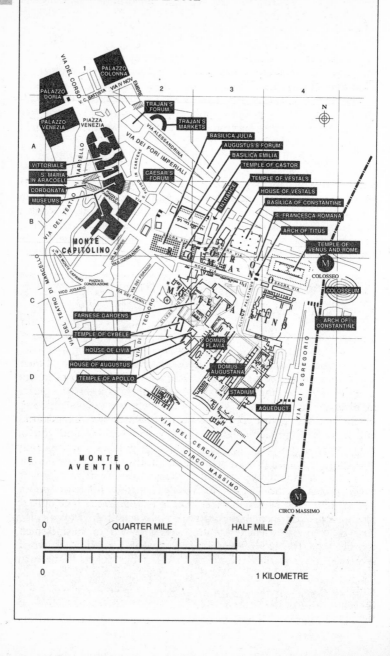

THE LEGEND OF ROME

The legend of Rome begins with rape, fratricide and attempted infanticide. Romulus and Remus were the offspring of Rhea Silvia, daughter of Numitor, the deposed King of Alba. She was a Vestal Virgin who had been (or, according to Livy, claimed to have been) raped by Mars. Her uncle, Amulias, who had seized the throne from Numitor, attempted to drown the babies in the Tiber, but the water receded and they were left on the banks of the river near the Palatine Hill. Here they were rescued and suckled by a she-wolf. The king's herdsman, Faustulus, discovered the twins and the wolf and took the boys to his cave, where they were cared for by his wife, Larentia. One version of the legend is that Larentia was a whore and that the wolf was apocryphal – in Latin the word for whore and she-wolf is the same: *lupa*. The boys grew up, and one day they were arrested on a false charge of stealing cattle. Numitor saw them, recognised them as his grandsons, and they killed his brother. Romulus and Remus decided to move out of Alba and establish a new town. Romulus and his party stood on the Palatine, Remus and his supporters on the Aventine, and they asked the gods which one of them should be its governor. Six vultures flew across the Aventine, then twelve swooped over the Palatine. The followers of each proclaimed their master to be king – those of Remus because his sign from the gods had come first; those of Romulus because his consisted of twice as many vultures. A battle ensued, during which Remus was killed. An alternative version is that Romulus had begun to build the walls of his new town, and Remus, showing that he had no intention of respecting the boundaries, leapt over them.

PIAZZA VENEZIA AND THE CAMPIDOGLIO (CAPITOLINE)

Piazza Venezia is dominated by the glacial Vittoriale, a piece of jingoisitic kitsch which outdoes anything dreamed up by the ancient emperors. The piazza itself serves as an arena for careering motorists, military jamborees and political demos. Five main roads, all of them bus routes, converge here, and as Roman drivers conform in one thing alone – ignoring zebra crossings – venturing across the piazza involves taking your life in your hands. There *is* a knack to it. Step out purposefully, with your head turned towards oncoming traffic, and glare at approaching drivers. They *will* veer around you or stop, because the rules of Italian insurance policies state that any accident involving a pedestrian is automatically the motorist's fault.

The piazza is flanked by what appear to be twin palaces with towers. One is the Palazzo di Venezia, former home to popes, ambassadors and Mussolini; the other is a *fin-de-siècle* fake built to house an insurance company. At the back, facing the Vittoriale, is a row of cafés, frequented by an eclectic crowd of businessmen, tourists and the *demi-monde*. The all-night Castellino is worth remembering if you need food, cigarettes or bus tickets in the early hours, though by then it will be full of some extremely dodgy types. Unless you're heading for the Capitoline or want to visit the dull museum in the Palazzo di Venezia, there's no reason to set foot in the piazza – traverse it aboard a bus.

The Vittoriale

The Vittoriale, officially known as the Altar of the Nation or Monumento Vittorio Emanuele (and unofficially as the wedding cake or typewriter), is a white marble stack so huge that it reduces the soldiers guarding it to Lilliputian proportions.

It was built at the turn of the century to celebrate the unification of Italy and to commemorate its first king, Vittorio Emanuele II. Now – given that the royal family is in exile, and that Italy's President recently cancelled the Republican Day parade because 'there isn't much to celebrate' – it's something of a white marble elephant. It has come in for more abuse than any other building in the city – though Kaiser Wilhelm considered it to be 'the maximum expression of the Latin genius'.

Although Peter Greenaway was given access to film *In the Belly of an Architect* on the Vittoriale, it has been closed to the public for years. If, however, you get a chance to climb inside, take it. The views are sensational.

Palazzo di Venezia, Mussolini and Claretta Petacci
Open Tues–Sat 9 a.m.–2 p.m.; Sun and hols 9 a.m.–1 p.m.

The palazzo was built in the mid fifteenth century for the Venetian Pope Paul II (ruled 1464–71). A great lover of sport and spectacle, he had the Roman Carnival shifted from Testaccio to the Corso so that he could watch the riderless horse races and other festivities from his windows. The races ended in what is now Piazza Venezia, with the horses, wearing nailed saddles to 'encourage' them, charging into a great white sheet. In the evenings Paul II entertained higher-class citizens at a banquet in front of the palace. Poorer people were allowed to eat the leftovers, then gathered outside waiting for Paul to throw down bags of money.

After being used for several centuries as an embassy, the palace was taken over by Mussolini, who had private apartments as well as his office here (he left the lights on all night, to give the impression that he never stopped working). The private rooms were used for entertaining his mistresses, most often Claretta Petacci. She would come in by a side door and spend hours waiting, lying on the divan upstairs, staring at the blue and gold ceiling, playing records, reading love stories, painting her nails and filling a notebook with reminiscences about picnics and skiing holidays with *Il Duce*.

By 1943 her affair with Mussolini had been going on for seven years; he was bored with her, and concerned about his reputation. On one occasion a policeman was given orders not to allow her into the palazzo, but she forced her way past him to confront Mussolini. 'I consider', he said coolly, 'the cycle closed.' But – partly owing to Claretta's obsessive persistence – it continued, and she remained

with him to the very end. She was shot, with Mussolini, in 1945,
and their corpses were strung up in a Milanese piazza.

The Palazzo di Venezia now holds a vast, heterogeneous assortment of paintings and decorative arts. It is hardly the most compelling collection in Rome, but it is worth a visit if you're interested in Florentine *cassoni* (decorated wedding chests), ceramics, silverware or Mannerist statuettes.

San Marco

Round the corner from the palazzo is the church of San Marco, with an arcaded Renaissance portico crowned by a loggia from which popes used to bless the people. Outside is an eroded statue of a busty woman, known as Madama Lucrezia. She is one of the city's four 'talking statues' (see p.57) and was probably named after a local woman. It is thought that the statue was originally an Isis from the temple built by Caligula near Piazza Minerva.

Inside the portico, low down on the wall to the right, is a plaque bearing an inscription to Alexander VI (Borgia)'s mistress, Vanozza Cattanei (see box, p.90) describing her as 'venerable' because she was the mother of Cesare, Lucrezia, Juan and Jofré Borgia, and 'illustrious' because she was old, wise, good and pious. Vanozza was originally buried in a chapel she endowed in Santa Maria del Popolo, and no one has any idea how the tombstone ended up buried in San Marco's portico, where it was unearthed a few decades ago.

The church itself is an appealingly colourful blend of the ancient and the Baroque, with a gilded coffered ceiling, steps covered with Cosmati tesserae, streaky Sicilian jasper columns and a ninth-century apse mosaic showing a procession of stylised lambs.

The Campidoglio
(Capitoline Hill and the Musei Capitolini)

Open Tues–Sat 9 a.m.–1.30 p.m.; Sun 9 a.m.–1 p.m.; Wed also open 5–8 p.m.; Sat also open 8–11 p.m.

Now completely screened from Piazza Venezia by the Vittoriale, the Capitoline Hill was the ancient citadel of Rome, betrayed in approximately 747 BC by the commander's daughter Tarpeia, who opened its gates to the Sabines seeking revenge for the mass rape of their women. The ungrateful Sabines, disliking traitors, promptly crushed her to death.

The Capitoline soon became home to Rome's three most important temples. One was dedicated to Jupiter Optimus Maximus Capitolinus, a divine version of the Roman father, with the power to protect or – if he was angry – to destroy the city; another was dedicated to Minerva, goddess of wisdom and war; and the third to Juno Moneta, protector of women and vigilante who could be relied upon to raise the alarm in times of danger. She – or, more precisely, the geese in her sanctuary – did indeed save Rome in 390 BC, waking the sleeping citadel guards by cackling as the Gauls, who had already devastated the rest of the city, mounted an attack. Juno's legendary vigilance was doubtless why her temple was selected to hold the ancient city's mint.

The Capitoline is now approached via an elegant ramp, the Cordonata, designed in the 1530s, along with the refined piazza at its head, by Michelangelo. Michelangelo's Cordonata is headed by two colossal statues of Castor and Pollux, which were discovered in the Ghetto. Until recently the piazza itself was dominated by a gilded bronze equestrian statue of Marcus Aurelius – a magnificent work which escaped destruction at the hands of the Christians because they thought it was Constantine. Recently restored, it is now displayed behind glass in the courtyard of the Palazzo Nuovo. Straight ahead is a statue of Minerva converted into the goddess Roma, the embodiment of the city, overlooked by the Palazzo Senatorio. This is the seat of the city government where, in 1957, the Treaty of Rome was signed, establishing the European Community. To the right is the Palazzo dei Conservatori, Renaissance headquarters of the city magistrates, and to the left the Palazzo Nuovo. The latter two house the collection of the Musei Capitolini.

Palazzo Nuovo

The richest half of the collection is in the Palazzo Nuovo, usually (and confusingly) known simply as the Museo Capitolino. Along with famous antique sculptures of men like the *Dying Gaul (Dying Galatian)* and a copy of Praxiteles' *Faun*, there are some brilliant statues of women. These include two haggard old Hellenistic women, one terrified, the other drunk; a topless, sour-faced Roman matron dressed as an improbable Venus; and one of the city's numerous copies of Praxiteles' X-rated *Venus of Cnidias* (see also p.161). There's also a romantic *Cupid and Psyche*; a statue of a little girl sheltering a bird; and, by way of contrast, a prophetic sculpture of the nasty Caracalla as a toddler, represented as Hercules happily strangling a snake.

His mother, Julia Domna, is one of many empresses and women from the Imperial family represented in the museum's collection of portrait busts. If you want to put faces to names, there are portraits of Livia (see p.199), Agrippina the Elder, Messalina (see p.126), Domitia (see p.197) and the Elder and Younger Faustinas, some of them with extraordinarily complex hairstyles.

ANCIENT ROMAN HAIRSTYLES

Augustus's wife *Livia* and his sister *Octavia* wore their hair fairly simply, plaited and raised on pads over the forehead, sometimes with a little knot at the nape of the neck. But hairstyles soon became more elaborate, and the *ornatrix* – or hairdresser and beautician – became an indispensable member of a wealthy woman's household.

Claudius's wife *Messalina* would have her hair moulded like pasta into spirals, curls and twists, but it was in the Flavian era (under emperors Vespasian, Titus and Domitian) that hairstyles reached the heights of ridiculousness. The final effect was akin to a snail-studded shower cap. 'See the tall edifice rise up on her head in serried tiers and storeys,' wrote Juvenal after describing a coiffeur scene in which the lady screams and lashes out at her cack-handed *ornatrix*.

Naturally, not all women were blessed with the copious quantities of hair necessary for such styles, so false hairpieces and wigs were used as well. By the time of Trajan one of Rome's main imports from India was hair. Dyeing and bleaching (with a mixture of beech ash and goat's fat) was also common, and red-gold became extremely modish in the early first century AD after the Germanic tribes were annexed to the Empire.

Palazzo dei Conservatori

The courtyard of the Palazzo dei Conservatori is where couples, just wed in the Palazzo Senatorio's registry office, come to pose for photos. They have a choice of backdrops: a personification of Rome or a head, foot, hand or knee which belonged to a giant statue of Constantine. Highlights of the main collection are a first-century BC bronze of a boy removing a thorn from his foot, a famous bronze she-wolf, dating back to the fifth century BC, suckling Romulus and Remus (Renaissance additions by Pollaiuolo), and a head of Medusa by Bernini, with writhing serpent dreadlocks.

Representations of women are varied. On the staircase Hadrian's wife Sabina is apotheosised; in the Hall of the Horatii and Curiatii, Mannerist artist Cavaliere d'Arpino represents the Sabine women half-heartedly resisting rape; while the Hall of the Throne is decorated with eighteenth-century medallions cataloguing the virtues of ancient Roman women. Far more interesting are a multibreasted cult statue of fertility goddess Diana (or Artemis) of Ephesus, reliefs of maenads and satyrs partying at a Bacchanalia, a glorious statue of a slinky Venus, and a delicately sculpted *Seated Girl* from the Orti Lamiani, one of a number of lavish gardens which occupied the Esquiline Hill in antiquity.

The Pinacoteca on the second floor holds a a small collection of paintings, much visited by Victorian travellers. George Eliot thought Guercino's immense *Burial of St Petronilla* (showing St Peter's hypothetical daughter being hauled up to Heaven) 'might as well have been left undone'. You might well feel the same about Pietro da Cortona's *Rape of the Sabine Women*, who clearly believed that when women say 'no' they mean 'yes'. The gallery's most self-sufficient representation of a woman is by Caravaggio: a fortune-teller who may or may not be telling the truth about his future to a dandy young man.

Paintings of Mary Magdalene range from a *déshabillée* courtesan by Tintoretto to a demure innocent by Guido Reni. Reni also supplies two bare-breasted women committing suicide: Cleopatra and Lucrezia. There are two *Rapes of Europa* – one by Veronese, the other by Elisabetta Sirani, a seventeenth-century Bolognese artist. There is nothing about Sirani's to distinguish it from the work of a man – indeed, even in her lifetime people refused to believe that her work was her own and not that of her artist father. Eventually she began to paint in public to prove herself. The ploy worked, and by the time she died, aged only twenty-seven, she was so famous that she was accorded a splendid public funeral and buried next to Reni.

Santa Maria in Aracoeli

A flight of steps to the left of the Cordonata climbs up to Santa Maria in Aracoeli, built on the supposed site of the temple of Juno Moneta, in which Augustus was informed of the coming of Christ. According to the twelfth-century guidebook, the *Mirabilia*, he had summoned the local Sibyl to the temple to ask her what she thought about the plans to deify him. As she was telling Augustus that 'the King of future centuries' was about to descend from the sun, he saw the heavens open to reveal an image of the Virgin, bathed in light and holding a baby. Two voices called out: 'This is the Virgin who will receive in her womb the Saviour of the World – this is the altar of the Son of God.' Apparently Augustus – who had doubtless hitherto considered himself the world's saviour – raised an altar (the Ara Coeli – Altar of Heaven) on the spot. True or not, it was this vision that allowed pagan Sibyls to join biblical prophets on the ceilings of churches throughout Italy.

The stark façade is no preparation for the chandelier-lit interior, with a gilded ceiling, Cosmatesque pavement, antique columns and frescoed episodes from the life of San Bernardino of Siena by Pinturicchio. Painted in the apse, above a Byzantine Madonna, Augustus and the Sibyl are present among the saints and angels.

There are also the tombs of two intrepid women travellers: St Helena (see p.222), who died while she was collecting sacred souvenirs in the Holy Land; and the unnamed Persian wife of a seventeenth-century traveller, Pietro della Valle. She died while he was in Asia, and he carried her corpse around for five years before burying it here.

The church is now best known for a miracle-working wooden statue of the baby Christ. Carved from the wood of an olive tree in Gethsemane, he is ruddy-cheeked, swaddled in gold and covered with jewels. Letters are sent to him from all over the world, often simply addressed to Il Bambino, Roma. They are left to lie in front of his altar for a while and then burnt, unopened. Traditionally, when people were ill, they could ask for the bambino to be brought to their bedside. Occasionally this still happens, though nowadays he travels by taxi. At Christmas he is placed within a crib scene, children recite poems to him, and shepherds from the Abruzzo come and play their bagpipes in his honour.

The Forum is linked to the Palatine, and you can visit both on the same ticket, though this demands considerable stamina, particularly as there are no cafés on either site. The best option is to take a picnic up to the Palatine, though you should be fairly discreet, as the guards may object.

The Roman Forum

Open winter: Mon and Wed–Sat 9 a.m.–3 p.m.; summer Mon and Wed–Sat 9 a.m.–6 p.m.
All year Tues and Sun 9 a.m.–1 p.m.

In the early days of the Republic the Roman Forum was much like an Italian piazza today – an open space where people would shop, gossip, catch up on the latest news and perhaps visit a temple. In the second century BC – by which time Rome was capital of an empire which included Greece, Sicily and Carthage (North Africa) – it was decided that the city needed a more dignified centre. The food stalls were moved out, and law courts and business centres were built. In time, as the Empire expanded and Rome's population boomed (with refugees and slaves rather than native Romans), the Forum became too small, and emperors began to build new fora to relieve congestion. But the Roman Forum remained the symbolic heart of the Empire. Emperors continued to renovate and embellish it; and in the wake of military victories they paraded prisoners and war booty through its precincts.

According to the Republican-era playwright Plautus, the Forum was full of liars, harlots, rent-boys, poseurs, gamblers and scandal-mongers. The part women played in Roman public and street life is not well documented, though there are some clues. Although the political power of women was nil (they had no vote), on occasions they did come into the Forum *en masse* to fight for their rights. They also attended the courts, as both spectators and participants, facing accusations of adultery, negotiating divorce settlements, bringing cases against rapists, and defending themselves against public order offences – like a prostitute who threw stones out of her window to get rid of an unwanted client. A few women were involved in business, inheriting their late husbands' tax-farming concessions or construction companies; acting as private moneylenders or pawnbrokers; and using skills acquired as slaves to set up as caterers or dye-sellers once they had been freed. Women also worked as midwives, wet-nurses, scribes, secretaries and even doctors, though whether they advertised or plied their professions in the Forum is unknown. Women of leisure may also have frequented the Forum, carried by slaves in a litter (a kind of sedan chair) until they decided to alight, whereupon a female slave would put sandals on their feet, and position a footstool so that they could step down.

When you first look at the Roman Forum you may assume that you'll never make any sense of it. You probably won't, without a little knowledge, a lot of imagination, a decent plan and a reconstruction (the latter two are included in most of the booklets on sale in the ticket office). If you don't feel like making the effort, you won't be the first: James Joyce was so unmoved by the site that he fell asleep.

Basilica Emilia

The Basilica Emilia – now a pastel pavement fringed with column stumps and a tufa wall – was a rectangular hall, founded in 179 BC, where Roman bankers, moneylenders and tax farmers met to wheel and deal. Women were not permitted to be bankers, but they did act as moneylenders (usually privately among the upper classes), and wives of members of the tax-farming consortia sometimes took over when their husbands died. These consortia – a particularly nasty Roman phenomenon – were associations of wealthy businessmen, known as *publicani*, contracted by the state to collect taxes throughout the Empire. Contracts went to the highest bidder, and an agreement was made whereby the *publicani* would guarantee the state a certain amount of tax revenue, then instruct their agents to collect as much money as possible. The consortia were allowed to keep anything in excess of the agreed sum – which made it a highly lucrative business.

The usurers were still at work in the fifth century when the Goths invaded, and clearly carried on business till the last moment. The pavement is spotted with tiny splashes of rust and verdigris: the remains of coins. The basilica was once decorated with a frieze of the Rape of the Sabine Women, and a fragment, with women being chased and carried off by Romans, is on display at the back.

THE RAPE OF THE SABINE WOMEN

The rape of the Sabine women, which became a favourite subject for sculptors and artists, is a legend, though Livy, writing at the time of Augustus, treated it as fact. It is, however, thought that at some point in the eighth century BC the Romans united with the Sabines, who lived on the nearby Quirinal Hill.

Livy reckoned that the rape was Romulus's method of ensuring that the Roman tribe (which was short of women) did not die out. The Sabines had refused to allow their women to marry the Romans, so Romulus decided to teach them a lesson. He invited them to a festival, and at the height of the fun he gave a prearranged signal, upon which the Roman men carried off all the young Sabine women. Livy claimed that as soon as the men had sworn that the motive behind the rape was passionate love, the women were quite happy.

Their parents and brothers, however, weren't, and in time war broke out between the Romans and the Sabines. The Sabines broke into the Roman citadel – thanks to Tarpeia, the daughter of its commander, who opened the gate (and was promptly crushed to death) – and the battle began. The women begged the men to stop fighting, and according to Livy:

> banished their natural timidity . . . and with loosened hair and rent garments . . . braved the flying spears and thrust their way in a body between the embattled armies. 'We are mothers now,' they said, 'our children are your sons – your grandsons: do not put on them the stain of parricide. If our marriage . . . is hateful to you, turn your anger against us. We are the cause of strife, and on our account our husbands and fathers lie wounded or dead, and we would rather die ourselves than live on either widowed or orphaned.'

Peace was made, and the Romans and the Sabines united.

Tabernae Novae and the Death of Verginia

The walls of a row of shops, the tabernae novae, stand in front of the Basilica Emilia, among a litter of fragmented columns, capitals and chunks of entablature. They were used by butchers, and according to Livy it was from one of these in the fifth century BC that a plebeian centurion, Lucius Verginius, seized a knife and killed his daughter Verginia. The motive? To prevent her from being abducted by the Decemvir Appius Claudius. Death was considered far less shameful than the forced loss of virginity, and for centuries Verginius's stabbing was held up as a prime example of how a good Roman father should act.

The Curia: The Senatorial Attitude to Women

This ugly brick building is a modern reconstruction of the Curia, or Senate House. The Senate was the chief council of the state, and all the Senators were male – though Nero allowed his mother, Agrippina the Younger, to listen to proceedings from behind a curtain. Many of the Senate's laws and debates reveal their attitude to women.

In 195 BC the Senate debated whether or not to repeal a law which forbade women to ride in carriages, own more than half an ounce of gold, or wear dyed clothes. It had been introduced as a kind of economy measure in 215 BC while Rome was at war with Carthage, but twenty years later it had still not been repealed. The debate raged for days, and women, becoming progressively angrier, began to demonstrate, unfortunately playing straight into the hands of diehard chauvinists like Cato. 'It made me blush to push my way through a positive regiment of women a few minutes ago to get here,' he thundered. 'Woman is a headstrong and uncontrolled animal . . . what they want is complete freedom – or to put it bluntly – complete licence. If you allow them one right after another, so that in the end they have complete equality with men, do you think you will find them bearable? Nonsense!' According to Cato, all women wanted was to have the chance to show off their wealth to inferiors: 'Do you want to inaugurate an era of competitiveness in dress? . . . When a woman's resources will stretch to something she will buy it; when she cannot, she will go to her husband for the money . . . If he does not find the money, some other man will . . .' The law was, however, repealed, though largely because it applied only to Roman citizens, not allies, which meant that foreign women looked more splendid than Roman ones.

FASHION AND MAKE-UP

It has to be said that Cato had a point, if only in the area of fashion. Wealthy Roman women (and the more foppish men) were amazingly extravagant, and as a result of their endless appetite for foreign fabrics, dyes, perfumes, precious metals and jewels, Rome clocked up a massive trade deficit.

Underclothes were simple: a loin cloth, breastband and tunic, which were also worn at night. By day, women donned a *stola*, a long tunic consisting simply of two rectangles of cloth sewn together and worn belted. The style barely changed over the centuries, and the main difference between those worn by the rich and the poor was the fabric. The availability of the more luxurious fabrics depended upon the success of the Imperial army. Once Augustus had secured Parthia (Iraq and Iran), cotton could be brought across from India and silk from China, ready to be dyed blue, yellow, red or purple.

After a wealthy woman's *ornatrix* (hairdresser and beautician) had tussled with her hair (see box, p.179), attention turned to make-up. Foundation was made from the grease of sheep's wool, and ingredients in other unguents included honey, barley meal and ground antlers. Brows and arms were painted white with chalk and white lead; lips and cheeks were reddened with ochre or wine sediment; and ash was used as an eyeliner and to darken eyebrows.

Plutei of Trajan The Curia now shelters the Plutei of Trajan, panels sculpted with reliefs, commissioned by either Trajan or his successor Hadrian to decorate the Rostra (see p.186). Unfortunately, you are not allowed to stand close enough to see them properly and staff shortages often mean the building is closed. On the left-hand panel, it's just possible to make out a number of books being piled up – these contained records of unpaid taxes, which Trajan ordered to be destroyed so that certain citizens would be freed from their debts. The right-hand panel shows Trajan standing on the Rostra, then sitting on a throne receiving a mother and child.

This is thought to represent his institution of the *alimenta*, an ancient form of child benefit, financed by the interest on loans made by the state to smallholders. Many parents who lacked the means to support children would abandon them, and for a child born into a poor family the payment could mean the difference between life and death.

ABORTION, CONTRACEPTION AND THE EXPOSURE OF CHILDREN

Augustus was so worried about the falling birth rate – and thus the future lack of citizens to serve in the army – that he introduced laws and incentives designed to encourage Romans to have children. Couples who had three children were rewarded; widows were obliged to remarry within two years, and divorcees within eighteen months. Some of the old rules forbidding marriage between classes were relaxed, and for the first time the freeborn could marry freed slaves.

There were many reasons for the low birth rate in Imperial Rome. Because dowries were high, fathers could be financially crippled by marrying off daughters. Infant girls were often exposed and left to die – a practice that was actually condoned by an ancient law (according to legend, introduced by Romulus) which stated that parents were obliged to raise all male babies but only the firstborn girl. There were even special places to leave unwanted children, where they could be picked up and kept as future slaves or prostitutes. Infanticide was not banned until the fourth century – even the usually shrewd Augustus forgot that girls were the future mothers of potential troops.

Large families were not popular. For the wealthy, numerous children meant dividing up the family property when they came of age; for the poor they posed the problem of too many mouths to feed. The bread dole [*annona*] was for men only (see p.208), and until Trajan introduced the *alimenta* there was nothing to help feed the children.

The recommended forms of contraception read like the script of a Pasolini or Almodóvar movie. There was quite a choice: a dose of snail excrement or pigeon droppings taken with wine and oil; mouse dung 'applied in the form of a liniment'; or the insertion of black pepper into the uterus after sex. It was also suggested that a woman could be turned off intercourse if her loins were 'rubbed with blood taken from the ticks on a wild black bull'. For those without the time to collect excrement and flea's blood, there were less kinky methods. Women were instructed to hold their breath at ejaculation, and to have a post-coital squat, sneeze and cold drink; and there may also have been primitive forms of familiar devices: diaphragms made of wool impregnated with gum, and goats' bladders used as condoms.

Abortion was also fairly common, and notwithstanding the Romans' sanguine attitude to infanticide, it was condemned by men. The reason? The woman was destroying the man's property. Ovid, discovering that his lover has aborted, is at first upset: 'Corinna got pregnant,' he wrote, 'and rashly tried an abortion. Now she's lying in danger of her life. She said not a word . . . I ought to be furious, but I'm only scared.' Later he *is* furious: 'Life is a prize well worth the waiting. Why probe your entrails with lethal instruments? Why poison what's still unborn?' A common accusation was that women aborted in order to maintain their figures.

Other theories about the reason for the low birth rate range from lead poisoning and cervical cancer to too many hot baths and mass alcoholism. Lead was present not only in make-up but in water and food – pipes, cups and pans were made of lead – and lead poisoning renders men impotent and causes miscarriages and stillbirths. The cervical cancer theory is based on the fact that Romans married young, and sex at an early age increases the risk of sexual disease; the impotence-through-alcohol notion is based on the fact that the alcohol content of Roman wine was 17%, and the poet Martial writes about drinking five pints of the stuff in a single afternoon. The most bizarre hypothesis, however, derives from the Romans' habit of taking a hot daily bath. Recent experiments in America have revealed that hot baths (and Roman hot baths were very hot) reduce sperm production.

Arch of Septimius Severus and The Syrian Empresses

This triumphal arch, one of the most striking monuments of the Forum, was erected in AD 203 to celebrate the tenth year of Emperor Septimius Severus's reign. It was dedicated to Septimius and his two sons, Caracalla and Geta – Septimius's wife, Julia Domna, is conspicuous by her absence. Julia was a Syrian princess who became the Emperor's second wife allegedly because he had read and liked her horoscope. She accompanied Septimius to England, where he was attempting to keep the Scots out, and after he died in York his sons (who loathed one another) returned to Rome with Julia. Julia supported Geta, but Caracalla had him stabbed to death while she was cuddling him, and surrounded her with spies, forbidding her to weep even in private.

Julia's sister, Julia Maesa, was made of sterner stuff, and after Caracalla and his successor had been assassinated (the latter on her orders) she succeeded in having her fourteen-year-old grandson, Elagabalus (who named himself after a Syrian sun god), placed on the throne. Vain, campish and completely insane, he entered Rome in the guise of the god, dressed in silver and gold, crowned with jewels, with his cheeks rouged and his eyebrows blackened. He built a temple to the god Elagabalus on the Palatine, where festivals were celebrated by Syrian strippers and copious quantities of rich wine. The Imperial palace was taken over by concubines and catamites who lounged all day on cushions stuffed with crocus petals, while Elagabalus, who had by then taken to dressing as a woman, gave all the most important jobs in Rome to his lovers, and raped a Vestal Virgin. The Romans were horrified, and Julia Maesa, realising that if Elagabalus fell she would be ruined, decided to have him and his mother assassinated. Thirteen-year-old Alexander Severus, son of her other daughter, Julia Mammaea, took over as emperor in 222. Julia Maesa died naturally in 226; Julia Mammaea and Alexander Severus ran the Empire together until 235, when they were murdered at an army camp by mutinying soldiers.

The Rostra and Female Dissenters

According to Shakespeare (who got his information from Plutarch), it was from this rickety stone dais that Mark Antony made his

'Friends, Romans, Countrymen' speech after Caesar's murder. It was also here that the head and hands of Cicero were displayed (apparently his tongue was skewered with a hairpin by Antony's wife Fulvia). Augustus (then known as Octavian) had condemned him to death because he feared that the ancient Republican statesman and powerful orator would become a focus for dissenters.

At the same time three hundred Senators and three thousand *equites* (wealthy men of property) were 'proscribed', and many were killed before they managed to escape. Their wives were allowed to remain, but 1400 of them were subjected to heavy taxes. They marched on the Forum, where Hortensia, daughter of an orator, made a speech: 'Why should we pay taxes when we do not share in the offices, honours, military commands, nor, in short, the government, for which you fight between yourselves with such harmful results?' The crowds were won over, and the next day the Triumvirate (a gang of three consisting of Octavian, Mark Antony and Lepidus) decided to tax only 400 of the women and to get the rest of the required revenue from wealthy men.

A few years later the Rostra was the scene of a very different form of female dissent. Augustus's daughter Julia, tired (after three arranged marriages) of being a pawn in her father's dynastic game, rebelled. She began to spend all her time with Augustus's enemies, and was accused of being promiscuous and making love on the Rostra. These accusations may have been false, but if they were true she could hardly have found a better way of ridiculing her father's new morality laws.

Temple of Saturn

In the fenced-off area behind the Rostra are eight columns forming one corner of a temple to Saturn. Saturn was the legendary god-king of Italy, who had introduced the art of agriculture and reigned over a mythical Golden Age in which the earth flourished and war, slavery and private property did not exist. His appeal to the lower classes is obvious, and the temple was the focus of the annual Saturnalia. From 17 December for between three and seven days schools closed, slaves would dine with their masters, presents were exchanged, and a fair and market were held in the Campus Martius. At first the only gifts on sale were little images made of earthenware or pastry, but – as with the Christianised version of the Saturnalia, Christmas – things soon became more commercialised. The presents haven't changed much – even then people were giving one another woolly slippers, socks and scarves – and the misogynistic poet Juvenal reckoned that the Saturnalia was an excuse for women to go on a shopping spree, buying crystal vases, myrrh jars and jewellery.

Lady Elizabeth Foster and the Column of Phocas

The column of Phocas was the last monument to be erected in the Forum, and stands on an overgrown podium. It was placed here in AD 608 in honour of the Byzantine Emperor Phocas, who had just given the Pantheon to the Pope. At the time Rome was part of (and effectively owned by) the Byzantine Empire, and the column may have been erected as a thank-you present.

The column had always been visible, but it wasn't until 1816, when the base was unearthed, that anyone knew what it was. The excavation was financed by Lady Elizabeth Foster, the widow of the fifth Duke of Devonshire. She came to live in Rome, and her *salons* became *the* fashionable focus of intellectual life among expatriates. She was passionately interested in the Classics, printed private editions of Horace and Virgil, and in her youth had so enraptured Edward Gibbon, author of *The Decline and Fall of the Roman Empire*, that he proposed to her. She turned him down.

The Basilica Julia

Julius Caesar began building this massive basilica in 54 BC, and after his assassination it was finished off by Augustus. In common with virtually every other building in the Forum, it suffered its share of fires and war damage, and today virtually nothing is left but its pavement and column bases.

Fortunately, activities in the basilica are well documented, as it was here that most of Rome's civil cases were tried. There was room for four cases to be tried at once, though as the 'courts' were split off from one another only by screens or curtains, lawyers with loud voices could be heard throughout the building. Matters were made worse by the use of professional clappers, an ancient Roman version of rent-a-mob, who hired themselves out to the highest bidder, and applauded riotously whenever 'their' lawyer made a positive point. This was supposed to impress the magistrates. The applauders spent the time in between cases playing chequers on the basilica's steps, as evidenced by the boards carved into the stone.

ADULTERY, MARRIAGE, DIVORCE AND THE EMANCIPATION OF WOMEN

In the beginning, Roman law, as it concerned women, was based on two premises: the weakness [*infirmitas sexus*] and light-headedness [*levitas animi*] of the female sex. Consequently, the leading male [*pater familias*] in a family had absolute power over his female relatives. The *pater familias* had the right to kill a woman for committing adultery or drinking wine, and when he died the custody of the women in his family passed over to the nearest male relative.

In the first century AD Augustus gave women the chance to emancipate themselves from their guardians as a reward for having three or more children. It is also obvious that few fathers actually killed adulterous daughters, because Augustus considered that making adultery a public offence, punishable by banishment to an island, would deter women from extramarital liaisons. Bleak as this was, it was hardly a fate worse than death. The most famous exile for adultery was Augustus's own daughter, Julia.

Although Augustus forbade men from having affairs with unmarried or widowed upper-class women, they were permitted to fraternise with prostitutes or slaves. Upper-class women were forbidden to have any extramarital affairs, and some protested by registering as prostitutes. This legal loophole was closed by Tiberius, Augustus's successor and – not entirely coincidentally – Julia's cuckolded husband. He banned women whose fathers, grandfathers or husbands were Senators or knights from applying to be prostitutes.

When a woman married she could either remain under the jurisdiction of her own family, or transfer to that of her husband. The former became increasingly popular. For the woman's family it meant that if she died, her property would revert to them; for her husband's family it meant that she had no rights to their property. For women it meant more freedom – they lived apart from the man who had absolute power over them, and with a man who had no formal power. Obviously, as the powers of the *pater familias* weakened, women became even freer.

Conservatives and chauvinists disapproved, and Roman poetry is packed with scandalous stories about the sexual exploits of women in the Late Republic and Empire. Augustus set up a special court to deal with cases of adultery, but by the end of the first century the law was virtually forgotten. Other emperors attempted to reintroduce it, but to little effect.

The chauvinists also deplored the fact that some women were intruding on traditionally male preserves. Juvenal mocks women who studied law, followed politics, discussed military strategies, indulged in literary criticism, or hunted, wrestled and fenced. Such women were probably aristocratic and exceptional, and if the funeral inscriptions on the tombs of less privileged women are anything to go by, the majority of women lived as obedient mothers and wives.

Divorce was easy. Men needed to be able to make and break their marriages (and often those of their children) to suit their political or financial purposes. Augustus's sister Octavia, his daughter Julia, and even his stepson Tiberius were so treated (although Octavia refused to divorce Mark Antony even when he was living with Cleopatra). All that was required was the couple's consent and seven witnesses. Women had the right to take a court action to reclaim their dowries, though deductions were made for misbehaviour, extravagance and the care of the children, who remained with their fathers. The reason for the return of the dowry was that Augustus was anxious for women to marry again, which was impossible without a dowry, and start producing more children. Women had the equal right to initiate divorce proceedings, and again became the butt of the chauvinist satirists. Juvenal mentions (or invents) a woman who has eight husbands in five years, while Martial reckoned that marriage had become a legalised form of adultery.

Temple of Castor and Pollux

Soaring above the Basilica Julia are three fluted columns supporting a slice of entablature, the ruins of a temple dedicated to Castor and Pollux. Better known as the twin brothers of Helen of Troy and the result of Jupiter's rape (in the guise of a swan) of Leda, they were also skilled horsemen. According to legend, the Romans were fighting against the Tarquins (deposed after one of them had raped Lucretia) when the twin gods appeared on the battlefield and made sure the Romans won. Immediately afterwards they materialised in the Forum, and the temple is said to mark the spot from which they gave the good news to the crowd.

THE VESTAL VIRGINS

The cult of Vesta, goddess of fire, is one of the oldest in Rome – priestesses devoted to keeping the communal fire burning, were at work back in the eighth century BC. The origins of the cult are easy to understand, for keeping a fire alight was obviously crucial for a primitive community's survival. In time, however, Rome became more sophisticated and no longer depended on a constantly burning fire for its wellbeing. Consequently, the priestesses' literal responsibility for the life of the community transmuted into a symbolic and moral one. Keeping their virginity intact was deemed to be as crucial to Rome's survival as the constant flickering of the sacred flame.

There were six priestesses, known as Vestal Virgins, who were selected by the chief priest, or *pontifex maximus*, from among the daughters of the nobility when they were between six and ten years old. Once they had been chosen, they were taken to the house of the Vestals, where they would live throughout their thirty-year period of duty. The first ten years were spent learning the sacred, secret duties; the next ten performing them; and the final ten teaching them to novices. They were bound by a vow of chastity, but were allowed to marry once their thirty years were up. Not surprisingly, few of them did.

When girls became Vestals their hair was cut off, and hung on a lotus tree as an offering. When it regrew it was parted six ways and arranged into little cushions supplemented by pads of artificial hair. They wore long white gowns, and when they were sacrificing they put on a white hood bordered with purple, which was held in place with a brooch – the only jewellery they were allowed. Apart from keeping the fire burning (no easy matter during wind and rain in a temple with a vent in its roof) their duties ranged from guarding secret documents and assisting at the consecration of temples to sweeping the temple and preparing special cakes to be offered at sacrifice. If a Vestal let the fire go out she was whipped by the *pontifex maximus* and expelled from the cult. If she broke her vow of chastity she was publicly whipped, and then buried alive (under present-day Piazza dell'Independenza). Her lover was flogged to death in the Forum. Whenever a Vestal was caught *in flagrante delicto* it was seen as a bad augury for Rome, and if the discovery of a misbehaving Vestal happened to coincide with a military defeat, it conveniently let the army off the hook.

The Temple of Vesta

This delicate temple, originally encircled by a double ring of Corinthian columns, was partially reconstructed in the 1930s. Although there have been numerous temples on the site (it burnt down several times) they have all been circular, probably to recall the round huts in which the earliest Roman tribes lived. In the centre of the temple is the *adytum*, a secret chamber which sheltered precious documents and a collection of weird and wonderful relics which Aeneas was supposed to have brought from Troy. They included a needle used by Cybele, the mother of the gods, and the Palladium, a wooden statue of Pallas Athena, the Greek virgin goddess of wisdom and victory. Only the Vestals and the *pontifex maximus* were allowed inside, but Emperor Elagabalus (who also raped a Vestal) ignored the rule, broke in, stole what he thought was the Pallas Athena, and placed it in his own temple on the Palatine. Fortunately, the Vestals had already hidden the original and replaced it with a fake.

The cult of the Vestals survived until AD 394 – long after the emperors had become Christians. It was eventually abolished by Emperor Theodosius, influenced by his niece, Serena, who was violently opposed to paganism, but hardly a model Christian: she stole a priceless necklace from the temple.

The House of the Vestals

The house where the Vestals lived was enormous. The current ruins, dating from the second century AD, include the foundations of about fifty rooms, and there were certainly two, if not three, upper floors. Most of the ground floor was probably used for storage and carrying out the more domestic of the Vestals' tasks, and it is thought that the *pontifex maximus* also lived in the house. Nevertheless, it is hard to imagine how all the rooms were used.

The courtyard is one of the loveliest parts of the Forum. A rose garden has been planted around three small ponds with water lilies and goldfish, and along one side is a row of (mostly headless) statues of Vestals. The rooms around the courtyard are well preserved, though unfortunately they are usually closed to the public. Along the east side is a large hall flanked by smaller rooms, and the series of small rooms along the south side includes a grinding room (with the remains of a mill) and a bakehouse, which were probably used for making the sacrificial cakes. A mossy staircase still leads to an upper floor.

Temple of Julius Caesar

These chunky, rubbly walls belong to a temple built by Augustus in 29 BC on the site where Caesar's body was cremated (the exact spot is marked by a round altar). Julius Caesar was assassinated in the Theatre of Pompey, having ignored the premonitions of his wife, Calpurnia.

Temple of Antoninus and Faustina

Converting pagan temples into churches was a common practice in medieval Rome, and this is a particularly striking example, with a Baroque pediment (which bears an odd resemblance to the 'Batman' motif) poking above a colonnaded porch. The temple was built by the Senate in honour of the late Empress Faustina, who had died in AD 141. Her husband Antoninus commemorated her in a more practical way, founding a charity to care for young girls. Antoninus outlived Faustina by twenty years, but when he died the temple was rededicated to him as well.

Temple of Romulus and a Republican Brothel

The fourth-century temple of Romulus, a circular domed brick building, was converted into the vestibule of a church, SS Cosma e Damiano, in the sixth century. Ironically, it stood right next to the remains of a Republican-era brothel – to the left of the temple there are still traces of a dank, weedy row of rooms with a corridor between them.

PROSTITUTION

Prostitution was legal in ancient Rome, husbands were permitted by law to attend brothels, and prostitutes were taxed. Many of the taverns doubled as brothels, and the women selected to work as waitresses and bar staff were usually chosen for their looks and expected to service clients in upstairs rooms.

Prostitution was so lucrative that pimps and madames considered it worthwhile to pick up abandoned baby girls and feed them until they were old enough to work. Masters often profited by sending their slaves (boys and men as well as women) to work as prostitutes in public baths and army barracks, and at sports arenas like the Circus Maximus. Poor freed- and freeborn women worked as prostitutes outdoors, traditionally under arches – the word fornicate comes from fornix, the Latin for arch.

Some masters, like Cato, charged their male slaves a fee for sex with their female slaves. It was also acceptable for masters to use female slaves as private whores, and wives were expected to condone this. When Scipio Africanus died, his wife gave his favourite slave-girl her freedom.

Roman poetry is full of scandalous stories about aristocratic women who slept with slaves or led double lives as whores. Messalina was accused of sloping off at night to have fun in brothels, as was Catullus's lover Lesbia. There may, however, have been more to the accusations than mere misogyny – some wealthy women registered as prostitutes in protest against the double standard which allowed only men to have extramarital sex.

Basilica of Maxentius and Constantine

The three colossal coffered barrel vaults dominating the eastern end of the Forum are all that remains of an immense basilica begun by Maxentius and completed after he had been killed at the Battle of the Milvian Bridge by his rival and co-Emperor Constantine. Both Bramante and Michelangelo studied the vaults when they were designing St Peter's, and the gilded tiles which once covered its roof were stripped off in the seventh century to adorn old St Peter's.

Santa Francesca Romana/a.k.a. Santa Maria Nova

This undistinguished-looking Baroque church is named for Francesca

Bussi, a fourteenth-century housewife from Trastevere (see box, p. 145) whose relics are kept inside. It is usually closed, but her body is supposed to be displayed on the ninth of every month.

For years on end, Francesca was consistently aware of her guardian angel watching over her. For this reason, she was made the patron saint of motorists – so next time you're wondering how Roman drivers have the nerve to be so reckless, remember they are being protected by Santa Francesca. On her feast day, 9 March, all the city's buses and trams are blessed, and the road outside the church is packed with cars whose drivers are seeking her blessing.

Arch of Titus

Domitian built this triumphal arch in AD 81 to honour the victories of his brother, Emperor Titus, and his father, Vespasian, in the Judaean War, a conflict which exploded partly because the Jews were sick of being fleeced by greedy Roman officials. The hostilities lasted for years, but eventually the Romans won, and sacked Jerusalem.

Among the eroded reliefs you may just be able to make out a procession of people triumphantly brandishing the spoils from Solomon's temple (including a seven-branched candelabra), and another procession in which a figure representing a defeated Jordan is carried on a stretcher. In the centre Titus, who was deified after his death, is shown being transported to Heaven by an eagle.

Antiquarium Forense

This museum, housed in the old convent of Santa Francesca Romana, is devoted to prehistoric graves, sculptured fragments and miscellaneous trinkets discovered in the Forum area. The museum itself is a sombre, old-fashioned place with dusty glass cases, labels calligraphed in faded ink, and yellowed photographs of august archaeologists. There are, however, some evocative finds – tree trunks containing crumbled bones, and a woman buried with her newly born child. Also worth a look are the iridescent glass vials, miniature statues of priestesses, lamps, and fragments of fine imported pottery discovered around the Vestals' house, which give some idea of the style in which the priestesses lived. On the upper floor (currently closed) is a sixth-century fresco of the Virgin as Queen of Heaven (Maria Regina), possibly the first time she was shown in such a role. It comes from the (closed) church of Santa Maria in Antiqua on the far edge of the Forum – the first church in Rome where ecclesiasts, instead of emperors, began to care for the sick and old, and to distribute food.

Temple of Venus and Rome

Built by Hadrian in the second century, this was the largest temple in Rome, though the site it occupies was merely the vestibule to Nero's Golden House (see p.217). It was designed by Hadrian, and when the architect Apollodorus of Damascus criticised him for creating statues which were too big for their niches, Hadrian had him killed. The temple looks pretty impressive today because many of the columns have been re-erected. There's no access, but there are good views of the temple from the upper tier of the Colosseum.

WOMEN AND RELIGION

There were two kinds of religion in ancient Rome: state-approved cults on which the survival of Rome was believed to hinge, and imported Greek and oriental cults which concentrated on the individual. The former were worshipped out of fear of what the Deity would do if he or she were neglected; the latter gave its initiates the chance to escape from the repressions of everyday life. Most important of the official religions was the cult of Vesta, and if any one of her priestesses lost her virginity it was considered a national disaster (see Vestals: box p.190). Other official religions, too, were designed to encourage female chastity. The specific cult to which a woman belonged depended on age and class, for Roman religions were as rigidly stratified as society.

Adolescent girls worshipped Fortuna Virginalis, and when they came of age they dedicated the togas they had worn as children to her. Afterwards they wore the long tunic known as a *stola*. On marriage women transferred to Fortuna Primigenia or Fortuna Lucina, the patroness of childbirth.

Upper-class women who remained with one husband throughout their lives (known as *univirae*) were permitted to attend the rites of the Bona Dea (Good Goddess) held annually in the house of the consul (who absented himself for the evening). In 63 BC they were held in Julius Caesar's house, and his wife Pompeia's lover, Publius Clodius, disguised himself as a woman and broke in. This also portended disaster for Rome, and Caesar promptly divorced Pompeia.

Other cults for *univirae* included Mater Matuta (the Good Mother) – at which a slave woman was ritually (and violently) expelled – and Patrician Chastity. After a woman named Verginia was excluded from the latter because she had married a plebeian, she founded a shrine dedicated to Plebeian Chastity. Within a year it was discovered that adulterous women were worshipping at the shrine, so the cult of Venus Obsequens (the compliant, or easy, Venus) was set up to shame them.

Prostitutes and women who were openly concerned about the quantity and quality of their sex lives worshipped Fortuna Virilis (Virile Fortune). To persuade them to mend their ways there was the shrine of Venus Verticordia, who was deemed to have the power to change a heart towards virtue. If the accounts of male authors mourning the moral degeneracy of Rome are to be believed, the ceremonies and shrines were much abused. Juvenal accused women of fixing a dildo on to the statue of Chastity. Many of the rites connected with the foreign cults were explicitly sexual. Initiates reached a state of ecstasy through sex, drink, dancing and possibly drugs. Priests castrated themselves in the service of the fertility goddess, Cybele (see p.200), and once men were admitted to the initially women-only rites of Bacchus, mass orgies ensued. In 186 BC a thousand Bacchantes were executed on a charge of immoral behaviour.

The most popular cult, however, for both women and lower-class men, was that of Isis (see p.82).

Same ticket and opening hours as the Forum

The Beverly Hills of ancient Rome, the Palatine is now the loveliest of Rome's ancient sites. Its slopes are shaded with pines, and in spring the relics of palaces and temples stand on a plateau sprinkled with wild flowers, fennel and acanthus. There's not a great deal left of the buildings, and making sense of their layout is pretty demanding, but it's a lovely place to wander, and with a bit of effort you *can* imagine its former splendour.

The Palatine was a twin-peaked hill on which, according to legend, Romulus and Remus were brought up by a she-wolf in a cave, and on which Romulus later founded the village that was to become Rome. The cave has yet to be located, but earlier this century traces of a ninth-century BC hut-village were discovered. The legend gave the hill a special significance, but in the late Republic it was the appeal of its leafy slopes, breezes and distance from the chaos of the city that made it Rome's most desirable residential area.

Home to the glitterati of the late Republic and some of the more scandalous members of the Imperial family, the Palatine was for centuries a hotbed of adultery, incest and political intrigue. In the last decadent years of the Republic the erotic poet Catullus lived here and had a steamy affair with Clodia Metelli, while her brother Publius Clodius embroiled Julius Caesar's wife Pompeiia in a ridiculous scandal which led to their divorce. Augustus was born and lived here, and both Tiberius and Caligula built palaces. Tiberius was no saint, but Caligula's exploits – if his biographer, Suetonius, is correct – were particularly nasty. He slept with and later exiled his sisters, banned catamites (despite his own delight in young boys), and forced respectable Roman matrons to parade in front of him so that he could select a partner for the night. He would then report on their performance to his cronies. His behaviour with his fourth wife Caesonia was no better. He displayed her naked before his friends, and spiced up their lovemaking by whispering threats of torture into her ear. Apparently Caesonia was more than a match for him.

The Site The cleft between the hill's two peaks, known as the Palatinus and Germalus, was filled in by Domitian to create a platform for a vast new palace, the Domus Flavia, which remained the Imperial headquarters for 300 years. After the fall of the Empire, Popes occasionally lived here; in the Middle Ages aristocratic families like the Frangipani built castles over the ruins; and in the sixteenth century Cardinal Alessandro Farnese laid out a vast botanical garden over the remains of the palace of Tiberius.

Contemporary accounts describe houses with bronze floors and ivory doors. Such easily reusable interior decor has long since vanished, but if/when the Palatine's museum, the Antiquarium Palatino, reopens, you should be able to see some fine Republican-era frescoes. There are also vivid *trompe l'œil* decorations in the so-called House of Augustus, and stuccoes and frescoes in a series of houses and a temple of Isis which lie underneath Domitian's palace. Unfortunately, these have been closed to the public for some time, and at present the only frescoes on show are the extremely faded ones in the so-called House of Livia.

One ticket buys access to both the Palatine and the Forum, and the sites are linked by the Clivus Palatinus. If you want to visit the Palatine first, the main entrance is on Via San Gregorio along the road from the Arch of Constantine.

LESBIA AND CATULLUS

Lesbia
  live with me
& love me so
we'll laugh at all
the sour-faced strictures of the old and wise . . .
(Catullus)

nothing is
left of me
each time I see her . . .
tongue numbed; arms, legs
melting, on fire; drum
drumming in ears
(Catullus translating Sappho)

The Lesbia of Catullus's poems was Clodia Metelli, wife of a politician. She ran a *salon* for bright young poets, lawyers and politicians, perhaps modelling herself on the intellectual courtesans, or *hetaerae*, of ancient Greece. Her relationship with Catullus was stormy, passionate and at times painful, and the moods of his poems range from deliriously happy to savagely vitriolic.

Clodia became embroiled in a vicious lawsuit when her brother, Publius Clodius, accused a lawyer and follower of Cicero of seducing her. Cicero, who also lived on the Palatine, was a leading figure in the conservative, senatorial party, and a bitter opponent of Publius. He retaliated by accusing Clodia in court of being a prostitute and of having an incestuous relationship with her brother. Catullus joined in the character assassination, writing poems in which Clodia/Lesbia hangs out in unsavoury taverns and on street corners offering sexual favours to all comers. Cicero's motives for destroying the reputation of an enemy's sister are clear; in addition, he was a conservative who considered that any woman who wasn't a demure, faithful wife must be a whore. As for Catullus, he was infatuated with Clodia, and one suspects that the source of his vitriol was an injured ego.

The Flavian Palace

When Domitian succeeded to the throne in AD 81 he decided to have a splendid new palace built. The site he selected was on the Palatine – which, as the traditional birthplace of Rome and former home of Emperor Augustus, was clearly a fitting location for the Imperial headquarters. The site, however, was problematic, for the western ridge was covered with temples and the eastern ridge was steeply sloped. The architect, Rabirius, decided to reshape the eastern ridge. He dug a massive step out of its steep southern slope and used the excavated soil to create a big flat platform at a higher level. In the process several buildings from the Republican era were buried and, incidentally, preserved (see below).

The palace was laid out on the two levels. The official residence, or Domus Flavia, was on the upper platform; the private wing, or Domus Augustana, was split-level; and the garden (commonly mistaken for a stadium) lay on the lower level.

Domitian and the Domus Flavia

According to the biographer of emperors, Suetonius, Domitian was vindictive, paranoid and hypocritical. In a crusade against public immorality he routed out corrupt magistrates, tightened up marriage laws, restored a shrine to Plebeian Chastity and conducted increasingly severe trials against Vestal Virgins accused of taking lovers. Yet he was no model of virtue himself, and used and abused the law as it suited him. He had numerous affairs with married women, yet introduced a law forbidding women of 'notorious bad character' to take up inheritances; he stole his wife Domitia from another man and had him executed for complaining; and having seduced and impregnated his niece, Julia, he forced her to have an abortion from which she died.

Column bases and fragments of walls mark the outline of the vast official wing. You can just make out the shape of the **Basilica**, where Domitian dispensed 'justice', the throne room (**Aula Regia**) where he held court overlooked by a row of colossal statues, and the **Lararium**, a shrine to the household gods which is now unceremoniously covered with a plastic corrugated roof. The **peristyle**, or courtyard, has a flower bed laid out like a maze in its centre, which follows the pattern of a fountain pool. Originally the courtyard's walls were lined with shiny selenite because Domitian, who was (not without reason) afraid of being assassinated, wanted them to act as mirrors, so that he could see if anyone approached him from behind.

The best-preserved room is the **triclinium**, or dining-room, which retains a flame-pink and yellow marble floor (unfortunately this is sometimes covered with a protective layer of gauze and gravel) and a dais backed by an apse in which the Emperor dined (presumably so that no one could creep up behind him). The floor was raised on brick pillars (you can see them in the centre) beneath which air, heated by an underground stove, wafted and warmed the room. On either side of the room you can make out the shapes of windows which still look on to two **nymphaea**, miniature oval rooms with the remains of decorative fountains.

Domitian was eventually killed after dinner in his bedroom. The hit man appears to have been Stephanus, the steward of Domitian's surviving niece, Domitilla, who brought Domitian a document and stabbed him in the groin while he was reading it. As Domitian had recently had Domitilla's husband executed on some flimsy charge (as well as being responsible for the death of her cousin, Julia) it is tempting to believe that Domitilla may have been behind the murder. Domitia was also suspected, perhaps because Domitian had executed her lover, Paris, with whom he was himself infatuated.

Domus Augustana The residential wing of the Domus Flavia is closed to visitors, which is a pity, as Rabirius gave his imagination free rein here. You have to make do with looking down on a sunken courtyard set around a decorative basin, and imagining the rest. Rooms were intricately shaped and paved with coloured marble, while staircases were lit by sun reflecting on pools lined with glass mosaic.

The Hippodrome This great sunken oval is usually referred to as a stadium or hippodrome, though it is more probable that it was planned as a garden. Column fragments and traces of arches in the brick walls mark the position of a two-storey portico, and the great curved recess in the south-west wall was probably for the Emperor to sit in. The running track was added by Theodoric, King of the Ostrogoths, in the sixth century.

To visit the rest of the Palatine's sites, return to the Domus Flavia and walk past the rubbly mound marked Temple of Apollo.

The Temple of Apollo and the Sibylline Books

All that remains of this temple, built by Augustus in 28 BC, is a rubbly mound. He deposited the Sibylline Books inside, secret tomes filled with prophecies about Rome, described by anthropologist James Frazer as a 'convenient farrago of nonsense'. The books were supposed to have been written (in Greek) by the Cumaean Sibyl, a prophetess of Apollo who lived in Cumae near Naples. If Rome had a problem, the Sibylline Books fixed it. As famine, plague or a foreign invasion was considered to be a punishment for the people's lack of faith, the solution was usually building a new temple, or performing a sacrifice to placate the god or goddess in question. Occasionally human sacrifice was called for – after a Celtic tribe had invaded up north in 225 BC the Romans obediently followed the instructions of the Sibyl and buried alive two Greek men and women and two Gauls in the Forum Boarium (Piazza Bocca della Verità). In the more cynical days of the Empire, after Rome had been ravaged by a fire (which was probably Nero's method of slum clearance) the Sibyl's solution – asking married women to sprinkle a shrine with sea water – was considered inadequate, so Nero took matters into his own hands and persecuted the Christians.

The Houses of Augustus and Livia

Augustus and Livia lived in a fairly modest late-Republican house on the Palatine which had once belonged to the orator Hortensius, father of the Hortensia whose speech in the Forum won tax exemption for a thousand women (see p.186). It is thought that the so-called House of Augustus was the public part of the Imperial household, and that the family occupied the House of Livia. Both houses are well preserved – inside and out – but usually only the House of Livia is open.

The couple lived a fairly frugal life, largely because Augustus wanted his family to set an example to other Romans. Livia and his daughter Julia were expected to spin and weave his clothes, and as Augustus felt the cold and wore four tunics, a woollen vest, underpants, gown and gaiters, they had their work cut out. For the slaves, feeding Augustus was an undemanding task, as he lived largely on bread, dates and grapes.

In order to preserve the frescoes which decorated the house they have been detached from the walls, but most of them hang in their original positions. Steps lead down to a narrow, mosaic-paved corridor which runs into a small courtyard. The frescoed walls were designed to look like marble, and though they are very faded you can still make out fake veining and moulding. Off the courtyard are three reception rooms. The central room has a barely visible scene showing the giant Polyphemus chasing the goddess Galatea into the sea, and a slightly better-preserved one of Hermes coming to rescue Io from her hundred-eyed guard, Argos. Fixed to the wall is a slice of lead piping engraved IVLIAE AV (Julia Augusta), one of Livia's official titles. The imaginary creatures which decorated the left-hand room have almost vanished, though you can just make out a symmetrical pair of griffins. A yellow frieze runs around the right-hand room, which was originally painted with miniature land- and cityscapes – all you can see now is a faded street scene.

LIVIA

Livia was born into one of Rome's oldest aristocratic families, the Claudians, and her ancestors included many powerful politicians. Livia's father had fought against the pro-

Caesar party (which was led by Octavian, the future Augustus) at Philippi and, like Brutus and Cassius, had committed suicide when they lost the battle. Her first husband, Claudius Nero, had also taken up arms against Octavian, and when Octavian and his army besieged Perusia (modern Perugia) Livia was probably inside the walls with her young son, Tiberius. Despite the fact that they were technically enemies, Octavian became obsessed with Livia, divorced his wife Scribonia, and took her away from her husband, although she was pregnant at the time. What Livia felt about this is not known.

According to the ancient historians, Livia was ruthlessly ambitious for Tiberius and eliminated all his rivals to the throne. Nevertheless, their relationship is described as fraught, and Suetonius has Tiberius accusing his mother of wanting to be his co-Emperor; telling her to remember that she was 'only a woman'; and, when she insisted that a certain citizen was enrolled as a juror, agreeing to do so only if the entry was marked 'forced upon the emperor by his mother'. Livia retaliated by showing him some of Augustus's old letters, in which he described Tiberius as sour and stubborn. Shortly afterwards Tiberius retired to Capri and, when Livia died, refused to attend her funeral or allow her to be deified.

The Temple of Cybele

There is virtually nothing to see of the Temple of Cybele, an Asiatic fertility goddess whose cult was once one of the most popular in Rome. The cult had been introduced on the advice of the Sibylline Books in 225 BC, when Rome was struggling against Hannibal. Cybele's three-day festival was celebrated from the 22nd to the 24th of March, and the third day was, with reason, called the Day of Blood. The high priest slashed his arms and presented his blood as an offering to the goddess; then the lesser clergy, accompanied by clashing cymbals, drums, bellowing horns and screeching flutes, danced themselves into a frenzy and hacked their bodies with potsherds and knives. This was probably followed by a castration ceremony, for such was the price of entering the service of the goddess. Apparently the novices' severed parts were dashed against the statue of Cybele, then buried in order to hasten the spring. Only foreigners were permitted to mutilate themselves – any Roman citizen who did so was banished.

The Cryptoporticus and Farnese Gardens

The Cryptoporticus is a long underground vaulted tunnel, built by Nero to connect the Golden House with the palaces on the Palatine. After the Domus Flavia had been built, another branch was added to the passage.

The palaces of Tiberius and Caligula were covered over by the Farnese Gardens, laid out for Cardinal Alessandro Farnese in the sixteenth century, but the Cryptoporticus still retains portions of its stuccoed ceiling, though it is more often vaulted by trees. At intervals mossy flights of steps lead up to the Farnese Gardens, whose neatly hedged pathways lead past rose gardens to a decayed pavilion and terrace, from which there are wonderful views of the Forum.

Wealthy Renaissance Romans were fond of having gardens away from their homes, where they could retreat for evening strolls and dinner parties. The Cardinal was at the centre of a ritzy set of brilliant men and beautiful courtesans, one of whom, Isabella da Luna, left a good deal of her considerable fortune to Alessandro. She owed her success as much to her quick tongue and sense of humour as to her looks, and one occasion, when she was issued with a summons for a debt she had refused to pay, she ripped it up and pretended to wipe her rump with the paper. She was imprisoned, taken to court and punished by having her bare bottom beaten in public. When the beating was over, she stood up, shook her skirts down, and managed to walk away without betraying any sign of pain or humiliation. After this episode her popularity increased, and she died a wealthy woman.

The Colosseum

Open 9 a.m.–6 p.m. (Oct–April 3 p.m.), except Wed and Sun 9 a.m.–1 p.m.

Within the arcaded travertine tiers of the Colosseum, audiences of 55,000 were entertained by gladiators fighting to the death and by the mass slaughter of wild animals. Today, looped by belts of traffic and with a metro line running virtually underneath it, the most famous ancient building in Rome is in danger of collapse from pollution and vibration. A major restoration is on the cards.

The Colosseum was built by Emperor Vespasian in the AD seventies on the site of an artificial lake in the grounds of Nero's Golden House. It was just two years since Nero had been assassinated, and his vast palace was a constant reminder of Imperial excess. By filling in the lake and building a public amphitheatre on top (blood sports had hitherto been held in temporary theatres) Vespasian intended to signal that a new era had begun. His propagandist, the poet Martial, relayed the message: 'What was formerly a tyrant's delight is now the delight of the people'.

What delighted the people was carnage on an unprecedented scale. At the inaugural games in AD 80, presided over by Vespasian's son and successor, Titus (Vespasian died in AD 79), nine thousand wild animals and scores of gladiators were killed by men and 'common women'. There is no record of how many women took to the arena, but gladiators were usually male slaves, war captives, or condemned prisoners, who lived and were trained in a nearby barracks. Successful male gladiators became instant sex symbols, and the glamour and kudos of standing in the arena fighting for one's life tempted some upper-class women to train as gladiators. According to Tacitus they usually made fools of themselves. Emperor Domitian, on the other hand, loved watching the women fight at night in the torchlit amphitheatre, and his contemporary Martial reported that a woman overcame and killed a lion. Tiberius attempted to ban upper-class men and women from fighting as gladiators, but some were so keen that they deliberately acquired criminal convictions, which, by the laws of the day, meant that they automatically forfeited their social rank.

The slaughter of men and beasts, known as a *munus*, had begun as a ritual intended to appease the gods and train soldiers, but by the late Republic such spectacles had become mere entertainment. Republican politicians, eager to buy popularity and votes, started to lay on the slaughter shows, and the emperors continued the tradition. By the time of Vespasian emperors financed 93 games and spectacles per year, and thanks to the Roman's insatiable appetite for wild beast fights, North Africa was emptied of elephants, Nubia of hippos, and Mesopotamia of lions.

The provision of so many entertainments, along with the dishing out of free corn, was also a highly effective form of social control. Most Roman men finished work by noon and at least 150,000 were unemployed. The emperors feared that so much spare time would lead to boredom and discontent, so they laid on savage spectacles and lavish entertainments. These not only earned the men's gratitude but kept them off the streets, provided endless topics of conversation, and distracted their attention from the fact that they no longer had any say in government. Even though women had no vote, a tier of seats was set aside for them. There was very little opposition to this wholesale slaughter of men and animals. Both Cicero and Pliny the Younger, writing a century apart, thought that the gladiators' fights exemplified the great Roman virtues of discipline, self-sacrifice and fortitude, though Cicero did oppose the wild beast hunts. Only Seneca attacked the spectacles outright: 'It is pure murder,' he wrote.

Visiting the Colosseum The Colosseum was originally surrounded by taverns, refreshment booths and wine stalls, though eating and drinking was banned within the amphitheatre itself. Entrance was by a tessera stamped with the numerals of one of the seventy-six numbered gateways. Once inside spoke-like passages crossed a system of concentric corridors with staircases leading up to the various levels of the oval auditorium.

To stamp out the flirting which was such a feature of race courses like the Circus Maximus, men and women were segregated. Women sat at the top, on wooden seats behind a colonnade, and slaves and foreigners sat in the section below. Beneath them were ranked marble seats divided into wedges by passageways known as vomitoria (as the name implies, they were designed to facilitate a swift exit). The top layer was reserved for middle-class men and the lower for those of the upper rank. The ringside terrace was set aside for the Emperor and his family, the Vestal Virgins, magistrates and priests.

Nowadays scarcely any seats are left, and only the concrete support arches remain. Although Renaissance architects praised the Colosseum, this did not stop them stripping away most of the marble to build palaces like the Venezia, the Cancelleria and the Capitolino. In 1744 Pope Benedict XIV put a stop to the pilfering and declared that the Colosseum had been sanctified by the blood of the martyrs who had died there (though there is actually no evidence that any did), and chapels and shrines were set up inside.

The platform which formed the arena was removed in the nineteenth century to expose the narrow corridors and cages through which the animals were filtered on their way to slaughter. Originally there was also a system of lifts, but these have obviously long since vanished. The exposed structure of the Colosseum may be an architect or engineer's dream, but you may find yourself wishing it still looked as it did in the eighteenth and early nineteenth centuries. Then, the Colosseum was overgrown with grass, shaded with trees and scattered with over 400 species of plants and flowers, some of them exotic importations whose seeds were introduced via the animals' faeces or fodder. It was probably the most written-about monument in Rome. Florence Nightingale, visiting Rome before she became a nurse, wrote: 'I am afraid its picturesque beauty will never make up to me for its sentimental [i.e. emotional] ugliness', though for most young women it was one of few secluded places to which they could escape for a a midnight tryst. Edith Wharton's *Roman Fever* hinges on such an encounter, and Henry James's heroine Daisy Miller dies of the dreaded Roman Fever (malaria) after a midnight rendezvous with her Italian boyfriend.

ANCIENT ROMAN GAMES

The night before a *munus* a lavish banquet was thrown for the gladiators, a spectacle which the public were also invited to watch. The next morning the gladiators, dressed in purple and gold, processed around the Colosseum's arena, after which weapons (checked for sharpness) were distributed, and lots were drawn to decide who should fight whom.

The entertainment sometimes began with 'comic' fights between obese women, dwarfs, clowns and cripples. Then, with a blast of trumpets, the true gladiators reappeared and the sword fights began, with the audience screaming for the gladiators on whom they had placed their bets. As soon as one gladiator had been slain, attendants, dressed as Charon, ferryman of the Underworld, checked to see that he was dead, then ordered assistants to carry the corpse out on a stretcher while they raked over the bloodstained sand ready for the next pair of combatants. Sometimes, if a gladiator was merely wounded but felt unable to carry on, he would raise his arm, and place himself at the mercy of the crowd. If they wanted him to be saved they raised their thumbs, and if the emperor agreed with their decision, he too gave the thumbs up. Thumbs down meant that the crowd did not consider that the gladiator deserved to live. The victor was showered with extravagant gifts, and became an instant hero and sex symbol. However, he would have to continue fighting and killing for some time before the emperor eventually decided he had earned his release.

The wild animal shows might also begin with circus acts: panthers pulling chariots, lions spitting live hares from their mouths, and elephants drawing Latin inscriptions in the sand with their trunks. Then there would be fights, in which a buffalo might be pitted against a bear or an elephant against a rhinoceros, and mock hunts, with men, armed with spears, firebrands and daggers, slaughtering leopards, tigers and lions. To add a further touch of realism, the arena was sometimes planted with greenery.

The Arch of Constantine

The Arch of Constantine, between the Colosseum and the foot of the Palatine Hill, was one of the last Imperial monuments to be erected in Rome, as shortly afterwards Constantine moved the capital of the Empire to Constantinople. It was dedicated in AD 315 to commemorate Constantine's victory at the Battle of the Milvian Bridge over his co-Emperor, Maxentius. Most of the reliefs and statues were plundered from pre-existing monuments, like the eight submissive Dacian prisoners on top, taken from Trajan's Forum.

The Imperial Fora

Thanks to Mussolini, a multilaned road, the Via dei Fori Imperiali, slices across the five Imperial fora, built by a succession of emperors ostensibly to cope with Rome's expanding population and an increasing legal and administrative load. Building a forum, however, was also an excellent opportunity to combine philanthropism with propaganda, and all but one was built to celebrate a major military triumph. Caesar's was built after he conquered Gaul; Augustus's after he had triumphed over Caesar's assassins and Antony and Cleopatra; Vespasian's celebrated his victory over Judaea: and Trajan's the annexation of Dacia. Nerva's forum – actually largely built by Domitian – was a simpler affair, little more than a corridor leading up to a temple dedicated to his favourite goddess, Minerva.

All five fora had temples, some had shops and law courts, while Trajan's included a library and Caesar's a heated public lavatory. Caesar was so besotted with Cleopatra that he placed her statue, along with one of himself and the goddess Venus, in his temple. Venus also appeared in Augustus's forum – as both he and Caesar claimed to be descendants of the goddess.

The fora are sunk below the level of the current city, scattered with eroded columns and fragments of masonry bearing the odd inscription or stylised acanthus leaf. With the exception of Trajan's – accessible from the market complex he built behind it – they can be viewed only from the pavement above. Be wary of getting too absorbed, though, as gypsies work the area and are only too adept at picking the pocket of a tourist puzzling over the layout of a temple.

The undoubted highlight is Trajan's Column. Two thousand five hundred Romans and Dacians spiral around its 38-metre stem, marvellously realistic figures engaged in the grim process of massacring one another. Originally they were painted, and were designed to be viewed from the roofs of libraries which stood on either side. Nowadays the upper reliefs are impossible to decipher without binoculars.

There are not many women, and apart from one scene, in which Dacian women torture Romans with fire, they appear only as prisoners. If you could see it, the final scene is the most moving. The Romans have triumphed, and the surviving Dacians – all old people, women and children – having been forced to abandon their homes, trail after their cattle searching for somewhere new to settle.

CLEOPATRA: THE TRUE STORY

Cleopatra was born in 69 BC, the third child of Ptolemy XII of Egypt. Egypt was a rich but volatile state, and by the time she was twelve both her elder sisters had usurped their father's throne, and both had been killed. Cleopatra succeeded to the throne when she was eighteen, along with her younger brother, ten-year-old Ptolemy XIII. Her first two years were beset with difficulties – the harvest failed, there were food shortages, whole villages of people disappeared in order to escape paying taxes, and her brother's regent, Pothinus, attempted to oust her.

Back in Rome, Julius Caesar and his joint ruler Pompey had quarrelled, and civil war had broken out. The Pompeians asked Egypt for aid, and were given ships and grain. A year later Pompey was defeated and fled to Egypt, but as soon as he landed he was beheaded. The Egyptians could not afford to be associated with losers.

Four days later Julius Caesar came to Egypt seeking cash. He met Cleopatra, they became lovers, and he arranged for Cleopatra and Ptolemy to marry (brother–sister marriages were a time-honoured Egyptian tradition) and rule jointly. Pothinus and the army attacked the palace, Cleopatra's younger sister Arsinoe proclaimed herself queen, and somehow Ptolemy drowned in the Nile. Caesar then married Cleopatra to her youngest brother and declared them joint rulers.

Shortly afterwards Caesar returned to Rome, leaving behind a pregnant Cleopatra. A few months later Cleopatra, Ptolemy and her baby, Caesarion, came to Rome and stayed as Caesar's guests until the Ides of March 44 BC, when he was assassinated. They left quickly.

By September Ptolemy was dead – perhaps murdered by Cleopatra, though there is no evidence. She made baby Caesarion co-ruler, and for the next three years maintained peace in Egypt. Meanwhile, Rome careered towards civil war. Octavian and

Mark Antony – both supporters of Caesar – wrestled for power, but eventually agreed to join forces and formed a dictatorship of three with the ineffectual Lepidus. In the meantime Caesar's assassins, Brutus and Cassius, had fled to the East and gained support. Both sides appealed to Cleopatra for funds, and for a year she stalled, knowing that if she picked the losing side, Egypt would be lost. Finally she *had* to act. She sent ships to Antony and Octavian, but they had to turn back because she was ill and a storm blew up.

Octavian and Antony defeated Cassius and Brutus at the Battle of Philippi in 42 BC, and Antony decided to conquer Parthia (modern Iran and Iraq). He came to Egypt, like other Roman leaders before him, to ask for funds. Cleopatra agreed to finance the expedition, and they became lovers.

Back in Rome, Antony's wife Fulvia engineered a rebellion against Octavian, failed, and fled to Greece. Antony left Alexandria for Athens – out of concern for his political career rather than his wife – and when Fulvia died, Octavian and Antony attempted to make amends. They divided the Roman Empire between them (Antony got the East), and to seal the agreement Antony married Octavian's sister, Octavia. Shortly after their wedding, Cleopatra gave birth to twins. For three years Antony and Cleopatra were apart. In 37 BC, having decided to invade Parthia the following spring, Antony returned to Alexandria. The reunion was not that of impassioned lovers – Cleopatra asked Antony for land; Antony asked her for a fleet of ships and provisions for his army. They did resume their relationship, however, because by May 36 BC, when Antony left for Parthia, Cleopatra was pregnant again.

The Parthian expedition was a disaster, and by the time Antony had retreated to Syria he had lost two-fifths of his men. He called for Cleopatra, who arrived (eventually) with money and clothes for the soldiers. Two months later he heard that Octavia was bringing supplies and reinforcements from Rome, and instructed her to turn back.

Antony had now unequivocally allied with Cleopatra rather than Octavian. He probably did love her, but he also reckoned he had a better chance of furthering his ambitions through her than through the Romans. Octavian began to persuade the Romans that Antony intended to make Alexandria the Imperial capital and demote Rome to a mere province. He probably did.

Antony and Cleopatra returned to Alexandria, raised money for military campaigns, and succeeded in vanquishing various rebels in Asia Minor. The victories were celebrated with a lavish triumph at which Antony handed out vast tracts of land to his children, and declared that Caesarion, Caesar's son, was the true heir to the Imperial Roman throne. Antony and Cleopatra began to prepare their ships and armies; Antony divorced Octavia; and two or three hundred Senators left Rome to join him.

The inevitable dénouement came in 31 BC in a naval battle at Actium off the west coast in Greece. The Romans won, but Antony and Cleopatra still had funds. Octavian's troops began to demand pay, but Octavian had no money. This gave Cleopatra hope: as long as he needed her money, she still had a chance of negotiating terms. She tried bargaining, but to no avail, so eventually she threatened to incinerate her treasure in the mausoleum where it was stored.

By now all three were desperate: Octavian to get his hands on the treasure; Cleopatra to save her dynasty; Antony (realising that he was finished) to save Cleopatra. On 1 August 30 BC the Egyptian fleet surrendered to Octavian, Antony's army followed suit, and Cleopatra locked herself up with three attendants in her mausoleum. Antony, believing that she was dead, stabbed himself, but he was still alive when a messenger arrived to tell him that Cleopatra was safe, and he was carried to the mausoleum to die in her presence. One of Octavian's men broke into the mausoleum just in time to prevent Cleopatra stabbing herself. She was allowed to attend Antony's funeral, but Octavian let it be known that he was keeping her alive to humiliate her in a triumphal procession when he returned to Rome. Although her suicide with an asp is one of the most famous in history, the instrument of her death could just as well have been a poisoned haircomb or hairpin. The only marks found on her body were two minute scratches.

Mamertine Prison/San Pietro in Carcere

This gruesome prison below the church of San Giuseppe dei Falegnami is one of the most chilling sights in Rome. It is built on two storeys, and originally the only entrance to the lower dungeon (which was originally a water cistern) was through a single hole in the roof. Prisoners were thrown through to die of starvation or to await execution. The only exit from the prison was into the city's main drain, the Cloaca Maxima, in which corpses were apparently deposited.

Among those who spent their final days here were the Catiline conspirators (who planned a coup and were sentenced to death on Cicero's advice) and Sejanus, Tiberius's rejected favourite. Its most famous inmate, however, was St Peter who, according to Christian tradition, was incarcerated here by Nero. The prison was consecrated as a chapel in his memory.

A staircase now leads down to the lower cell, a dank pit with mouldy walls lit by two naked lightbulbs. An altar has been installed in memory of Peter, and a spring bubbles into a pool, which the saint is supposed to have caused to spring up so that the other prisoners could drink. He also converted some of the prisoners and two prison guards to Christianity, and baptised them with the water.

Trajan's Markets

Open winter Tues–Sat 9 a.m.–1.30 p.m.; Sun 9 a.m.–1 p.m.
Summer Tues, Thur and Sat also open 4–7 p.m.

Trajan's Markets, a dour red-brick complex of 150 shops laid out on five levels, was the ancient Roman equivalent of the shopping mall. Built on Trajan's orders in the first decade of the second century and designed by the architect Apollodorus of Damascus (whom Hadrian later had killed), they sold everything from meat and fish (kept fresh in sea- and fresh-water tanks) to spices, fruit, flowers, oil, wine and fabrics. The complex had the same impact on the city as supermarkets do today: the small specialist markets like the Forum Boarium (meat) and Forum Holitarium (fruit and vegetables) lost trade.

Most trading seems to have been done by men, but some freed women *were* involved in commerce, selling food, clothing and luxury items like dyes and perfumes. As for shopping, Roman frescoes and funeral reliefs give the impression that wealthy women visited only dressmakers and cobblers – sometimes with their husbands (shown waiting while they try on clothes or boots); sometimes with female friends. The market complex is well preserved, and is often used for art and sculpture exhibitions. There's a two-storey hall, probably used for distributing the corn dole (see box below), a paved street, the Via Biberatica, with shops opening on to it, and – most impressive of all – a three-storeyed crescent standing directly behind Trajan's Forum. It was originally closed off from the forum by a wall, but nowadays you can walk straight into the forum from the ground floor.

THE CORN DOLE [ANNONA]

Trajan's Markets were also used for administering and distributing free corn, a benefit introduced in the late Republic by politicians who wanted to buy votes. The emperors continued the practice, principally because keeping stomachs full kept the lid on potential unrest. The dole went to men, as only they had the vote, and only they were likely to create a serious disturbance. Under Caesar and Augustus the number of men eligible for the dole fluctuated between 150,000 and 320,000, though Trajan, anxious to create a supply of healthy young men for the army, allowed 5000 boys to receive it. The dole portions, however, were only enough for one, so corn still had to be bought to feed the rest of the family. Elsewhere in Italy Trajan established a cash allowance for children – girls got less than boys, and in one town from which records survive there were 300 boy recipients and just 36 girls. This is unlikely to be a reflection of the number of girls and boys in the town – families could probably claim for only one child, and naturally favoured boys. There were a few private schemes to help poor girls, but the first state allowance was established only in the mid second century, when Antoninus Pius instituted a (modest) fund for girls in memory of his wife Faustina.

OUTSIDE THE CENTRE

The contrast between Rome's *centro storico* and the outer districts is acute. You leave behind the quaint tangled streets for the rural expanses of the Aventine and Celian hills, the urban disaster on the Esquiline, or the Fascist-era suburb of EUR. Enjoying the outlying sights can depend a lot on the kind of neighbourhood they're in, so take this into account before rushing off to see the vivid mosaic-covered interiors of the Esquiline's churches or the surreal pyramid and weird hill of potsherds in Testaccio. You must be in the right mood.

The historic women you'll encounter are largely saints, many of them martyred virgins or the owners of houses in which churches were founded. Most are shadowy figures, whose lives have been lavishly embroidered with ecclesiastical fictions. There are, however, a few formidable characters such as the prostitute-turned-empress Theodora, St Helena, intrepid traveller and aged collector of Holy Relics, and the already familiar figures of Vanozza Cattanei (see p.90) and the courtesan Imperia (see p.224).

The most relaxing areas to visit are the Celian and Aventine, leafy hills sprinkled with ancient churches. The bleakest is the Esquiline, where the desperation of the city's junkies, homeless and immigrants provides an ironic commentary on the wealth and splendour of its magnificent churches. Testaccio, a gutsy working-class quarter which has become fashionable with the alternative set, has a certain bizarre appeal, as does EUR, a planned suburb of broad boulevards and clinical travertine. Parioli, one of the city's wealthiest suburbs, is worth a visit for the catacombs of Priscilla, a refreshingly untouristy alternative to the commercialised catacombs along the Via Appia. If you like mosaics, don't miss Santa Costanza on the fringe of the dreary African District, built by Constantine's unprincipled daughter.

Although you may have got used to the leers and comments of passing men while wandering around central Rome, in the suburbs, where you are far more conspicuous, things can feel much more threatening. If you're alone, avoid Testaccio and parts of the Esquiline (notably the area around Termini and Piazza Vittorio

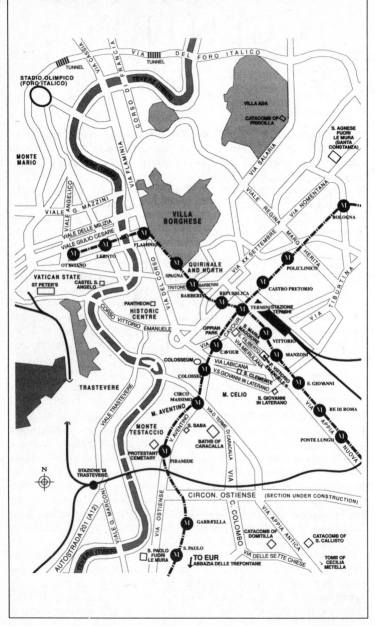

Emanuele) at night, and when you're sitting in a park – whether it be on the seemingly innocent Celian or Aventine or the more obviously dodgy Oppian – be on your guard.

TERMINI AND THE ESQUILINE HILL [ESQUILINO]

During the Republic the Esquiline Hill was allegedly haunted by witches and used for burying paupers and crucifying undesirables. Parts of it became fashionable under Augustus, but Suburra, at its foot behind the Imperial Fora, was a permanent fixture. This was a raffish workers' quarter of taverns and brothels, where Claudius's wife Messalina was said to have come to satiate her sexual appetite. As late as the fifth century the Esquiline was much-frequented by rather more respectable women, who came to worship during and after pregnancy at the shrine of a mother-goddess, Juno Lucina.

The area was ruthlessly developed in the final decades of the last century, and though it is no longer haunted by witches or the ghosts of the crucified, it is beset with the evils of the twentieth century. Congested streets, deafening traffic, gagging fumes and grimy buildings are the least of it. This is the land of Rome's dispossessed, the people the city would prefer to forget. Outside Termini station is a vast bus terminus littered with sandwich wrappers, pop cans, fag ends and wine bottles, and smelling as places do smell when men relieve themselves on the pavement. It is almost permanently populated by gypsies, loitering groups of North African youths, and old men boozing as they play cards. Alongside, dwarfed by the station's clean-cut Fascist-era travertine arcades, are Eritrean cafés and African fabric shops, where Rome's unfairly maligned street vendors attempt to create a home from home; down the road junkies and alcoholics sleep among discarded syringes in the gardens of Piazza Vittorio Emanuele.

Among all this mess are magnificent churches, their mosaics and marbles glittering testimonies to the wealth of the Church, their grimy façades victims of the polluted air. Three of them – Santa Bibiana, Santa Prassede and Santa Pudenziana – were built to commemorate the lives of (sometimes fictional) female martyrs; while the most important, Santa Maria Maggiore, was founded in the fifth century in the hope that the cult of a Christian mother would seduce women away from that of the pagan mother-goddess Juno Lucina. Fans of Michelangelo might consider braving the crowds to see his **Moses** in San Pietro in Vincoli, while anyone who is beginning to feel that Rome's historic centre is just *too* quaint need only take a stroll through the Oppian park to change their mind. Though the area is better avoided at night, it's fine by day, as long as you walk around fairly purposefully.

Santa Bibiana
Via G. Giolitti

At the far end of Termini station, huddled below an elegant helter-skelter-like tower and rattled by passing trams, is the grubby yellow church of Santa Bibiana. Bernini's first foray into architecture, it was built on the site of the family palace of Bibiana (Vivian), who was flogged to death with leaded cords under Julian the Apostate for refusing to sacrifice to pagan idols. Inside the church, in a cage beside the left-hand door, is a stubby column against which she was supposed to have been beaten. On the altar is Bernini's first ever sculpture of a clothed woman – Bibiana blindly swooning against a column, a bunch of lashes clutched in her hands.

Piazza Vittorio Emanuele

This huge square was laid out in the 1870s, just after Rome became the capital of the newly unified Italy. Today it houses the city's main market, its stalls piled high with a fantastic range of fruit and vegetables, pasta, pulses and spices, cheese, salamis, fresh meat and offal. Under the square's dingy arcades a Pakistani importer sells baggy trousers and hookah pipes, a chiromancer or two tell fortunes, and bag-ladies and tramps rummage through bins. In the central garden winos and junkies loll on grass sprinkled with used syringes and empty bottles.

If you feel like braving the garden, there are a couple of historical relics in one corner: an ancient brick tower (now inhabited by junkies) and, behind it, a gate known as the Porta Magica. This is all that is left of a Renaissance villa in which an alchemist once stayed and left, as a thank-you present to the owners, a list of magic formulae designed to turn metal into gold. Generously enough, the owners had the formulae engraved on their front door, though it never led to anyone making their fortune.

Auditorium of Maecenas
Largo Leopardi
Open Tues–Sat 9 a.m.–1.30 p.m.; Sun 9 a.m.–1 p.m.
1 April–30 Sept also open Tues, Thur and Sat 4–7 p.m.

A short walk from Piazza Vittorio Emanuele, set on a small wedge of land beside the busy **Via Merulana**, is all that remains of the villa of Maecenas (died 8 BC), flamboyant homosexual, *bon vivant*, lavish patron of the arts and adviser to Emperor Augustus. The so-called auditorium, a brick, partly subterranean building with an apse, has been reroofed, and as well as being open for visits it is occasionally used for concerts, plays and meetings.

The auditorium was probably a summer dining-room, with water cascading down the flight of steps at the back and running along a channel beside which tables would be set. Guests probably included poets and philosophers – like Horace who, when he wasn't yearning after women who had rejected him, or attacking those he had tired of, addressed many of his poems and epistles to Maecenas, his patron.

Once your eyes are accustomed to the dim light, you can begin to make out traces of frescoes on the walls – fake windows with views of gardens, ornamental urns, flowers and birds, and, at the back, a miniature frieze of a Dionysiac procession, including, at the left side, a drunken Dionysus being helped along by a satyr.

Santa Maria Maggiore

Piazza S. Maria Maggiore
Nothing about the grubby Baroque shell of Santa Maria Maggiore prepares you for the interior, a sumptuous gold-coffered mosaic-covered hall, flanked by two of the city's most outrageously opulent chapels. The church, dating back to the fifth century, is the most important of the city's 'Mary' churches, and one of three basilicas in Rome to enjoy the privilege of extraterritoriality (which simply means that they belong to the Vatican). Santa Maria is also one of the city's main pilgrimage churches, and certain chapels are often out of bounds as groups of pilgrims – many of them having travelled all the way to Rome by coach from Eastern Europe – celebrate Mass.

The church stands between two piazzas, Esquilino and Santa Maria Maggiore, with cars and coaches sardine-packed around the former's obelisk (taken from outside the Mausoleum of Augustus) and the latter's column (from the Basilica of Constantine). You can enter through doors on either side of the apse at the back or by the main façade, a light, two-storeyed affair flanked by palatial travertine-trimmed brick wings designed by the late Baroque architect Ferdinand Fuga. The loggia which forms its upper storey shelters a series of medieval mosaics, illustrating a legend which grew up around the foundation of the church, now unfortunately closed to the public. On a hot August night in 352 the Virgin appeared to Pope Liberius and a patrician named John, and informed them that in the morning they would discover a patch of snow on the Esquiline marking the spot on which they were to build a church. The snow fell, Liberius drew up a plan, and John financed the building of a church named Santa Maria della Neve (St Mary of the Snow). In fact, work did not begin on Santa Maria Maggiore until the early fifth century, and so far no trace of an earlier building has been found. Nevertheless every year on 5 August the legend is celebrated by a papal Mass in the Borghese chapel in which white petals (symbolic snowflakes) are dropped from the ceiling.

As far as anyone knows, Santa Maria Maggiore was founded

by Pope Sixtus III in the fifth century. He chose to build it on the Esquiline because women were still celebrating the pagan cult of the mother-goddess Juno Lucina in a temple on the hill. Mary had just been proclaimed the Mother of God (which is not as obvious as it may sound . . . God, after all, has always existed, and wasn't simply born in a stable in Bethlehem – a point made by the Patriarch of Constantinople, who was promptly denounced as a heretic and excommunicated), and Sixtus clearly felt that this was a good opportunity to replace the cult of a pagan mother with that of a Christian one. The design of the church itself has more than a little in common with ancient Roman basilicas – as you'll see as soon as you pass through the Baroque shell into a rectangular, flat-roofed hall with marble columns forming its nave and aisles.

High up on the walls of the nave are panels of fifth-century mosaics which are almost impossible to see, even with binoculars. The Cosmati floor, inlaid with tesserae of burgundy, bottle-green, grey and cream marble, dates from the twelfth century, while the coffered ceiling was allegedly gilded with the first load of gold which Columbus shipped back from America in 1492. The gold was a gift from Isabella of Castile and Ferdinand of Aragon to fellow Spaniard the Borgia Pope Alexander VI.

The mosaics covering the chancel arch date from the fifth century, and include an Annunciation, in which Mary is dressed up as a Byzantine empress, and an Epiphany, in which the baby Christ sits on an enormous jewelled throne graciously receiving the three Magi. In the twelfth-century apse she appears again in all her Byzantine finery, this time sitting with Christ on a throne as he crowns her Queen of Heaven. By commandeering the trappings of earthly monarchs for a heavenly queen, the Roman Church intended to indicate that its power was temporal as well as spiritual.

When you've tussled for long enough with the subtleties of medieval Mariology, head for the gloriously unsubtle Capella Sistina. Built in the late sixteenth century by Sixtus V as a memorial to himself, it's a riot of gilt, stucco and multicoloured marble – most of it scavenged from ancient monuments, Sixtus's pet method of symbolising the triumph of Christianity over paganism. Underneath the high altar (behind a usually locked gate) is what's left of a Presepio, or Nativity scene, which collapsed as it was being moved, on Sixtus's orders, from its old location outside the church, into his new chapel. Only the Magi, Joseph and some animals survived.

The relics of Christ's crib – five pieces of wood bracketed with iron – are kept in the even more lavish Capella Borghese (a.k.a. Paulina), on the other side of the church. This was built in the early seventeenth century by Paul V, a member of the hyperwealthy Borghese family, to house an ancient icon of the Virgin – one of scores attributed to the artistic skills of angels – which is now believed to date from the twelfth or thirteenth century. Not only is it completely overwhelmed by its setting, a ridiculously extravagant altar encrusted with lapis lazuli, amethyst, jasper and agate, but the Virgin herself has been studded with jewels.

PRASSEDE AND PUDENZIANA: TWO FICTIONAL SAINTS

The story of Saints Pudenziana and Prassede could have been scripted by an absurdist playwright. Neither of them existed, and Pudenziana owes her existence to a linguistic error. The church now dedicated to her was thought to have been built over a house used for Christian worship belonging to a man named Pudens, and became known as the *ecclesia Pudenziana* (the Pudensian church). In time the adjective Pudenziana evolved into a woman. It was decided that Pudenziana was the daughter of Pudens, and as St Peter was supposed to have lived in Pudens's house for seven years, it seemed entirely natural that he would have converted the daughter of the house to Christianity. By the early Middle Ages Pudenziana had become a martyr. Only in 1969 was she declared a non-person and removed from the register of saints.

Prassede's origins are also uncertain, but according to legend the church of S. Prassede was built on the site of her house. Confusingly, she developed into Pudenziana's sister, and the story went that she too had been converted by St Peter, and that the two of them had watched twenty-three Christians being killed. Prassede and Pudenziana were then supposed to have mopped up their blood with a sponge, and placed the sponge in a well. In 1969 Prassede too was declared to be a counterfeit saint.

Santa Prassede

Via di S. Prassede

A simple red-brick church tucked away on a back street, Santa Prassede was built by Pope Paschal II in the ninth century on the legendary site of a *titulus*, a private house where Christian services had been held in secret during the first and second centuries. To decorate the church Paschal imported mosaic artists from Byzantium, whose work remains in the choir and in the jewel-box-like Capella di San Zenone.

The most striking of the choir mosaics are the geometrically stylised Elders on the inner arch and the representations of the spurious saintly sisters, Pudenziana and Prassede, in the apse. Bejewelled, haloed and dressed in gold, they stand on either side of Christ, with the arms of Saints Paul and Zeno lying across their shoulders. The fact that the sisters did not exist did not prevent them having 'corpses' which are buried in a tomb below the choir in the crypt.

Prassede and Pudenziana also appear in the Capella di San Zenone, sharing the glittering gold walls with angels, saints, Christ, flowers and birds. The chapel was built by Paschal I as a mausoleum for his mother, Theodora Episcopa, who is depicted wearing a square halo (indicating that she was still alive at the time) in the company of Prassede, Pudenziana and the Virgin Mary.

Santa Pudenziana

Via Urbana
Sunk well below the current street level, Santa Pudenziana is one of the oldest churches in Rome, built in the fourth century over a second-century bath-house. Though it doesn't look much from the outside – the result of an uninspired nineteenth-century restoration – it's worth a visit if you're interested in seeing a rare fourth-century mosaic, or in descending through the chill, damp rooms of the three superimposed Roman houses which lie below the church.

Before entering, look at the eighth-century frieze preserved in the façade, in which Saints Prassede and Pudenziana are crowned like Byzantine empresses. Inside, Roman columns are clumsily embedded in plaster piers, and lines on the pavement indicate the layout of the foundations of the Roman baths which lie just below. The apse is covered with a subtly coloured fourth-century mosaic in which the Apostles look like Classical statues and the architecture in the background looks Roman. It is one of few mosaics in Rome surviving from the period before the art was influenced by Byzantine stylisation. Unfortunately, a clumsy sixteenth-century restoration has cut off two Apostles and the bottom halves of many of the bodies.

You'll need to find the sacristan in order to visit the Roman houses beneath the church and baths. Built of brick and with fragments of mosaic pavements, they range in date from the early second century AD to the second century BC.

San Pietro in Vincoli

Piazza S. Pietro in Vincoli (foot of Via delle Sette Sale)
This church was founded in the fifth century by Eudoxia, wife of Emperor Valentinian III, to house one of the chains with which St Peter had been bound in prison in Jerusalem before being miraculously rescued by an angel. A few years later the other chain was also brought to Rome, and the two halves were magically united. Ever since, San Pietro has been one of the most popular pilgrimage churches in Rome.

The piazza in front is packed with souvenir stands, snack wagons and coaches; inside, the church reverberates to the multilingual commentaries of tour guides, as the crowds elbow their way to a tomb strobed with camera flashes, and a tarnished chain in an illuminated glass reliquary.

Adding to the church's popularity is a statue of Moses by Michelangelo, part of a tomb he was designing for Pope Julius II.

When Julius II commissioned Michelangelo to build it, the artist was so thrilled that he immediately abandoned work on a fresco in Florence, rushed off to see the Pope, and then spent eight months in a quarry choosing marble. He produced numerous designs, each one more ambitious than the last, but eventually settled on an 800-metre-square combination of mausoleum and sarcophagus adorned with over forty statues. Unfortunately, Julius lost interest in the project, ignored Michelangelo's pleas for more funds, and eventually forced him to abandon the tomb altogether in order to paint the ceiling of the Sistine Chapel. Michelangelo managed to complete a pair of dying slaves (now in Paris and Florence) and the statue of Moses, which now sits, along with statues carved by his less talented pupils, in a modest six-niched façade.

When Cecil B. De Mille was planning to make *The Ten Commandments* he came to see the statue, and immediately decided that his cinematic Moses had to look like the stone one. Charlton Heston got the part after De Mille had scribbled a beard on his photo and declared the resemblance astonishing.

Torre Dei Borgia
Piazza S. Pietro in Vincoli
From the corner of Piazza San Pietro in Vincoli a flight of steps leads down to Via Cavour, passing below a scuffed tower. According to Livy (who never overlooked an opportunity to give women a bad press) it was here that Tullia, daughter of a sixth-century BC king of Rome, drove over the corpse of her father, murdered by assassins in the pay of either herself or her husband, Tarquin, in order that he could succeed to the throne. The tower itself, now incorporated into the monastery of S. Francesco di Paola, was once the home of Vanozza Cattanei (see box, p.90), formidable businesswoman, hotelier, mistress of Pope Alexander VI and mother of Cesare and Lucrezia Borgia. On 14 June 1497 she threw a party here for Cesare, on the way home from which her eldest son, the Duke of Gandia, was murdered, possibly by Cesare.

The Oppian Park and Nero's Golden House

Access from Via delle Sette Sale or Via Nicolo Salvi
The Oppian Hill, once the swankiest peak of the Esquiline, is now occupied by a neglected park where Muslims pray after a visit to the nearby soup kitchen; the homeless sleep in the ruins of two ancient bath-houses; street kids wash in the fountain; winos pass out; and old men, with nothing else to do, while away the hours playing cards or staring into space. Further down the hill is a rose garden where the scene is slightly less heavy; old women knit, a bag-lady feeds cats, and mothers play with their children.

Ironically, the Oppian Park rises over the ruins of a section of **Nero's Golden House**, or Domus Aurea, the most lavish palace ever to have been built in Rome. After his slum-clearance scheme of AD 64 (he set Rome on fire), Nero decided that in order to be 'housed like a human being' he simply *had* to have a palace which spread over all the Palatine, most of the Celian and the Oppian peak of the Esquiline – an area of something like 50 hectares. What Nero wanted he got, though as he committed suicide in AD 68, he had little time to enjoy it.

Beneath the hill, a number of damp vaulted rooms with mildewed frescoes were discovered, but since a landslide in 1984 they have been closed to the public. Renaissance artists like Raphael certainly groped around the dank rooms, for the miniature grotesques with which they are decorated influenced his work at the Villa Farnese. Michelangelo also hurried along when it was announced that the Laocoön had been discovered in one of the rooms. Until the place reopens, however, you'll have to make do with accounts by Suetonius and Tacitus.

According to Suetonius, the colossal gilded statue of Nero stood in a mile-long vestibule formed by a triple portico, while the lake was surrounded by pastures, ploughed fields, vineyards, woodlands where wild beasts roamed, and buildings 'which gave the impression of cities'. The palace itself was inlaid with gold and studded with gems and mother-of-pearl, and there were rooms roofed with ivory panels designed to sprinkle perfume or flowers on the people below. The dining-room was a spinning rotunda, and sea water and sulphurous water flowed through the baths.

If the historian Tacitus is correct, only the most decadent women were invited to Nero's garden parties. Banquets were laid out on a barge towed by gold-and-ivory boats rowed by debauched youths; aristocratic women slummed it in lakeside brothels; and naked prostitutes kept the party swinging with lewd comments and obscene gestures. Nero apparently 'disgraced himself with every kind of abomination, natural and unnatural, leaving no further depth of debauchery to which he could sink'.

Anxious to stamp out all traces of the loathsome man, future emperors did their utmost to destroy the Golden House. His successor, Vespasian, covered Nero's artificial pond with the Colosseum. Both Trajan and Titus both built bath-houses over the buildings on the Oppian, and Hadrian destroyed the vestibule to make room for his temple of Venus and Rome.

THE CELIAN HILL [*CELIO*] AND THE LATERAN DISTRICT

Largely undeveloped except for an immense military hospital and a handful of churches, the Celian Hill rises, green and tranquil, across a busy main road from the Palatine. The Lateran district, just to the east, is by contrast a grey, hectic urban area. Although the basilica for which it is named, San Giovanni in Laterano, is second only to the Vatican in the world's ecclesiastical pecking order, its appeal for non-Catholics is limited.

There is little point in going to the Celian unless you're interested in churches, for apart from the lush Villa Celimontana Park, there's virtually nothing else up there. Though it was heavily populated in the late Empire, most people moved out in the 530s once the Goths had cut the aqueducts (jagged fragments of which you can still see) and deprived the elegant villas and apartment blocks of their water supply. The churches which remained were sacked by Robert Guiscard and his Norman army in 1084, since when the hill has remained virtually uninhabited. Apart from nuns and the occasional fellow tourist, the only people you're likely to meet are those working at or visiting the hospital.

Women may not be particularly prominent in the Celian's history, but there are still a few memorable characters in the churches. Saddest are the saints whose gory martyrdoms grace the walls of Santo Stefano Rotondo, but you'll also come across some more powerful figures: notably the Byzantine Empress Theodora and St Helena, the mother of Emperor Constantine, who legendarily discovered the True Cross and a staircase from Pontius Pilate's house.

San Clemente

Via S. Giovanni in Laterano
Sandwiched between Via Labicana and Via San Giovanni in Laterano, in the unprepossessing neighbourhood at the foot of the Celian Hill, the church of San Clemente is somewhere to go if you want to indulge in a bit of time travel. Superimposed one atop the other are Republican buildings burnt down in Nero's AD 64 fire, a first-century apartment block and palazzo, a late-second-century temple, and two churches – one dating from the fourth century, the other from the twelfth. The Republican relics have yet to be excavated, but you can descend through the other layers, passing from vivid twelfth-century mosaics, via the ghostly frescoes of the fourth-century church, to the dank, mouldy ruins of the palazzo's courtyard and temple, which resound surrealistically to the noise of traffic above.

The works of art in the upper church alone span over a thousand years, ranging from the pretty eighth-century *scola cantorum* or choir enclosure, salvaged from the lower church, to the brashly gilded eighteenth-century ceiling. The splendid mosaics vaulting the presbytery were created for the new church in the twelfth century, but probably used themes from the decoration of the fourth-century church. The centrepiece is a dazzling apse, with the crucified Christ represented as the tree of life growing from foliage watered by the four rivers of Paradise. Leafy tendrils spiral over the entire apse basin, symbolising the new life that was given to the world.

San Clemente is also one of the few churches in Rome to have really excellent Renaissance frescoes. These are in the Capella di Santa Caterina, and were painted by two stars of the early Florentine Renaissance: Masolino and his even more talented pupil, Masaccio. They have been undergoing restoration for years, but once they are revealed again, they should be magnificent. They include an Annunciation, a Crucifixion, and scenes from the life of St Catherine of Alexandria. St Catherine, best known for giving her name to a firework, may never have existed, as although she was supposed to have lived in the fourth century, a 'life' was dreamed up for her only in the ninth. In fact, she owes much of her fame to the fact that the dramatic martyrdom invented for her appealed to the gory imaginations of artists. She was supposed to have refused to marry the Emperor because she was a 'bride of Christ'; to have knocked dead the arguments of fifty philosophers, brought in to show her the errors of Christianity; and to have been martyred because she continued to protest about the persecution of Christians. The famous wheel on which she was tortured collapsed, injuring the audience, so she was eventually beheaded.

Steps lead down into the lower church which, after being severely damaged by Guiscard and his band of marauding Normans in the eleventh century, was filled up with rubble so that a new church could be built on top. The rubble was not shovelled out until the mid nineteenth century – a job which took forty years to complete. What was revealed was a three-aisled basilica with a narthex, whose walls still bore the images of frescoes. The most intriguing of these is in the right aisle, thought to be a sixth-century portrait of Empress Theodora, later converted into a Madonna and Child by the simple addition of a haloed child.

EMPRESS THEODORA (c. 497–548)

Theodora, the dark, beautiful and – by all accounts – witty daughter of a dancer and a bear-keeper, herself became a dancer, mime artist, comedienne and prostitute. She eventually became the mistress of a high-ranking official, through whom she met the future emperor, Justinian, who fell madly in love with her. In order to marry her, he changed the law which forbade marriage with a prostitute, and when, two years after the wedding, he acceded to the throne, he made Theodora his co-ruler, Empress of the Eastern Empire. Theodora not only participated in her husband's plans and strategies, but in order to give women more power, she passed a law giving them more property rights, and made pimping a criminal offence. She established a convent for reformed prostitutes, and often bought girls who had been sold into prostitution, freed them, and gave them money to see them through the future. Unfortunately, contemporary (male) historians could not cope with the idea of a powerful woman, and represented her as a sex ogre, whose perversions (tellingly enough) included presiding over the castration of men.

At the end of the left aisle, a narrow flight of steps descends to a series of dank rooms smeared with vibrant green slime. These are the foundations of the Roman apartment block and palazzo which were filled with rubble and debris in the fourth century so that the church could be built above. As soon as they were excavated, water began to seep in, and until 1912, when a drainage tunnel was bored, they lay almost completely submerged. You can walk through the rooms which bordered the courtyard of the palazzo, but the ruins of the apartment block are difficult to make sense of, as sometime in the late second or early third century a temple devoted to the cult of Mithras was built in its courtyard. Women were excluded from this mysterious but hugely popular cult, which in the third century had more adherents than Christianity. Certain scholars have suggested that if women had been permitted to take part, Mithraism might have survived Christianity.

There were, however, parallels between the two religions: followers of Mithraism believed that Mithras had brought life to the world by spilling blood (albeit that of a bull); that he had ascended to the heavens after a banquet (with the sun-god Apollo), and that faith in Mithras guaranteed salvation. As well as initiation ceremonies, which included trials by terror, ice, fire, hunger and thirst, followers of the cult participated in ritual banquets, in which it is thought only bread, wine and water were served. The room in which this ceremony took place, the *triclinium*, retains its stone benches and an altar of Mithras slaying the bull. There is also a room, assumed to be a school for novices, with stuccoed vaults and a mosaic floor.

Santi Quattro Coronati

Via dei S. S. Quattro Coronati
The Church of the Four Crowned Saints (no one is quite sure who they were) lies just above San Clemente up a quiet narrow lane bordered by creeper-covered walls at the beginning of the Celian Hill. Its flaking fortress-like entrance dates from the Middle Ages, when it protected the nearby Lateran, seat of the popes, from attack. Since the sixteenth century it has been home to a closed order of Augustinian nuns who maintain their vow of silence by giving out the key to the bizarrely frescoed Oratorio di San Silvestro (and taking L1000 in return) by means of sign language and a revolving hatch.

Quattro Coronati's fortifications did not prevent it from being virtually destroyed by Guiscard and his army in 1084, and though it was rapidly rebuilt, the new church was much shorter. This is why there are now two courtyards – the inner one, still with columns embedded in its wall, was part of the original nave. A door on the right-hand side leads into the lobby of the Oratorio, where you pay for the key.

It's an intimate little chapel, with fetchingly naive frescoes illustrating the life of San Silvestro. As pope between 314 and 335 he was so ineffectual that in later years a more exciting life was invented for him. The frescoes show him curing a spotty Emperor Constantine of the plague, baptising him in a basin and bringing back to life a bull (shown standing on its head) which had been killed for sacrifice. More significant, however, is a scene in which Constantine is shown handing Silvestro a red-and-white-checked tiara. This illustrates a notorious eighth-century ecclesiastical con trick. At the time the Byzantine emperor and pope were engaged in a massive power struggle, during which the Church authorities conveniently 'discovered' a document in which Emperor Constantine had handed over temporal power to Silvestro. It was, in fact, a forgery, but no one noticed until the sixteenth century.

The final fresco in the cycle is devoted to Constantine's mother St Helena, an innkeeper's daughter who was divorced by Constantine's father as soon as he became emperor. Constantine Junior revered her, and it may have been her influence which persuaded him to convert to Christianity. She certainly converted others, built churches, intervened in religious controversies and, at the age of seventy, went off to the Holy Land in search of the True Cross. She found it (or at least managed to convince everyone that she had), and the fresco shows her pointing out which of the three crosses on Golgotha was the genuine article. Helena probably didn't realise what she was starting. There are now enough fragments of the True Cross scattered in the churches of the world to make several crucifixes – most of them made by medieval fakers.

The church itself is considerably less entertaining, though it does have a mellow Cosmatesque floor paved with zigzags, circles, squares and octagons of multicoloured marble. It also has a *matroneum* or women's gallery, to which the female members of a congregation used to be confined. Ring the bell on the door to the left and you'll be let into a diminutive cloister with a fountain, a goldfish pond and column capitals carved to resemble the leaves of water lilies.

San Giovanni in Laterano is just a five-minute walk from the top end of Via dei Santi Quattro Coronati: if you're not bothered about seeing it take a sharp right at the junction along Via di S. Stefano Rotondo to see the other churches of the Celian.

Santo Stefano Rotondo

Via di S. Stefano Rotonda
Open Mon–Fri 8.20 a.m.–12.20 p.m.

A short walk from Santi Quattro Coronati, past the huge military hospital complex and a stretch of Claudius's aqueduct with a modern water tower clamped above it, is the recently restored church of Santo Stefano Rotondo. As its name suggests, the church is round; in the fifth century, when it was built, it was one of the largest circular churches in the world, its three concentric rings stretching to a diameter of 65 metres. In the fifteenth century the outer ring was removed, but it is nevertheless wonderfully light and spacious. Once the sacristan has checked that your shoes are clean and that you are not about to spit chewing gum on his newly polished parquet floor, prepare yourself for a series of sixteenth-century frescoes: sadistic voyeuristic scenes of saints martyred by Roman emperors. Among them are Margaret of Antioch, lying naked and blood-spattered on a rack as she is prodded with pincers, Saints Felicity and Perpetua being devoured by wild beasts, and most disagreeable of all, Saint Agatha, who was tortured by having her breasts removed. She is still believed to have the power to protect against breast disease.

Santa Maria in Domnica (Santa Maria della Navicella)
Via della Navicella

Nicknamed after the *navicella*, a sculpted boat which was probably a votive offering by Roman sailors to the goddess Isis, now incorporated into a fountain outside, this church is a popular place for weddings. The first church on the site was probably built over a house belonging to a virtuous Roman matron, Santa Cyriaca, but the present building dates from the ninth century. In the early sixteenth century Sansovino added a porch decorated with lions' heads – a punning reference to Pope Leo X who commissioned it. The joke continues inside on a *trompe-l'œil* frieze designed by Raphael's star pupil Giulio Romano a few years before he was kicked out of Rome for illustrating a set of pornographic poems by his friend, Aretino.

The main reason for entering the church, however, are the apse mosaics. Far from being stiff and stylised like many in the city, they show the wind stirring the drapery of the angels who stand on either side of a large-eyed Madonna and Christ, and licking the gowns of the Apostles as they stroll through a field scattered with flowers. The two Roman sarcophagi in the right aisle are also worth a look – one carved with two embracing couples, the other with a wife holding her head in her hands as she mourns the death of her husband.

Santi Giovanni E Paolo and the Villa Celimontana
Via S. Paolo della Croce

Passing through the arch of Dolabella – dedicated to a Consul, but later used to support Nero's aqueduct – you reach a small lane which runs alongside the walls of the lush Villa Celimontana Park – a good place for a read or a picnic. The lane continues to the twelfth-century church of Santi Giovanni e Paolo. The church is lovely from the outside, its campanile inset with coloured marble, its apse daintily arcaded, and its buttresses arching over the street, and it is one of many in the city which were built over the ruins of a Roman house. These are currently undergoing restoration, but should be well worth seeing once they reopen, as they apparently contain traces of some exquisite frescoes – pagan scenes of youths and spirits, and a Christian one showing a woman at prayer.

THE LIFE AND DEATH OF IMPERIA

San Gregorio Magno, now a speckled travertine Baroque church strikingly positioned atop a sweeping flight of steps, was the burial place of Imperia, one of the most successful courtesans of the Renaissance. It has been completely rebuilt, and Imperia's tomb in the atrium is now occupied by the corpse of a canon, while its inscription – which may, unusually, have made reference to her profession as well as praising her beauty – has long been lost. Imperia, whose mother was also a courtesan, was born in 1481 close to the Vatican, whose cardinals were the source of much of a prostitute's income. When Imperia was eighteen her mother married for the first time, and shortly afterwards she and her husband built two new houses on the recently built Via Recta (today's Via dei Coronari), almost certainly financed by Imperia's earnings as a courtesan. Imperia was, by all accounts, extraordinarily beautiful, though the descriptions of her by awestruck poets are so vague that it is impossible to tell what she looked like. She may have posed for Raphael – perhaps as Sappho or Calliope in *Parnassus* on the walls of the Vatican, or as Psyche or Galatea in the Villa Farnesina – but this is all speculation. She certainly knew Raphael, and there is evidence that she posed nude as Venus for him – a fresco which may have been painted on the façade of her house.

By the time Raphael came to Rome, Imperia was famous, and had already been the cause of a murder. She lived in great style, her house furnished with embroidered gold wall-hangings, velvet and brocade, vases of alabaster, porphyry and serpentine, and – to impress on clients that she had a brain as well as a beautiful body – lavishly bound books (in Latin as well as Italian) and musical instruments. She was also said to have written sonnets and madrigals.

Imperia had many wealthy, powerful lovers, most famously the multimillionaire banker Agostino Chigi, the owner of what is now known as the Villa Farnesina, by whom she had a daughter, Margherita. By the age of twenty-nine Imperia, realising that her charms were not going to last for ever, set about preparing for her future, buying land and property. She was also determined that her first daughter, Lucrezia, would not become a courtesan (she knew that Agostino would provide for Margherita) and placed her in a convent.

Everything seemed fine, but then, perhaps for the first time in her life, Imperia fell passionately in love with a long-standing client, Angelo del Bufalo. No one knows what happened, but it seems probable that Angelo told her he had fallen in love with someone else. One night in August 1512 Imperia poisoned herself. Chigi immediately sent the best doctors in town to try to save her, but they failed. She recovered sufficiently to make a will, leaving two dresses and two rings to Margherita and virtually everything else to fourteen-year-old Lucrezia. Two days later she died.

Piazza S. Giovanni in Laterano

The Lateran complex stands between two ugly piazzas where the only places to rest are grubby plastic café tables where you are deafened by the row of engines, klaxons and car alarms. It consists of Rome's cathedral, San Giovanni in Laterano, the Lateran Palace, a baptistry and the famous Holy Staircase which St Helena carted back from the Holy Land.

San Giovanni is one of the most revered Christian monuments in the city, occupying the site of the first Christian basilica which Constantine built in Rome. It is still the 'mother and head' of the world's Catholic churches. The palace was the official residence of popes for a thousand years, and has witnessed and given its name to some of the most important councils in the history of the Church – most recently the Lateran Treaty of 1929, when Mussolini gave the Vatican State total autonomy and 81 million dollars, and placed marriage in Italy under canon law – the reason why divorce became legal only in 1970.

Constantine founded the complex shortly after he converted to Christianity in 312; in 313 he promulgated the Edict of Milan, which gave Roman citizens freedom of worship. A basilica, baptistry and palace were built on land which had formed part of the dowry of his wife, Fausta, better known for having her stepson executed on a false charge of attempted rape. She wanted to ensure that one of her own sons inherited the Empire, but Constantine discovered the ruse and retaliated by suffocating her to death in the hot steam room of a bath-house.

Barbaric behaviour did not cease with Christianity, and in 897 the church was the scene of one of the sickest episodes in ecclesiastical history. Popes often loathed their predecessors, but in the ninth century Stephen VII took his dislike to extremes, and put the corpse of former Pope Formosus on trial for having crowned a barbarian emperor. Not surprisingly, the decaying cadaver was unable to defend itself, so Stephen sliced three fingers off the benedicting hand and chucked the rest of the body into the Tiber. The fact that the basilica then collapsed in an earthquake was taken to be a sign of God's wrath, so Formosus's supporters strangled Stephen.

The consequence of divine judgement, earthquakes, marauding Vandals, and a series of fires is that little of the original buildings survives. The church was revamped by Borromini in the 1650s and given a new façade in the eighteenth century; the palace was rebuilt for Sixtus V in the seventeenth century; and the baptistry has been reconstructed and modified on numerous occasions.

The Basilica The basilica has two façades. The main one is an eighteenth-century confection with statues of saints and Christ perched on the roof; the other has a two-storey loggia and twin towers. The naves and aisles are Borromini's work, but on the fourth pillar of the right aisle there's a lonely relic of a fourteenth-century version of the church: a fragment of a fresco by Giotto showing Pope Boniface announcing the first ever Holy Year, which was held in 1300 and attracted an estimated two million pilgrims and inestimable profit to the city.

At the head of the nave is a gaudy, glittery fourteenth-century *baldacchino* (a kind of canopy), the repository for the church's most prized relics – the heads of St Peter and St Paul, and part of a table upon which Peter was supposed to have celebrated Mass. Also worth seeing are the thirteenth-century cloisters with slender twisted, fluted and mosaic-striped columns, and a small museum whose loveliest exhibit is a charcoal-and-pencil drawing by Raphael of a sandal-wearing Madonna, sitting on the ground watching the young Christ and St John at play.

Baptistry and Holy Staircase The octagonal baptistry retains some beautiful fifth-century mosaics, an ancient green basalt font and a pair of doors from the Baths of Caracalla. On Piazza di Porta San Giovanni is the entrance to the famous Holy Staircase (*Scala Santa*). It's easy to miss – look out for a couple of souvenir stands on the pavement outside. The staircase is supposed to have come from Pontius Pilate's house, and Christ is reputed to have walked down it after he had been sentenced to death. It was brought to Rome by St Helena (see p.222).

The Holy Staircase, now protected by wooden boards, can be mounted only on the knees, so when you enter the building don't be surprised to see frail old women painfully crawling up one step at a time, heaving their shopping bags with them. There are stairs at either side for the non-devout, but the penitential atmosphere can make one feel extremely intrusive. Not that the church is squeamish about profiting from its precious relic – there's a booth at the foot of the stairs selling Holy Staircase car stickers.

If you do decide to mount to the top, there's not much to see – just a dusty, shadowy chapel visible through a grille. This is the Sancta Sanctorum (holy sanctuary) built in the thirteenth century as a private chapel for the popes, and never open to the public. You may, however, just be able to see a portrait of Christ inside, allegedly painted by angels.

Santa Croce in Gerusalemme
Piazza S. Cioce in Gerusalemme

To see another of St Helena's souvenirs from the Holy Land and other gruesome relics, head down Via Carlo Felice to the church of Santa Croce in Gerusalemme. Its curvaceous Rococo façade rises between two ancient ruins – a hall known as the Temple of Venus and Cupid and the elegant Amphitheatrum Castrense, an amusement hall built for the delectation of the court of Emperor Alexander Severus.

The church itself is built over Helena's fourth-century palace, part of which was converted after her death into a chapel to house a fragment of the True Cross which she had picked up on her travels to the Holy Lane. Although it has been rebuilt many times – most recently under Mussolini – it has remained one of the city's main repositories of relics. These are kept in the Chapel of the Relics, a Fascist-era confection and yet another place of homage for pilgrims. As well as the chip off the True Cross, there are two thorns from Christ's crown, a nail used in the Crucifixion, and a finger belonging to St Thomas.

Also worth seeing is St Helena's chapel, decorated with mosaics and with an ancient statue of Helena above the altar – actually a modified statue of the goddess Juno, which was discovered at Ostia.

THE AVENTINE HILL [*AVENTINO*]

Rising above the Tiber to the south-west of the Palatine, the double-peaked Aventine Hill is a lush, leafy and highly desirable residential area, with a handful of early churches scattered among its secluded villas and convents. Although it's in the centre of Rome it's remarkably peaceful, and for once the sound of birdsong is louder than the noise of traffic. Even if you're not particularly interested in churches, a stroll around the Aventine is an easy way to escape the chaos of the city for a while, with a couple of small parks frequented – in mid afternoon, at least – by mothers and primary-school children.

At the foot of the Aventine in ancient Rome was the Circus Maximus, the city's main chariot-racing arena. The hill itself was the focus of the rites of Bacchus, a cult which was originally confined to women only but which, as soon as men were admitted, deteriorated into boozy orgiastic parties. The Bacchanalia were banned in 186 BC, and thousands of men and women were sentenced to death for participating.

Ironically enough, the two women now associated with the Aventine are saints, though their lives are more than a little elusive. One church is dedicated to Sabina, who was converted to Christianity by her Greek slave; another, San Saba, may have been built on the site of the nunnery to which Pope Gregory the Great's mother Silvia retired, devoting part of every day to cooking vegetable stews for her son.

Finally, the Aventine has no bars, so whether you want to

spend a Bacchanalian afternoon, or simply eat something, make sure you bring your own supplies. As a last resort, there are a number of roadside cafés on the busy Viale Aventino which slices between the hill's two peaks, the Aventine proper and the miniature Piccolo Aventino.

Circo Massimo

They pack us close . . . My sweet,
Your dress is brushing the ground, you really should gather
It up – no, let me. There you are. Oh dear,
What a mean old dress to keep such beautiful legs hidden!
M'm. The more one looks . . .
(Ovid, *Amores* Book 3; translated by Peter Green)

As Ovid noted, men and women sat together in the Circus (in many other entertainment areas they were segregated), so it provided the ideal opportunity for anyone on the pick-up. Ovid bluntly admits that he had absolutely no interest in horse races, but relished the chance to sit next to his crush of the moment, pressing up against her accidentally-on-purpose and flicking non-existent flecks of dust from her gown, as well as gallantly picking her trailing hem from the dust for a glimpse of her ankles.

By the time Ovid became a race-goer in the first century AD, the Circus Maximus, between the Palatine and Aventine, was probably around 700 years old, and was to go on being used for chariot races until the sixth century. The most popular entertainment arena in ancient Rome is now a lumpy grass oval circuited by multilaned highways where motorists play Ben Hur in Fiats and Lancias, overlooked by the headquarters of FAO, the UN's Food and Agriculture Organisation.

The circus once had seats for 385,000 people, who would pour in to watch not only chariot races but wild beast fights, athletics and (as it could be flooded) mock sea battles. It was also used for crucifixions, with the crosses set up along the low wall that ran down the centre.

Originally spectators simply sat on the hillsides while the charioteers raced round two posts staked into the marshy ground below, but over the centuries the sport became increasingly more sophisticated. Pompey had iron barriers erected to protect spectators during a fight between elephants and armed warriors (though these collapsed as the animals hurled themselves against them in a vain effort to escape); Caesar enlarged the arena, surrounded it with a moat, and had tiers of seats dug into the hillsides; while Augustus built a royal box for his family, and embellished the arena with an obelisk from Heliopolis (now in the Piazza del Popolo). Future emperors added stone seats for VIPs, wooden seats for ordinary citizens, and surrounded it with arcades, where wine sellers, snack vendors, astrologers and prostitutes traded.

The Roseto Comunale and Parco Savelli
Piazzale Amalfa and Via di S. Sabina
In May or early June, as you're trekking along the Circo Massimo, the fumes of carbon monoxide are suddenly overlaid with the heady scent of roses from a gorgeous public rose garden. If the traffic is too intrusive, continue up Via di Santa Sabina to the small Parco Savelli. It's set within the walls of a medieval fortress; there are great views of the city from its belvedere, spanning from the Vittorio Emanuele monument to St Peter's and the Janiculum.

Santa Sabina

Piazza S. Pietro Illiria (Via di S. Sabina)
Open 6.30 a.m.–12.45 p.m.; 3.30–7 p.m.

Santa Sabina was founded in the fifth century on the reputed site of a house belonging to Sabina, a Roman widow converted to Christianity by her slave, Serapia, both of whom were martyred for their beliefs. Set on a small tree-shaded piazza with a fountain spilling from a grotesque mask, Santa Sabina is a serene, immediately likeable church, which has been run since the thirteenth century by Dominican monks. The vestibule shelters ancient Christian sarcophagi, and leading into the church is a remarkable wooden door, dating from the fifth century and carved with scenes from the life of Christ, featuring comically disproportioned figures.

   The interior is cool and gracious, a classic basilica, with light spilling through windows of selenite on to elegant fluted Corinthian columns and subtle mosaics. Unfortunately, the apse is marred by a garish fresco – all that remains of a Baroque facelift after extensive restoration work earlier this century – but the west wall is decorated with mosaic – a gold inscription on a blue background remembering the founder of the church, one Peter of Illyria, flanked by female figures representing the churches of the converted Jews and Gentiles. Finally, if you can manage to find one of the Dominican monks who live in the adjacent monastery, ask to see the cloisters.

Piazza dei Cavalieri di Malta
At the end of Via di S. Sabina, past the grubby mustard church of Sant'Alessio, another little park and a string of primary schools, is the Piazza dei Cavalieri di Malta. Designed by Piranesi – better known for his etchings of nightmarish prisons – it has a weird, almost hallucinatory feel. It was built in the eighteenth century out-

side the Priorato di Malta, residence of the Grand Master of the Knights of Malta. Miniature obelisks flank stone collages of shields, belts, chains and panpipes, set against a leafy screen of pines and cypresses belonging to the neo-Romanesque church of Sant'Anselmo next door.

Adding to the piazza's dreamlike quality is the telescopic view through the keyhole in the door of the Priorato: St Peter's, on the other side of the Tiber, appears to be an arm's length away at the head of a tunnel of trees.

San Saba
Via di S. Saba

Via di Sant'Anselmo leads down to the hectically trafficked Viale Aventino, which runs along the cleft between the Aventine proper and the diminutive Piccolo Aventino. A little way up the hill is the church of San Saba, secluded in a walled garden screened with trees. It was founded in the seventh century, close to the nunnery to which Silvia, mother of Pope Gregory the Great, had retired, by monks who had escaped from the Arab invasions of Syria and Jordan. Although it has been rebuilt several times since, fragments of sculpture surviving from the earliest church are displayed in the Renaissance loggia, notably an oriental-looking horseman with a falcon. Inside is an old Cosmati floor, an *Annunciation* set among pink Renaissance buildings, and in a fourth, short aisle, faded frescoed scenes from the life of the fourth-century Saint Nicholas of Bari. The most interesting one shows him handing out three gold balls to three girls lying naked on a bed. The girls were the daughters of a poor, respectable father who, because he had no money for their dowries, feared that the only way they could make a living was by prostitution. Nicholas came to the rescue with three balls of gold – one of many charitable acts which led to him becoming the most famous saint of all: Santa Claus.

TESTACCIO

A working-class neighbourhood since ancient times, Testaccio is in many ways stubbornly traditional, and certain bars are still basically no-go areas for women. The result of recent gentrification, and the development of a somewhat self-consciously alternative night scene is an uneasy clash of trendy and proletarian left-wing cultures. Wholefood shops have opened in an area where for years the main employer was an abattoir; gay clubs sit next door to car repair garages where workers ogle every passing female; and as the yuppies move in and rents rise, banners fly from the windows of squats bearing slogans like *Testaccio ai Testaccini* (Testaccio for the Testaccians).

There are three 'sights' in Testaccio – a pyramid, a hill made of ancient smashed pots, and the cemetery where Keats and Shelley are buried – along with a great food market, but it's the strange mood and incongruous juxtapositions of the place which will probably make the biggest impact. By day expect curious, even suspicious stares; at night it really is not advisable to go alone.

Pyramid of Gaius Cestius

Piazzale Ostiense

Slotted into the Aurelian wall alongside the ancient turreted Porta di San Paolo, a marble pyramid rises amid the heavy traffic, trams and litter-strewn pavements of the Piazzale Ostiense. The late first century BC, in the wake of the Caesar/Antony/Cleopatra scandal, saw a craze for Egyptian exotica. Most Romans were content to haul back the odd obelisk or immerse themselves in the cult of Isis, but Gaius Cestius, tribune of the people and official party-thrower to the state, decided to build himself a pyramid as a tomb. True pyramid-builders would doubtless have been appalled at the short cuts taken by Gaius's builders – they made it of brick and simply faced it with marble – but it has survived the centuries in a virtually pristine condition.

The Protestant Cemetery

Via Caio Cestio

Open Thur–Tues 8–11.30 a.m.; 2.20–4.30 p.m.

As attitudes to death go, that of Gaius, determined that he would never be forgotten, and of John Keats, totally convinced that he would be, could hardly be more different. Keats was buried just down the road from Gaius, in Rome's pine- and cypress-shaded Protestant cemetery, after his death in 1821, in a house beside the Spanish Steps. He was twenty-five, and though the physical cause was consumption, his condition was exacerbated by scathing reviews and his unrequited love for Hampstead girl Fanny Brawne. In fact he was himself convinced that he was dying of a broken heart. Eventually he could no longer bear to read the letters Fanny sent him, and they were buried, unopened, in his grave. On his request the tombstone was inscribed with the words 'Here lies one whose name was writ in water'.

Among the graves of famous men – including Keats's friends Shelley and Joseph Severn – is that of Rosa Bathurst, a beautiful young Englishwoman who was drowned in 1824 when her horse slipped as she was riding along the banks of the Tiber.

Monte Testaccio

Via del Monte Testaccio

Monte Testaccio owes its existence to the dockers of ancient Rome, who broke enough amphorae while unloading Spanish wine at the nearby docks to create a hill of pottery shards. It was soon discovered that the shattered pots kept cool throughout the year, so caves were dug into its sides for storing wine; nowadays they are given over to car repair workshops and clubs.

Walking around the rubbly overgrown hummock (ignoring the puzzled stares of garage workers) you eventually come to the Mattatoio, an abandoned abattoir which is home to an old people's day centre, a stable for the horses which pull carriage loads of tourists around the city's sites, and two savage Alsatians. There have been plans to turn it into a cultural centre for years, but apart from an occasional series of raves and politically slanted gigs, nothing permanent has yet materialised.

THE SOUTH: EUR TO SAN PAOLO FUORI LE MURA

Unless you're into funfairs or Fascist architecture, there is little to entice you to the southern suburbs of Rome, except perhaps the chocolate- and liqueur-selling Abbazia di Tre Fontane. Nor have women figured particularly strongly in its history, although the massive basilica of San Paolo fuori le Mura owes its existence in part to the Roman matron who rescued and buried St Paul's decapitated corpse on the site.

South of Testaccio the drab Via Ostiense leads down past the gas works and main wholesale market to San Paolo, a cool, forbidding basilica surrounded by garages, a bus terminus and thieving gypsy children. The quickest way to reach both the church and EUR beyond is by metro – if you want to take in all three, head to EUR first, as its museums close in the afternoon. EUR is a chill, sanitised suburb planned during the Fascist era, with Neo-Nazi graffiti scrawled on the otherwise spotless walls of its surreal travertine buildings. In 1937 Mussolini decided to mount a universal exhibition (Exposizione Universale di Roma – hence EUR) devoted to the Progress of Civilisation, to show the world that Italian Fascism, following in the footsteps of the ancient emperors, was the way to the top. The date was set for 1942, and the reactionary classicist architect Piacentini was given the job of creating a monument to modernism and megalomania. An area to the south of Rome was cleared, crisscrossed with broad boulevards and landscaped with parks and a huge artificial lake. Work began on vast pavilions and colonnades, and plans were afoot for an immense aluminium arch which would span the entire exhibition area. But then in 1940 Italy entered the war. Work stopped a year later, and in 1943 Rome was bombed and the Fascist regime collapsed.

Rather than allow EUR to become a white elephant, it was decided to turn it into a residential and business complex. The wartorn, half-finished buildings of the first phase were completed, new ones were erected, and government offices and big businesses moved to the site. The intellectual needs of residents were supposedly met by a series of pompously didactic museums; their physical needs by sports centres and parks; while the immense Luna Park funfair was expected to fill their leisure hours. The area, connected to the centre by a dual carriageway and the metro, continues to develop, and the original nucleus is now surrounded by business parks and freeways worked day and night by prostitutes.

There is, however, a certain banal appeal to EUR's modernistic optimism. Streets celebrate electronics, aeronautics, tourism and chemistry; and mosaics, dating back to the Fascist era, glorify miners, assembly-line workers and mothers. The presence of the latter is hardly surprising: Mussolini was so keen to persuade women to have vast families that he once brought ninety-three of the most prolific mothers in Italy to Rome – between them they had produced 1300 children – to act as role-models for the nation's females.

As for the architecture, most of it reworks the building styles of Imperial Rome, notably the colonnaded approach to the Museo della Civiltà Romana (paid for by the late Fiat boss Giovanni Agnelli) and the Palazzo della Civiltà del Lavoro, with its audaciously simple tiers of travertine arches, and proud dedication to a nation of 'poets, artists, heroes, saints, thinkers, scientists, navigators and emigrants'.

Museo della Civiltà Romana

Piazza Agnelli (Via della Civiltà Romana)
Open Tues–Sat 9 a.m.–1.30 p.m.; Sun 9 a.m.–1 p.m. Tues and Thur also 3–5 p.m.

Consisting entirely of plaster casts of statues and monuments, along with a scale model of ancient Rome, the Museo della Civiltà Romana showcases articles made for two exhibitions – one devoted to archaeology in 1911; the other to the achievements of Augustus in 1937. This was exactly two thousand years after he came to power, and – not entirely coincidentally – the year in which Mussolini was feeling confident enough of his achievements to plan the universal exhibition.

Though it is an undeniable advantage to have ancient Rome presented logically and thematically in 59 rooms, instead of scattered haphazardly in the city, around Italy and in the far-flung corners of the ex-Roman Empire, there are times when you feel you might just as well be sitting at home with a book of photographs and reproductions. The museum was opened after Mussolini's demise, yet the comments on the information boards (in English as well as Italian) are so unquestioningly flattering of the achievements, and gloss so slickly over the limitations, of the emperors that they might as well have been written by Fascist apologists. That said, if you want a superficial history lesson, the museum is worth a couple of hours of your time.

Women are scantly represented, as the museum is very much devoted to the triumphs of Great Men. Cleopatra makes a brief appearance with her son, Caesarion; while Augustus's female relatives – Livia, Julia, Octavia – are merely named. The scale model of Rome at the time of Constantine is fun, though you can buy good posters of it from souvenir shops throughout the city. The one exhibit really worth seeing – plaster casts of the frieze which winds up Trajan's Column, which is virtually impossible to see properly *in situ* – is not always open.

Museo Nazionale delle Arti e Tradizioni Popolare

Piazza Marconi
Open Mon–Sat 9 a.m.–2 p.m.; Sun 9 a.m.–1 p.m.

This museum, devoted to popular traditions and folk art, is entertaining, though naturally the emphasis is on the jolly simplicity of Italy's peasants, rather than their economic struggles. There are gorgeously decorated carts and puppets from Sicily; rustic musical instruments (including a conch shell with a brass mouthpiece welded on); elaborate filigree jewellery, and amulets worn as a protection against the Evil Eye. Also worth a look is an eighteenth-century Nativity scene, set in a Naples complete with inns, market and eels squirming on the pavement; baby clothes, cradles and a highchair with a hole for a potty; and a collection of love-gifts, including a cake decorated with clasped hands and the message 't'amo'.

The highlight, however, is a collection of ecclesiastical kitsch (presumably included to illustrate the touchingly naive faith of peasants) ranging from wax ex-votives (the daftest is a foot with painted toenails) to a representation of the Holy Trinity in a miniature plastic TV.

EUR's Other Museums

Overstaffed by guards who spend their days gossiping and smoking, the Museo dell'Alto Medioevo and Museo Preistorico Etnografico are of limited appeal. There's some pretty Byzantine jewellery in the former (you could always pop in if it's raining, as the museum is free) and the latter contains a large collection of Etruscan hut urns, along with a magpie-ish collection of Alaskan dolls, beaded Indian jackets and dinosaur bones.

Via Laurentina
Open daily 6 a.m.–7 p.m.

Just outside EUR, tucked away at the end of a tree-lined drive off busy Via Laurentina, is the Abbazia delle Tre Fontane. Surrounded by palms, eucalypti and conifers, with a mossy fountain trickling into a sarcophagus and nuns and monks hurrying over the gardens to Mass, it's a soothing, even rural place which seems miles as well as centuries away from the sanitised modernism of EUR.

In the nineteenth century the abbey was forlorn and neglected, surrounded by marshes and occupied by a few pallid, malarial monks. It was handed over to the Trappists, who drained the site and planted eucalyptus trees, considered to be protection against malaria as well as consuming vast quantities of water. The Trappists are still here, along with a community of nuns, making and selling a eucalyptus liqueur, an aromatic vinegar (*Aceto Galenico*) which cures headaches caused by the *sirocco* wind, and a chunky range of chocolate and *torrone* (a rich nougat).

The monastery was founded in the fifth century on the site where, after he had been decapitated, St Paul's head bounced three times, causing three springs to sprout. There are, appropriately enough, three churches. Two date from the Baroque era, but the main abbey church, SS. Vincenzo e Anastasio, rebuilt in the thirteenth century, is simple and austere, with light filtering through slivers of marble, a high beamed ceiling and narrow naves, and aisles divided by thick, heavy brick arcades. Try if you can to visit at 5.15 p.m., for the chanted Mass. The most interesting of the other two churches is San Paolo alle Tre Fontane, which has an ancient mosaic from Ostia Antica embedded in its floor.

San Paolo fuori le Mura

Piazzale S. Paolo
If you decide to visit San Paolo fuori le Mura, you can either take bus 223 from outside the Abbazia delle Tre Fontane, or get there from EUR or the city centre by metro line B. A third option is to take any bus down Via Ostiense from Testaccio.

Considerable effort is required to imagine the former loveliness of San Paolo, for the eighth-century basilica burnt down in 1823 after a couple of workmen repairing the roof spilt a bucket of burning coals. Some of the original church did survive, but the nineteenth-century architects were so enthusiastic about their new design that they virtually disregarded the ancient bits. The result was aptly described by Augustus Hare as a railway station. It is, nevertheless, an important site for pilgrims.

After St Paul had been decapitated and his head had bounced three times (see Abbazia di Tre Fontane), his torso was buried by a Roman matron named Lucina. A couple of centuries later Constantine built a shrine over his grave, and in the late fourth century Emperors Valentinian II and Theodosius began work on a splendid basilica. This was later decorated with mosaics by Theodosius's daughter, Galla Placidia, one of many powerful women in the Byzantine royal family, who ruled the Western empire from the age of fifteen as regent for her younger brother; shared power with him when he came of age; then ruled again after his death on behalf of her son.

Dodging the gypsy children, drawn to tourist/pilgrim sites like bees to honey, you enter the church via a courtyard with a prinked lawn, manicured hedges, perfect flowerbeds and a sword-brandishing statue of St Paul. In the bare, echoing five-aisled interior daylight dribbles through tiger-striped alabaster windows on to cold granite columns and polished marble. High up along the walls, the mosaic heads of 265 popes from St Peter to John Paul II look down from medallions. There is room for only another eight papal portraits, and according to tradition, when space runs out the world will end.

On this sobering note you pass beneath the triumphal arch, adorned with Galla Placidia's mosaics (restored after the fire) and including, appropriately enough, the Elders of the Apocalypse as well as Christ and the symbols of the Evangelists. A number of other relics from the old church also survived: an elaborately carved Paschal candlestick, a gold and cream Gothic *baldacchino* by Arnolfo di Cambio which shelters Paul's tomb slab (though his headless corpse was probably stolen by Saracens in the ninth century) and a (heavily restored) thirteenth-century mosaic in the apse, featuring Christ and saints standing among palm trees which resemble half-closed umbrellas. At either end of the transept are opulent malachite altars, donated to the church in the nineteenth century by Tsar Nicholas I of Russia.

To the right a door leads into the one truly lovely part of the church: an intimate medieval cloister, with twisted, ribbed and zigzag-decorated columns surrounding a pretty rose garden. Just off it is a chapel devoted to reliquaries, most strikingly one in the shape of an arm and another in the form of a hand.

Finally you reach the Pinacoteca, where the church's scanty collection of art (including a minutely detailed *Flagellation* attributed to Bramantino) tends to receive less attention from visitors than the ecclesiastical souvenir stand.

VIA APPIA ANTICA: THE BATHS OF CARACALLA TO THE CATACOMBS

As Roman baths are popularly imagined to have been male pre-serves and hotbeds of homosexuality, it comes as something of a surprise to learn that they were used by women too – though after a series of bathtime scandals Hadrian banned mixed bathing. The Baths of Caracalla, overlooking the first stretch of the Appian Way (now a six-lane dual carriageway), is the best preserved of the city's bath complexes. As the site is quite taxing, you might prefer to visit on a summer night instead, when the old 'hot bath' is used as an arena for opera.

Beyond the baths, Via di Porta San Sebastiano continues along the route of the old Via Appia, passing through the city's Roman walls at the Porta San Sebastiano. The most potentially interesting sights *en route* are closed to the public, and it is not really until you reach the catacombs on and around the Via Appia Antica (so called to distinguish it from the Via Appia Nuova highway further north) that there's anything worth stopping for. Three catacombs are open to the public, of which those of San Callisto and Domitilla have the strongest associations with women. St Cecilia was buried in the for-mer, and the latter was built on land belonging to Domitian's niece.

Appia Antica Practicalities Walking along the Via Porta di San Sebastiano and the Via Appia Antica is not much fun; the narrow cobbled roads are choked with traffic, and besides having to watch your toes, you have to put up with cheery choruses of *Ciao bella* from passing motorists. Bus 118 runs along the Via Appia Antica, can be caught from outside the Baths of Caracalla, and drops you at the entrance to the grounds of San Calisto, after which there's a pleasant ten-minute walk across fields to the catacombs. Alternatively, you could catch bus 218 (just beyond the junction of the Appia Antica and Viale di Porta Ardeatina), which continues to Largo Martiri at San Calisto's other entrance – a two-minute walk from the catacombs, and a hairy ten-minute walk to those of Domitilla (the road is full of blind corners). If you want to continue along the Via Appia Antica, the tremendous tomb of Cecilia Metella, daughter of a Roman property speculator, is worth a look. Beyond this the traffic virtually ceases, but though the sight of tombs decaying among fields has a certain romance, reports of mug-gings make it inadvisable to go alone.

Make sure to have a bus ticket with you for the return journey, as there is nowhere to buy one along the Via Appia.

OUTSIDE THE CENTRE

Via delle Terme di Caracalla
Open Tues–Sat 9 a.m.–1 hour before sunset
Sun and Mon 9 a.m.–1 p.m. (exit by 2 p.m.)

In ancient Rome, going for a daily bath was one of the major social events and – particularly for poor women – the main chance of getting out of the house and meeting people. When the first public baths opened in the second century BC there were separate establishments for men and women, but by the first century AD there was nothing to stop the sexes bathing together. Women who went to the mixed baths risked their reputations – the satirist Juvenal is particularly nasty about what they got up to with the masseurs – but the smaller, women-only baths had no facilities for working-out before bathing. Consequently, women who wanted to keep fit as well as clean had little choice. Scandals were rife, and eventually Hadrian banned mixed bathing, setting aside separate sessions in the same establishments for men and women.

These baths, begun by Septimius Severus in 206 and completed by his son Caracalla eleven years later, had a capacity of 1600, and continued to be used until the sixth century when the Goths sabotaged the city's aqueducts. There was more to do here than work-out and wash: there were gardens, shops selling food and drink, a library and lecture rooms, and – inevitably doing a roaring trade – a host of pimps, gigolos, rent-boys and prostitutes.

The baths' well-preserved dull red-brick walls soar above multi-laned Via delle Terme di Caracalla, alongside which modern Romans work themselves into a sweat jogging along its tree-lined verge. Sweating, in fact, is something that is hard to avoid, for although the ancient steam baths are roofless and the heating system is defunct, the high walls trap the heat. In hot weather, be sure to bring something to drink – the contemporary equivalents of Caracalla's food and drink vendors now operate from wagons at the site's entrance.

Unfortunately, the routes across the complex are arranged in a way that makes it impossible to follow that taken by the ancient Roman bathers, so although the ruins are pretty substantial, they can be confusing. Things are even more frustrating in summer, when the vast *caldarium* (hot bath) is used as an arena for opera and concerts, which means that parts of the complex are cordoned off and the *caldarium* itself is filled with tiers of seats and stage sets. Make life easy and buy a plan at the ticket office.

The Site   The bath complex is bounded by a wall which curves on either side around two halls with apses, which were probably gymnasia. The back wall, now covered with creepers, bowed out behind a stadium, with tiers of seats behind and small halls on either side holding libraries. The main bath buildings occupied a block in the centre of the gardens, with two hot steam baths [*laconia*], two gyms [*palaestrae*], two changing rooms [*apodyteria*], and two vestibules symmetrically arranged on either side of the circular hot bath [*caldarium*], a lukewarm bath [*tepidarium*], a vast rectangular hall [*basilica*], and an open-air swimming pool [*frigidarium* or *natatio*].

The current route takes you through to one of the indoor gyms, with fragments of a wavy-patterned green, red and white mosaic pavement, and fractured mosaic pictures of athletes propped up against its walls. From here you can peer into various smaller, roped-off rooms, where wrestlers (women as well as men) were probably massaged and smeared with a mixture of oil and wax to make the skin more supple, then sprinkled with dust to stop them being slippery, before engaging in matches.

You now enter one of the two changing rooms, long halls with undulating black-and-white mosaic floors, leading off the two vestibules. Some sports (notably wrestling) were done in the nude, but people usually remained dressed for activities in the outer gymnasia, so they would have to return to the changing room to remove their clothes before bathing. They then headed back through the indoor gyms to one of the two hot steam bath rooms designed to induce sweat. The next stage was a hot bath, in an immense bronze tub surrounded by cubicles in which the more modest could bathe in private. After this, the skin was scraped to remove dirt. The rich were scraped, rubbed, massaged and perfumed by slaves, but the less wealthy had to manage as best they could, scraping as much of their bodies as they could reach, then improvising by rubbing their backs against the walls, unless they could afford to pay one of the bath-servants. They then passed to the *tepidarium* for a lukewarm bath, before plunging into the cold waters of the open-air swimming pool.

Via di Porta San Sebastiano and Around

Without the constant traffic, the ten-minute walk along this narrow cobbled road, squeezing between high walls lushly curtained with creeper, would be idyllic. In fact, the reasons for heading up to the Porta di San Sebastiano are hardly compelling. The Parco degli Scipione is pretty enough, but its two ancient tombs, the Tomb of the Scipios – hollowed out under a low hill – and the Columbarium of Pomponius Hylas – built for a wealthy first-century Roman and his wife, and decorated with mosaics, stucco and frescoes – are usually closed to the public. You could, however, cut across the park to see San Giovanni a Porta Latina, a medieval church with a campanile, an ancient cedar in its courtyard, and alabaster windows, leaning columns and faded frescoes inside. It is dedicated to St John the Evangelist, who supposedly emerged unscathed from a cauldron of boiling oil on nearby Via della Porta Latina – the site is marked by a tiny octagonal chapel.

Back on the other side of the park, the **Porta San Sebastiano**, with ancient marble arches and crenellated medieval brick towers, is the most striking of the city's gates, but the Museo delle Mura, with its illustrated information boards on construction methods, and sentry-path walk, is likely to thrill only aficionados of Roman masonry.

In the early sixteenth century, Imperia (see box, p.224) bought land here, which was converted into a pleasure garden. The area still attracts philandering men at night, nowadays serviced by transvestites. Even by day, however, if you're walking along the Ardeatina, cars slow down to check you out – so avoid the road if you can.

Via Appia and the Catacombs

The Via Appia, begun in 312 BC, was eventually extended right across Italy to the port of Brindisi. It was Rome's first major highway, four metres wide, paved with immense flags of stone, some of which can still be seen. As burial was forbidden within the city walls, it soon became lined with tombs, and in the early Christian era catacombs, basically underground cemeteries, were dug, usually on land belonging to a Christian family. There is little of interest until you reach the Catacomb of San Calisto, though you can spot the occasional derelict tomb, tucked behind a petrol station or sheltering below the spans of a concrete bridge.

Contrary to popular belief, catacombs were not places in which Christians hid to escape persecution. The authorities knew about the catacombs, and most of the time they left the Christians free to bury their dead and pray at their tombs. They were closed twice in an attempt to disperse the Christian community, but the Christians disregarded the ban, and a number were killed within the underground galleries.

Because space was limited, after one layer of tunnels and caverns had been filled with bodies another was hollowed out underneath. There is, however, a slightly dubious theory that the Christians opted for catacombs because they were spooky, and they knew the pagans were scared of ghosts.

Bodies were wrapped in white sheets, covered with quicklime – to ensure a swift decomposition – and placed in a variety of tombs. Poorer Christians were simply deposited in shelves, which were closed with a stone slab; richer ones were buried in family rooms, sometimes in elaborately carved sarcophagi. Over half the bodies in the catacombs are babies, many of them abandoned pagan children rescued from the streets of Rome by charitable Christians.

Via Appia Antica
Open 8.30 a.m.–noon; 2.30–5.30 p.m. (closes earlier in winter)
Closed Wed

If you take bus 118, you could pop into the little church of Domine Quo Vadis first, to see the supposed footprints of St Peter, who apparently met Christ here as he was running away from Rome to escape crucifixion. He asked Christ where he was going ('Domine, quo vadis?') whereupon Christ retorted that he was going to Rome to be crucified a second time. Peter was suitably shamed, and turned round to meet his own death.

From here a ten-minute walk across fields, scattered with poppies in spring, brings you to the catacomb entrance, with a coach park, souvenir shop, loos and notices reminding you that you are about to enter a holy place. Guided tours (in English) take you through just over a kilometre of San Calisto's twenty kilometres of corridors, their dull tufa walls hollowed out into layers of shelves which once held the bodies, and in places frescoed with ancient Christian symbols – Jesus as a shepherd, the Magi bowing before Mary and Christ, doves and fish (the latter a pun on the word Ichthus, which is both the Greek for fish and an acronym of the phrase Jesus Christ Son of God).

The most moving of the catacomb's crypts is the one built to hold the body of Saint Cecilia (see p.147). Her sarcophagus was moved to Santa Cecilia in Trastevere in the ninth century, but a copy of Stefano Maderna's sculpture of the saint, based on a sketch of her undecayed, thirteen-hundred-year-old body, looks all the more vulnerable lying on its side among offerings of plastic roses in the dim, underground cavern.

Catacomb of Domitilla

Via delle Sette Chiese
Open 8.30 a.m.–noon; 2.30–5.30 p.m. (closes earlier in winter)
Closed Tues

There are many versions of the story of Domitilla, a niece of Emperor Domitian who was martyred, along with her husband, for being a Christian. The most popular (and outrageous) is that because Saints Nereus and Achilleus were her eunuchs, she succeeded in preserving her virginity. Domitilla's name has long been removed from the calendar of saints, though her alleged toy boys are still considered sufficiently *bona fide*. Naturally the Church prefers the evidence that they were Roman soldiers specialising in execution, who converted to Christianity and were themselves killed for their faith.

These catacombs date back to the late first century, but they really rose to fame only 300 years later, when a basilica was built over the tombs of Nereus and Achilleus. Unfortunately, in order to situate the church as near as possible to the holy corpses, the catacomb's oldest, upper galleries were destroyed. The basilica, partly underground, is cool and lofty, and has plenty of sarcophagi and fragments of inscriptions to occupy you while you wait for tours to begin. You are then hurtled at breakneck pace through a small section of the catacombs, with brief pauses to see faintly frescoed *cubicula*, small rooms hollowed out to house sarcophagi. The most interesting is the Cubiculum of Veneranda, burial place of a Roman woman who had the financial clout to ensure that she was interred right next to the body of Saint Petronilla, and to commission a fresco showing herself and Petronilla entering Paradise together. All that is known about Petronilla is that she was one of Domitilla's relatives, and that she was martyred, but a fictitious biography written in the sixth century decided that it was more interesting to make her the daughter of St Peter, who refused to get married and died after a three-day hunger strike.

Tomb of Cecilia Metella
Via Appia Antica
Open Tues–Sat 9 a.m. to between 4 p.m. and 7 p.m., depending on the time of year. Sun and Mon open 9 a.m.–1 p.m.

A short walk (or 118 bus ride) along the Via Appia Antica is the immense cylindrical tomb of Cecilia Metella, just beyond the ruins of the fourth-century Circus of Maxentius (open Tues–Sat 9 a.m.–1 p.m.; Tue, Thur, Sat also 4–7 p.m.; Sun 9 a.m.–12.30 p.m.), where *Ben Hur* was filmed. Little is known about Cecilia except that she was the daughter of a property speculator who made his fortune buying up properties seized from political undesirables during Sulla's reign of terror. Whether the size of his daughter's tomb was intended to signify the extent of his love for her, or simply to advertise his wealth, is unknown.

In 1300 the Pope, Boniface VIII, handed the tomb over to his relatives, the Caetanis, who turned it into the keep of their fortress by adding a few gap-toothed brick crenellations and used it to commandeer the road, forcing travellers to pay tolls. The exterior of the travertine-faced tomb, ringed with a frieze of fruit garlands and bulls' heads, is magnificent, but the interior is littered with fag ends and drink cans, and echoes to the cooing of pigeons.

Parioli is one of Rome's wealthiest suburbs, verdant, hilly and scattered with villas and apartments. The adjacent African District, so called because many of its streets are named after African countries, is ugly, urban and working-class, its grim grey blocks of flats largely dating from the days of Mussolini. Neither neighbourhood is particularly appealing, unless you feel like spending a Sunday afternoon in a café surrounded by Parioli's beautiful young things. Café car parks are crammed with glossy motorbikes and gleaming cars – most of them birthday presents from doting parents: many of them to be spotted later in the evening parked on lovers' lanes on the fringes of the massive Villa Ada Park. Meanwhile, in humbler bars, Filipina maids collapse over ice creams on grubby plastic chairs, making the most of their afternoons off, and inside Villa Ada boys from the rougher parts of town discreetly peddle drugs.

Apart from the Bar San Filippo (see p. 294), which serves some of the best ice cream in Rome, the main reasons to visit the northern suburbs are the gorgeous church of Sant'Agnese fuori le Mura and the Catacomb of Priscilla. Fans of postmodern architecture might also want to see Paolo Portoghesi's current work-in-progress on Via della Moschea – the city's new mosque – financed in part by the Egyptian government, whose embassy now occupies the ex-hunting-lodge in the Villa Ada.

Sant'Agnese fuori le Mura

Via di S. Agnese (off Via Nomentana)

Sunk below Via Nomentana, a major road lined with extravagant villas, Sant'Agnese fuori le Mura is an endearing mellow brick church with a pantiled roof, standing above the catacombs in which St Agnes was buried after her ordeal in Piazza Navona and its brothels (see p.56). The first chapel was built on the site not long after the Imperial executioners slashed Agnes's throat in AD 304, but the current building dates from the seventh century. It has been rebuilt many times – most recently in 1855, after the floor collapsed while Pope Pius IX was saying Mass. The congregation crashed into the basement, but Pius floated – an event which only furthered his claim (which he succeeded in making Catholic doctrine in 1870) that popes were infallible.

The main entrance on Via Nomentana is usually closed, which is a shame, as the flight of steps leading down to the church has walls covered with inscriptions from the catacombs below – including a relief of Saint Agnes taken from her tomb. Usually you have to enter from Via di Sant'Agnese, through a courtyard shaded with cypresses and palms. On the far side is a fake grotto devoted to Bernadette's vision of the Virgin at Lourdes, laden with fresh flowers and ex-votives – many of them home-made – thanking the Virgin for saving the life of a child or husband. The interior of the church has been tampered with over the years, but despite the gilded rosettes, angel heads and coats of arms on its coffered ceiling, and undistinguished nineteenth-century paintings on the chancel arch, it retains its basic seventh-century shape. The nave and aisles are divided by ancient grey, white and apricot marble columns, and originally its male and female congregations were segregated by confining the women to the gallery, or *matroneum*, above. The remains of Saint Agnes lie below the high altar, along with those of her foster-sister Emerentiana, who was stoned to death while praying at her tomb. The peculiar statue of Saint Agnes, with an alabaster torso and bronze head and feet, is actually a sixteenth-century adaptation of an ancient statue of Isis (see p. 82). Above the altar, in the basin of the apse, is a seventh-century mosaic of Agnes, kitted out in Byzantine finery, flanked by two tonsured popes, Symmachus and Honorius.

If the sacristan is in a good mood, you may be able to persuade him to guide you round the catacombs. If he's not, head up to the circular church of Santa Costanza (to the left of Sant'Agnese) founded by Constantine's daughter Constantia.

Santa Costanza

According to legend, Constantia caught leprosy and was cured after spending a night sleeping beside Agnes's tomb. She is then supposed to have converted to Christianity and become a nun, though she was in fact married to a particularly vicious provincial governor, and is reported to have shared his insatiable bloodthirstiness. She did, however, build a chapel over Agnes's tomb, a massive basilica nearby (you can still see the high walls of its apse in a field to the right of Santa Costanza) and a mausoleum for herself, which was converted into a church in the thirteenth century. Though the exterior is dull, the interior is magnificent, and consequently a popular place for weddings. The vaults are still covered with fourth-century mosaics, which, as biblical scenes are completely absent, do nothing to support the Church's claim that Constantia was a Christian. Instead, there are delicate vines, stylised flowers, exotic birds and cartoonish vintage scenes with recalcitrant carthorses being furiously whipped, which suggest that Constantia may indeed have had a sadistic streak, not to mention a penchant for alcohol. Booze also features heavily on her porphyry sarcophagus (actually a cast – the original is in the Vatican), which is covered with carvings of energetic cherubs picking grapes and squashing them with their knees.

Villa Ada
Open 7 a.m.–sunset

A vast sweep of wild, wooded hills fringed with formal and land-scaped gardens, the Villa Ada is one of the largest of Rome's public parks, and occupies the site of a Sabine city. More recently it was a royal hunting reserve, and nowadays the royal villa, the Villa Ada proper, is the Egyptian Embassy. Attracting the usual mix of jog-gers, mums with prams, dope-pushers and loitering men, it is, as ever, a more comfortable place to walk than to sit. Heading off alone into the extensive hilly pine woods is not advisable, even if it's only to save yourself the embarrassment of interrupting an amorous couple.

Catacomb of Priscilla

Entrance at *Via Salaria 430*
Open Tues–Sun 8.30 a.m.–noon; 2.30–5 p.m. Closes 6 p.m. in summer

If you visit only one catacomb, make it the Catacomb of Priscilla, where the frescoes include the world's oldest representation of the Virgin. Tunnelled to a depth of thirty-five metres under the Villa Ada Park, these catacombs are named after the wife of a Christian condemned to death by Domitian for his beliefs. Far from acting as a deterrent, the martyrdom inspired Priscilla and her family to embrace Christianity, and they permitted local Christians to tunnel under their home in order to create space for the tombs of their dead. The catacombs are now entered through a convent, where nuns sit knitting and reading in a tiny courtyard before donning anoraks to escort occasional visitors through the subterranean labyrinth.

ACCOMMODATION

Rome is one European city in which there is absolutely no need to stay in a functional, anonymous purpose-built hotel. In fact, most of the hotels in the centre occupy old palazzi, antique villas and even ex-monasteries. The disadvantage is that these old buildings are not readily adaptable to the needs of people with disabilities, that very few have space for swimming pools, and that the only gardens are roof terraces.

On the positive side, you can still stay in Campo dei Fiori and around Piazza Navona, the main hotel areas during the Renaissance, when Rome was flooded with visiting ecclesiasts and cardinals; or in the streets around the Piazza di Spagna, as did the Grand Tourists of the eighteenth and nineteenth centuries. The advantages of such central locations cannot be overstated – there are enough people around at night to make them safe, and in summer, when it's baking hot, there's nothing like being able to pop back to your room for a shower and a siesta without wasting time on a long walk or bus ride. Areas outside the historic centre worth considering include the Aventine, where you can stay in exquisite villas among lush gardens; Trastevere, where there are just two cheap hotels, convenient for the area's bars and restaurants; and the Villa Borghese area, where there is a hotel with a garden and a swimming pool. The area around Termini station is better avoided, unless you can afford to stay in the Grand (and use taxis at night). We have, however, included a couple of good hotels in relatively safe streets, in case you can't find accommodation elsewhere.

Rome's hotels run the full gamut, from luxurious nineteenth-century and contemporary extravaganzas to tiny, basic establishments which have a few dingy rooms without bathrooms. They are officially classified with one, two, three, four, or five stars according to facilities, and prices are set by the state (they should be displayed in your room). Breakfast is often extra, and unless you're really hungry it's really NOT worth paying L20,000 plus: go to a café instead. You are frequently charged extra for air-conditioning, too, which can bump up the price of a room considerably. The prices we quote range from the cheapest single to the most expensive double, though you'll be quoted only the lowest rates in winter. Sometimes hotels have a discount in August. In slack periods, and if you're staying for over a week, it is always worth haggling over prices. As well as excluding breakfast and air-conditioning, the price you are quoted may not include tax (19% in upper-class hotels, 9% in the rest) or service. Even if service is included, you should tip bellboys and chambermaids, for they are not well paid.

Standards and prices vary widely within the categories – some three-star hotels have beautifully decorated air-conditioned rooms with minibars; others are dated and basic – but you usually pay for what you get. There are also a few extremely comfortable two-star hotels, though in a one-star hotel you shouldn't expect much more than a clean room. There are also rooms in convents and hostels, none of them particularly conveniently located. The former are not restricted to Catholics, though in both you'll be expected to observe a curfew.

If at all possible you should book well in advance, for finding a room, even in April and November, can be very difficult. As the Italian postal service is so unreliable, it is wiser to phone or fax. Some hotels will ask you to send a deposit; others will simply ask you what time you are arriving. In this case, add an hour or so to your flight arrival time, and phone again from the airport. If you don't, and are later than you've said, you may get to the hotel only to find that your room has been given away. Incidentally, except for the cheapest hotels, most will have someone who can speak enough English to take a booking. Travellers on a budget may have problems finding somewhere affordable in a safe location, for the vast majority of the budget hotels are in the unsavoury streets around Termini (those to the north are better than the ones to the south). You may need to book a month in advance to get into the cheaper hotels we recommend, even longer if you want to stay in a convent. If you do arrive on spec, head straight for Enjoy Rome, Via Varese 39 (tel. 445 1843). (Open   Mon–Fri 8.30 a.m.–1 p.m. and 3.30–6.30 p.m., Sat 8.30 a.m.– 1 p.m.) They have a list of hotels, rigorously inspected for quality and safety in all categories, and make no charge for reserving rooms. Go straight up Via Marghera (turn right as you leave the platform area and keep on walking). Via Varese is the third cross-street on the right. Alternatively the tourist office will reserve you a room, but it could be anywhere. If none of the hotels listed below has vacancies, you'll obviously have to take whatever is available, but if you're not happy with either the location or the establishment, it's worth trying again the next morning.

For budget hotels the best time to phone is between 8 a.m. and 10.30 a.m., in smarter hotels between 10 a.m. and noon, by which time the owners should know how many clients are checking out.

If you arrive at Termini late at night without anywhere to stay, and can't find a room, Enjoy Rome has an emergency line open until 10 p.m. Otherwise go to the police station at Termini, though the amount of help you get will depend very much on the mood of the duty officer.

It's also worth considering taking a package, which can work out much cheaper than going independently. If you're on a tight budget, some companies now include simple rooms without bathrooms in their brochures. You'll also find that some of the hotels we recommend are offered on packages.

Single travellers are very badly catered for – even in the more expensive hotels single rooms are often tiny, and frequently have only a shower and a loo rather than a complete bathroom. In cheaper establishments, single rooms tend to be the last ones to have bathrooms installed. Annoyingly, the inferior quality of single rooms is not reflected in the price – at the very least you'll pay 60% of the price of a double, usually you'll pay 70%, and sometimes it can be an outrageous 90%. If you *are* being asked to pay more than 70%, make sure it's a decent room – many hotels will give you a room with a double bed [*matrimoniale*] for the price of a single. If you're coming to Rome on business, and need to work in your room, you must ensure that the room is a good size. If you arrive and discover it is not, insist on changing.

If you're staying for a fortnight or more, consider renting a flat. Agencies like the American-run International Services (see directory) make this extremely easy to do from abroad, and have studios and flats all over the city – some of them in the historic centre. It not only works out cheaper than staying in a hotel, but can be far pleasanter. Another alternative is a *Residenza*, which combines the facilities of hotels with the freedom of staying in a flat. Prices range from L500,000 to L3,000,000 per week, and the tourist office in London should be able to supply you with details.

Children are welcome in virtually all hotels, and though virtually none has babysitters on site, they will try to arrange one for you, though it's worth requesting this in advance, preferably as you book. Though some hotels have cots, many expect babies to share their mothers' beds! If the latter suits you and your baby, you will probably not have to pay extra. Prices for cots, however, can be the same as for an extra bed (as much as 35% of the room rate). Incidentally, nearly all hotels have extra beds.

Staying Alone
Small, friendly, family-run hotels are most comfortable if you're

staying alone, as the staff will soon get to know you. And if you think you're going to want company during your holiday, consider staying in one of the hotels used by package companies, where there should be plenty of your fellow countryfolk to chat to. Large hotels full of politicians and businessmen – particularly those on Via Veneto – are the least enjoyable, and if you see other solo women sitting in their bars, they will probably be high-class call girls. With a few exceptions, drinking alone in the bars of large hotels is pretty dreary unless you take your work with you or have something to write or read. Despite glowing references in many restaurant guides, Roman gastronomes do not rate the city's luxury hotel restaurants highly, so don't go out of your way to eat in them.

The occasional flirty waiter or barman may invite you to the Trevi Fountain at midnight, or some such nonsense. Things are extremely unlikely to go any further – you have to trust that they value their jobs too much – but it is worth avoiding giving out your room number in a bar, just in case there are any unprincipled fellow guests around. Most hotel rooms lock securely from the inside, but most internal phone numbers are simply the room number!

Staying in Rome on Business

Many international companies are based outside the centre at EUR and Magliana, and most industry is concentrated in Pomezia, forty kilometres south of the city. Neither is a particularly appealing place to stay, and you'd be better advised to select a hotel in the centre, so that you can make the most of any time off. Classic business hotels can be terribly impersonal, and unless you need business facilities on site, consider staying in a small four-star or one of the better three-star hotels. Virtually all hotels have fax machines, on which clients can send and receive messages, and many have meeting-rooms which can be hired.

Unless otherwise stated, you can assume that your hotel will have the following facilities:

IDD phones in rooms

24-hour reception or door keys given to guests

Breakfast

Bar

Fax service for clients (if, of course, it has a fax number)

Laundry service

Babysitting on request

Map grid references are supplied when a hotel appears on one of our detailed maps. For hotels on the Aventine and around Termini, and for the hostels and convents, you will need a reliable street map like the F.M.B. or Roma Facile.

Book well in advance for any of these, and remember you have to observe a curfew. The Protezione della Giovane will help women under twenty-five to find a room in a convent or in their hostel, though they can't guarantee to be successful if you arrive on spec. Enjoy Rome are far more likely to come up trumps (see p.247). In university holidays, you can stay extremely cheaply at a hall of residence.

PROTEZIONE DELLA GIOVANE
Termini Station,
tel. 482 7594

Hostel at Via Urbana 158, 00184
ROMA, tel. 488 1489. Metro to
Cavour.

YWCA
Via C Balbo 4, 00184,
tel. 488 0460. Walk from Termini.

Single, double and triple rooms for women only. The hostel is close to Termini, and is not in a particularly pleasant area.

OSTELLO DEL FORO ITALICO
Viale delle Olimpiadi 61,
tel. 3236279. Bus 3 from Termini or
(weekdays until 9 p.m.) 53 from
Piazza San Silvestro.

Rome's youth hostel – which is miles out of the centre. For International Youth Hostel Association members only, but you can join on the spot.

RESIDENZA UNIVERSITARIA DE LOLLIS
Via Cesare de Lollis 20, 00185
ROMA. Bus 71 from Piazza San
Silvestro or 492 from Termini.

A university hall of residence in the San Lorenzo area, which offers bed and breakfast during the vacation. For information and booking, contact AIG, Via Cavour 44, 00194 ROMA, tel. 487 1152.

ISTITUTO MADRI PIE
Via A de Gaspari 4, 00165 ROMA,
tel. 631 967. Bus 62 from Termini.

Singles and doubles, with and without bath, for women only. Near the San Pietro train station. Single room without bath L35,000 (about L5000 extra for a single room with bath).

CONGREGAZIONE SUORE DELLO SPIRITO SANTO
Via della Pineta Sachetti 227, 00168
ROMA, tel. 305 3101. Bus 49 from
Piazza Cavour or Piazza Risorgimento
near the Vatican.

Single, double and triple rooms, with and without bathroom, for single women, couples or families. A long way from anywhere except the Gemelli Hospital.

Campo dei Fiori

If you want to stay in the bustling heart of historic Rome, to be able to breakfast at 6 a.m. with the market folk, and drink till 3 a.m. in raffish bars; to choose between dinner in a simple trattoria or an exclusive restaurant; and to browse in artisans' workshops cluttered with Baroque bric-à-brac, this is the place to be. Most of these hotels are in a little web of interlinking piazzas just off the market square, and the first time you go it's easy to get lost. If you do, head down to Piazza Campo dei Fiori and ask!

Bracketed phone numbers in listings below will come into operation sometime in 1993.

TEATRO DI POMPEO** *Map ref. [D/E 3] p. 86

Largo del Pallaro 8, 00186 ROMA, tel. 687 2566, fax 654 5531. Bus 46, 62, 64, 81, 87, 90 to Sant'Andrea della Valle (on Corso Vittorio Emanuele). Walk alongside the church down Via de' Chiavari. Largo del Pallaro is off to the right.

Tucked into a quiet wedge-shaped square, the Teatro di Pompeo is a small, intimate hotel built over the relics of Pompey's Theatre. There are just 12 rooms (all doubles) with beamed ceilings, bathrooms and tasteful furnishings. All have minibar, safe, TV (with CNN) and radio, and hair dryers are available on request. There's also a pretty bar, and breakfast is served in a room beneath the arches of the ancient theatre. Service is personal, helpful and courteous. It's also worth considering if you're coming to Rome on business and want to stay somewhere with character – it even has a conference room within the ruins of the theatre. Room L155,000. Breakfast L21,000; air-conditioning L20,000 per day. Credit cards: Master, Visa, Amex, Diners, Eurocard.

CAMPO DE' FIORI **Map ref. [D/E 3] p. 51

Via del Biscione 6, 00186 ROMA, tel. 654 0865 (6880 6865), fax 687 6003. Transport: see Teatro di Pompeo. Walk down Via Chiavari and take the first right (Piazza Paradiso). Via del Biscione is to the left, across the tiny adjoining Piazza Pollarola.

A well-above-average two-star hotel in a well-kept coral-painted stone-trimmed building just off Piazza Campo de' Fiori. The decor is unusual – a corridor with an illusionistic fresco and mirrors endlessly reflecting mock Corinthian columns, and bedrooms individually furnished in styles ranging from the rustic to the romantic. There's a roof garden with dizzying views, and a small breakfast room. Nine of the 27 rooms have bathrooms, but all 7 singles are without private facilities. Rooms L60,000–L100,000. Breakfast L20,000; air-conditioning L10,000 per day. Credit cards: Master, Visa, Eurocard. No bar or laundry service.

SOLE **Map ref. [D/E 3] p. 51

Via del Biscione 76, 00186 ROMA, tel. 654 0873 (6880 6873), fax 689 3787. Transport: see Teatro di Pompeo. Walking route: see hotel Campo de' Fiori.

A newly refurbished hotel in an old palazzo a couple of minutes' walk from Piazza Campo de' Fiori. The decor is somewhat bizarre – lino floors twinned with painted beamed ceilings – but the rooms are clean and comfortable. There are lots of tiny sitting areas scattered about, and a leafy courtyard garden (with a drink and snack machine). There are plenty of single rooms, and almost half of the rooms have their own shower and loo. Rooms L60,000–L105,000. Credit cards: no. No breakfast, bar, air-conditioning, babysitting or laundry service.

PICCOLO** Map ref. [D/E 3] p. 51
Via dei Chiavari 32, 00186 ROMA, tel. 654 2560 (6880 2560). Transport: as for Teatro di Pompeo. Walking route: as for Pomezia.

A clean, neat hotel run by a reserved old couple. There are 16 rooms: most of the doubles have private showers but no loos, but the 3 singles are without facilities. Breakfast is served in a small bar area with smart polished granite tables. Rooms L58,000 –L107,000. Breakfast L8000. Credit cards: no. No air-conditioning, babysitting or laundry service. Reception closes at 1 a.m.

POMEZIA** Map ref. [D/E 3] p. 51
Via de' Chiavari 12, 00186 ROMA,

tel. 686 1371. Transport: as for Teatro di Pompeo. Via de' Chiavari runs straight down the side of Sant'Andrea della Valle.

Twenty-two spotless, recently renovated rooms in a friendly hotel in the heart of the Campo de' Fiori neighbourhood. Half of the rooms (including 3 of the 5 singles) have their own bathroom. There's no bar, but drinks are available from reception. Rooms L40,000–L110,000. Breakfast L15,000. Credit cards: Master, Visa, Amex. No air-conditioning, laundry service or babysitting.

DELLA LUNETTA **Map ref. [D3] p. 51
Piazza del Paradiso 68, 00186 ROMA, tel. 686 1080, fax 689 2028. Transport: see Teatro di Pompeo. Walking route: see Campo de' Fiori.

On a quiet piazza between Corso Vittorio Emanuele and Piazza Campo de' Fiori, the Della Lunetta is a clean, tidy, and conveniently located hotel. There are 36 fairly basic rooms – at present 10 doubles and 3 singles have their own shower and loo. There's a leafy internal garden, and a roof garden is to be laid out in the near future. Rooms L40,000–L92,000. Credit cards: no. No breakfast, bar, air-conditioning, babysitting or laundry service.

Piazza Navona and Around

There's nothing *quite* like having Piazza Navona and its effervescent fountains on your doorstep, crossing it several times a day so that you know *exactly* how its moods shift with the hours. The *Raphael* is directly off the square, close to the antique shops of Via dei Coronari and the neighbourhood's trendy bars. The *Due Torri* and *Portoghesi* are tucked behind Corso Rinascimento, in a pocket of streets which remains neighbourly, with restorers and jewellers at work, and little unpretentious bars and grocery shops nestling alongside classy restaurants.

RAPHAEL****Map ref. [C3] p. 51

Largo Febo 2, 00186 ROMA, tel. 650 881 (683 8881), fax 687 8993. Any bus along Corso Rinascimento to the beginning of Via Zanardelli. Largo Febo is just off Via dei Coronari.

The Roman residence of champagne Socialist leader Benito Craxi, the Raphael is a prestigious hotel in a gorgeous ivy-curtained palazzo just off Piazza Navona. Antique statues and pieces of contemporary sculpture stand in the large reception/lounge area, and there are more antiques in the restaurant. Tables are well spaced here, so it's not a bad place for either solo dining or business lunches. The bar is tiny, and unless you want to get into conversation (meeting a Socialist politician could help to oil the wheels in business dealings) it's better to drink in the small lounge leading off it. Rooms are kitted out with eighteenth-century-style furniture, and all have air-conditioning, satellite TV, minibar, and hair dryer. There is just one small meeting-room. Rooms L250,000–L385,000. Breakfast L22,000. Credit cards: Master, Visa, Amex, Diners, EC.

DUE TORRI*** Map ref. [B3] p. 51

Vicolo del Leonetto 23–5, 00186 ROMA, tel. 687 6983 (6880 6956), fax 686 5442. Bus 26, 70, 87, 186 to Piazza Cinque Lune or Via Monte Brianzo. Vicolo del Leonetto is off Via del Cancello, which runs between Via dell'Orso and Via Monte Brianzo.

Concealed in a backwater alley, the Due Torri is a pleasant hotel with affable staff. It's very convenient – a few minutes' walk from both Piazza Navona and Piazza di Spagna – and extremely quiet. Some of the 25 bedrooms are elegant; some are rather plain; but none is particularly large. All have bathroom, TV, radio, minibar, safe and hair dryer. Rooms L65,000–L170,000. Breakfast L25,000; air-conditioning L20,000 per day. Credit cards: Master, Visa, Amex, Diners, EC.

PORTOGHESI*** Map ref. [B3] p. 51

Via Portoghesi 1,00186 ROMA, tel. 686 4231 (6880 5133), fax 687 6976. Buses as for Due Torri as far as Piazza Cinque Lune. Via Giglio d'Oro leads up from Piazza Cinque Lune to Via dell'Orso where you turn right.

A lovely location at the end of Via dell'Orso, opposite the Torre della Scimmie and a few minutes' walk from Piazza Navona, makes the Portoghesi worth considering, though its rooms are rather drab and dated. All have bathroom, hair dryer and TV, and though there's no bar, beer and soft drinks are available. There's also a small roof terrace. Rooms L80,000–L130,000. Breakfast L10,000; air-conditioning L20,000 per day.

NAVONA* Map ref. [D3] p. 51
*Via dei Sediari 8, 00186 ROMA,
tel. 686 4203. Bus 26, 81, 87, 90,
90b, 186, 492 to the first stop on
Corso Rinascimento. Via dei Sediari is
to the right directly off Corso
Rinascimento.*

A *pensione* with basic rooms
(including three singles with
bathroom) in a brilliant location – a
minute's walk from Piazza Navona
and two minutes from the Pantheon.
It's run largely by the owner's
daughter and her Australian husband,
who have their own young child and
are happy to babysit. There's no bar,
but you can usually buy water, and
cans of beer. Rooms
L40,000–L80,000. Breakfast L8,000.
Credit cards: no. No air-conditioning
or laundry service.

Around the Pantheon

You're not going to escape the crowds here, but the locations are
safe and convenient as well as picturesque. Not only are you near
the sights, but two of Rome's best *gelaterie* are close by, along with
some good cafés and bars.

Holiday Inn Minerva*****
Map ref. [D4] p. 51
*Piazza della Minerva 69, 00186
ROMA, tel. 684 1888, fax 679 4165.
Any bus to Largo Argentina. Walk
straight up Via Cestari to Piazza della
Minerva.*

An austere seventeenth-century
palazzo, just behind the Pantheon,
stunningly refurbished by postmodern
architect Paolo Portoghesi. The
interior is fun: *trompe-l'œil* designs on
doors, eggs balancing on columns, and
a lounge canopied with milky pink,
blue and green glass. Bedrooms are
less flamboyant, decorated in muted
shades of beige, coral and pale green,
and the junior suites are among the
few in the city to have separate offices.
All rooms are spacious, and – of
course – air-conditioned, with satellite
TV, radio, minibar, and safe, along
with hair dryer and power shower in
the bathroom. Though it's not a vast
hotel (135 rooms) the public areas,
restaurant and bar are somewhat
impersonal, and it's preferable to do

your eating and drinking elsewhere,
though there is 24-hour room service
for snacks. The best public space is the
roof terrace, which has wonderful
views. Children under nineteen are
free if they're sharing their parents'
bedroom – which can work out very
reasonably. It is also virtually the only
hotel in the centre to have rooms
designed for people with disabilities.
Rooms L320,000–L492,000.
Breakfast L30,000. Credit cards:
Master, Visa, Amex, Diners, EC.

SOLE AL PANTHEON**** Map
ref. [C4] p. 51
*Piazza della Rotonda 63, 00186
ROMA, tel. 678 0441, fax 684 0689.
Any bus to Largo Argentina. Up Via
Cestari across Piazza della Minerva,
and continue along Via della Minerva
until you reach the front of the
Pantheon.*

Former guests of the Sole, founded in
1467, range from Ariosto to Simone
de Beauvoir. The location is wonderful
– right opposite the Pantheon – and

though it has been comfortably modernised, some rooms retain their original coffered ceilings, and the breakfast room has detached frescoes on its walls. Sixty per cent of the 26 rooms have a jacuzzi, and all have air-conditioning, TV, radio, minibar, safe and hair dryer. Many of the rooms are rather small, so they're not ideal if you need to work in them. Rooms L220,000–L380,000. Breakfast L25,000. Credit cards: Master, Visa, Amex, Diners, EC.

Piazza di Spagna and Piazza del Popolo

There's a surprisingly wide range of hotels scattered around the Piazza di Spagna area – from the stately *D'Inghilterra* to the basic *Fiorella*. You've got designer Rome on your doorstep, constantly entertaining streetlife, and you can escape to the Pincio Park when the bustle becomes too much. You can also treat yourself to English breakfasts at Babington's. Bus 119 is useful once you're in Rome, as it does a circuit of the *centro storico*, but the easiest way to get to the area by public transport when you arrive is by Metro. This can involve quite a walk, so consider using a taxi.

HASSLER VILLA MEDICI**** Map ref. [E2] p. 108
Piazza Trinità dei Monti 6, 00187 ROMA, tel. 678 2651, fax 678 9991. Metro to Spagna. Walk straight up the Spanish Steps. The hotel is at the top.

A splendid location and a roof garden with magnificent panoramic view make this the ideal choice for businesswomen who want to make the most of their time off. Founded in the late nineteenth century, it has played host in the past to the royalty and glitterati of Europe and America. Though those halcyon days are over, a solid reputation, discreet staff and good business facilities (secretarial and interpreting as well as a range of prestigious meeting-rooms) means that your stay will probably be irritation-free. The rooms are pretty and fairly spacious, with marble bathrooms, and though public rooms are pleasant rather than sumptuous and lack the atmosphere of somewhere like the Grand, you're unlikely to have any complaints. Rooms L380,000–L750,000. Credit cards: Master, Visa, Amex, Diners, EC.

D'INGHILTERRA**** Map ref. [F2] p. 108
Via Bocca di Leone 14, 00187 ROMA, tel. 672 161 or 679 0889, fax 684 0828. Metro or bus 119 to Spagna. The second left as you head down Via Condotti from Piazza di Spagna.

A venerable old hotel, founded in 1850, whose former guests include the likes of Liszt and Hemingway. A good place to stay if you want to do Rome in style, and one of the upper-notch hotels which is sufficiently genteel and where the staff are usually sufficiently vigilant for you to be able to drink alone in the English-style bar undisturbed. The rooms are not particularly large, but are classically, though individually, decorated and furnished. The main drawback is that the single rooms have only showers and loos rather than full bathrooms.

All rooms, of course, are air-conditioned, most have desks, and all have satellite TV, minibar, safe, and hair dryer. Some come with a balcony. There's a pretty restaurant/breakfast room frescoed with garden scenes, and a smart black-and-white-marble-tiled lunch room. A prestigious temporary address if you've come to Rome on business. Rooms L285,000–L446,000. Breakfast L25,000. Credit cards: Master, Visa, Amex, Diners, EC.

DEI BORGOGNONI**** Map ref. [F/G 2] p. 108

Via del Bufalo 126, 00187 ROMA, tel. 678 0041, fax 684 1501. Any bus to Piazza San Silvestro. Walk up Via Pozzetto from Piazza San Silvestro – it leads into Via del Bufalo.

A recently opened hotel, popular with businesspeople, in a quiet but centrally located street just off Piazza San Silvestro and about five minutes' walk from Piazza di Spagna. Its peacefulness, discreet staff and lack of holidaymakers make it a good choice if you need to concentrate solely on work. The lounge is spacious, with well-spaced seats where you can have a conversation without being overheard, and there's a small bar in the corner. Rooms are medium-sized, with pale-blue fabric walls, and some have terraces overlooking the courtyard garden. All are air-conditioned with satellite TV, radio, minibar, safe and hair dryer. There are only 2 singles, and 10 of the 50 rooms have shower and loo only, so specify if you want a bath [*vasca*]. There are two meeting-rooms, and the staff can arrange translation services. You'll have to go out for dinner, as the hotel serves only snacks. Rooms L275,000–L440,000, breakfast included. Credit cards: Master, Visa, Amex, Diners.

SCALINATA DI SPAGNA*** Map ref. [E2] p. 108

Piazza Trinità dei Monti 17, 00187 ROMA, tel. 679 3006, fax 684 0598. Metro to Spagna. Walk straight up the Spanish Steps. The hotel is on the right.

An endearing hotel in a pretty eighteenth-century villa superbly located at the top of the Spanish Steps, which is ideal if you want a sociable holiday, as guests breakfast together at a single dining table watched by a parrot. The staff are extremely friendly, and service is genuinely personal – which has made the hotel a favourite with visiting celebrities who want to escape the formality of a luxury hotel. But there's nothing pretentious about the Scalinata – photos of famous guests share wall space in the tiny reception room with a bookcase crammed with well-thumbed paperbacks. There are some lovely bedrooms with coffered ceilings and antiquey furniture, and a couple of rooms with private roof terraces. All 15 rooms are air-conditioned, with bathroom, minibar and hair dryer – TV provided on request. There's no lounge or bar, but drinks are available and there *is* a roof terrace decked with flowers and plants, with gorgeous views over the city. Rooms L200,000–L260,000, breakfast included. Credit cards: Master, Visa, EC.

CONDOTTI*** Map ref. [E2] p. 108

Via Mario de' Fiori 37, 00187 ROMA, tel. 679 4661, fax 679 0457. Metro to Spagna. Take the first right as you walk down Via Condotti from Piazza di Spagna.

An ideal location for designer shopaholics (all the big-name shops are within a few minutes' walk), the

Condotti may not look much from the outside, but inside it is at once elegant and welcoming. There are books and magazines to browse through in the country-houseish reception/bar area, and rooms are modern and tastefully decorated. There are no single rooms, but single use of double is not too expensive, and all rooms have TV and minibar. Three rooms open on to a terrace; one room has a private terrace. Rooms L70,000–L133,000. Breakfast L25,000; air-conditioning L20,000 per day. No babysitting.

GREGORIANA*** Map ref. [F3] p. 108

Via Gregoriana 18, 00187 ROMA, tel. 679 4269, fax 678 4258. Metro to Spagna. Walk up the Spanish Steps. Via Gregoriana is to the right.

A slick, stylish hotel close to Piazza di Spagna, popular with the fashion crowd. The decor is slightly offbeat – leopard-print walls in some corridors, William Morris in others, and rooms with twenties fashion drawings and black lacquer doors – but the location and genial staff make it a good bet for solo women. All 19 rooms have bathroom and TV. Rooms L56,000–L142,000. Breakfast L25,000; air-conditioning L20,000 per day. Credit cards: no. No babysitting or bar.

CARRIAGE *** Map ref. [E1/2] p. 108

Via delle Carrozze 136, 00187 ROMA, tel. 699 0124, fax 678 8279. Metro or bus 119 to Spagna. Via delle Carrozze is directly off Piazza di Spagna.

The Carriage exudes elegance. In the reception area there are silky striped sofas and gilded framed mirrors, while the 24 rooms are decorated in serene powder blue, and some have pearly 1930s telephones. There's a pretty terracotta-tiled roof garden, and 3 of the rooms (including 1 single) open on to other roof terraces. All rooms are air-conditioned with bathroom, satellite TV, minibar and hair dryer, but there are only four single rooms. Rooms L160,000–L185,000. Breakfast L25,000. Credit cards: Master, Visa, Amex, Diners, EC. No bar.

MOZART*** Map ref. [E1] p. 108

Via dei Greci 23B, 00187 ROMA, tel. 684 0041, fax 678 4271. Metro to Spagna. Walk along Via del Babuino. Via dei Greci is off to the left.

A pleasant hotel on a quiet street which runs between Via del Babuino and the Corso. The cool, tranquil reception area is stone-flagged, hung with antique Venetian mirrors, and has plenty of pastel flowery sofas to collapse into. Bedrooms have tiled or parquet floors, flowery walls and brass bedsteads. All have bathroom (all but two have shower only), TV, radio, safe and minibar. Though there's no bar, there's a stylish café next door. Rooms L148,000–L203,000. Breakfast L23,000; air-conditioning L30,000 per day. Credit cards: Master, Visa, Amex, Diners.

LOCARNO*** (Off map)

Via della Penna 22, 00186 ROMA, tel. 361 0860, fax 321 5249. Metro to Flaminio. Walk through Porta del Popolo, across Piazza del Popolo and down Via di Ripetta. The first right, Via Oca, runs into Via della Penna.

The Locarno, on a noisy road between the Tiber and Piazza del Popolo, was founded in the 1920s and retains some original Art Nouveau details and

ACCOMMODATION

accessories – a Tiffany lamp and grandfather clock in reception, a wrought-iron cage lift, and a curvaceous polished wood bar in the lounge (which has a real fire in winter). There's also a small patio with a fountain. At the time of inspection the bedrooms were about to be refurbished – it's worth checking when you book that this has been completed, as they were rather worn at the seams! Rooms L125,000–L160,000. Breakfast L25,000; air-conditioning L20,000 per day. Credit cards: Master, Visa, Amex.

MANFREDI *** Map ref. [E2] p. 108
Via Margutta 61, 00187 ROMA, tel. 320 7695, fax 320 7736. Metro to Spagna. Walk along Via del Babuino and turn right up Vicolo Alibert. Via Margutta is the first left.

An excellent choice for solo women. The Manfredi is a courteously and carefully run small hotel on a pedestrianised cobbled street lined with art galleries, just off Piazza di Spagna. There's a small, pretty breakfast room/bar with a tiny balcony; bedrooms are tastefully decorated in restful shades of powder blue and dove grey. All 17 rooms have bathroom, TV, radio, minibar and safe. Rooms L70,000–L170,000. Breakfast L25,000; air-conditioning L20,000 per day. Credit cards: Master, Visa, Amex, EC. No babysitting.

PIAZZA DI SPAGNA*** Map ref. [E2] p. 108
Via Mario de' Fiori 60/61, 00187 ROMA, tel. 679 6412, fax 679 0654. Metro to Spagna. Walk down Via Condotti and take the first right.

A smart, rather genteel little hotel at the heart of the designer shopping area. Bedrooms are a good size, and all 16 have private loo and shower, while some have bath and a couple have jacuzzi. There's only a tiny breakfast room, so most people choose to have breakfast in bed. Rooms L90,000–L139,000. Breakfast L15,500; air-conditioning L20,000 per day. Credit cards: Master, Visa, Amex. No bar, no cots, no babysitting.

MARGUTTA** Map ref. [D1] p. 108
Via Laurina 34, 00187 ROMA, tel. 679 8440/322 3674. Metro to Flaminio. Walk through Porta del Popolo, across Piazza del Popolo and down Via del Corso. Via Laurina is the second left.

On another quiet street between Via del Babuino and Via del Corso. The Margutta's public areas are dingy and dated, but the recently refurbished rooms are very pleasant, with white walls and bottle-green wrought-iron bedsteads. All rooms are doubles (3 have roof terraces), but the prices are fairly reasonable and it's worth negotiating a price for single use of a double. Rooms L94,000. Breakfast L9500. Credit cards: Master, Visa, Amex, Diners, EC. No air-conditioning, babysitting or bar (but soft drinks available).

FIORELLA* Map ref. [D1] p. 108
Via del Babuino 196, 00187 ROMA, tel. 361 0597. Metro to Flaminio. Pass through the Porta del Popolo, across Piazza del Popolo and down Via del Babuino. The hotel is a little way down on the right.

Budget accommodation on one of the classiest streets in Rome, close to Piazza del Popolo and a brief walk from Piazza di Spagna. There are 8 rooms without bathroom, decorated and furnished *ad hoc* with orange-and-green-tiled floors and flowery bedspreads. Rooms L25,000–L60,000. Breakfast L5000. Credit cards: no. Phone in reception. No bar, babysitting, air-conditioning or laundry service.

Via Veneto to Villa Borghese

Via Veneto itself is rather forlorn now, though there are frenzied attempts to resuscitate La Dolce Vita. There are, however, a couple of decent, quiet hotels nearby. The Villa Borghese area is worth considering if you want to relax as well as sightsee – though it's not as appealing (or as peaceful) as the Aventine (see below).

ALDROVANDI PALACE*****
Map ref. [A4] p. 108
Via Ulisse Aldrovandi 15, 00197 ROMA, tel. 322 3993, fax 322 1435. Trams 30b and 19 run outside (but are not very useful – 30b takes a very circuitous route from the Colosseum). Take a taxi.

The Aldrovandi is a luxury hotel outside the city centre on the edge of the Villa Borghese park. Though the road outside is fairly busy, the hotel itself is extremely peaceful, and one of very few in Rome to have a garden and a swimming pool. If you want to combine a lazy poolside holiday with city sightseeing, it's ideal – though you'll have to use taxis even during the day as there's no direct public transport connection with the centre. Public areas are sumptuous, one of the two restaurants overlooks the lush garden, and the bedrooms are decorated in subtle shades of grey and peach, though some of the bathrooms could do with updating. Try to get a room facing the garden. All rooms are air-conditioned, with satellite TV, radio, minibar and hair dryer, and one floor has been set aside for non-smokers. There is also access for people with disabilities. Rooms L275,000–L500,000, breakfast included. Credit cards: Master, Visa, Amex, Diners, EC.

BAROCCO**** Map ref. [F4] p. 108
Piazza Barberini 9/ Via della Purificazione 4, 00187 ROMA, tel. 487 2001, fax 485 994. Metro or any bus to Piazza Barberini. The hotel is on the Via Veneto side of the piazza.

A new hotel in a restored palazzo, ideal for anyone in Rome on business wanting to stay in a small, serious hotel, as all bedrooms have work areas, and some have curtains to screen off the bed. Internal rooms are completely silent, but though the rooms overlooking busy Piazza Barberini are double-glazed, there is a bit of traffic noise. All 28 have a bathroom (13 with shower only) and all are air-conditioned, with satellite TV, radio, minibar, safe and hair dryer. At the time of inspection there was only a bar, but a restaurant was in the process of being built. There are very few singles. Rooms L215,000–L290,000. Breakfast L15,000. Credit cards: Master, Visa, Amex, Diners.

ACCOMMODATION

VILLA BORGHESE*** Map ref. [D4/5] p. 108

Via Pinciana 31, 00198 ROMA, tel. 844 0105, fax 844 2636. Bus 910 passes the hotel, but it's difficult to spot. Take a taxi.

A small hotel in a villa on a busy road fringing the Villa Borghese park, where the owner welcomes you as if you were a guest at a country house party. Apart from a serious lapse of taste in one of the two little lounges (a frescoed nude gripping her nipples) the decor is lovely – Persian rugs and chintzy soft furnishings in the intimate public rooms, and paisley or pastels in the small but comfortable bedrooms. All have bathroom (some with shower only), TV and minibar, and you can borrow a hair dryer. There's also a gorgeous patio canopied by an ivy-covered pergola, which is ideal for a shady mid-afternoon read. Rooms L125,000–L160,000. Breakfast L28,000. Credit cards: Master, Visa, Amex, Diners.

LA RESIDENZA*** Map ref. [E4] p. 108

Via Emilia 22, 00187 ROMA, tel. 488 0789, fax 485 721. Any bus up Via Veneto. Via Emilia runs parallel on the left. The hotel is between Via Ludovisi and Via Liguria.

La Residenza is a tranquil hotel on a quiet road just off Via Veneto. Public rooms are elegant, strewn with Persian carpets and kilim rugs, though the 27 bedrooms (just 4 singles) are rather dull. All have satellite TV, radio and minibar. There are only 2 rooms with private terraces, but there's a roof garden and a raised, sheltered patio above the pretty front courtyard. A good choice if you want peace and quiet as well as a central location. Rooms L90,000–L210,000. Breakfast L25,000. Credit cards: Master, Visa, EC. No air-conditioning. Give advance notice if you need a babysitter.

The Aventine

A perfectly peaceful hill above the Circus Maximus, with some gorgeous hotels in villas with gardens. Book well in advance, as the hotels are frequently used by UN staff working at nearby FAO.

SANT'ANSELMO***

Piazza Sant'Anselmo 2, 00153 ROMA, tel. 574 5174, 574 3214, 574 5232, fax 578 3604. Bus 94 from Piazza Venezia to Piazza Albania or Via Santa Sabina. Via Santa Sabina is closer, but it's not easy to get off at the right stop, so ask someone. Turn left along Via Sabina towards Piazza Cavalieri di Malta, and then down Via Porta Lavernale to Piazza Sant'Anselmo. Piazza Albania is a busy junction on Viale Aventino. Via

di Sant'Anselmo leads off it, climbing the hill to Piazza Sant'Anselmo and the hotel. Alternatively, take a taxi!

An idyllic hotel in an ochre-and-russet-washed villa on the lush, leafy, peaceful Aventine Hill. The decor, particularly in the public rooms, is exquisite – inlaid marble floors, stencilled flowers on walls and ceilings, flowery soft furnishings, and glinting chandeliers – and there's a secluded garden with wrought-iron chairs and tables under a trellis. Some of the 46 rooms are rather plain; others have buttermilk, pink and aqua hand-painted and gilded antique furniture whose colours and motifs are echoed on the embroidered bedcovers. Rooms L120,000–L175,000. Breakfast L18,000. Credit cards: Master, Visa, Amex. No air-conditioning. TV on request (L10,000).

VILLA SAN PIO***
Via Sant'Anselmo 19, 00153 ROMA (check in at the Sant'Anselmo). Phone and fax as for Sant'Anselmo, transport as for Sant'Anselmo.

Another very special hotel in a yellow and ochre villa, set within a garden studded with Classical statues. As in the Sant'Anselmo, the public rooms are beautiful, and here too some of the bedrooms have embroidered soft furnishings and flower-stencilled furniture. Though there's no bar, drinks can be ordered in the garden or from bedrooms. Rooms L120,000–L175,000. Breakfast L18,000. Credit cards: Master, Visa, Amex. No air-conditioning.

AVENTINA**
Via San Domenico 10, 00153 ROMA (check in at Sant'Anselmo). Phone and fax as for Sant'Anselmo, transport as for Sant'Anselmo.

Though much simpler than either the Sant'Anselmo or Villa San Pio, the Aventino is also set in a villa, and many of the rooms open straight on to its lovely garden. Rooms L45,000–L98,000. Breakfast L18,000. Credit cards: Master, Visa, Amex. No air-conditioning.

DOMUS AVENTINO**
Via di Santa Prisca 11B, 00153 ROMA, tel. 574 6135/574 6189, fax 5730 0044. Any bus to Piazza

Albania, or bus 94 to the first stop on Via di Santa Prisca.

A spotless, recently refurbished hotel in a fourteenth-century convent, run by a friendly couple. Rooms are simple and spacious, and many have balconies overlooking the church next door. There's also a vast roof terrace. All rooms have satellite TV, minibar and hair dryer. Rooms L120,000–L160,000, breakfast included. Credit cards: Master, Visa, Amex. No air-conditioning.

Vatican

ATLANTE STAR**** Map ref. [B3] p. 151
Via G Vitelleschi 34, 00193 ROMA, tel. 687 9558 (687 3049), fax 687 2300. Hotel has own bus shuttle service to and from the airport (L30,000).

This hotel should be considered only if you need business facilities on site. All rooms are small, singles are tiny, the place lacks any atmosphere, and though the views from the roof garden restaurant are magnificent, the food and service are not. As you would expect in a four-star hotel, all rooms are air-conditioned with satellite TV, radio, minibar and hair dryer. The business office and conference room are equipped with video, fax and telex. Rooms L210,000–L420,000. Breakfast L27,000. Credit cards: Master, Visa, Amex, Diners.

COLUMBUS*** Map ref. [B3] p. 151
Via della Conciliazione 33, 00193 ROMA, tel. 686 5435, fax 686 4874. Bus 64 to Via Corridori (the terminus). Via Rusticucci cuts from Via Corridori to Via della Conciliazione. The hotel is a short

walk down the road, heading away from St Peter's.

For anyone whose main reasons for coming to Rome are religious, the Columbus is ideal. It's just down the road from the Vatican, and retains the rather austere, contemplative atmosphere of the ex-monastery it occupies. Rooms are adequate, if slightly dated, and the beds are ascetically narrow! All rooms (both with and without bathroom) are air-conditioned, and have TV, minibar and hair dryer. Rooms L65,000–L150,000. Credit cards: Master, Visa, Amex, Diners.

Trastevere

MANARA* Map ref. [E3] p. 141
Via Luciano Manara 25, 00153 ROMA, tel. 581 4713. Any bus along Viale Trastevere to the junction with Via San Francesco a Ripa. Turn up Via San Francesco a Ripa (away from the church). Via Luciano Manara is just off it on the left.

A tiny, very simple hotel with a friendly, helpful owner, well positioned if you're intending to spend evenings in Trastevere's bars and restaurants. All rooms are without bath but though there are no singles, the doubles are good value. Rooms L52,000. Credit cards: no. No bar, breakfast, air-conditioning or babysitting. No phones in rooms.

CARMEL* Map ref. [F3] p. 141
Via G Mameli 8, 00153 ROMA, tel. 580 9921. Bus 75 to Via Morosini. Via Mameli leads straight off Via Morosini. The hotel is on the left.

A great little hotel, with just 10 rooms (only 1 single) on the edge of Trastevere. The rooms are simple and spotless; some open straight on to a roof terrace, and virtually all have bathroom. Book well in advance, as the old lady owner closes when she thinks there isn't much work! She's not keen on having too many children in the hotel, so you should check first if you're travelling with yours. Rooms L50,000–L80,000. Breakfast L10,000. Credit cards: no.

Termini

Though the area immediately around Termini is not recommended for solo women at night, the streets to the north of the station are reasonably safe and quiet. None of the hotels recommended involves getting off a bus or metro at Termini.

LE GRAND HOTEL***** Map ref. [F/G 5/6] p. 108
Via Vittorio Emanuele Orlando 3, 00185 ROMA, tel. 4709, fax 474 7307. Metro to Repubblica. The hotel is just off Piazza della Repubblica.

Despite its setting, on a busy, ugly road, Le Grand is arguably Rome's most opulent hotel. The nineteenth-century public rooms are stunningly extravagant: decorated with playful cherubs, swags of fruit and flowers, gilded panelling and hand-embroidered brocades, lit with chandeliers and strewn with sumptuous rugs. The bar is warm and welcoming, with a pink-and-gilt ceiling, brocade curtains and comfortable sofas, and the restaurant really is worth eating in. Bedrooms vary – some are graciously furnished with antiques; others are hallmarked with the taste of more recent eras (notably the vibrant green tiles in some of the bathrooms). Naturally all are air-conditioned, with satellite TV, radio and minibar, and though hair dryers have not yet been installed in all bathrooms, you do get a bathrobe! Service is attentive without being too formal. Rooms L280,000–L624,000. Breakfast L30,000. Credit cards: Master, Visa, Amex, Diners.

CANADA***

Via Vicenza 58, 00185 ROMA, tel. 495 7385/445 7770, fax 445 0749. Metro to Castro Pretorio. Walk straight along Viale Castro Pretorio. Via Vicenza is off on the right.

An above-average mid-bracket hotel, with helpful, friendly staff, used by some of the better package tour companies. Rooms are thoughtfully designed and extremely comfortable – all are air-conditioned, with TV, radio (speakers in the bathrooms too!), safe and hair dryer. The decor and furnishings vary from room to room, but all are tasteful. Rooms L110,000–L180,000. Breakfast L20,000. Credit cards: Master, Visa, Amex, Diners, EC.

GEXIM*

Via Palestro 34, 00185 ROMA, tel. 446 0211/444 1311 Bus 492 or 75 to Piazza Indipendenza. Walk straight up Via San Martin della Battaglia and turn left along the second cross-street, Via Palestro.

Don't be put off by the scruffy, graffiti-scrawled façade of the palazzo housing the Gexim (along with a number of other small hotels). Its 9 rooms and communal bathrooms are immaculate, with pastel-painted walls and prints of Impressionist paintings. Rooms L38,000–L70,000, breakfast excluded. Credit cards: no. No air-conditioning, babysitting or bar. Pay-phone in reception.

EATING AND DRINKING

EATING

The thought of eating alone – particularly in Italy – can be nerve-racking. If you haven't done it before, you may feel self-conscious walking into a crowded restaurant, be convinced that everyone is looking at you, and find that it helps to have a book to read or a letter to write while you eat. But as you grow more accustomed to it, you really can relax and enjoy yourself.

For eating alone in Rome can be wonderful. In spring and summer you can dine outside, often with streetlife to keep you occupied. In cold weather you can eat in chaotic neighbourly trattorias, and eating alone gives you the chance to key into the life that most tourists miss. Most satisfying of all is becoming a regular. It doesn't take long for the staff and other habitués to recognise you, and even if you don't speak Italian, you'll soon feel a part of things. For times when you want to be alone, the larger, more anonymous trattorias or formal upmarket restaurants are the places to go.

The vast majority of places we recommend for eating and drinking are in and around Piazza Navona, Campo dei Fiori, Piazza di Spagna and Trastevere. Trastevere can be slightly rowdy, though you'll soon get used to it, but the other neighbourhoods are usually full of tourists and respectable Italians as well as young things out on the town. But if you're not used to eating alone, you need to build your confidence. The trick is to act confidently. There's no harm in assuming an 'I've-been-doing-this-all-my-life' expression, nor in feigning oblivion to all that is happening around you. It's also worth being assertive (with a smile) to the waiters. Where you sit is incredibly important, especially as in many pizzerias and trattorias the tables are only a couple of inches apart. Look or wait for a table at which you'll feel comfortable, and ask for it. There's no point in accepting a table which is right next to a group of boisterous men, because unless you want to talk to them, you'll have a miserable time. If the waiter won't oblige, it really is better to walk out and go elsewhere.

Occasionally, men will start to talk to you. If you want to be alone, blank them immediately; if you want to talk, don't look too eager, even if you're desperate for company. Aim to give the impression that you're quite content alone, but happy to chat. If you have second thoughts, either make firm excuses and leave, or (much easier) discreetly ask the waiter to order you a taxi. If you get on well, you can agree to join them for a coffee or *digestivo*, or even go on elsewhere, though it's wise to pick somewhere close to your hotel so that you can make a swift exit if necessary.

DRINKING

All bars and cafés sell alcohol as well as soft drinks and beverages, and as there are no restrictive licensing hours you can (and people *do*) start the day with a grappa. The most basic establishments have stainless-steel bars, a shelf of lurid liqueurs, a steaming coffee machine, photos of football teams, a tray of *cornetti*, a few sandwiches, a rack of chewing gum, and floors sprinkled with sawdust, cigarette stubs and paper napkins. Most have standing room only – or a couple of tables at most – and are places for a quick drink or sandwich. If you *do* take one of the tables, you'll pay extra. Most are open from around 8 a.m. to 8 p.m.

For a leisurely drink or snack, you need a café or bar with tables – preferably outside. On major piazzas like Navona and Popolo these can be very expensive, but you *can* dawdle for as long as you like, and sitting on a café terrace watching the streetlife is one of the most enjoyable aspects of being in the city. If you're alone in the evenings, you may be approached – see Sexual Harassment (p.26) for hints on how to deal with it.

Many cafés are open from 8 a.m. till after midnight, so if you find one you like, you can have breakfast and lunch, as well as doing your evening drinking there. Not only does drinking somewhere familiar make you feel more confident, but you can track the shifts in atmosphere: from the leisurely emptiness of early morning, through the chaos of the day, to late at night when the waiters carry away the tables, leaving the city's last drinkers isolated on deserted piazzas.

That said, getting wasted is not something Romans tend to do – which is partly why the city's streets at night feel less threatening than they do in Britain. Buying another round as soon as someone's glass is empty is not customary, and it's not unusual for people to sit all night over one drink, which can take some getting used to. In the more raffish bars and alternative clubs the drinking is heavier – though a good number of those knocking back the alcohol are likely to be expat Brits. Whatever you do, don't get drunk alone.

The most comfortable places for solo drinking are the wine bars (known as *vinerie* or *enoteche*), where most of the habitués are too civilised to give you any hassle. 'Sophisticated' bars like Hemingway's and Le Cornacchie are not ideal: you'll be terribly conspicuous, and even if no one makes a move, you're likely to feel pretty self-conscious. However, if the *demi-monde*-ish life of bars appeals, if you want strange encounters with ageing transvestites, self-styled gurus, jaded expats and angry young things, you *can* do it, and it *is* exhilarating. You need to speak Italian, you need to know exactly what you're doing, and it helps if you can come across as sassy, streetwise and someone who can't readily be pigeonholed – the last thing you want is to give the impression that you're an innocent, an alcoholic or a nymphomaniac. Select somewhere like Goldfinch or San Calisto, stand or sit at the bar, and initiate the conversation yourself – with the barman, barwoman or fellow drinkers. You *are* playing with fire, but it *can* be done without getting your fingers burnt, especially if you remain sober.

Coffee and Tea

Cappuccino is traditionally drunk only in the morning. The rest of the day it's a case of popping into a bar for an espresso – a short sharp shot of caffeine – usually referred to simply as *un caffè*. Italians spend minutes carefully stirring sugar into their cubic inch of coffee, then down the solution in seconds.

Coffee comes in numerous forms: *caffè macchiato* (with a dash of hot milk); *latte macchiato* (a glass of milk with a dash of coffee served hot [*caldo*], lukewarm [*tiepido*] or cold [*freddo*]); *caffè coretto* (spiked with alcohol – specify what you want); *caffè lungo* (a double espresso); and *caffè decaffeinizzato* (decaffeinated and usually referred to simply as *Hag*). There's also *caffelatte* – cappuccino without the froth. In summer you can have iced coffee, *caffè freddo* (which usually comes with sugar, but you can ask for it without: *senza zucchero*) or *granita* – frozen coffee.

Tea [*tè*] is available everywhere: expect to be given a cup of hot(tish) water, with a teabag on the side. You'll be asked if you want it *al limone* (with a slice of lemon) or *con latte* (with milk – sometimes warm, and usually long-life). Herbal and fruit teas are extremely popular. *Camomilla* (camomile) is most common, but there's often *menta* (mint) and occasionally *finocchio* (fennel seed), which is wonderful if you have digestive problems. In summer, iced tea [*tè freddo*] is popular. It's usually very sweet, and flavoured with lemon or peach.

Soft Drinks

The cheapest thing to drink is mineral water [*acqua minerale*]. If you don't specify *senza gas*, it will be carbonated [*gassata*]. As well as Coke, Sprite and Fanta, there are various home-grown fizzy drinks: LemonSoda and OranSoda are good. Fruit juices and freshly squeezed fruit juices are widely available – *succo* should be unsweetened; *nectar* will have sugar. The most common juices are orange [*arancia*], pineapple [*pina*], peach [*pesca*] and pear [*pera*]. A freshly squeezed juice [*spremuta*] (usually orange or lemon) is obviously far more expensive, and a favourite waiter trick is to bring foreigners a *spremuta* when they asked for a *succo*. Send it back. Milkshakes are common – but look for somewhere that makes them with fresh fruit [*frullati*] rather than synthetic syrup [*frappé*]. There are also various non-alcoholic aperitifs, which usually resemble cough medicine.

Alcohol

Beer [*birra*] is nearly always lager, and comes in cans, bottles and on tap. The most common Italian brand is Peroni, but there are also a lot of German beers, and familiar Mexican beers feature in trendy bars, served with a slice of lemon. It's cheapest to have an Italian beer [*birra nazionale*] on tap [*alla spina*]. A *birra piccola* is .20 litres (the equivalent to a half-pint); a *birra media* is .40 litres. Vodka, gin and brandy are all common, as is grappa – fiery, powerfully potent, and pretty cheap. You'll also find Cinzano, Martini and Campari – a Campari Soda comes ready mixed in a bottle (but can be improved by being diluted with orange juice and spiked with vodka).

There are scores of liqueurs. The nicest are *amaretto* (almond) and *sambuca* (aniseed). Ask for the latter with a *mosca* – literally a fly, but actually a coffee bean. You then set the drink alight and watch the caffeine grains appear. *Digestivi* – usually herbal-based after-dinner drinks – are well worth investigating (and really do settle the stomach after a big meal). *Averna* is dark, syrupy, comforting and sweet; *Fernet Branca* is rather bitter; and *Centerbe* is bitter-sweet and made from a hundred different herbs.

The most common wine in Rome is from the Castelli Romana – the local hill villages. Most famous is Frascati, but the unnamed versions are usually drinkable. Other wines worth looking out for are Arneis (a refined white), Velletri (a robust red), Est! Est! Est! (which comes in both dry and demi-sec versions), and Grottaferrata (a sharp, aromatic white). Dry sparkling wine, *prosecco*, is available in most wine bars – it's usually white, but there is also a rosé version.

Breakfast, Snacks, Takeaways

The typical Italian breakfast is a cappuccino and *cornetto* – a plain, jam, custard, chocolate or raisin-filled croissant – traditionally consumed standing up at the bar. If you don't like sweet breakfasts you can usually get a *toast* (toasted ham and cheese sandwich), but before nine o'clock you'll often find that the more interesting sandwiches have not yet been prepared. For a really healthy breakfast you'll need to picnic: bakeries, *alimentari* selling yoghurt and juice, and the fruit and vegetable markets all open by nine o'clock.

Along with the obligatory burger bars, there are scores of small outlets selling *pizza al taglio* – rectangular slices of pizza sold by weight. Many are open from mid-morning till the early hours. Some have benches, a few have tables, but in most people stand leaning against the walls, or cluster outside. If you prefer to take your pizza away and eat in peace, ask to have it wrapped up [*mi fa un pachetto per favore?*]. For something more substantial, go to a *tavola calda* – these sell hot stuffed vegetables, pasta, and meat dishes to take away.

Virtually all bars and cafés sell sandwiches. Italian bread is excellent, apart from the cotton-woolly white sliced used in *tramezzini*. There are all sorts of crusty rolls; *focaccia*, a kind of pizza bread; and *piadina*, pockets of unleavened bread which are a bit like pitta. Despite its popularity in Britain, *ciabatta* is rare. Ham, prosciutto, salami and mozzarella with tomato or spinach are the most common sandwich fillings, but there are also more interesting combinations like *bresaola* and *rughetta* (sometimes with creamy *mascarpone* cheese as well).

Italian ice cream – as long as you pick your *gelateria* carefully – is every bit as good as it's cracked up to be. Some establishments sell hundreds of bizarre flavours, such as fig or avocado, though strawberry, chocolate and pistachio are hard to beat. Even a small ice cream [*un piccolo*] gives you two generous scoops, and you'll usually be asked if you want *panna* – a complimentary dollop of whipped cream. Skipping a dessert at a restaurant, and going for a late stroll with an ice cream around the *centro storico*, is a pleasant way to end an evening.

PIZZA AL TAGLIO

There are *pizza al taglio* outlets all over the city. Outstanding ones are included in the listings, but here are some streets to target if you need a quick snack while sightseeing. Most open from around 10 a.m. to 2 p.m. and from 5 p.m. until late.

Via Tor di Millina (off Piazza Navona)

Via dei Pastini, Via Giustiniani and Via Minerva (near the Pantheon)

Via San Vincenzo, Via del Lavatore (near the Trevi Fountain)

Borgo Pio (south of the Vatican and St Peter's)

Viale Trastevere

Via della Croce (south of Piazza di Spagna)

RESTAURANT OPENING TIMES AND BOOKINGS

Few trattorias or pizzerias will take bookings, and if you arrive at a popular one after 9 p.m., you'll probably have to queue. It's always worth reserving a table in more expensive restaurants, and essential on Friday and Saturday nights.

Most restaurants, trattorias and pizzerias open lunchtime from around 1 p.m. to 3 p.m. and in the evenings from 7.30 p.m. Few people eat before nine in the evenings, and orders are rarely taken after 11 p.m. – to be on the safe side, don't arrive much after 10.30 p.m.

Credit cards are not accepted unless otherwise stated.

Most bars and restaurants close in August: here are a few which stay open:

Lo Scoppetaro (see p.293)
La Tana di Noantri (see p.292)
Caffè Colombia (see p.278)
Bar San Calisto (see p.293)
Burghy (see p.280)

Bracketed phone numbers in listings below will come into operation sometime in 1993.

MENU

Basics

These are words worth learning!

piatto del giorno	dish of the day
pane e coperto	bread and cover charge
il conto	the bill
il coltello	knife
la forchetta	fork
il cucchiaio	spoon
la bicchiere	glass
il piatto	plate
la tassa	cup
il portacenere	ashtray
la carta	menu
antipasti	starters
primo	pasta, soup, risotto
secondo	fish or meat course
contorno	vegetable or salad
dolce	sweet
formaggio	cheese
carne	meat
pesce	fish
insalata	salad
pane	bread
grissini	bread sticks

sale	salt
pepe	pepper
olio	oil
aceto	vinegar
maionese	mayonnaise
caldo	hot
freddo	cold
cornetto	croissant
marmellata	jam
espresso/caffè	short, strong coffee
cappuccino	frothy coffee
tè	tea
cioccolata calda	hot chocolate
vino	wine
rosso	red
bianco	white
secco	dry
amabile/abboccato	medium-sweet wine
dolce	very sweet wine
birra	beer
acqua minerale	mineral water
con/senza gas	fizzy/still
granita	fruit/coffee crushed ice drink
spremuta	freshly squeezed juice (expensive)
succo	juice

Pizza

forno al legna	wood oven (makes the most authentic pizza)	Margherita	with mozzarella, tomato and often basil
calzone	folded pizza with mozzarella, salami or ham, tomato or egg, baked or deep-fried	marinara	with tomato and garlic but no mozzarella
capricciosa	usually a wild mix of toppings	quattro stagione	with four different toppings
		quattro formaggi	with four different cheeses
cardinale	with ham and olives		
funghi	with tinned sliced mushrooms	Napoli	with tomato, anchovies and olive oil
frutta di mare	with seafood		

A–Z Food and Cooking Terms

A

abbacchio	roast baby lamb
acciughe or alice	anchovies
aceto	vinegar
acqua minerale	mineral water
affumicato	smoked
aglio	garlic
agnello	lamb
albicocche	apricots
al forno	baked
alla brace	barbequed
amaretti	bitter almond biscuits
amatriciana	tomato and bacon pasta sauce (usually with bucatini)
ananas	pineapple
anguilla	eel
animelle	sweetbreads
antipasto misto	mixed cold meats and cheese
aragosta	lobster
arancia	orange
arrabiata	tomato and chilli pasta sauce (usually with bacon)
arringa	herring
arrosto	roast
asparagi	asparagus

B

baccalà	dried, salted cod
banane	bananas
basilico	basil
bistecca	steak*
bollito misto	mixed boiled meats and salami
Bolognese	meat and tomato sauce
bresaola	cured beef; very finely sliced
brocoletti	miniature broccoli
bruschetta	doorstep of bread toasted with oil and garlic
bucatini	thick hollow spaghetti
burro	butter

C

caccia	game
calamari	squid
calzone	folded pizza
cannelloni	large tubes of stuffed pasta
capperi	capers
carbonara	spaghetti sauce with ham and beaten egg

carciofi	artichokes	forno al legna	wood-fired oven (makes the best pizza)
castrato	castrated lamb		
cavolfiori	cauliflower		
ceci	chickpeas	fragole	strawberries
cervello	brain	fragolini	tiny wild strawberries
cilegie	cherries		
cinghiale	wild boar	frittata	omelette
cioccolata	chocolate (also cocoa)	fritto	fried
		frullati	milkshake
cipolla	onion	frutta di mare	seafood
coco	coconut	frutti di bosco	fruits of the forest
coda di bue	oxtail	funghi	mushrooms
coniglio	rabbit	funghi porcini	very expensive wild mushrooms; meaty taste; usually dried, in a pasta sauce
cornetto	croissant		
cotiche	pork skin, cooked till jellified		
cotolette	chops		
cotto	cooked	**G**	
cozze	mussels		
crostata	flan	gamberetti	shrimps
crostini	bread dipped in egg and baked; often with cheese	gambero	prawns
		gelato	ice cream
		gnocchi	potato-dough pasta – usually buttons
crudo	raw		
		Gorgonzola	soft blue cheese
D		granchio	crab
		granita	slushy iced coffee or lemon
dentice	dentex (a white fish)		
dolce	sweet/dessert	alla griglia	grilled
F		**I**	
fagiano	pheasant	insalata	salad
fagioli	beans (pulses)	insalata mista	green and tomato salad (and often onion and grated carrot)
fagiolini	French beans		
farfalle	butterfly-shaped pasta		
fave	broad beans	insalata selvatica	wild green salad
fegatini	chicken liver	insalata verde	green salad
fegato	liver		
fettucine	thin pasta ribbons	**L**	
fighi	figs		
finocchio	fennel	latte	milk
fiori di zucchini	courgette flowers	lepre	hare
focaccia	hot flat bread made with oil (basically like plain pizza bread)	limone	lemon
		lingua	tongue

M

macedonia	fruit salad
maiale	pork
mandorle	almonds
manzo	beef
mascarpone	more like cream than a cheese – very rich. Vital ingredient in tiramisù
matriciana	tomato and bacon pasta sauce
mela	apple
melanzane	aubergines
merluzzo	cod
Milanese	fried in egg and breadcrumbs
milze	spleen
minestrone	vegetable and pasta soup
mortadella	salami
mozzarella	the famous pizza cheese, but common in sandwiches and salads
mozzarella alla bufala	the best mozzarella – made with buffalo milk

O

olio	oil
olive	olives
ossobucco	stew with veal marrow
ostriche	oysters

P

pagliata	intestines of unborn calf
pane	bread
panino	bread roll/sandwich
panna	cream
panna cotta	crème brûlée (with or without the brûlée)
Parmigiano	Parmesan
patate	potatoes

patatine fritte	chips
pecorino	pungent sheep's cheese
penne	small tubes of pasta
penne primavera	penne tossed with mozzarella, tomato and fresh basil
pepe	pepper
peperoni	peppers
pere	pears
pesca	peach
pesce spada	sword fish
pesce S. Pietro	John Dory
pesto	pasta sauce of basil, garlic, pine nuts and oil
piadina	unleavened circular bread – like pitta
piccione	pigeon
piselli	peas
polenta	boiled cornmeal – can be grilled/toasted as well
polipo	octopus
pollo	chicken
pomodoro	tomato
prosciutto crudo	raw cured ham
prosciutto cotto	roast or boiled ham

Q

quaglio	quail

R

radicchio	chicory (sometimes red)
ragù	meat sauce for pasta
ravioli	largeish squares of pasta stuffed with meat or ricotta and spinach
ribollita	veg and white bean soup, poured over bread
ricotta	soft white cheese, good with pasta

rigatoni	large tubes of grooved pasta	toast	toasted ham and cheese sandwich
ripieno	stuffed	tonno	tuna
riso	rice	torta	cake
risotto	risotto	tortellini	knots of pasta stuffed with cheese or meat
rognone	kidney		
rughetta	rocket – nutty-tasting salad leaf – more bitter than the UK variety	tramezzino	sandwich made of white sliced bread
		triglia	red mullet
		trippa	tripe
S		trota	trout
salame	salami	**U**	
sale	salt		
salmone	salmon	uova	egg
salsiccia	sausage	uve	grapes
saltimbocca	veal with ham, mozzarella and sage, sometimes in a Marsala sauce		
		V	
		vitello	veal
sarde	sardines	vongole	clams
seppie	cuttlefish	vongole veraci	big clams
sogliola	sole		
spaghetti alle vongole	spaghetti with clam and tomato sauce	**Y**	
spaghettini	thin spaghetti	yoghurt	yoghurt
spinaci	spinach		
stracetti	thin slices of cooked meat	**Z**	
suppli	crumbed deep-fried rice balls (with bits of meat, and sometimes with cheese in the middle)	zucchero	sugar
		zucchini	courgettes
		zuppa	soup
		Zuppa Inglese	trifle

*Italians eat their steaks very rare (*sangue* means – and is – bloody). *Ben cotto*, which means well-done, is not! *Molto ben cotto* (very well-cooked) is the equivalent to the British well-done.

T

tacchino	turkey
tagliatelle	same as fettucine
testarella	head

Map grid references are supplied when an establishment appears on one of our detailed maps. For places outside the centre, you will need a reliable street map like the *F.M.B* or *Roma Facile*.

The prices given for restaurants are approximate, but based on a full Italian meal (in *pizzerias* on a pizza and beer). Remember to take account of inflation.

In Italy as a whole, most people eat their lunch at home, and over 50% have their main meal at lunchtime – which means there are an awful lot of women tied to the kitchen midday. In Rome and the big cities, however, the proportion of people eating out at lunchtime is far higher. The traditional lunch break is two hours or more – usually from around 1.30 p.m. to 4 p.m. – but a number of firms have adopted Northern-European-style one-hour breaks, which does not leave time for employees to go home for lunch, or to have a full meal.

Lunching or dining healthily is easy, as long as you like pasta. There are usually vegetable-based sauces (and you get far less sauce with your pasta than in British Italian restaurants). Some of the sauces with offal or bacon can be a bit fatty, and main meat courses can be greasy in trattorias – peep at what other people are eating before ordering.

You need a large appetite to consume an entire Italian meal, but it's perfectly acceptable to have only a pasta or meat course and salad (if you opt for the former, it keeps the price down). Traditionally, however, you begin with an *antipasto: prosciutto*, mozzarella, salami, or a selection of vegetables or seafood. Typically Roman *antipasti* include *carciofi* (artichokes) in various forms: *alla giudea* (deep-fried), *alla Romana* (stuffed with mint and garlic) and *alla mattone* (beaten flat and fried). Then comes the *primo* – pasta or soup. Roman specialities are *bucatini all'Amatriciana* (hollow spaghetti with tomato and bacon sauce), *spaghetti alle vongole* (spaghetti with clams), *gnocchi* (tiny potato dumplings, often served simply with Parmesan), and *spaghetti alla carbonara* (spaghetti with beaten egg and bacon). Other common pasta dishes are *penne alla primavera* (pasta tubes with cubes of mozzarella, raw tomato and basil leaves added at the last moment) and any pasta with artichokes. Pasta dishes with offal sauces are also popular – the delicacy above all delicacies is *pagliata* or *paiata*, the innards of an unborn calf removed from its mother's womb. It looks like hollow worms and tastes like mild liver.

You then move on to the *secondo*, the main fish or meat course. Roman specialities are *abbacchio* (unweaned lamb roasted with oil, vinegar, sage, rosemary and garlic); *saltimbocca alla romana* (slices of veal cooked with *prosciutto* and mozzarella, sometimes served with Marsala sauce); *trippa alla romana* (tripe stewed with tomato and mint); *involtini* (stuffed rolls of veal); *scottadito* (grilled lamb chops); and *coda alla vaccinara* (stewed oxtail). There's also quite a bit of game [*caccia*] in season. If none of these appeals, there is usually something plainer like grilled steak, but if you don't specify how you want it cooked, it will be extremely rare. *Ben cotto* is roughly the equivalent to medium-rare.

There are always salads, the most interesting being *insalata selvatica*, a green, bitter salad with wild leaves. For dessert [*dolce*] there is usually ice cream and fruit (look out for wild strawberries [*fragolini*] in May and June). Among the more decadent desserts are *zabaglione* and *tiramisù* (properly a kind of trifle with mascarpone cheese, sponge cake, cream, liqueur and chocolate, but there are lots of commercial fakes).

Pizzerie and Trattorie

An authentic trattoria is a neighbourly place, serving simple, home-cooked food. A pizzeria traditionally serves nothing but pizza. Nowadays, however, some pizzerias serve pasta, some trattorias serve pizza, and many trattorias have become large, anonymous places catering for tourists. But there are plenty of traditional trattorias in Rome – family-run establishments where the cook doubles as a waitress, and the decor hasn't changed for decades. Expect teak-effect Formica walls covered with photos of football teams, sheets of paper on the tables, and to have the menu reeled off (usually at top speed) by the waiter. Quite often there *is* a written menu, so it's always worth asking.

Most trattorias have a limited selection of bottled wine, but the house white – from the Castelli, the local hill towns (which include Frascati) – is usually drinkable: clean-tasting, dry and uncomplicated. Sometimes, though, it's adulterated with chemicals, and even modest quantities can result in a headache the next morning. It's wise to order water as well. Don't be surprised if you get only one glass for both wine and water – like their ancient ancestors most Romans dilute their wine.

The cheapest place to eat is a pizzeria, though as these tend to attract big groups of lads, they're not ideal for solo eating. In the best pizzerias you should expect to queue, and you should decide in advance what you want to order. There will usually be a menu board – if you can't see it, most of the standard pizzas will be available, and if you speak Italian, you can order a customised pizza.

Trendy Restaurants and Wine Bars

Rome has a number of young, trendy restaurants which are ideal for solo dining, as they attract a fairly cultured clientele. They tend to serve healthy New Wave Italian food – salads, herb and vegetable pasta sauces, and little meat. Some of the wine bars [*vinerie* or *enoteche*] are also excellent places for lunch or light dinner, serving a wide – and often sophisticated – range of salads, pâtés, regional cheeses, cured meats and salamis. Again, these are frequented by an arty/intellectual crowd.

EATING AND DRINKING

Snacks, Fast Food, Takeaways

PIZZA AL TAGLIO Map ref.
[C/D 2] p. 51
*Via del Governo Vecchio 28. Open
Mon–Fri 8.30 a.m.–2 p.m.; 5–7.30
p.m.*

A brilliant little place which is packed
at lunchtime. You order a slice of
plain pizza bread and specify what
you want on it – *bresaola*, *rughetta*
and tomato is a delicious
combination. There's also wine and
water – usually people help
themselves.

DA QUINTO Map ref. [C3]
p. 51
*Via di Tor Millina 15. Open 1 p.m.–2
a.m.; closed Wed.*

Ice cream, fresh fruit juices and
milkshakes.

CREPERIE Map ref. [C3] p. 51
*Via di Tor Millina 8. Open 10.30
a.m.–2.30 p.m.; closed Tues.*

Takeaway sweet and savoury crepes.

BAR Map ref. [B3] p. 51
*Via dell'Orso 29. Open 7 a.m.–8
p.m.; closed Sun.*

Good ham-and-cheese-filled *focaccia*.

Ristoranti, Trattorie, Pizzerie

LA MONTECARLO Map ref.
[D2] p. 51
*Vicolo Savelli 12, tel. 686 1877.
Closed Mon in winter, open daily in
summer. L15,000.*

Not a place to come for a peaceful
meal, but good fun if you're in the
mood for some exuberant Roman
chaos. This recently opened pizzeria is
immensely popular, so expect to wait
for a table, to sit two inches away
from your neighbour, and to have to
duck your head occasionally as the
waiters dash around with extra chairs.
In summer there are tables outside,
where the chaos continues. The pizzas,
which come in three sizes, are thin and
crispy, served blistered and bubbling
from the wood-fired oven. The menu

is posted on the wall in the entrance,
so make your choice before you sit
down.

NAVONA NOTTE Map ref. [C3]
p. 51
*Via del Teatro Pace 44. Closed Wed.
L15,000.*

Navona Notte is an unrefined place
with a slightly raffish late-night
clientele, atrocious frescoes and a fish
tank, and it's the only place in the
centre where you can eat until 3 a.m.
The pizza is better than the pasta, and
if you're in need of an aphrodisiac
after a few hours on the dance floor,
they sometimes have pizza with
oysters.

TRATTORIA Map ref. [C 1/2] p. 51
Via dei Banchi Nuovi 14. No phone.
Open Mon–Fri 1–3 p.m. L25,000.

A tiny trattoria, with football posters, a copy of Cézanne's *Absinthe*, and photos of the owners, when young, at grape harvest on the family vineyard on its wood-veneer walls. A neighbourly, old-fashioned place, open lunchtimes only for good, simple Roman fare cooked on a single gas cooker in a tiny kitchen. There's a daily choice of one pasta dish and two or three *secondi*, and pudding consists of crisp shortbready biscuits served from an antique tin, best eaten dunked in a glass of the no-frills house white. It's frequented largely by locals, but the elderly lady owner – who's been here for over twenty years – makes newcomers welcome.

DA FRANCESCO Map ref. [C2] p. 51
Via della Fossa 29 (corner Via del Corallo). Tel. 686 4009. Open Wed–Mon 12.15–3 p.m.; 7–12.55 a.m. L20,000–L35,000.

A relaxed, unprettified trattoria best known for its pizza, with amiable down-to-earth, leer-free waiters. In summer there are tables outside – get there early if you don't want to wait for one – and it's also one of the few places where you can eat after midnight. There's a good selection of *antipasti*, laid out for self-service, and the pizzas – particularly *al salmone* (with smoked salmon) and *ai funghi porcini e rughetta* (with *porcini* mushrooms and rocket) – are memorable.

L'INSALATA RICCA II Map ref. [D3] p. 51
Piazza Pasquino, tel. 6830 7881.

Closed Mon. L25,000–30,000. All major credit cards except Diners.

A pretty but uncluttered restaurant whose light, simple food reflects the healthier eating habits of Italy's younger generation. Though it's busy at weekends, it's very peaceful midweek, and as long as you don't mind the slow (and sometimes rather absent-minded) service, it's a good place to come if you're slightly apprehensive about eating alone.

Pasta courses include *tonarelli* with salmon, risotto with fresh seafood, and tagliatelle with pesto; for *secondi* there's veal steak with lemon, scamorza (a cheese shaped like a miniature rugby ball grilled to gooiness) and omelettes. As you might expect from the name, there's a good range of salads.

L'ANTICO CARBONARO Map ref. [C2] p. 51
Vicolo di Monte Vecchio 27, tel. 687 9471. Closed Wed. L30,000.

Though the *tagliatelle ai carciofi* is magnificent, closely packed tables and an owner whose brusqueness is legendary mean that this trattoria is best saved for a night when you're not alone.

TRE MAGHI Map ref. [D3] p. 51
Piazza Pasquino 77/8, tel. 683 0774. Closed Sun. L40,000–50,000. Visa.

Trendy but civilised restaurant, with a monthly-changing menu inspired by New Age themes (horoscopes, seasons, the four elements, etc.). Dotty pretensions notwithstanding, the food is excellent, and though it's not strictly vegetarian, most dishes are meatless. Pasta sauces range from the delicately aromatic to the fiercely piquant; salads are inventive; and *secondi* might include falafel or spinach, nut-and-ricotta rissoles. The wines, for once, are carefully chosen – the perfumey, honeyed Pinot Bianco is particularly fine.

L'ORSO 80 Map ref. [B3] p. 51
Via dell'Orso 33, tel. 686 4904/686 1710.
Closed Mon. L40,000. All major credit cards.

An animated restaurant–pizzeria frequented by middle-aged couples, thirtysomethings and businessmen. There's a stunning array of *antipasti* and the pasta dishes (*spaghetti alle vongole* and *bucatini alla amatriciana*) are good, but the pizza can be soggy. The fish dishes are well prepared but, as ever, bump up the price.

DA PASSETTO Map ref. [C3] p. 51
Via Zanardelli 14, tel. 654 0569 (688 6569). Closed Sun. L80,000. All major credit cards.

Da Passetto is over 130 years old, with a glamorous list of ex-patrons including Jean Cocteau, Bette Davis, Charlie Chaplin and Elizabeth Taylor – ask the waiter if you can see the autograph book. Nowadays it's frequented mostly by politicians and businessmen. It was recently taken over by new management – a father and two sons – who have succeeded in creating an atmosphere which is at once friendly and gracious. The dining-rooms are elegantly panelled with wood, and in summer there's a terrace outside. Food – the responsibility of the youngest son – is a mixture of Italian and international, and specialities include *cannelloni passetto* (stuffed with *porcini* mushrooms and meat) and an *ossobucco* enriched with cream and cognac – so it's not somewhere to come if you're concerned about cholesterol.

Cafés

TRE SCALINI Map ref. [C3] p. 51
Piazza Navona 28.
Open 8 a.m.–12.30 a.m.; closed Wed.

The most famous café–restaurant on Piazza Navona has been smugly resting on its laurels for a few years now, and though their famous *tartufo* ice cream is as good as ever, service is dismissive and the food from its restaurant is unexceptional. It's not a bad place for breakfast, but there are more inviting cafés on the piazza, so do as most Italians do – drop in late evening for a stand-up or takeaway *tartufo*. It's unforgettable: a slab of dark chocolate ice cream studded with shards of bitter-sweet chocolate and served with a smear of whipped cream.

CAFFÈ COLOMBIA Map ref. [C3] p. 51
Piazza Navona. Open 8.30 a.m.– 1.30 a.m.; closed Thur in winter.

Situated directly behind Bernini's Four Rivers fountain, the Colombia, run by a young Welshman, is usually a little more relaxed, and its waiters are a little more cheerful than the Tre Scalini's. Seats outside are good for observing – and occasionally eavesdropping on – the crowds flocking around the fountain, and though the covered arcade around the corner is ugly, it's the only place on the piazza where you can sit outside during bad weather.

Vinerie

IL PICCOLO Map ref. [D3] p. 51
Via del Governo Vecchio 74/5. Open daily 6 p.m.–2 a.m.

Arguably the most inviting wine bar in the city, an intimate, warm, relaxed place popular with the intelligentsia, where you can happily stay for hours drinking, reading and writing. If the owner, Lanfranco, is there, he'll probably come and chat for five minutes to put you at your ease, and if you return another evening, he'll greet you like an old friend. There's a vast, carefully selected choice of wines, and they create a sensational fruits-of-the-forest sangria served in a goblet with a spoon and straw. There are also delicious light snacks and nibbles. There are a few tables outside in summer, but there's room for only six tables inside, so go early in winter if you want to sit.

CUL DE SAC 1 Map ref. [D3] p. 51
Piazza Pasquino 73, tel. 654 1094 (6880 1094). Open 12.45–3 p.m.; 7.30 p.m.–12.30 a.m.; closed Mon and July.

One of the first of Rome's wine bars, Cul de Sac 1 is now more a place for a light lunch or dinner than somewhere simply to drink. Conversation is subdued, the clientele is fairly cultured, and though at times it can feel rather dull and sanitised, it's ideal if all you want is a quiet evening. There are over a thousand wines to choose from, starting at around L9000 per bottle, and as well as a massive choice of Italian cheeses and salamis there are home-made pâtés, soups, salads and smoked fish.

BEVITORIA Map ref. [C3] p. 51
Piazza Navona 72. Open 6 p.m.–12.30 a.m.; closed Sun.

This small wine bar, with cellars in the foundations of Domitian's Stadium (the owner will show them to you if he's not too busy), is the most civilised and secluded of Piazza Navona's watering holes. In autumn and winter they serve mulled wine – *vin brûlé* – and year-round there's a vast choice of wines, with prices starting at L2000 for a glass. In winter, when there are no tables outside, go early if you want to sit down.

Bars

BAR DELLA PACE Map ref. [C2/3] p. 51
Via della Pace 5. Open 10.30 a.m.– 2 a.m. (approx – sometimes still serving at 3 a.m.); closed Mon.

A beautiful *fin-de-siècle* bar with a beamed ceiling, helicopter fans and marble tables, packed in the late evening with the *jeunesse dorée* and the media crowd. If you don't look the part, expect curt service. It is, however, very quiet during the day, and sitting at one of the outside tables, backed by an ivy-curtained wall, is a pleasant way to kill an hour on a hot afternoon.

TAVERNA DI BACCÒ DI SANTORI PIETO Map ref. [C2] p. 51
Via della Pace 1. Open evenings only (tel. 686 5771 for details). Closed Sun.

A friendly little bar playing jazz and lit by candles stuck into Grolsch bottles. Habitués occasionally take over the (out-of-tune) piano for an impromptu jam. Not a bad place to spend an hour.

EATING AND DRINKING

JONATHAN'S ANGELS Map ref.
[C2] p. 51
*Via della Fossa 29. Open 1 p.m.–2.30
a.m.; closed Mon.*

Sandwiches and cakes during the day,
cocktails and booze at night in a
kitschily cluttered bar frescoed with
swooning Venuses and Cupids.
Popular with young US travellers.

PANICO Map ref. [C2] p. 51
*Via del Panico 17. Open Sun 5 p.m.–
2 a.m.; closed July/Aug.*

A friendly, laid-back lesbian club,
where you can sit around drinking
and eating quiche, pasta and salads,
play pool, and – from 10.30 – bop. A
good place to go if you want company
– you won't be alone for long!
Straight women are welcome, but can
expect to be quizzed about their
sexuality.

Around the Pantheon

Snacks, Fast Food, Takeaways

LA MERIDIANA Map ref. [B4]
p. 51
*Via Campo Marzio 47. Open
7.30 a.m.–midnight; closed Sun.*

A large, clean, bright self-service
tavola calda, popular with office
workers at lunchtime. Also good for a
solitary drink in the evenings.

BURGHY Map ref. [C4] p. 51
*Piazza della Rotonda 14A. Open
9 a.m.–1 a.m.; closed Wed.*

A burger bar opposite the Pantheon,
where you can sit outside without
paying extra. Good orange juice, too –
at a third of the price of the other
cafés on the piazza.

PANINOTECA Map ref. [B3]
p. 51
*Via della Scrofa 16. Open
7.30 a.m.–8.30 p.m.; closed Mon.*

A clean, modern bar serving a good
range of sandwiches and snacks,
hearty home-made soup, and a variety
of teas.

GELOCREMERIA DELLA PIGNA
Map ref. [D4] p. 51
*Via della Pigna 58. Open 7.30
a.m.–8.30 p.m.; closed Sat.*

One of the quietest bars in the
neighbourhood – an ideal retreat for a
peaceful drink, ice cream or sandwich.

ROSTICCERIA SALSAMENTERIA
Map ref. [B3] p. 51
*Via della Scrofa 30. Open 8 a.m.–
8 p.m.; closed Sun.*

A delicatessen with some of the best
hot takeaway pasta, rice, meat and
vegetable dishes in the city.

CAMILLONI A SANT'EUSTACHIO
Map ref. [C4] p. 51
*Piazza Sant'Eustachio 54. Open 6.30
a.m.–1 a.m.; Aug 4 p.m.–1 a.m.;
closed Mon.*

A better-than-average range of
sandwiches, pleasant staff and usually
not too crowded. Their *tartufo* ice
cream rivals that of Tre Scalini.
There's also a piano bar upstairs, but
no one ever seems to go there.

Tazza d'Oro Map ref. [C4] p. 51

Via degli Orfani 84. Open 7 a.m.–5 p.m.; closed Sun.

A stand-up bar in a shop roasting what many reckon to be the best coffee in Rome. Thick, foamy cappuccino, coffee liqueurs and a delicious *granita di caffè* with whipped cream. Pay at the till first, then order at the bar.

Ristoranti, Trattorie, Pizzerie

Vino Buffet Map ref. [B4] p. 51

Piazza della Torretta 60, tel. 687 1445. Closed Sun. L20,000.

A yuppyish, civilised wine and food bar, good for lunch or a light dinner, included in this section because it's not really a place simply to drink. There's a wide choice of rice and main-course salads; hearty *crostini con mozzarella* (doorsteps of toasted bread and mozzarella) served with rocket and prawns or *porcini* mushrooms; roast meats, soups, and bread with asparagus, artichoke or mushroom and truffle pâté.

Il Leoncino Map ref. [A4] p. 51

Via del Leoncino 28, tel. 687 6306. Closed Wed (open evenings only at weekends). L15,000.

Over fifty years old and still largely undiscovered by tourists, Il Leoncino is one of the best and most authentic *pizzerias* in Rome: you sit at simple tables watching the chef prepare your pizza.

Cafés

Gran Caffè Map ref. [C5] p. 51

Piazza di Pietra 65. Open 7.30 a.m.–midnight; closed Mon.

A refined, though expensive café which is ideal for a leisurely breakfast, brunch, lunch – or a late-night champagne cocktail. As well as good sandwiches and mini pizzas, there are interesting salads, pasta dishes and quiches.

Ciampini Map ref. [B4] p. 51

Piazza San Lorenzo in Lucina 29. Open 7.30 a.m.–9 p.m.; closed Sun.

A pavement café on an appealing piazza which does good sandwiches and salads, and an exceptionally velvety truffle ice cream. Also pleasant for evening drinking.

Alemagna Tea Room Map ref. [C5] p. 51

Via del Corso 181. Open 7.30 a.m.–11.30 p.m.; closed Mon.

A large, crowded self-service cafeteria with hot meals, pizzas, sandwiches and cakes. Plenty of room to sit down inside, and waiter service outside – if you don't mind sitting on busy Via del Corso.

Cafeteria della Maddalena Map ref. [C4] p. 51

Piazza della Maddalena. Open 6.30 a.m.–8.30 p.m.; closed Sun.

Sandwiches, quiches, salads and stuffed focaccia, most pleasantly eaten on outside tables opposite the frilly façade of the Maddalena church. It's also one of the few cafés where you can make a phone call in peace – there are lots of phones downstairs.

EATING AND DRINKING

CAFFÈ SANT'EUSTACHIO Map ref. [C4] p. 51
Piazza Sant'Eustachio 82. Open 8.30 a.m.–1 a.m.; closed Mon.

A small, smart stand-up café (with a few outdoor tables) serving some of the best coffee in town. Specialities include a rich, smooth espresso, velvety cappuccino, and coffee ice cream and granita. It's jam-packed on Sunday mornings and afternoons.

Gelaterie

GELATERIA DELLA PALMA Map ref. [C4] p. 51
Via della Maddalena 20. Open 8 a.m.–2 a.m.; closed Wed.

Some people reckon the Palma's ice cream is the best in Rome. There are over a hundred flavours, so if you agree, you'll be kept busy trying them all. You pay at the till first, then jostle at the ice-cream counter waiting to be served.

GIOLITTI Map ref. [B/C4] p. 51
Via degli Uffici del Vicario 40. Open 7 a.m.–2 a.m.; closed Mon.

One of central Rome's oldest *gelaterie*, and with as many aficionados as Palma. Pay at the till first, then order at the counter if you want to take away – or go to the elegant period parlour for an indulgent sundae. Whenever squabbling politicians from nearby Palazzo di Montecitorio (the House of Deputies) want to prove to the country that they've patched up a quarrel, they head down here to eat ice creams in front of the TV cameras.

Bars

MISCELLENEA Map ref. [C4] p. 51
Via Paste s/n (runs between Via dei Pastini and Via del Seminario). Open lunchtime–4 a.m.; closed Sun.

A lively bar, frequented largely by American students. There's a heavy pick-up scene at night, but good food at lunchtime, cooked by Livia Borghese (see p.72 for stories about her ancestors).

Campo dei Fiori and the Ghetto

Snacks, Fast Food, Takeaways

PIZZERIA Map ref. [E4] p. 51
Via Santa Maria del Pianto 64/5. Open mid-morning–8 p.m.; closed Sun.

Great *piazza al taglio* and fizzy Pinot Chardonnay on tap in an amiable little establishment which gets packed at lunchtime. If there's no room inside, you can squat round the corner in Piazza Costaguti.

IL FORNO DEL GHETTO Map ref. [E4] p. 51
Via Portico d'Ottavia 2. Open 8 a.m.–8 p.m.; closed Mon.

A tiny Jewish bakery, best visited at around 5 p.m., when you join a queue of locals of all ages for roast pumpkin seeds or a slice of freshly baked cake studded with raisins, cherries and angelica. It sometimes shuts down at lunchtime.

IL FORNO DI CAMPO DE' FIORI
Map ref. [D3] p. 51
Piazza Campo dei Fiori 22/22a. Open 6 a.m.–2 p.m. and 5–7.30 p.m.; closed Sun.

One of the best traditional bakeries in Rome, selling freshly baked pizza as well as a wide variety of breads. Prepare to elbow your way through to the counter at lunchtime.

BAR FILETARO SANTA BARBARA
Map ref. [E3] p. 51
Largo dei Librari 88. Open 5 p.m.–10 p.m.; closed Sun.

A tiny, stark café with Formica-topped tables (including a few outside) serving nothing but battered cod, which you eat with your fingers. Attracts a cross-section of young tourists, elderly locals, and the occasional pair of fur-coated contessas.

Ristoranti, Trattorie, Pizzerie

IL GROTTINO (A.K.A. DA SERGIO)
Map ref. [E3] p. 51
Via delle Grotte 27, (opposite Palazzo Spada), tel. 686 4293. Closed Sun. L30,000.

If you want pizza, but don't want to brave the boisterous chaos of Monte-carlo and the like, Il Grottino is a good choice. It attracts a slightly older clientele than many of the centre's pizzerias – along with a number of tourists – and though the service is pretty brusque, tables are well spaced, the pizzas are crispy and aromatic, and in summer you can eat outside. Book if you want to eat after 10 p.m.

COSTANZA
Map ref. [D3] p. 51
Piazza del Paradiso 63–65, tel. 686 1717 (6880 1002). Closed Sun.

L40,000.

In summer you can sit outside in a tiny cobbled alleyway; in winter you dine in rustic vaulted rooms adorned with antique kitchen utensils and a couple of ancient olive presses. The pasta is wonderful (the *secondi* less so, and overpriced) but service can be poor, and waiters flirty. The delicately flavoured *riso con fiori di zucchini* (rice with courgette flowers) and *ravioli pieni du carciofi* (home-made ravioli stuffed with artichokes) are memorable, and if you're in need of a vitamin C boost, the *crudités* (an immense bowl of whole raw vegetables served with a saucer of oil) should do the trick.

PATRIZIA E ROBERTO DEL PIANETA TERRA
Map ref. [E3] p. 51
Via Arco del Monte 94/5, tel. 686 9893 (6880 1663). Closed Sun. Over L100,000. All major credit cards.

An extremely exclusive, self-consciously formal restaurant in which exquisitely presented *nouvelle cuisine* is served with great ceremony by impassive waiters. Women eating with men are given a menu without prices – so if you are intending to pay, you must make it clear from the start!

The restaurant is best known for its fish and seafood, and every dish is prepared without butter or cream. *Zuppa di Boyle* is a light tomato and aubergine soup with seafood; *papillote* is John Dory with prawns, parsley and tomato baked in a paper parcel; and *pesce con pecorino* is also John Dory, cooked with fresh tomato, mint and pungent pecorino cheese. Desserts range from wild strawberry sorbet and zabaglione to delectable chocolate, ricotta, coconut and apple cakes. The fish *menu a degustazione* cannot be recommended. Each dish is nice

enough in itself, but after the fourth
variation on the theme of white fish
and tomato, your tastebuds fall asleep.

DA GIGETTO Map ref. [E/F5] p. 51
*Via Portico d'Ottavia 21A, tel. 686
1105. Closed Mon. L50,000.*

A typical Roman Jewish restaurant in
the heart of the Ghetto, where in
summer you eat outside by the
columns of the Portico d'Ottavia. The
carciofi giudea, whole artichokes
crunchily deep-fried, are wonderful,
and if you don't fancy *rigatoni con
pagliata* (pasta tubes with the innards
of an unborn calf), there are less
barbaric pasta dishes like *spaghetti
carbonara*, *penne arrabiata* and
fettucini con carciofi. *Secondi* include
ossobucco, *abbachio*, scampi and sole.

LA CARBONARA Map ref. [D3] p. 51
*Piazza Campo dei Fiori 23, tel. 686
4783. Closed Tues. L50,000. Amex or
Visa.*

A long-established Campo dei Fiori
restaurant in which clusters of
Communist Party leaders and media
men sit darkly besuited among closely
packed tables of animated Romans
and holidaying foreigners. It's worth
arriving fairly early so that you can
choose where you sit – after 9 p.m.,
expect to wait for a table. The service
is slow, but the food is good and
traditional. Pasta dishes include
taglioni ai funghi porcini, *tagliolini ai
carciofi* and *ravioli di ricotta e spinaci*,
and *secondi* range from a surprisingly
delicious deep-fried *cervello e carciofi*
(brains and artichokes) to vegetable-
based dishes like *melanzane alla
Parmigiano* (baked aubergines with
Parmesan).

PALLARO Map ref. [D/E3] p. 51
*Largo del Pallaro 15, tel. 654 1488.
Closed Mon. L25,000.*

A traditional, no-frills neighbourly
trattoria in which the flustered cooks
double as waitresses. Ordering is
simple – there's a daily four-course set
menu (and vegetarian alternative)
which comes with house wine.

DA PIERLUIGI Map ref. [D2] p. 51
*Piazza de'Ricci (on the corner with
Via del Monserrato), tel. 686 1302.
Closed Mon. L30,000–40,000.*

A popular, amiable trattoria at its best
in summer, when you can sit outside
on a shabby lamplit piazza. There's a
wonderful array of *antipasti*, fish and
seafood on display, so you can point if
you don't speak Italian. If you want
pasta, the waiters reel off the menu at
top speed – listen out for spaghetti
with *fiori di zucchini* (courgette
flowers), *brocoletti* (mini-broccoli),
vongole (clams) and *radicchio* (red
chicory). In spring it's worth asking
for an *insalata selvatica* or wild salad,
and you could finish up with a bowl of
cherries, served in ice.

EVANGELISTA Map ref. [E3] p. 51
*Via delle Zoccolette 11A, tel. 687
5810. Closed Sun. L50,000. Credit
cards: Visa.*

An elegant up-market restaurant,
specialising in Jewish food, offal and
game, with a frequently changing
menu. Starters might include *carciofi
al mattone* (flattened, fried artichokes)
and lentil, chickpea and artichoke
soups; pasta dishes can range from
tagliolini with salted herring [*arringa*]
and rocket [*rughetta*] to *fettucine* with
asparagus tips; and main courses are

dominated by game and offal. Desserts tend to be Sicilian/Arab-influenced, and very sweet.

Cafés

FIORI DI CAMPO Map ref. [E3] p. 51
Piazza Campo dei Fiori. Open 6 a.m.–1.30 a.m., closed Sun.

The best place for drinking solo on Campo dei Fiori, particularly in good weather, when you can sit outside watching the bustle of the market. Early morning you drink with the stall-holders; later in the day it attracts a mixture of tourists and Romans; in the late evening it's considerably calmer than the nearby Vineria, but still a good vantage point for watching the raffish streetlife of the Campo.

PASTICCERIA FARNESE Map ref. [E2] p. 51
Piazza Farnese/corner Via Baullari. Open 7 a.m.–12.30 a.m.; closed Sun.

A small, pleasant café where you can sit outside and look at the exquisite Palazzo Farnese, with glimpses, as darkness falls, of the frescoes inside. Good cakes and sandwiches, and herbal teas as well as coffee and alcohol.

OM SHANTI Map ref. [E3] p. 51
Piazza Campo dei Fiori 53. Open 8 a.m.–2 a.m.; closed Mon.

The most sedate of Piazza Campo dei Fiori's cafés, and a comfortable place to stop for a drink or snack during the day. The inside room is pretty, tranquil and popular with women, and the terrace attracts a mixture of tourists and Romans. Recently the owners decided to make dining obligatory in the evenings, and if this

is successful, it will probably become a full-blown restaurant. If the meals are of the same standard as the salads and snacks they used to serve, the restaurant should be worth a try.

BERNASCONI Map ref. [D4] p. 51
Largo Argentina 1. Open 8 a.m.–11 p.m.; closed Mon.

Bernasconi's tempting selection of exquisite cakes and pastries, along with delicate sandwiches, attracts a combination of genteel ladies, businessmen and casual passers-by – who all stand at the bar nibbling. In summer you can sit outside – though Largo Argentina's soundtrack of revving buses is hardly the perfect accompaniment for *petits fours*.

Gelaterie

ALBERTO PICA Map ref. [E3] p. 51
Via della Seggiola 12. Open 8 a.m.–1 a.m.; closed Sun.

Prize-winning ice creams (and some rather good savoury snacks) to eat inside, outside or take away. It's nice and peaceful mid-afternoon.

Vinerie

LA VINERIA Map ref. [E3] p. 51
Campo dei Fiori 15. Open midday–midnight or later (depending on how lively things are); closed Sun.

A no-nonsense family-run wine bar and off-licence on the old centre's main marketplace. Lunchtimes and afternoons are reasonably quiet, and a fair number of single women pop in for a swift *prosecco* or beer and sandwich. At night a crowd of locals, alternative types, hippies, expats and young tourists spill onto the piazza, sitting on Vespas, leaning against cars and squatting on the steps. In summer there are tables outside – a better option if you're drinking alone than squashing inside the bar. Service at the tables can be pretty slow – but there's plenty to watch while you wait.

IL GOCCETTO Map ref. [D1] p. 51

Via dei Banchi Vecchi 14. Open 10 a.m.–1.30 p.m.; 4.30–9 p.m.; closed Sun.

An old wine shop with an original stencilled coffered ceiling and walls lined with shelves of wine. As well as selling wine, it's also a friendly place for a light lunch or an evening snack of cheese, bread and salami (eaten at marble-topped tables).

Bars

OSIRIS Map ref. [E3] p. 51

Largo dei Librari 82A. Open daily from around 6.30 p.m.–4 a.m.

The owner, Pilar, is a playwright, which might be why, when you step into her dimly lit bar to confront a plastic pair of stockinged legs, and the torso of a

male dummy, you can feel as if you've walked into the plot of an existentialist play. Nothing *ever* seems to happen. Perhaps someday the women-only night *will* happen at 10 p.m. on Friday . . . or 6 p.m. on Wednesday . . . and perhaps one day you *will* go along to find a disco in the cellar. But none of this really matters at Osiris. Just go. Chat to Pilar (who speaks English) and wait for some of the gently *demi-monde*-ish habituées to drop by. There probably won't be more than five of you, but you can expect an interesting, if slightly unreal, evening.

GOLDFINCH Map ref. [D3] p. 51

Piazza Pollarola 31 Open 10 p.m.–3 a.m. plus.

There's no name or number outside, but it's a few doors beyond the kitchen shop labelled Number 36. Goldfinch is a late-night drinking den, frequented by a raffish mix of gay men, local artisans, and the alternative crowd from the Vineria; and if you're up to delving below the surface of Campo dei Fiori, this is the place to do it. It's virtually empty before 11 p.m., if you feel like a quiet drink with the occasional oddball.

Piazza di Spagna and Piazza del Popolo

Snacks, Fast Food, Takeaways

FIOR FIORI Map ref. [E1/2] p. 108

Via della Croce 16. Open 8 a.m.–3 p.m.; 5 p.m.–7.30 p.m.; closed Sun.

Pizza al taglio and freshly baked olive bread to eat in or take away.

COSE FRITTE Map ref. [D1] p. 108

Via di Ripetta 3. Open noon–3 p.m.; 5–10 p.m.; closed Sun.

Crispy deep-fried snacks, ranging from courgette flowers and aubergines to chickpea balls.

PANEFORMAGGIO Map ref. [D1] p. 108
Via di Ripetta 7–8. Open 7 a.m.–9 p.m.; closed Sun.

A spotless, reasonably priced café–bakery, popular with local women and businessmen. Freshly baked breads, cakes, sandwiches and filled focaccia.

CAFFÈ SOGO Map ref. [D1] p. 108
Via di Ripetta 245. Open 7 a.m.–10 p.m. (opens 9 a.m. on Sun); closed Mon.

A dimly lit Japanese sushi bar (which also serves crusty Italian sandwiches and a range of *antipasti*) with lots of comfy seats. A good place for lunch.

CAFFÈ ACCADEMIA Map ref. [G3] p. 108
Via del Triton 54. Open 7.30 a.m.–8.30 p.m.; closed Sun.

A clean, bright café with plenty of tables, specialising in ice cream, freshly squeezed fruit juices and milkshakes.

AL SALONE MARGHERITA Map ref. [F2/3] p. 108
Via Due Macelli 74. Open 5.30 a.m.–7.30 p.m.; closed Sun.

A virtually tourist-free café in the foyer of a variety theatre just beyond Piazza di Spagna. Delicious fresh sandwiches and filled focaccia to eat standing by the bar or at marble tables.

PALAZZO DELLE ESPOSIZIONE Map ref. [H4] p. 108
Via Nazionale s/n. Open 10 a.m.–9 p.m.; closed Tues.

As well as a cinema, design shop and exhibition spaces, the Palazzo delle Esposizione has a cool, minimalist café and a roof-garden restaurant. The latter is slightly clinical, but the former is a good, quiet place to escape during the day for a snack or lunch.

Cafés

ROSATI Map ref. [D1] p. 108
Piazza del Popolo 5. Open 7.30 a.m.–12.30 a.m.; closed Mon.

A classical, antique café with marble inlaid floors and glossy carved wooden fittings, with a delectable range of sticky pastries, good ice creams and some unusual sandwiches. Although it's at the top of busy Via di Ripetta, sitting outside is good fun if you like watching tourists and moneyed Romans at work and play.

TOY'S BAR Map ref. [D1] p. 108
Via Laurina 32. Open 8.30 a.m.–8 p.m.; closed Sun.

A trendy but amiable bar, pleasant for lunch as well as early-evening drinks. There are well-spaced tables at the back and an interesting selection of *piadine*, *bruschette* and *crostini*.

BABINGTON'S Map ref. [E2] p. 108
Piazza di Spagna 23. Open 9 a.m.–8.30 p.m.; closed Thur.

Babington's (see p.121) is jaw-droppingly expensive, but worth the price if you want a serene, leisurely lunch and one of the good cups of tea on which the establishment's reputation hangs. Food is traditionally British: rarebits, club sandwiches, muffins, omelettes, shepherd's pie, scones and jam, plum cake and cinnamon toast.

CAFFÈ GRECO Map ref. [E/F2] p. 108.
Via Condotti 86. Open 8 a.m.–4 p.m.; closed Sun.

Inattentive service from snooty waiters, stale sandwiches and a recent brush with the city's Environmental Health Department hardly make this the most recommendable café in Rome. But it's been going since 1742, and was frequented by most of the big-name artists and writers who visited Rome in the eighteenth and nineteenth centuries. If you want to look at their portraits (most of them are men), you may feel it's worth the price of an *acqua minerale*.

CAFÉ DE PARIS Map ref. [E4] p. 108
Via Veneto 90. Open 8 a.m.–3 a.m.; closed Wed.

The café scenes in *La Dolce Vita* were filmed here, which is doubtless why it's the only one of Via Veneto's cafés to be even marginally busy during the day. There are, however, some sumptuous inside rooms, and if you can cope with paying L6500 for an espresso on the terrace, it's not a bad place to sit and watch life go by. If you sit alone at night on the terrace, expect to be pounced on.

CIAMPINI AL CAFÉ DU JARDIN Map ref. [E2] p. 108
Open spring and summer only, 9 a.m.–1 a.m.

A pretty open-air café, surrounded by creeper-curtained trellises with a small lily pond in the centre. The sandwiches, light snacks and ice creams are good and not *too* pricey, though service is slow. It's also a pleasant place to come for an evening cocktail or aperitif.

VANNI Map ref. [F2] p. 108
Via della Frattina 94. Open 7.30 a.m.–11 p.m.; closed Mon.

This *pasticceria* is a great place for lunch or afternoon tea. There's a wide variety of sandwiches, pasta, chicken and rice salads, and delicious cakes, which you can eat in a wood-panelled tea room in winter, or outside in summer, watching tourists, businessmen on Vespas and designer-dressed boutique assistants flowing by.

DOLCI E DONI Map ref. [E2] p. 108
Via delle Carrozze 86. Open 10 a.m.–8 p.m.; closed Mon.

An elegant, tranquil tea room run by women, ideal for an unhurried breakfast, lunch, tea or early-evening drink. There's a wide range of teas and coffees (including coffee with chocolate or cream); savouries include quiches, salads and crepes; and there are usually scones, cheesecake, carrot cake and chocolate cake from the adjoining *pasticceria*. It is as yet undiscovered by tourists.

Ristoranti, Trattorie, Pizzerie

EDY Map ref. [D1] p. 108
Vicolo de Babuino 2, tel. 323 5618. Closed Sun. L35,000. Amex, Visa.

Edy's has been run by the same family for almost twenty years, and the mother, Luciana's, scrumptious homely food has a steady, select following. The restaurant itself is welcoming, candlelit, and ideal for a tranquil, leisurely meal. Luciana often waits on tables as well as cooking, so service is slow, but the food is well worth waiting for. Her tagliatelle with ricotta and artichokes is unforgettable, but also comes with aubergines, carbonara or *porcini* mushrooms. *Secondi* include an exceptional *abbachio arrosto*, and *stracetti*, finely sliced pork, served with artichokes, rocket or *porcini* mushrooms. The home-made tiramisù is the best in Rome – though you may have to wait an hour while it's prepared – and the house white is deliciously dry and appley.

BUCA DI RIPETTA Map ref. [E1] p. 108
Via di Ripetta 36, tel. 321 9391.
Closed Sun evening and Mon.
L35,000.

A friendly, relaxed restaurant, popular with middle-aged Romans and British expats. The urbane owner is to the fore, welcoming diners, waiting on tables, and recommending the best dishes of the day. If you're served by one of the less forthcoming waiters, make sure you ask about dishes which are not on the menu. The food is traditional – *rigatoni all'amatriciana, penne all'arrabbiata, bolliti* (mostly with offal) and *involtini*.

DAL BOLOGNESE Map ref. [D1] p. 108
Piazza del Popolo 1/2, tel. 361 1426/322 2799. Closed Mon. L70,000–80,000. Diners, Visa.

Bologna is the meat capital of Italy, and this Emilia-Romagnan restaurant is a must for carnivores, and a safe bet for entertaining business clients. It's smart and classical, service is polite and rapid, and the waiters are knowledgeable. The home-made pasta is delicious, but the real specialities are the *secondi. Bollito misto* is the most famous – beef, tongue, veal head, sausage, chicken and *prosciutto* served with piquant *mostarda di Cremona* –

spicy, pickled candied figs, pears, cherries and mandarin oranges – or *salsa verde* – parsley, root vegetables and celery in salt, oil and vinegar. If that doesn't appeal, there are more straightforward steaks, chops and cutlets. Book in advance.

DA ANDREA Map ref. [E4] p. 108
Via Sardegna 26, tel. 482 1891.
Closed Sun. L80,000. Amex, Diners, Visa.

Exquisite food and discreet service make Da Andrea a perfect place in which to entertain business clients or eat alone. There are a number of rooms, all tables are well spaced, and many of them are very secluded. Only the best ingredients are used – as you'll realise as soon as you taste *antipasti* like prawns with rocket, mixed seafood, buffalo mozzarella and *olive all'ascolana*; there's a superb *l'astice alla catalana* – a casserole of tomato, potato and lobster; and among the pasta dishes there's *tonarelli d'Andrea* (with tomato, peas and mushrooms), *pennette* with artichokes and courgettes, oyster risotto, and home-made egg ravioli stuffed with ricotta and spinach. Main courses include an excellent mixed grilled fish, fillet steak cooked in Barolo, and *carpaccio* with Parmesan and rocket. There's also a tempting selection of desserts, and a wine list which is updated every season.

TULLIO Map ref. [F4] p. 108
Via San Nicolà da Tolentino 26, tel. 475 8564. Closed Sun. L50,000. Amex, Diners, Visa.

Tullio's generous portions of good honest Tuscan food, and polite rapid service, attract journalists and politicians as well as tourists, making it a good choice for a business lunch. The *pasta e fagioli* and *spaghetti all' checca* (with raw tomato and basil) are delicious, the steaks are tender and juicy, and in late spring you shouldn't miss the wild strawberries.

Vinerie

ROFFI ISABELLI Map ref [E1/2] p. 108
Via della Croce 76A. Open 9 a.m.–1.30 p.m.; 5–8. p.m.; closed Sun.

More of a wine shop than a bar, but nevertheless a good place to go if you want to rub shoulders with the elegant set. Pop in at lunchtime or early evening for a *prosecco* and a miniature caviare sandwich.

THE VICTORIA PUB Map ref. [E1] p. 108
Via Gesù e Maria 18. Open 6 p.m.–1 p.m. (5 p.m.–1 a.m. Sun).

An English pub which is also popular with Italians, where you can be guaranteed to meet people – lots of expat British and American women go here. It's as friendly as English pubs are supposed to be (but rarely are). A must for anyone who feels intimidated by Rome.

Trastevere

Snacks, Fast Food, Takeaways

CAFFÈ DI MARZIO Map ref. [E3] p. 141
Piazza Santa Maria in Trastevere 14B. Open 7 a.m.–2 a.m.; closed Mon.

A pleasant place for breakfast or an early-evening drink (there are usually lots of local women there at around 5 p.m.), especially when the weather is good and you can sit outside on the piazza.

LA CASA DEL TRAMEZZINO Map ref. [E4] p. 141
Viale Trastevere 81. Open 7 a.m.–3 a.m.; closed Tues.

A vast and inventive range of sandwiches – and open late if you get the munchies in the early hours (though going alone at 3 a.m. is not recommended).

MCDONALD'S Map ref. [E4] p. 141
Piazza Sonnino 40 (also branches on Piazza della Repubblica and Piazza di Spagna). Open daily 10 a.m.–midnight (1 a.m. Sat).

Everything you'd expect – including highchairs – but better cakes and salad than you get in UK branches. Lots of clean loos, too (and it's easy to sneak in).

BAR SETTIMIANA Map ref. [D2] p. 141
Via Porta Settimiana 1. Open 7.30 p.m.–2 a.m.; closed Mon.

The bar – just down the road from the Villa Farnesina – is usually full of (mostly female) American students from nearby John Cabot University. Good sandwiches (some in wholemeal rolls) throughout the day; salads and hot dishes at lunchtime.

Ristoranti, Pizzerie, Trattorie

ENOTECA FERRARA Map ref. [E3/4] p. 141

Via dell'Arco di San Calisto 36, tel. 581 7011. Closed Sun in summer, Tues in winter. L25,000 plus.

A tiny, gently refined vaulted food and wine bar run by two sisters, Lina and Mary, who will guide you through their selection of 230 wines. There are just eight tables for four, so you should book in advance. Unless you go early (before 9 p.m.) they may not be able to guarantee a table to yourself. The food is good – roast *scamorza* stuffed with mushrooms and *prosciutto*, vegetable or pulse soups, along with a choice of Italian cheeses and salamis. The home-made desserts are delicious.

IL GENERALE Map ref. [D3] p. 141

Via del Moro 1A, tel. 580 3769. Closed Sat evening and all day Sun. L25,000.

Il Generale is one of the few trattorias in Trastevere untouched by the neighbourhood's trendification. The decor and furniture are stark and functional, the food is cooked (in a tiny kitchen) and served by a motherly woman, and it's frequented largely by locals. If you get there reasonably early in summer, you can eat outside in a tiny garden. The food is simple: their *penne primavera* – pasta tubes with diced mozzarella, raw tomato and basil leaves added at the last minute – is one of the best in Rome, and in spring and summer there's a good, bitter wild salad. *Secondi* include *coniglio arrosto* (roast rabbit), *abbacchio al forno* (roast baby lamb) and *trippa alla romana* (tripe stewed

with tomato and mint), and for dessert there's usually fresh fruit or ice cream.

DA AUGUSTO Map ref. [D3] p. 141

Piazza de' Renzi 15 (just off Via Pelliccia), tel. 580 3798. Closed Sun. L25,000.

You need to be feeling confident to enjoy eating at Da Augusto. The trattoria's reputation rests partly on its traditional Roman food, and partly on the grumpiness of its owner and the chaotic, exuberant atmosphere. People who know the ropes grab the first empty table, lay it themselves (with a sheet of paper) and order and collect their food from the kitchen hatch. It's also the kind of place where, if you're alone, other diners are fairly likely to invite you to join them. The menu changes according to the season and day of the week – *primi* to listen out for include *fettucine fatte in casa* (home-made fettucini) and *bucatini amatriciana* (bacon, tomato and chilli sauce); and *secondi* include *bollito* (mixed boiled meats) and *pollo con peperoni* (chicken with peppers). Dessert is usually tiramisù or a fruit flan [*crostata di frutta*]. Beware of the house white – it tastes fine, but even in modest quantities it can leave you with a bad hangover.

DA GILDO Map ref. [D3] p. 141

Via della Scala 31A, tel. 580 0733. Closed Wed in winter; rest of the year closed Sun. L40,000 (L25,000 for pizza and salad).

A respectable middle-of-the-road pizzeria and trattoria, and a good choice if you're not overly confident about eating alone. *Antipasti* include *olive ascolane* (stuffed, crumbed, deep-fried olives), a salad of raw mushrooms and slivers of Parmesan, and smoked swordfish and smoked salmon; there are a couple of unusual *primi* – spaghetti with rocket [*rughetta*] and *penette* (small pasta tubes) with courgettes [*zucchini*] or beans [*fave*] as well as standard sauces like *carbonara*, *primavera* and *amatriciana*. There are unusual salads, inventive pizzas, *calzone* and *crostini*, and a number of meat dishes, including *ossobucco* and steaks.

LA TANA DE NOANTRI Map ref. [E3] p. 141
Via della Paglia 1–3, tel. 580 6404. Closed Tues. L40,000. Visa.

A large restaurant just off Piazza Santa Maria in Trastevere, popular with tourists. In season, there are tables outside; out of season, especially midweek, it's a good place to come for a quiet meal with a book. Service is courteous, but as the food is in no way outstanding – the cream-based pasta sauces, especially, tend to be overly bland – opt for something cheap like pizza.

API SUR MELE Map ref. [D3] p. 141
Via del Moro 17, tel. 588 2881. Closed Wed. L30,000.

A minuscule restaurant run by two gay women, with a gay and straight clientele. There are just five tables, so don't come if you're not prepared to talk to people. It's also wise to book. There's a short select menu of starters and *secondi* – the *bresaola*, Parmesan and *rughetta* salad is good, as is the hearty polenta with *salsicce di Norcia* (one of Italy's best salamis). Wines are also carefully chosen.

IL CIAK Map ref. [D3] p. 141
Vicolo del Cinque 21, tel. 589 4774. Closed Mon. L45,000.

A highly popular Tuscan restaurant which is a must for meat- or game-lovers. As well as Tuscan standards like *ribollita* (a hearty meat-and-vegetable soup) and beefsteak, there are wild boar [*cinghiale*] steaks and salamis; polenta with sausage [*salsiccia*] or hare [*lepre*]; grilled *porcini* mushrooms, grilled *scamorza* with *porcini* or truffle pâté, and various game dishes. Book in advance.

CUL DE SAC 2 Map ref. [E5] p. 141
Vicolo dell'Atleta 21 (runs between Vias Genovesi and Salumi), tel. 581 3324. Closed Mon lunchtime, Sun evening. L80,000. Amex, Diners, Visa.

A refined restaurant serving what is widely reckoned to be the best and most sophisticated food in the city. Dishes include lasagne with sole and artichokes, steamed lobster with parsley, a potato and saffron salad, and guinea fowl breast with wild asparagus. Desserts are also delicious, and there are over 600 wines to choose from.

Gelaterie

CECERE Map ref. [E/F4] p. 141
Via San Francesco a Ripa 20. Open 6.30 a.m.–2.30 a.m.; closed Thur.

Scrumptious zabaglione ice cream, along with gorgeous cakes and rich, buttery croissants.

BAR SAN CALISTO
See below. This rough bar is also the purveyor of wonderful home-made ice cream.

Bars

BAR SAN CALISTO Map ref. [E3] p. 141
*Piazza San Calisto 4. Open 7 a.m.–
1 a.m.; closed Sun. Aug closes 1 p.m.–
5 p.m. but stays open on Sun.*

Slightly dodgy at night, but not a bad
place to drink during the day or early
evening, as you don't pay to sit outside.

TRASTÈ Map ref. [E4] p. 141
*Via della Lungaretta 76. Open 5.30
p.m.–midnight; closed Mon.*

Trastevere's most cultured bar, and
the most comfortable place in the
neighbourhood for solo drinking. Low
travertine tables and bench seats at the
front, chairs and tables at the back,
papers and magazines to read; bottled
beers, herbal teas and a range of light
snacks.

MAGO DI OZ/OMBRE ROSSE Map ref. [D/E3] p. 141
Piazza Sant'Egidio 12. Closed Sun.

The Mago di Oz was about to be
refurbished at the time of writing, and
reopened as the Ombre Rosse. Should
be worth checking out, as the woman
owner is friendly and welcoming.

CAFFÈ DELLA SCALA Map ref. [D3] p. 141
*Via della Scala 4. Open 8 a.m.–1 p.m.;
5 p.m.–1.30 p.m.; closed Wed.*

A relaxed, low-key bar where people
drink, chat, or play cards to a jazz
soundtrack. There are tables outside in
summer – a prime position for
watching Trastevere's animated
streetlife.

The Archaeological Zone and Outside the Centre

Ristoranti, Trattorie, Pizzerie

ULDERICO
*Via San Giovanni in Laterano 106
(opposite S. Clemente), tel. 735 924.
Closed Sun. L25,000.*

This is virtually the only authentic,
tourist-free trattoria close to the
archaeological zone, and is worth
coming to either for lunch or for
dinner. *Spaghetti alla carbonara* or
alla vongole is good, and second
courses include roast rabbit, roast
veal, trout and mixed fried fish.

LO SCOPETTARO
*Lungotevere Testaccio 7 (just after
Ponte Sublicio), tel. 574 2408. Closed
Tues. L35,000.*

There aren't many restaurants in
Testaccio which can be recommended
for solo women, largely because
getting to them involves walking
through the quarter, which is not
advisable at night. However, Lo
Scopettaro is on the main road by the
Tiber with a busstop close by, and as
it's considered one of the best in the
area, it's frequented by a fairly eclectic
– albeit predominantly male – crowd.
Nevertheless, you must be in the mood
for 'real Rome' to enjoy it. Offal
features heavily on the menu, but if
you're too squeamish for pasta with
pagliata, there's *carbonara* and
amatriciana. Meat dishes include tripe
and veal, but there's also steak and
chicken.

EATING AND DRINKING

TRAM TRAM
Via dei Reti 44/6 (runs between Via Tiburtina and Scalo S. Lorenzo), tel. 490 416. Closed Mon. L35,000.

This trendy restaurant and bar in the lefty-studenty quarter of San Lorenzo is not an ideal place to go alone, but if you've got wheels and company, it makes a good start to a night on the town. There are unusual salads – spinach and salmon, rocket with Parmesan and pear, *bresaola* with mushroom and rocket – and hearty pasta courses like spaghetti with clams and artichokes; and you can continue drinking afterwards at the bar until it's time to go clubbing.

DA VINCENZO
Via Castelfidardo 6 (off Via XX Settembre), tel. 484 596. Closed all day Sun and Mon lunchtime. L50,000. Amex, Diners, Visa.

A useful restaurant to know about for a not-too-formal business dinner. Da Vincenzo is famous for its fish, and the restaurant is usually packed with aficionados. There's no menu – the waiter reels off the dishes at the speed of a 100-metre sprint commentator – so listen out for *astice* (lobster), *dentice* (sea bream) scampi and *calamari*. The pasta courses – particularly *spaghetti alle vongole* – are substantial, so unless you're ravenous, wait for the fish. There's no fish on Mondays because they can't be sure of getting it fresh, but the meat is also said to be good. There are some good desserts (like *panna cotta* with *frutti di bosco*) but the wine list isn't brilliant. In summer you can eat outside.

Gelaterie

SAN FILIPPO
Via di Villa San Filippo 10 (off Piazza Bligny). Open 7 a.m.–midnight; closed Wed.

Worth making a detour for if you're up at Villa Ada in Parioli. A tiny, old-fashioned, unprettified bar and *gelateria* selling some of the best fruit ice creams in the city. On Sundays it's full of Filipina maids who work for the wealthy of Parioli.

GIOLITTI
Viale Oceania 90. Open 8 a.m.–1 a.m.; closed Mon.

Branch of the famous gelateria (see p.282) close to the artificial lake in EUR.

Vinerie

CAVOUR 313
Via Cavour 313, tel. 678 5496. Open 12.30–2.30 p.m.; 7.30 p.m.–1.30 a.m.; closed Sun.

A civilised wine bar in an old-beamed wine shop where you eat and drink at polished wooden tables. There are 500 wines to choose from, and the food, carefully selected from all over Italy, should satisfy most gastronomes. As well as a wide choice of cheeses, salamis, smoked fish and cured meats, there are inventive salads, savoury flans and polenta – with wild mushrooms, herbs or Gorgonzola. A perfect place to lunch after visiting the archaeological zone, or to bring a book or letters to write in the evening.

 Though Rome is on the cutting edge of neither Classical nor youth culture, it is nevertheless a good city to be in at night. Since Italian House hit the dance floors of Europe in the late 1980s, the club scene has energised; there are some skilled and inventive DJs around; and a number of up-and-coming US artists have come to work in Rome, where there's more chance of getting a break than there is at home. Radio Centro Suona (see p.16) has its own recording label. Jazz is big, and many international groups which bypass London call in at Rome. The optimum time for jazz is summer, when many artists stop off *en route* to the prestigious Umbria Jazz Festival in Perugia. If you're into Brazilian and South American music, there are scores of tiny clubs where you can dance all night to salsa, and recently African music has become popular.

In late June, July and August, there's *Estate Romana*, a festival of cinema, jazz and rock with events in outdoor venues which change every year. Though no longer as dynamic and adventurous as it was when it was first established in the 1970s by the city's then left-wing government, there are usually some things worth seeing or hearing.

The standard of classical music, dance and theatre is some way below that in London – in both quantity and quality – though in summer there are opera and concerts in prestigious outdoor venues like the Baths of Caracalla and the Theatre of Marcello.

Map grid references are supplied when a venue appears on one of our detailed maps. For venues outside the centre, you will need a reliable street map like the F.M.B. or Roma Facile.

Bracketed phone numbers in listings below will come into operation sometime in 1993.

CLUBS AND GIGS
Though touring megastars prefer to hit the hipper city of Milan,

Rome does attract a fair number of credible US and UK bands. And there are often hard-hitting alternative and indie bands playing the Forte Prenestino, a squatted anarchist club in the suburbs. If you're going to gigs alone, bear in mind that most of the big venues are outside the centre, so check the time of the last bus back before you set out. The amount of attention you'll receive as a solo foreign woman depends entirely on the audience – you know best the kind of following your favourite bands attract – so base your decision on that.

There are also a host of smaller venues, many of them in Trastevere (which is fairly unhairy at night) and Testaccio (which can be dodgy). You are virtually guaranteed to be the only solo woman, so expect attention. The same goes for clubs. If you speak Italian, however, and have the skill to control encounters as you want to, you can have a good time.

Most women find clubbing alone in Rome something of an ordeal, and unless you're very self-assured or on the pick-up you'd be better advised to wait until you have someone to go with. If you do decide to go alone, you'd do best to stick to the alternative clubs, where a large proportion of the men do not come out with the sole aim of picking up a woman. The scene *will* seem a bit dated and provincial if you've come from New York or London, but it *is* good fun, especially if you like bopping to old Jam, Clash and Police hits. The majority of Rome's discos are cattle markets, and the swish nightclubs – many of them around Via Veneto – cannot be recommended unless you are determined not to go to bed alone. You need to look sexy, or at least glamorous, to get in; and if you see any other single women, they will probably be call girls.

In summer the mainstream club and disco scene shifts to the beaches of Fregene and Ostia. Most have swimming pools, and dancing is punctuated by party games and three-legged races. There are usually one or two lesbian nights in clubs (most recently at Il Castello), but these are always changing. Straight women who want a night in a male-free environment are not catered for – and if you go alone to a lesbian club, you'll attract just as much attention as you do in a hetero club. For up-to-date information on the gay scene, ask the women at Panico (see p.280).

In straight clubs, too, the in places and nights to go are in constant flux. The best source of information is, of course, word of mouth, but failing that, you could ask the staff at the trendy Cantiere del Nord boutique and booking office (see below), or consult *Trova Roma*.

The main clubbing nights are Thursday, Friday and Saturday, so entrance (and often drinks) are cheaper during the week, when there will be a mixture of theme nights, one-offs and private parties (some advertised in *Trova Roma*; others by invitations left in bars or handed out on the street; a few by word of mouth). At weekends, entrance to most clubs is at least L15,000, but in classier joints you can pay as much as L50,000. Some clubs require membership – you can usually join on the door, and fees are not that much more than you pay for a one-off entry elsewhere. This usually entitles you to free entrance on quieter nights.

Trendy Bars

These are the hip places to go before moving on to clubs, and the places to be to find out what's happening – look out for free invitations to clubs piled on the tables. Most stay open till late, and if all you want to do is carry on drinking, you could do worse than stay put.

PICASSO Map ref. [D4] p. 51
Piazza della Pigna 23. Open 9 p.m.–approx 4 a.m.; closed Sun.

A minimalist bar playing loud music till the early hours, which also showcases art and photography. Cool without being pretentious.

HEMINGWAY Map ref. [C4] p. 51
Piazza delle Copelle 10. Open 10 p.m. till late; closed Sat.

A pricey, sophisticated cocktail bar, popular with the moneyed and media crowd. Too many high-class sleaze-balls for comfortable solo drinking, but entertaining people-watching if you have company. If you don't arrive too late, you can sit on deep squashy sofas – otherwise you have to stand up or perch at the bar.

LE CORNACCHIE Map ref. [C4] p. 51
Via del Pozzo delle Cornacchie 53 (runs from Via della Scrofa to Piazza Maddalena). Open 9 p.m.–3 a.m.; closed Mon.

An expensive cocktail bar which attracts a slightly younger crowd than the Hemingway. Not a bad place to drink alone, but you will be conspicuous.

LA VETRINA Map ref. [C2] p. 51
Via della Vetrina 20.

A small bar/club which keeps closing down but invariably reopens. In its last reincarnation it was playing a pretty conventional mix of music (Queen, REM, Jam and fifties classics) to some of the city's less conventional dressers. It's definitely worth heading down on a Thursday or Friday night to see if anything's happening.

ALDEBARAN
Via Galvani 54. Open 9 p.m.–2.30 a.m.; closed Sun.

A relaxed cocktail bar in Testaccio, close to the Mattatoio and the clubs of Monte Testaccio.

Clubs

ARGONAUTA
Lungotevere degli Artigiani.

A vaguely alternative crowd (lots of habitués of the Campo dei Fiori Vineria) plus a scattering of music journalists pile on to the *Argonauta* on Friday and Saturday nights. It's a boat, moored on the Tiber just beyond Trastevere by the Testaccio bridge, with a dance floor below deck and lots of tables on top. Expect to queue to get in. Drinks – served in plastic cups – are expensive, but fatally strong.

ENTERTAINMENT

SOUL II SOUL Map ref. [E3] p. 141
Via dei Fienaroli 30D (off Via Arco S. Calisto).

A small but popular club which usually moves to an outdoor location in the summer – check *Trova Roma* for details. A brilliant mix of black music – ranging from soul classics and dance to reggae-rap and Zaïrois – attracts an equal mix of blacks and whites.

UONNA
Via Cassia 871.

Miles out of town, and a magnet for punks and the alternative set. Underground music, and often a venue for foreign indie and metal bands. Don't go alone unless you're used to the scene.

BLACKOUT
Via Saturnia 18.

The most exciting indie club in Rome. Music ranges from Lush and the Cocteau Twins to Ministry, Fugazi, Pixies and Nirvana. It's in the Porta Latina area, just off Piazza Epiro. Take bus 4 from Termini.

ALPHEUS
Via del Commercio 36.

If you're determined to club alone, Alpheus is not a bad choice, as it simultaneously hosts discos, gigs and sometimes exhibitions and theatre. There are a couple of bars and a restaurant, and it's large and busy enough for you to be relatively inconspicuous.

IL CASTELLO
Via di Porta Castello 44.

A club in a former cinema which attracts a fairly young, alternative crowd. Every night is different – Seventies Revival, Gay, Lesbian, Rock – and entrance is cheap for Rome (around L10,000).

ALIEN
Via Velletri 13.

The hippest disco in Rome, with art shows and exhibitions as well as two dance floors.

Live Music

You're going to be conspicuous in the small jazz and Brazilian clubs, but if you're feeling sassy, have a go (but drink moderately). For your first solo foray into Rome clubs, choose somewhere in Trastevere – preferably after you've familiarised yourself with the neighbourhood. Think twice before going solo at night to Testaccio: though there *are* night trams running from Piramide to the Colosseum, it's wiser not to walk around Monte Testaccio alone.

The venues for stadium concerts and other big gigs are all outside the centre, so be sure you take a taxi phone number with you or check on bus times for the return journey before setting out. Bus numbers are included in the listings for the out-of-town venues.

As ever, details of what's on are in *Trova Roma*.

CIRCOLO DEGLI ARTISTI
Via Lamarmora 28.

Housed in part of the old milk distribution centre, the Circolo degli Artisti hosts a range of gigs and politically orientated events. Studenty feel, but a dodgy location between Termini and Piazza Vittorio Emanuele.

CAFFÈ LATINO
Via di Monte Testaccio 96.

Small, slightly ropey, sweaty venue tunnelled under Monte Testaccio. There are three rooms – one for jazz (get there early for concerts, or you won't find a table), the other two for a Friday- and Saturday-night disco.

CLUB PICASSO
Via di Monte Testaccio 63.

A neon-lit white plastered tunnel under Monte Testaccio, free on Fridays. Live music every night, ranging from underground to funk, blues and rock. Friendly bar staff.

CAFÉ CARUSO
Via di Monte Testaccio 36.

Another whitewashed tunnel. Live and taped South American and salsa, and dope-smoking in the loos.

BIG MAMA Map ref. [F4] p. 141
Vicolo San Francesco a Ripa 18.

A long-established venue for jazz and blues on the east side of Viale Trastevere.

CLARABELLA Map ref. [F3] p. 141
Piazza San Cosimato 39.

A small, friendly Trastevere club serving milkshakes, ice creams and crepes as well as alcohol. People come to play board games from around 6 p.m., and there's live Brazilian music from 9.30 p.m. in winter and around 10 p.m. in summer.

DRINK MUSIC Map ref. [E/F3] p. 141
Via Natale del Grande 4.

A tiny, scruffy venue for live Brazilian bands. Friendly.

YES BRAZIL Map ref. [F4] p. 141
Via San Francesco a Ripa 103.

Cocktails, Brazilian bands, and spontaneous dancing.

PALAEUR
Piazzale dello Sport.
Metro B.

If a megastar condescends to play Rome, it's often here – a vast sports arena in EUR.

STADIO OLIMPICO (IN THE FORO ITALICO)
Viale dei Gladiatori. Bus 48.

Sports stadium used for jazz concerts and major gigs.

PALLADIUM
Piazza B Romano 8. Bus 92 or 770.

Venue for touring bands – anyone from Run DMC to the Cowboy Junkies and Lush – as well as home-grown fare.

TEATRO TENDASTRISCE
Via Cristoforo Colombo 393. Bus 93.

A permanent tent used for some of the more exciting offbeat Rome gigs – touring artists as well as Italians.

FORTE PRENESTINO
Via Chiovenda. Bus 14.

Miles out, but on the 14 bus route. Old fortress occupied by the anarchists, and a venue for the wild bands of Europe, and other alternative happenings. Once you get off the bus, just follow the graffiti.

IL MATTATOIO
Via di Monte Testaccio.

There have been plans to turn Testaccio's ex-abattoir into a permanent venue for years, but so far nothing has materialised. Listen out, though, because it's spasmodically used for raves and various right-on happenings.

THE ARTS

Rome has three orchestras – the Santa Cecilia, which is pretty good, the RAI, which is passable, and the Teatro dell'Opera, which can be awful. There are also a number of musical associations which organise regular seasons of concerts. International orchestras rarely visit, foreign soloists and chamber ensembles sometimes do. Despite the fact that some of the leading composers of this century have been Italian – Berio, Maderna, Nono, Bussotti and Dallapiccola – there are very few contemporary concerts in the city.

The most appealing aspect of music in Rome is that concerts are not performed only in halls – there are also performances in churches, the cloisters of Santa Maria della Pace, and in palaces like the Cancelleria. There are also outdoor concerts in summer – notably in the Baths of Caracalla (along with operas) and the Teatro di Marcello.

Opera in Rome is not of the standard of that in Milan or Naples, though during the summer, when operas are staged in the Baths of Caracalla, the evocative setting is some compensation. International opera stars do visit, but getting tickets is difficult.

Ballet is slightly more dynamic, and there are a fair number of contemporary dance performances. If you speak Italian, you're unlikely to be bowled over by the standard of theatre, but there are some interesting fringe groups – keep an eye out for posters and listings in *Trova Roma*.

Booking Italy is still a cash culture, and credit-card phone bookings have not yet caught on. Though you can phone to reserve a ticket in advance, you will usually have to pay and collect the ticket from the venue or go in person to one of the booking offices around town.

Venues

TEATRO DELL'OPERA
Piazza Beniamino Gigli 1, tel. 488 1755.

Home to Rome's opera company. Performances shift to the Baths of Caracalla from late June to early September.

ACCADEMIA NAZIONALE DI SANTA CECILIA Map ref. [B3] p. 151
Via della Conciliazione 4, tel. 654 1044 (6880 1044).

Home venue for Rome's best orchestra.

AUDITORIO DI FORO ITALICO
Piazza Laro de Bosis, tel. 3686 5625.

Usually the venue for RAI concerts.

TEATRO GHIONE
Via delle Fornaci 37, tel. 637 2294.

Solo and chamber music recitals.
Sometimes talks.

SALA BALDINI Map ref. [E3]
p. 51
Piazza Campitelli 9, tel. 481 4800.

Solo and chamber music recitals

organised by the Euterpe and Claudio
Monteverdi associations.

AUDITORIUM DEL SERAPHICUM
*Via del Serafico 1 (off Via
Laurentina), tel. 592 3034.*

More concerts organised by Euterpe.

ORATORIO DEL GONFALONE
Map ref. [D1] p. 51
*Via del Gonfalone 21A (off Via
Giulia), tel. 687 5952.*

Thursday concerts by the Coro
Polifonico Romano.

Cinema

The Italian film industry is in a slightly more healthy state than its UK counterpart. Major American directors still come to shoot at Rome's film studio, Cinecittà, the only place in Europe to have the full range of production facilities, and new Italian directors can get a substantial state subsidy for making their first film. Unfortunately, the system has been much abused, with directors claiming that their budgets are a few million lire larger than they really are, and pocketing the difference. The law is currently being tightened up.

The industry is still dominated by men, but there are a couple of very successful women directors. Liliana Cavani makes serious but usually popular big-budget movies, though her recent *San Francesco*, with Mickey Rourke as the saint, was a notable exception. Look out for *La Pelle, Il Portiere dei Notte, Al di là del Bene e del Male* and *Milarepa*. Lina Wertmuller is another bankable director, creating thoughtful comedies – one of her best is *Mimi Metallurgico Ferito nell'Onore*, about a southern Italian who leaves home for the factories of Turin. Among the younger female directors, Francesca Archibugi is the rising star – *Mignone è Partita* and *Verso Sera* are both worth seeing.

There is just one English-language cinema in Rome, the *Pasquino*, Vicolo del Piede 19 (tel. 580 3622) just off Piazza Santa Maria in Trastevere. It's an engaging place, a tiny old-fashioned cinema run by the sixty-year-old son of the late film director Gaetano Amata, showing a different film virtually every night. If you phone, the receptionist, Suzanne, will give you a blunt critique of the night's offering.

Most films shown in Rome, however, are dubbed American products, though if you can tolerate Kevin Costner talking Italian, you can catch US movies long before they are released in Britain. Roman cinemas are categorised into Prima Visione (new releases, shown in the most comfortable cinemas) and Seconda Visione (older films shown in grottier establishments). There are also a number of tiny arty cinemas; *Cinema d'Essai* usually shows foreign films with subtitles – all are listed in the newspapers. Finally, in summer, there's a major theme film season, forming part of the summer festival *L'Estate Romana*. Films are shown at makeshift open-air cinemas, with the locations changing from year to year.

TICKET AGENCIES

Orbis, Piazza Esquilino 37.
Open Mon–Sat 9.30 a.m.–1 p.m.; 4–7.30 p.m.
Classical and rock/pop. Bookings in person only.

Il Botteghino Via del Lavatore 88
Open Mon–Sat 9.30 a.m.–1.30 p.m.; 2.30–6 p.m.
Bookings in person only. Classical music and theatre.

Pronto Spettacolo, tel. 3938 7297
Open Mon–Fri 10 a.m.–5 p.m.
Theatre, rock/pop, classical and sports. Telephone bookings.

Babilonia/Il Cantiere del Nord, Via del Corso 88, tel. 678 6641.
Bookings in person or by phone for rock/pop concerts.

SHOPPING

Shops and Markets

Although there are scores of designer boutiques and an increasing number of bijou ethnic shops, Roman shops are in many ways old-fashioned. There are hardly any supermarkets in the centre – you go to the local *alimentari* for basics, cheese and cooked meats, to a market for fruit and veg, to the butchers for fresh meat, to a *vineria* for wine and a *forno* for bread. There are also lots of tiny jewellery shops where craftsmen (and the very occasional craftswoman) sit inside creating filigree earrings and setting stones, and hundreds of carpentry and restoration workshops, crammed with Baroque oddities and smelling of spirit and linseed oil.

'Just looking' is not the norm in Italy – so when you walk into a shop, expect to be pounced on by an assistant and followed around. If you intend to go inside any of the exclusive designer shops around Piazza di Spagna, it's well worth putting on your best clothes. You're unlikely to be refused admission, but the immaculate label-clad assistants have a talent for making you feel as if you're something the cat brought in. Mainstream clothes are slightly more expensive than in Britain, but if you need something desperately and don't have much money you can always go to the San Giovanni clothes market, one of the cheaper department stores, or a second-hand clothes shop. High-street clothes are rarely particularly interesting – expect to see exactly the same fashions as you do in Britain. Alternative clothes shops are few and far between.

Books, and cassettes, records and CDs are more expensive in Italy than in the UK, but if you run out of reading matter there are plenty of shops selling British and American paperbacks. Many books are cellophane-wrapped – browsing in bookshops is only just beginning to catch on – and you may have problems persuading the assistants to unwrap a book for you. As you might imagine, given the country's cultural heritage, the illustrated art and archaeology books are superb.

Rome is a great city for looking at antiques – from Roman sarcophagi and porphyry busts to gilded Baroque altarpieces and eggshell-cracked stucco cherubs. Unless you know what you are doing, it's unwise to buy anything really expensive, as many objects are not quite what they seem. The main antique streets are Via dei Coronari and Via del Babuino, but the streets around Piazza Navona and Campo dei Fiori are packed with little restoration workshops. For collectables and junk, the best place is the Sunday-morning flea market at Porta Portese in Trastevere.

Jewellery is also worth investigating – the historic centre is full of gold- and silversmiths – and there are an increasing number of shops selling ethnic and outlandish contemporary pieces. There are still places where you can take a stone and design the setting yourself with the help of the jeweller.

Though Milan is the design capital of Italy, there are a few shops in Rome selling state-of-the-art household objects by the big-name (and big-price) Italian designers. There are also some great kitchenware shops, ranging from trendy Habitat-like stores to corner shops where you can pick up a hob-top espresso maker for L12,000.

THINGS TO TAKE HOME

Espresso maker (Bialetti are best; get spare rubber rings at Standa)

Miniature espresso cups and saucers

Toothbrushes (all sorts of trendy designs and colours)

Matchboxes (brilliant designs)

Marble ashtrays

Messalina T-shirt (from the Vatican)

A dinner plate stamped with the Pope's portrait

Kitsch period jewellery (from **Moon**)

Dried pasta (Latini or Martelli are the best)

Sun-dried tomatoes (soak them in warm water when you get home, and bottle them with fresh basil, garlic cloves and olive oil)

Dried *porcini* mushrooms (soak in lukewarm milk and water before cooking)

Parmesan, pecorino and other hard cheeses

Coffee beans

SHOPPING HOURS

Most shops are open from 9 a.m. to 1 or 1.30 p.m. and again from 4 p.m. to 7 p.m. (in winter) and from 5 p.m. to 8 p.m. (in summer). Virtually all shops except *alimentari* (food shops) are closed on Monday mornings, and *alimentari* close on Thursday afternoons. The up-market clothes boutiques rarely open until after 10 a.m., and the same goes for the trendy one-off design, clothes and ethnic shops in Trastevere (many of these, however, stay open late in summer). A few shops now stay open all day (*orario non-stop*).
Pasticcerie (cake shops) are usually open on Sunday mornings.

Some shops have no name! In this case, we list just the address.

Markets

CAMPO DEI FIORI
Exuberant fruit and veg market on a shabbily beautiful piazza in the *centro storico*. Every morning Mon–Sat.

PIAZZA SAN COSIMATO
Lively food market in Trastevere – excellent cheese and salami stalls. Every morning Mon–Sat.

PIAZZA TESTACCIO
Wonderful food market – and the most appealing introduction to Testaccio. Famous for its fish – one of the stalls is owned by Marcello Mastroianni's cousins – and a stall devoted solely to tomatoes. Every morning Mon–Sat.

PORTA PORTESE
A Sunday-morning flea market in Trastevere. Army boots and Bakelite phones, filmscripts and furniture, soutanes and chandeliers, Corinthian capitals and rusty tins of Iranian caviare, along with South American crafts, jade buddhas, Algerian RAI cassettes and paeons to Mussolini inscribed on ceramic tiles. **Watch out for pickpockets.**

MERCATO DI SAN GIOVANNI
Via Sannio.

New and second-hand clothes, every morning except Sun.

PIAZZA VITTORIO EMANUELE
Central Rome's biggest food market (along with a nice selection of acrylic trousers and synthetic 'Last Supper' wall hangings) installed around a garden full of junkies and down-and-outs. Every morning Mon–Sat.

LARGO FONTANELLA BORGHESE
Weekday-morning market of old prints, second-hand books, and antique oddities. Look out for Piranesi prints of old Rome, and books on art and architecture. Be prepared to bargain.

BEFANA
Piazza Navona.
Christmas kitsch and toys. Annually from mid Dec to 6 Jan.

Department Stores

COIN
Piazzale Appio 7/Viale Libia

61/Cinecittà Due (shopping mall)
Viale Togliatti 2.

All branches are outside the centre,
but if you come to live in Rome,
Coin's clothes and home furnishings
are well worth investigating.

RINASCENTE
*Via del Corso (corner Largo Chigi)/
Piazza Fiume.*

Good-priced clothes, and familiar-
brand cosmetics and toiletries. The
home furnishings and kitchen
departments are worth checking out if
you move to Rome.

STANDA
Corso Francia 124/Corso Trieste

200/Via Cola di Rienzo 173/Viale
Regina Margherita/Viale Trastevere
60.

The Viale Trastevere branch of this
economic, slightly down-market
department store is the most central.
As well as being the cheapest place to
buy toiletries and cosmetics, it also has
one of central Rome's rare
supermarkets.

UPIM
*Piazza Santa Maria Maggiore/Via
Nazionale 160, and 211/Via del
Tritone 172.*

Similar to Standa. Budget clothes and
household goods.

Clothes: Offbeat and Second-hand

AVANT DE DORMI
Piazza della Torretta 25.

Funky pyjamas – at a price.

MEDISON
Via Gregoriana 6.

Handmade pyjamas (from around
L150,000).

CANTIERI DEL NORD
Via del Corso 187.

Camden Town on the Corso – a
shrine to leather, Lycra, studs,
Perspex, plastic and PVC. Red or
Dead shoes, too.

DAKOTA
*Via del Seminario. Open 10 a.m.–
8 p.m.*

End-of-line clothes and shoes – if you
take size 1 or 8 shoes, you might pick
up a pair of Converse for L14,000 –
along with a miscellaneous collection

of collectables – anything from a
Bakelite phone to a jukebox or an ex-
bar espresso machine.

MISS FRANCE
Via della Scrofa 13.

Period clothes.

MOON
Via del Governo Vecchio 89a.

Stunning selection of vintage clothes,
ranging from twenties silk dresses to
designer beaded flares. The owner is a
true aficionado, and the shop was
designed expressly for shoppers to sit
around and chat. Ask her to show you
her collection of kitsch jewellery.

SEMPREVERDE
Via del Governo Vecchio 26.

Period clothes shop which changes its
entire stock every month.

VIA DEL GOVERNO VECCHIO 85

Good for second-hand leather jackets and lace blouses.

LABORATORIO ARTIGIANALE
Via del Governo Vecchio 67.

Second-hand and period clothes.

SCALA QUATTORDICI
Via della Scala 14.

Simple linen dresses run up by the owner, who sits at her sewing machine in the shop.

VICOLO DEL CINQUE 30B.

Streaky dyed leggings and jackets.

Clothes: Designer

IL DISCOUNT DELL'ALTA MODA
Via Gesù e Maria 16a.

As the name suggests, discounted designer fashion, but still an awful lot of zeros on the price tags.

ARMANI
Via del Babuino 102.

Quintessential Italian elegance.

EMPORIO ARMANI
Via del Babuino 140.

Armani's cheaper line: clothes for the *jeunesse dorée* of Parioli. You pay for the label rather than the quality of fabric, design or finishing.

MISSONI DONNA
Via del Babuino 96a.

Designer knitwear.

MARIO VALENTINO
Via Frattina 84.

Shoes, bags and suits. The choice of colours appears to have been inspired by Smarties.

MAXMARA
Via Frattina 28.

Crisp, sharply tailored suits and separates in neutral and children's paintbox colours.

GALASSIA
Via Frattina 21.

Young – often wild – designs by Gaultier, Comme des Garçons, Joseph Tricot and Ozbek.

GIVENCHY
Via Borgognona 21.

Feminine chic from a French designer.

BYBLOS
Via Borgognona s/n (opposite Givenchy).

Co-ordinating variations on the Classics with wacky touches – polka-dot shoes and the like.

VERSACE
Via Borgognona 29.

Insane prints and fizzing colours.

VALENTINO
Via Bocca di Leone 15–18.

Kitsch for millionaires and a window display which is always worth a detour. Keep an eye out, too, for exhibitions in his palazzo headquarters on Piazza di Spagna.

FENDI
Via Bocca di Leone 36a.

As well as the famous stripy bags and infamous fur coats, some dubiously witty clothes.

LAURA BIAGOTTI
Via Borgognona 43.

Unpredictable. Sometimes brilliant, but sometimes the clothes wouldn't look out of place in a thrift store.

HERMÈS
Via Condotti 60.

The famous scarves plus lots of accessories.

MILA SCHÖN
Via Condotti 64.

Austere cuts and zinging colours.

Conventional Clothes

ENERGIE
Via del Corso 487.

US-style clothes – jeans, Converse, print shirts and baseball caps.

ODEON
Via Frattina 57.

Usually has something of good value – like silk vest tops for L14,000.

Shoes, Leather, Luggage

DE BACH
Via del Babuino 128.

Stop-and-stare shoes.

GUCCI
Via Condotti 8.

As safe as ever. The famous loafers, along with bags and classic clothes.

THE CONDOTTI STREET VENDORS

Come 2 p.m. when the designer emporia close, the vendors of fake Gucci, Chanel and Louis Vuitton start trading.

OLIVER
Via del Babuino 60.
Valentino's cheaper line. Kitschy.

KOOKAÏ
Via Frattina 113.

Lots of Lycra. Often good imitations of major designers – look out for wild Versace-style print leggings.

STEFANEL
Via Frattina 31.

One of many branches. Wider range than in the UK. Good for cotton jeans.

MR BOOTS
Piazza Trilussa 34.

One of the few shops in Rome where you can get DMs – twice as expensive as they are in the UK.

VIA DELLA LUNGARETTA S/N
(*on the Tiber side of Viale Trastevere*).
Open Mon–Sat 6 a.m.–noon.

Shoe repairs.

PASCUCCI
Via di Pallarcorda 11.
Open Mon–Fri 9 a.m.–7 p.m.

Bag repairs.

I CERVONE
Via del Corso 99.

Mid-price shoes – at last visit a
rainbow of suede pumps.

BARRILÀ
Via del Babuino 33.

A range of reasonably priced shoes
along with expensive customised ones.

BELTRAMI
Via Condotti 19.

Famous make of shoes and handbags.

FERRAGAMO
Via Condotti 73–4.

Arguably the most famous designer
shoes in Italy. Exquisitely crafted.

DOMINICI
*Via del Corso (near junction with Via
Brunetti).*

Trendy, stylish shoes.

MADA
Via della Croce 57.

Expensive shoes – but subtly offbeat
designs.

PELLETTERI
*Corner Via de' Baullari and Piazza
della Cancelleria.*

If you can't fit all your purchases in
your suitcase, there's a range of
cheapish travel bags here, along with
more up-market brands like Samsonite
and Delsey.

Jewellery

AMATI E AMATI
Via Pianellari 21.

Conversation-stopping armwraps and
neckbands made of stained glass and
metal, along with hand-printed fabrics
and other designer pieces. It's also the
only place in Rome selling futons!

BULGARI
Via Condotti 10.

Jewellery for the elite in a sumptuous
shop – if you have the nerve to enter.

SIRAGUSA
Via delle Carrozze 64.

Handmade designs incorporating
archaeological fragments.

NAMELESS JEWELLERS
Via dei Coronari 193.

Unconventional costume jewellery
made of semi-precious stones, relief
metalwork or painted glass.

ODDI E SEGHETTI
*Via del Cancello 18 (off Via
dell'Orso).*

Traditional craftsmen who create
jewellery to the client's specifications.

VIA DEI PETTINARI 80
Nameless jewellers with a good range
of Art Nouveau pieces plus interesting
modern creations by two female
artisans who work in the shop.

VIA DEL GOVERNO VECCHIO 89
Reasonably priced selection of antique
jewellery and knick-knacks.

Kitchenware

C.U.C.I.N.A.
Via del Babuino 18.

The place to come if you can't live any
longer without a pecan-sheller or
pineapple-corer. Most stock is
American, but there's also a good
selection of Alessi.

BOFFI
Piazza Nicosia 32.

Smart kitchen shop – with a great
range of pans, if you can face carrying
them home.

CROFF
Via Tomicelli 137/Via Merulana 143.

Italy's answer to Habitat, with
comparable prices. Virtually the only
place in the city where you can buy a
mug!

ART DE LAMAI
Via de'Baullari 146.

From copper pans and Alessi to plain
white crockery.

CASALINGHI
Via del Governo Vecchio 72.

Basic kitchen shop where you can pick
up a hob-top espresso maker for
L12,000.

LEONE LIMENTARI
*Via Portici d'Ottavia s/n (opposite
Sant'Angelo in Peschiera).*

A cellar crammed with piles of pans
and crockery, used by restaurateurs
and the kitchenware cognoscenti. The
cheapest place to buy an Alessi kettle
or espresso maker.

Cosmetics etc.

ANTICA ERBORISTERIA ROMANA
Via di Torre Argentina 15.

Founded in the eighteenth century,
this herbalist sells natural cosmetics
and cures in an antique shop.

BODY SHOP
Via del Corso 168.

The full range of Body Shop products
at twice the price.

BOLLE DI SAPONE
Via della Lungaretta 63.

Trendy toiletries, funky toothbrushes
and natural soaps – including mint,
which is supposed to be cooling in hot
weather.

LA TASTE
Via Bergamaschi 60.

Herbal cosmetics, teas and soaps.

AL TEMPO RITROVATO
Piazza Farnese 103.

Rome's sole women's bookshop. Wide range of Italian feminist magazines, a good selection of books (even a few Virago novels), and a focal social point for Rome's feminists. Check out the noticeboard and the posters stuck to the door, and ask the owner for information about women's events and other happenings.

CORNER BOOKSHOP
Via del Moro 48.

Cosy bookshop with a good range of English books, run by a friendly English woman.

LOUISE MACDERMOTT
Via Giubbonari 30 (Flat 9), tel. 654 5285.

A wonderful range of books in English about Italy (ask at the Corner Bookshop for a catalogue). Louise runs the book-dealing business from home – phone for an appointment, and prepare to spend a pleasant half-hour or so chatting about Rome and browsing through her books. All sorts of treasures and out-of-print books – many of them extremely reasonable.

LION BOOKSHOP
Via del Babuino 181/Via della Fontanella 3.

Great bookshop for browsing, lots of paperbacks and a reasonable range of children's books.

ECONOMY BOOK AND VIDEO CENTRE
Via Torino 136.

English and American books, videos and magazines and lots of second-hand paperbacks. Also a trade-in scheme.

AMERICAN BOOKSHOP
Via delle Vite 57.

English and American books.

LA GROTTA DEL LIBRO
Via del Pellegrino 169.

Discount and remaindered books; usually has the full range of guides (in Italian) to each neighbourhood in Rome.

LIBRERIA LUNGARETTA
Via della Lungaretta 90e.

Italian novels and art books, in a relaxed shop with a sofa for browsing.

RINASCITA
Via delle Botteghe Oscure 1–3.

Good for maps and travel guides.

FELTRINELLI
Largo Argentina 5a/Via del Babuino 41. Open Mon–Sat 9 a.m.–8 p.m.; Sun 10 a.m.–1.30 p.m.; 4–7.30 p.m.

Major Italian bookshop chain.

MESSAGERIE BOCCA
Via delle Carrozze 50.

Good selection of art books – some with English text.

RIZZOLI
Largo Chigi 15.

Vast bookshop, with a large academic department. Virtually all Italian.

JCCC
Via Bergamaschi 49.

Comic strips and kitsch and cartoony postcards.

LIBRERIA SCORZINI
Via delle Vite 43.

New and second-hand Italian books. Good for history.

JUST LIKE HEAVEN
Via Torpignattura 55.

Trendy music shop – indie, Gothic, psychedelia, etc. – but miles out of the centre.

DISFUNZIONI MUSICALI
Via degli Etruschi 4–14.

Near the university in San Lorenzo. New and second-hand records, CDs and cassettes. Mostly rock and pop.

MAKUMBA CENTER
Via del Vantaggio 28.

Senegalese, Zaïrois and Afro-Caribbean tapes and records.

RICORDI
Via del Corso 506/Piazza dell'Indipendenza 24/6.

Rome's biggest music store – classical as well as rock and pop.

Design, Crafts, Antiques

APOLLODORO
Piazza Mignanelli 17 (near Piazza di Spagna).

A *trompe-l'œil* door gives access to a gallery/shop showcasing household objects designed by the likes of Paolo Portoghesi (who owns the place), Giò Ponti, Robert Venturi and Michael Graves.

ARTEMIDE
Via Margutta 107.

State-of-the-art lighting by – among others – Ettore Sottsass Jnr.

CASSINA
Via del Babuino 100.

Limited-edition cover-versions of furniture by Wright, Le Corbusier, Charles Rennie Mackintosh and Giò Ponti. Resembles a minimuseum of twentieth-century design.

STIL DOMUS
Via del Babuino 54.

Minimalist furniture and accessories for the home. The kind of stuff foreigners consider quintessentially Italian.

CERAMICHE DE SIMONE
Via Margutta s/n.

Modern, reasonably priced, bright and cheerfully painted mugs, plates and dishes. Some wonderful crockery for kids.

FABRIZIO LOMBARDI
Via dei Coronari 31.

Twentieth-century kitsch and collectables. Former customers include Bono and Michael Jackson (unless Fabrizio bought the signatures displayed on the wall).

LA GIARA
Via dei Coronari 54.

Gorgeous majolica – traditional-painted Italian ceramics – ranging from tiles and ashtrays to giant plates and urns.

BOTTEGANTICA
Via di San Simone 70 (just off Coronari).

Antique majolica and rustic bits and pieces.

PIETRO TALONE
Via dei Coronari 135.

Lighting: from Baroque to Art Deco.

MARMI LINE
Via dei Coronari 113.

Inlaid coffee tables, marble urns, busts of Romans.

MOSAICUM
Via della Scrofa 113.

Antique jewellery, along with Turkish and Caucasian rugs.

KILIM GALLERY
Via del Panico 8.

As the name suggests, gorgeous kilim rugs.

IMMART
Vicolo delle Cinque 24b.

A trendy Trastevere art gallery.

LEGGATORI DI LIBRI
Via Bellina 53.

An old-fashioned bookbinder's.

LO SCRIGNO
Via della Lungaretta 7/8.

Ethnic bags, jewellery and belts.

VIA LUNGARETTA 96
South American crafts, T-shirts and cassettes; and titanium, stained-wood and silver jewellery.

PROPOSTA
Via del Moro 28.

Handmade and hand-printed silk cushions, scarves, wall hangings and lampshades.

MOSAICI
Via Gigli d'Oro 9.

Byzantine-style mosaics.

Posters and Stationery

L'IMAGE
Via della Scrofa 67.

Posters and postcards – some arty, some dubiously humorous.

LE SCATOLE
Via della Stelleta 27.

Pretty marbled boxes, notebooks, files and writing paper.

GRAFFITI
Vicolo delle Cinque 22.

Crafts and paper goods.

DESIGN, CRAFTS, ANTIQUES

SHOPPING

SALUMERIA ROSSI
Piazza della Rotonda 4.

An excellent deli stocking some of Italy's best brands of dried pasta. Look out for Marcelli or Latini.

AI MONASTERI
Piazza delle Cinque Lune 76 (Corso Rinascimento).

Monks' produce – chocolate, honey, and herbal liqueurs.

IL FORNAIO
Via de' Baullari 5.

Trays of pizza, olive-studded focaccia, and scores of different breads (including wholemeal).

PASTICCERIA VALZANI
Via del Moro 37b. Closed July and Aug.

The oldest and most authentic *pasticceria* in Rome, creating traditional sweetmeats for traditional festivals. They also produce wonderful *cornetti* and chocolate throughout the year.

GARGANI
Via Lombardia 17.

Scrumptious deli just off Via Veneto. Roast beef, salads, stuffed aubergines, olives, cheeses and hams.

ANTICO CAFFÈ DEL BRASILE
Via dei Serpenti 21.

Suppliers of coffee beans to the Vatican. The papal blend is called *miscela del papa*.

BUCCONE
Via di Ripetta 19.

Excellent wine shop.

MORIONDO & GARIGLIO
Via della Pilotta 2.

Handmade chocolates – filled with fondant, zabaglione, coffee, rum, fruit and coconut.

DELUCHI
Via della Croce 75.

Rome's best fruit shop.

PASTA ALL'UOVO
Piazza Campo dei Fiori 55.

Wonderful fresh-egg pasta – if you have access to a stove.

FORNO
Piazza Campo dei Fiori 22.

Brilliant fresh bread and pizza.

Only in Rome . . .

TROMPE L'ŒIL
Via dei Coronari 107.

The place to come if you want a mock loggia, garden or statue painting on the walls of your palazzo. If you don't have a palazzo, pop in and look at the frescoes in the shop and leaf through the portfolio.

DE RITIS
Via de' Cestari 1.

Monstrances, chalices, incense-burners and ecclesiastical garb.

SOUVENIRS
There are stands outside every major site. Plaster *pietàs*, Colosseum ashtrays, papal benedictions (in the Vatican) and candles, plates and key rings bearing a portrait of the Pope.

CHILDREN, BUSINESSWOMEN, GETAWAYS

CHILDREN

If your children are going to enjoy Rome, you need to involve them. Let them have a go at navigating the mazy streets by tracing a route on the map and looking out for street signs; let them learn a bit of Italian with you, and order in cafés, shops and restaurants; and make sure they know what there is to do and see, so that you can plan your days together. (The listings below are designed to be used by children.)

Children are unlikely to have a good time in Rome if they feel as if they're on a school trip. *Asterix the Gladiator* is the most fun book about Ancient Rome, and if you do your homework and tell them stories and anecdotes about the city's history, they'll enjoy it all the more. With a few exceptions, most of the stories in this guidebook can be adapted for children. There are some good illustrated children's history books, but leave them at the bottom of the suitcase until your children start wanting to find out more.

Rome's museums are decades behind their British counterparts, technology-free zones with no opportunity for interactive learning, so you have to work hard to make them exciting. As well as pre-selecting what you think will interest your children and having a few stories up your sleeve, give them a chance to discover things for themselves. And unless there's something they specifically want to see, don't drag them around the Vatican Museums.

They are, of course, going to need time to play. The Villa Borghese Park has a zoo, miniature train and boats to hire, and there's a pleasant open-air swimming pool at EUR, but before going to the city's biggest – though old-fashioned – funfair, LUNEUR, make sure your children know it is not a hi-tech rival to Alton Towers or EuroDisney. As well as day trips to the beach and Lake Bracciano, many children enjoy the fountains in the Villa d'Este, which you could follow up with a picnic in the Villa Adriana.

As for eating and drinking, you don't see many children eating with their parents in the evenings, though yours will be made welcome, particularly in the more homely trattorias. If they don't like pizza and pasta, resign yourself to picnicking and burger bars. Kids are unlikely to be impressed by Italian chips (except in McDonald's), and finding plain grilled meat other than steak is not easy. Children often accompany their parents to cafés in the evenings, and as Romans eat late you may find it a better idea to have your main meal at lunchtime and make do with a café snack in the evening, followed by a visit to a *gelateria*. As well as ice cream, milkshakes and *granita* (sloppy lemon- or coffee-flavoured crushed ice) are widely available. If your children are miserable without breakfast cereals, you can find them – at a price – in the more up-market *alimentari*.

Children are welcome in virtually all hotels, and most will supply cots and extra beds. They will also organise babysitters – though in smaller hotels you should give the staff plenty of warning. If you're not staying in a hotel, you'll find English-speaking babysitters advertising in *Wanted in Rome*, and sometimes on the noticeboard of the Anglican church, All Saints on Via del Babuino.

Rome is not an ideal city to which to bring very young children and babies. You never see anyone breastfeeding in public; and loos are often cramped (and none too clean), which makes changing nappies awkward. Bear in mind, too, that the hectic streets (and in spring and summer the heat) are likely to make even the sweetest-natured child fretful. Nappies, baby food and powdered milk are available at most *farmacie*, though they're cheaper in supermarkets like Standa (Viale Trastevere).

Culture for Children

MUSEO DELLA CIVILTÀ ROMANA (SEE P.233)
A miniature model of ancient Rome.

MUSEO DELLE ARTI E TRADIZIONI POPOLARE (SEE P.234)
Old-fashioned toys, an antique potty, puppets and a Christmas crib scene.

MUSEO DEL FOLKLORE (SEE P.146)
Action-packed paintings of old Rome and waxwork tableaux.

MUSEI CAPITOLINI (SEE P.177)
A wolf feeding baby Romulus and Remus, some statues of children, and marble heads of ancient Roman women with very peculiar hairstyles.

VILLA GIULIA (SEE P.136)
A walk-in Etruscan tomb and some wonderful jewellery.

SANTA MARIA DELLA CONCEZIONE (SEE P.131)
Ghoulish caverns decorated with bones and skeletons.

CATACOMB OF PRISCILLA (SEE P.245)
Spooky underground galleries where Christians were buried, a friendly nun

who speaks English to take you round, and the Villa Ada Park to explore afterwards.

SANT'IGNAZIO (SEE P.83)
A trick ceiling. See if you can tell which bits are real and which bits are painted.

THE COLOSSEUM (SEE P.201)
Good views of Rome from the top. The floor in the middle has been removed, and you can see the corridors which the wild animals walked along on their way to fight gladiators.

ST PETER'S (SEE P.154)
The most exciting thing is the dome – hundreds of steps up, but brilliant views from the top.

SAN CLEMENTE (SEE P.219)
Two churches and an ancient Roman house piled on top of each other.

SANTA PRASSEDE (SEE P.215)
Gorgeous brightly coloured mosaics in the Capella San Zeno.

SANTO STEFANO ROTONDO (SEE P.222)
A round church with revolting paintings of saints being killed on the walls.

SANT'AGOSTINO (SEE P.70)
A painting of the Virgin Mary with dirty toenails.

TREVI FOUNTAIN (SEE P.109)
A fountain with seats in front where you can sit and watch water gushing over sea horses and monsters.

FONTANA DELLE TARTARUGHE (SEE P.99)
A fountain with tortoises sitting on the rim.

FONTANA DELLE QUATTRO FIUMI (SEE P.56)
Four muscly river gods and some weird monsters hiding in the water.

TRAJAN'S MARKETS (SEE P.207)
An ancient Roman shopping centre.

SPANISH STEPS (SEE P.120)
A good place to sit and watch people.

Food for Children

BURGHY (SEE P.280)
A burger bar opposite the Pantheon, with seats outside.

MCDONALD'S (SEE P.290)
Much better salads and cakes than in Britain.

GIOLITTI AND GELATERIA DELLA PALMA (SEE P.282)
Try the ice creams from both of these *gelaterie* and decide which is best.

CAFFÈ ACCADEMIA (SEE P.287)
Fresh-fruit milkshakes made while you watch.

LEONCINO (SEE P.281)
An old-fashioned pizzeria where you can see the pizzas being made.

GHETTO BAKERY (SEE P.282)
Scrumptious homemade fruit cake.

FIORI DI CAMPO (SEE P.285)
A good café to sit in and watch the chaotic old-fashioned Italian market on the piazza outside. There's usually a knife-grinder working next to it, sharpening knives on a pedal-powered wheel.

BAR FILETARO SANTA BARBARA (SEE P.283)
Deep-fried fish.

CHILDREN

COSE FRITTE (SEE P.286)
Deep-fried everything – even fruit and cheese!

Playing and Entertainment

PISCINA DELLE ROSE
Viale America (EUR).

A pretty open-air swimming pool surrounded by roses.

LUNEUR
An old-fashioned amusement park with a big wheel and a big dipper.

VILLA BORGHESE/PINCIO (SEE P.132)
A big park around an art gallery. Miniature train rides, boats and bikes to hire (with child seats), and a zoo.

MARIONETTES AND CHILDREN'S THEATRE
There are usually marionette shows on Piazza Garibaldi on the Janiculum. Other events are listed in *Trova Roma* (see p.11).

Shops

As well as the following shops, it's also interesting to peep into the workshops in the streets around Piazza Navona, where craftsmen repair and paint antiques or make jewellery.

LA CITTÀ DEL SOLE
Via della Scrofa 65.

A brilliant toy shop, with games for adults as well as children.

LETTINI
Piazza Navona.

Hundreds of very expensive stuffed, fluffy and furry toys.

MASKHARA
Via della Scala 66.

Weird and wonderful masks.

JCCC
Via Bergamaschi 49.

Comic strips and cartoony postcards.

L'IMAGE
Via della Scrofa 67.

Good posters and cards.

BRUMMEL
Via Frattina 86.

Fun but practical clothes for children.

JACADI
Via dei Greci 29.

Stylish children's and baby clothes.

NAJ OLEARI
Via dei Greci 32.

Pretty – usually flowery – girls' dresses.

IL PALLONCINO ROSSO
Via dei Pettinari 49.

Wacky leopard-print leggings, sequin pumps and the like.

BUSINESSWOMEN

The most famous businesswomen in Italy are connected with the fashion industry – the Fendi sisters, Giuliana Benetton and Giovanna Stefanel – but women are certainly not limited to such 'feminine' fields. The country's second-largest steel empire, Danieli, is run by the founder's granddaughter, Cecilia, and until her recent death, Marisa Bellisario not only headed the state telecom equipment manufacturers, Italtel, but was the highest-ranking non-media executive in the world. Out of the limelight, too, facilitated by the country's childcare provision, women are making progress, though business is still dominated by men.

Doing business in Italy can be great fun. Flirting is almost obligatory, and if possible you should be relaxed about it. Most Italian men genuinely like women, and do not make flattering comments about a woman's appearance in order to embarrass or disempower her. Once you grow accustomed to it, it simply makes the working day more pleasurable – Italians really do seem to have a talent for getting the most out of life!

Italian businesswomen power-dress by looking glamorous or stylishly flamboyant, generally in designer clothes. Don't be surprised if your Italian counterparts arrive at work wearing vibrant colours, short skirts and glitzy costume jewellery, for they know they are still going to be taken seriously – far more so, in fact, than if they donned a safe navy suit. The men, too, are clothes-conscious. Suits are rare (they wear contrasting jackets and trousers), but they're terribly fond of English-gentlemanly accessories like mock regimental or college ties. Taking – and being seen to have taken – care over one's appearance accrues respect.

Italians are hospitable, and if they know you're alone, they'll often invite you for dinner, to a party, or to join them for a day trip at the weekend. As most of their income goes on clothes and cars rather than houses, entertaining tends to be done outside the home. A considerable amount of business, too, is done in restaurants, usually over a long lunch. Italians are modest drinkers, so don't assume that you'll be able to clinch a deal when your client is tipsy.

The Italian business world is not as lethargic and disorganised as its reputation might suggest – things *do* get done . . . eventually. That said, making contact can be difficult. Try to do all your phoning before lunch – all government offices close at 1.30 p.m. or 2 p.m. – preferably first thing in the morning. If you leave a message, don't expect to have it returned – Italians are very skilled at playing hard to get, and may try to make you do all the running. Although it's better not to look too eager (they'll assume you're desperate), if you've continually failed to make contact by phone, it's worth going along in person. Once you have ceased to be simply an anonymous voice on the other end of a telephone, things can begin to happen.

USEFUL ADDRESSES

Faxing
Most hotels allow clients to send and receive messages, but see 'communications' for addresses of public fax offices.

Photocopying
24 Via di San Doroteo (tobacconist in Trastevere)
Open 8 a.m.–1.45 p.m.; 4.30–9 p.m.

Eurocopie di Pienicci Valler
79 Via Monte Brianzo (behind Via dell'Orso)
Open 9 a.m.–1 p.m.; 3.30–7.30 p.m.

D'Antimi
1 Foro Traiano (behind Trajan's Forum)
Open 8.30 a.m.–1.30 p.m.; 3.30–6.30 p.m.

Translation/Interpreting
David Geddings, tel. 666 3347.
English/Italian and Italian/English interpreting and translation.

Angela Ricci, tel. 686 9252.
English/Italian and Italian/English interpreting and translation.

Temporary Offices
Rome at Your Service
Centro Uffici
Via Vittorio Emanuele Orlando 75, tel. 484 583.
Offices, with access to computers, fax, secretarial services, to rent by the day or week.

Car Hire/Limousine Services
Ezio Ciarelli
Via Vallelunga 110, 00166 ROMA, tel. 62 43 589.
Reasonable rates (comparable to taxis for transport to the airports) and extremely courteous service. Recommended.

Bevilacqua
Via San Nicolo da Tolentino 20, tel. 483 756/488 2896.
Cars with chauffeur.
Approx L320,000 up to 70 km plus L1000 per subsequent km.

Budget
Via Boncompagni 14C, tel. 482 0966/482 0967

or

Fiumicino Airport, tel. 652 9133

or

Ciampino, tel. 7934 0137.
From approx L87,000 inclusive per day.

Travel Agent
Viaggiare
Via San Nicolo da Tolentino 18, tel. 474 6751.
Reliable family firm with an English-speaking owner (ask for Marco Chelo).

Italians prefer to do business with people they know. This is why so many businesses, from corner shops to international empires, are family-run, and on a more sinister level, it is also why corruption is endemic, and why many of the most successful businesses are those with Mafia connections and a few politicians in their pockets. Even Italians find it impossible to get a job or secure business without knowing the right people. Personal recommendations can smooth your way considerably, so forage around for contacts before you leave, and use them mercilessly. Even the friend of a friend of a friend can help. Once you have made contact, things can happen very quickly, especially if the person you have met likes you. Coming across as the formal representative of your company may not get you very far – you need to strike them with your personality as well as your purchasing power.

Although the Italian business game is more informal than in Britain or the US, there is far more bureaucracy and red tape to cut through. Again, some of this can be bypassed if you know the right people – doing things 'by the book' is not inevitably the best policy.

GETAWAYS

Wonderful as Rome is, there's nothing like escaping for a day. Most Romans do, heading up to Lake Bracciano or across to the coast on sunny weekends. Except in August, the crowds can largely be avoided if you go to such places midweek. If you're not already surfeited with culture, the ancient town of Ostia and Emperor Hadrian's retirement villa near Tivoli are both easily accessible. Tivoli itself is worth a visit for two glorious gardens: the fountain-studded terraces of the Villa d'Este, created for Lucrezia Borgia's son; and the wild, romantic valley of the Villa Gregoriana. All destinations below are accessible by public transport, but you could hire a car or a Vespa for the day (see directory p.39). Alternatively, major sights, like the Villas of Tivoli and Ostia Antica, can be visited on coach excursions, bookable at virtually all hotels.

Bus from Lepanto to Trevignano (tel. 386 406). Twelve per day on weekdays, five per day on Sundays and holidays. Get off the bus beyond Anguillara – the busstop is after the restaurant sign 'Aquarella'.

About forty kilometres north of Rome is Lake Bracciano, a huge expanse of water filling a volcanic crater. Most people head to one of its resorts – Bracciano itself, Trevignano or Anguillara – but it's immeasurably more pleasant to go instead to one of the small, lakeside restaurants, where you can not only eat, but swim and sunbathe in peace. **La Valletta**, between Anguillara and Trevignano, is little-known and attracts a select group of regulars – most of them families or British expats – and is somewhere you really can relax, whether you're alone or with your children.

To get to the restaurant once you're off the bus, walk back to a stony white side road, signposted the Sabate Boat Club: **La Valletta** (open daily in summer) is just off here. The food is splendid – the *spaghetti alla carbonara* is probably the best you'll taste – served with cool bottles of local white wine. There's space to sunbathe on the grassy lakeside, and there are pedalos and sailing boats (including a speedy catamaran) to hire by the hour.

Villa Adriana and the Gardens of Tivoli

Bus from Rebibbia to Tivoli (tel. 591 5551 for details). Ask to be let off the bus at the 'Bivio Villa Adriana', from which there's a ten–fifteen-minute walk (signposted) to the site entrance. The opening hours of the three villas change according to season, so check with the EPT in Rome before setting out.

Even if you've had your fill of ancient ruins, it's worth considering a picnic trip to the Villa Adriana though the entrance ticket is not cheap, shaded by pines and beautifully set in wide-open country. It's an ideal place, too, for your children to let off steam, as they can run around without you having to worry about traffic.

The complex, covering 180 acres, is vast, a magnificent private retreat begun by the emperor in AD 126, with bath-houses, libraries, a fire station, temples and theatres as well as a palace. Hadrian, a keen architect, had been deeply impressed, on his travels through the Empire, by buildings in Greece and Egypt, and had some of them reproduced here.

There are plans and leaflets about the site on sale in the bar, and next door, a model of the complex gives some idea of its former extent and luxury. There's really too much to absorb in a single visit, so concentrate on some of the more outstanding relics. The most pleasant place to picnic is the Terrace of Tempe, named after a famous valley in Greece where Daphne legendarily escaped the amorous clutches of Apollo by becoming a laurel tree.

Close to the entrance is the so-called Teatro Marittimo, actually a tiny circular palace surrounded by a canal and portico, where, it is thought, Hadrian retired to write and paint – he was a contemplative, as well as a military man. Though he was married to Sabina – in what appears to have been a fraught and loveless relationship – Hadrian's great passion was a beautiful Greek youth named Antinous. Antinous drowned in AD 130 near the temple of Serapis at Canopus in Egypt. Grief-stricken, Hadrian deified the youth, combining his cult with that of Serapis, the god of the dead. In Antinous's memory he reconstructed the Temple of Serapis in the grounds of the villa, an exquisite monument fronted by a canal still partially lined with statues (including one of a crocodile). Watch out for the geese living hereabouts: they bite.

From outside the site, there are buses every half-hour to Tivoli, an unexceptional, largely modern town, splayed around a sturdy castle. The only reason to come is to visit either of the two gardens here. The Villa d'Este was built for Lucrezia Borgia's cardinal son, Ippolito d'Este, in the 1550s. The villa, caked with Mannerist frescoes, gives access to fabulous gardens, steeply raked on terraces and studded with extravagant – though decaying – fountains, furred with moss and creepers. If Renaissance artificiality does not appeal, head instead to the wild, lush gardens of the Villa Gregoriana, where paths wind down the steep, wooded valley, giving views of a magnificent waterfall, the Grande Cascata. There are also two wonderfully well-preserved ancient temples – access is from the Ristorante Sibilla (closed Mon) above the gardens.

Ostia Antica

Open daily 9 a.m.–one hour before sunset

Overland metro from Magliana to Ostia Antica. The site is about five minutes' walk from the station. There are no refreshments there, so bring your own.

The extensive remains of the ancient port town of Ostia are among the best-preserved in Italy. Nevertheless, they are fairly demanding, and seeing everything would take around six hours. The site itself is lovely, the ancient creeper- and ivy-covered walls rising from long grass scattered in spring with wild flowers.

According to legend, Ostia was founded in the sixth century BC, though archaeologists believe it was established two hundred years later. It was originally a walled fortress built at the mouth of the

Tiber to protect Rome; later it became a port and naval base. Eventually a new and larger port was built by Claudius, and by the time of Hadrian, in the second century AD, Ostia had become a residential suburb for the middle and working classes. By then most businesses had moved out, and Ostia's main function was to store the grain for the *annona*, or corn dole (see p.208). By the fifth century Ostia had virtually been abandoned, and gradually the Tiber's silt moved the coastline further west. The site is now several kilometres from the sea.

To get the most out of Ostia Antica, you'll need a plan – which involves a ten-minute walk up to the bookshop (signposted from the main street, the Decumanus Maximus). While you're there you could pop into the nearby Museum (open 9 a.m.–1 p.m. only) to see some wonderful reliefs of everyday life in the ancient town. Most evocative is a maternity scene (the woman is held down on a chair while the midwife forages for the baby); but there are also scenes of women selling poultry and vegetables. Before leaving the museum, ask if it's possible to have access to the ancient brothel, the Casa delle Volte Dipinti (see below).

Among the more interesting buildings are the Baths of the Cisiarii, set up by the wagon-drivers' guild, with mosaics showing the members transporting citizens about the town; the Piazzale delle Corporazioni, surrounded by the former offices of the town's maritime businesses, each one with a black-and-white mosaic floor depicting its trade (most of them are cargo ships); and a couple of Horrea, corn warehouses.

There are also indications of how ancient Ostians spent their time off. Abutting the Piazzale is a large theatre, and down the street is the Casa di Diana, an up-market apartment block, complete with loo, balcony and cistern. Across the road is the Thermopolium, which served wine and hot snacks, and retains a marble bar and courtyard for *al fresco* eating and drinking. There's also a twenty-seater public lavatory, or Forica, and a frescoed house, the Casa delle Volte Dipinti (see above for access), which was converted into a brothel – as is clear from some naughty illustrations on the walls.

Ostia's Beaches

Overland metro from Magliana to Ostia Lido or Cristoforo Colombo.

If you're desperate you could head to Rome's nearest beach, Lido di Ostia, a couple of stops down the line from Ostia Antica. It does, however, have an appalling reputation for pollution, and you can be sure – at weekends, at least – that there will be plenty of *burrini* (see p.55) around. South of Ostia, the duney sands get quieter, but as prostitutes solicit along the roadside, the beaches here are not exactly ideal for solo women. If you do decide to go, take the metro to Cristoforo Colombo, then catch bus 07/ along the Via Litoranea coast road. There are stops at each of eight gates which give access to the sands.

Sabaudia and San Felice Circeo

Bus from EUR Fermi (tel. 591 5551).

If you want to go to a beach, it's preferable to take a bus down to Sabaudia or San Felice Circeo. Sabaudia, a clinical resort built in Mussolini's time, has a lovely long duny beach, accessible by a shuttle bus from the Rotonda, where the Rome bus stops. The beach is lined with restaurants and bars, most of which have sunbeds and pedalos for hire, and it gets crowded only on sunny weekends and during August. If you're alone, make sure you have left your valuables behind, and ask the restaurant staff to look after your bag while you swim. La Caravella is reckoned to be the best of the seaside restaurants, specialising in fish.

If you have your own transport, you could head to the Parco Nazionale del Circeo, which stretches from the marshes around Sabaudia to Monte Circeo, a wood-cloaked mountain jutting out into the sea. Walking routes have been laid out through the woods, and information on these and the park's wildlife can be picked up from the Visitors' Centre, signposted from the coast road south of Sabaudia.

On the other side of Monte Circeo is San Felice Circeo, a picturesque old village of stone houses which became trendy in the 1970s. It (and the mountain) are named for the legendary enchantress Circe, who turned men into beasts and was supposed to inhabit one of the caves which riddle this dramatically serrated coastline. Her most famous appearance is in the *Odyssey*, though in Homer's version she lives on an island. Prevented from transforming Odysseus into a pig (he threatens her with his sword), she is nevertheless sufficiently sexually powerful to persuade him to dally with her. When he does eventually tear himself away, she advises him to fill the ears of his men with wax and to tie himself to the mast of the boat, so that they cannot be seduced to their deaths by the singing of the Sirens.

In season, you can take a boat from San Felice to the alleged cave of Circe [*Grotta della Maga Circe*] or simply join the beautiful people tanning on the artificial beaches. If you have transport, you should be able to find a quiet spot on the rocky coast for solitary sunbathing (though the sea here is usually too rough for swimming). Drive along the road signposted to the lighthouse [*Faro*], from which a number of rubbly tracks lead to the coast.

BACKGROUND

RECOMMENDED BOOKS

Women in Ancient Rome

Goddesses, Whores, Slaves and Wives, Sarah Pomeroy, Schocken Books, 1975.
An objective, meticulously researched, and readable account of women in ancient Rome (and Greece) from various social strata.

Women's Life in Greece and Rome, Mary R. Lefkowitz and Maureen B. Fant, Duckworth, 1992.
A fascinating, and at times alarming, collection of extracts concerning women from literature, history and tombs. Covers everything from ancient gynaecology to how to select a wet-nurse. Great to dip into, and some of the extracts have a startling immediacy.

Sex in History, Reay Tannahill, Cardinal, 1989.
An entertaining and illuminating survey of sex, racily written and packed with surprising facts. There's a good chapter on ancient Rome.

The Erotic Poems, Ovid, Penguin, 1982.
Raunchy, ironic love poems, a manual on the art of cosmetics, and the *Ars Amores*, a handbook for cynical lovers, for which the poet was banished from Rome.

Sixteen Satires, Juvenal, Penguin, 1974.
Spirited, though often viciously misogynistic, poems.

The Poems of Catullus, Penguin, 1966.
Sometimes pornographic, sometimes malicious, but occasionally heartbreakingly lovely poems about women.

Cleopatra: Histories, Dreams and Distortions, Lucy Hughes Hallett, Vintage, 1990.
An erudite but entertaining account of the ways in which, for almost two thousand years, the image of Cleopatra has been moulded and remoulded by male fantasy.

The Twelve Caesars, Suetonius, Penguin, 1989.
Biographies of Roman rulers from Julius Caesar to Domitian, and
the source of much of the scandal associated with the women who
surrounded them.

The Caesars, Allan Massie, Cardinal, 1983.
A sort of popular modern rewrite of Suetonius which draws also on
the writings of other ancient historians. Doesn't leave you much the
wiser about the empresses, though it is very readable.

Daily Life in Ancient Rome, Jerome Carcopino, Peregrine, 1941.
Over fifty years old now (and some of the information on women
relies rather too heavily on Juvenal), but nevertheless a vivid and
memorable account of everyday life in Imperial Rome.

Roman Society, Donald Dudley, Penguin, 1970.
A concise account of the history of Rome from the ninth century BC
to the fourth century AD. Recommended if you want a broad
overview which includes culture, politics and economics.

Roman Architecture, Frank Sear, Batsford, 1989.
An accessible account of Roman architecture and building techniques, with lots of diagrams and illustrations. Makes you see the
ancient ruins with new eyes.

Women in General

Courtesans of the Italian Renaissance, Georgina Masson,
Secker & Warburg o/p, 1975.
An intelligent, revealing and sensitive survey of the most famous
courtesans of the fifteenth and sixteenth centuries.

Ragionamenti, Pietro Aretino, Libra o/p.
Renaissance porn: three raunchy, satirical dialogues about the lives
of nuns, married women and courtesans.

Women of the Renaissance, Margaret L. King, University of
Chicago Press, 1991.
A stimulating survey of women's lives in Europe from the mid fourteenth to mid seventeenth centuries. Insight into the experiences of
ordinary as well as famous women.

Women and Religion

Alone of All Her Sex: The Myth and Cult of the Virgin Mary,
Marina Warner, Picador, 1976.
An impressively researched, but occasionally oversubjective account
of the history and facets of the cult of the Virgin.

Eunuchs for the Kingdom of Heaven, Uta Ranke-Heinemann,
Penguin, 1990.

A challenging, formidably erudite and engagingly witty critique of the Catholic Church's attitude to sex from St Jerome to John Paul II. An unforgettable read.

Women and Art

Women Artists, Frances Borzello and Natacha Ledwidge, Camden Press, 1986.
Highly entertaining, but concise, informative and thought-provoking survey of women artists by a lecturer at the National Gallery, London. Brilliant cartoons, too. The best book to start with.
Women, Art, and Society, Whitney Chadwick, Thames & Hudson, 1990.
A more in-depth introduction to women artists and the obstacles they have faced over the centuries. Sections on most of the female artists whose works you'll see in Rome.
Feminism and Art History: Questioning the Litany, Norma Broude and Mary D. Garrard (eds), Harper & Row, 1982.
An eclectic collection of feminist essays, including a chilling account by Garrard of the rape of Artemisia Gentileschi.
Refiguring the Renaissance, Marilyn Migiel and Juliana Schiesari (eds), Cornell, 1991.
Many of the essays are heavy going, but if you've become intrigued by the various representations of Judith and Holofernes in Rome's art galleries, Elena Ciletti's exploration of the subject is a must.

General Books on Art

Art and Architecture in Italy 1600–1750, Rudolf Wittkower, Pelican, 1958.
Everything you ever wanted to know about Baroque – a reliable, revealing, though demanding survey.
Bernini, Howard Hibbard, Pelican, 1965.
An accessible account of Bernini's work.
Mannerism, John Shearman, Pelican, 1967.
A stimulating, and eye-opening encounter with Mannerist art, architecture, literature and applied arts.

Miscellaneous

Rome: The Biography of a City, Christopher Hibbert, Penguin, 1985.
An engaging, effortlessly readable account of Rome's history from the Etruscans to Mussolini. Lovely illustrations too.
The Blue Guide to Rome, published by Black Norton, 1989.

Rome without the people, but covers virtually every church and palace in the city.

Roma e Dintorni, TCI (Updated edition due end 1992).
The most comprehensive guide available to the monuments of Rome and its surroundings. Worth it if you're studying and read Italian.

Roma: Guida ai Ristoranti, Trattorie, Pizzerie, Enoteche e Sfiziosità, published by Gambero Rosso.
The best guide to eating and drinking in Rome, published every year as the offshoot of the country's best gastronomic magazine. Good sections on food shops as well as restaurants, trattorias and pizzerias. Useful even if you don't read Italian.

Edible Italy, Valentina Harris, Ebury Press, 1988.
A mouth-watering guide to the food of Italy.

Italian Regional Cookery, Valentina Harris, BBC Books, 1990.
A great collection of authentic Italian recipes – though in Britain you'll need to hunt hard for some of the ingredients.

Getting it Right in Italy, William Ward, Bloomsbury, 1990.
At once street-wise and informed, this is not only invaluable if you're moving to Italy, but packed with pithy facts, surprising statistics and shrewd observations.

Novels, Travel Books, Short Stories

The City and the House, Natalia Ginzburg, Paladin, 1990.
Ginzburg at her best. A series of letters imperceptibly draws you into the insecurities of her characters and the poignant minutiae of their lives.

Family Sayings, Natalia Ginzburg, Paladin, 1986.
An autobiographical novel first published in 1963, this is a quirky, though sad, evocation of Jewish family life in Mussolini's Italy.

Woman at War, Dacia Maraini, Lighthouse Books, 1984.
A compelling record, in diary form, of a woman's increasing self-awareness. A rich book encompassing strange characters, political argument and a wonderfully evoked sensuality.

The Train, Dacia Maraini, Camden Press, 1989.
A sharp satire of student life in the sixties, following a group of friends on their way to an international socialist gathering in Finland.

The Silent Duchess, Dacia Maraini, Peter Owen, 1992.
This richly evocative story of Marianna, a highly intelligent deaf-mute duchess, is also a subtle description of – and commentary on – the social, political and intellectual life of upper-class Italian women – and men – in the Age of Enlightenment.

History, Elsa Morante, o/p, 1980.
Brilliant evocation of everyday life for a woman in Rome during World War II.

A Woman, Sibilla Alermo, Virago, 1979 o/p.
First published in 1906 – a classic story of a girl growing up, torn between her love for her father and her need to break away.

The Memoirs of Hadrian, Marguerite Yourcenar, Penguin, 1986.
A sombre, reflective novel, written as if by Hadrian as he approaches death. It can take some time to get into it (and it certainly isn't ideal holiday reading), but persevere: it's powerful.

Roman Fever, Edith Wharton, Virago, 1983.
Published in 1911, this is a stinging short story about two old American ladies in Rome, dangerously reminiscing about the past.

The Marble Faun, Nathaniel Hawthorne, Penguin, 1990.
Published in 1860, this quaint moralising novel about two women artists in Rome was described by American sculptor Anne Whitney as 'a detestable book'. It's actually quite a page-turner, and the risibly cardboard characters say much about the conventional nineteenth-century view of the ideal female.

Augustus, Allan Massie, Sceptre, 1986.
Tiberius, Allan Massie, Sceptre, 1990.
Massie knows his ancient history, and he's a talented, sensitive novelist as well. These two fake autobiographies, though perhaps rather more sympathetic to the two emperors than they deserve, make them – and their wives and families – come alive.

I Claudius and *Claudius the God*, Robert Graves, Penguin, 1986 (First published 1934).
Damning portraits of most of the Imperial women (though Livia is almost sympathetic) and some turgid political passages. But it *does* put flesh on the bones of history. Massie is better, though.

Vendetta, Michael Dibdin, Faber & Faber, 1990.
An excellent thriller set in a deftly evoked contemporary Rome.

A Time in Rome, Elizabeth Bowen, o/p, 1960.
A personal and disarmingly unintellectual response to the city, which will appeal mostly to dedicated Bowen fans.

aedile	an official – one of whose main functions was to provide entertainment
amphora	a vase used for oil, wine and other liquids
apodyterium	the changing room in an ancient Roman baths
architrave	the lowest part of an entablature (see below)
atrium	a forecourt
attic	the top storey of a classical building
basilica	a rectangular hall (see also CHURCHES)
caldarium	the hot (usually steam) room in ancient Roman baths
cavea	the auditorium of an ancient theatre
cella	the sanctuary of a temple
circus	a stadium (usually oval) used for chariot races
consul	the supreme political office in the Republic, held by two men for a period of a year. During the Empire, emperors often took the position themselves.
Corinthian	the most elaborate of the three Classical orders; the decoration on the capital is based on acanthus leaves
Doric	the plainest of the three Classical orders
entablature	the upper (horizontal) part of a Classical order, lying across the columns. It consists of three elements: the architrave, the frieze and the cornice
exedra	a semicircular recess
forum	an open space in a city – a place for markets, meetings or official buildings
freeborn	as it sounds, but usually refers to people of the lower class
freedwoman	a liberated slave-woman
frigidarium	the cold bath in an ancient baths
Hellenistic	refers to objects created in Greece from the mid fourth century BC to the death of Antony and Cleopatra; sculpture from this period is often exaggerated and mannered

household god	each Roman household was believed to be under the protection of a guardian spirit, or Lar, to whom they would erect a shrine and make sacrifices
insula	an ancient Roman apartment block
Ionic	the second Classical order; the most distinctive feature is the capital, with volutes (scrolls)
nymphaeum	a sort of ancient summerhouse, often with fountains
oinochoe	a wine jug
order	a column with base, shaft, capital and entablature
patrician	an aristocrat
peristyle	a courtyard or garden surrounded by a portico
plebeian	a non-aristocratic Roman citizen
pontifex maximus	chief priest
portico	a porch in front of a Classical building; also a covered walkway with a roof supported on columns or pillars
rostra	a podium from which speeches were given
Senate	the chief council of state; only men of property could become Senators
tepidarium	a room for warm baths in an ancient Roman baths
thermae	bath-house
triclinium	dining-room
triumphal arch	as it sounds – a ceremonial arch erected to commemorate a military victory
univira	a woman who had been married only once

Art and Architecture

abside	the apse – a semicircular recess at the back (usually east end) of a church
baldacchino	a canopy supported by columns, usually over an altar
Baroque	Refers to seventeenth- and early-eighteenth-century art and architecture. Characteristics of the architecture are exuberant decoration, voluptuous curves and a fondness for complex spaces. Artists described as Baroque are a mixed bunch; ranging from the realist

	Caravaggio to masters of illusionism like Lanfranco and Baciccia (a.k.a. Gaulli)
basilica	a church with aisles but no transepts
campanile	bell tower
capella	chapel
caryatid	a column in the form of a woman
cassetone	coffering (i.e. a panelled ceiling – usually wood or stucco)
chiesa	church
chiostro	cloister
confessio	the crypt below the high altar (usually contains the relics of a saint)
cortile	courtyard
Cosmati/cosmatesque	marble mosaic named for the Cosma family of medieval mosaic-makers
cupola	dome
escutcheon	a shield bearing a coat of arms
ex-voto	a thank-offering to a saint (often representing the part of the body the saint is believed to have cured
fresco	a wall-painting technique (the paint is applied to wet plaster)
Greek cross	a cross with equal-length arms
grotesque	weird miniatures – either painted or stuccoed – inspired by ancient Roman decorations discovered during the Renaissance in Nero's Golden House. Sphinxes, fantasy birds and animals, and flowers and foliage sprouting human heads are common motifs
icon	a painting of Christ, the Madonna or a saint on a wooden panel, deriving from Byzantine Greece
Latin cross	a cross with a long vertical arm
loggia	a covered gallery or balcony
Mannerism	used to refer to art and architecture from the mid to late sixteenth century; often characterised by playing games with Classical rules, by the exaggeration of form, and the diminished importance of content
matroneum	women's gallery – common in early churches
narthex	the vestibule of a church
palazzo	palace (also used for modern apartment blocks)

pediment	the gable above a portico; also a similar feature above a door or window
pietà	a representation of the Virgin with the dead Christ
pilaster	a flat, shallow column projecting just slightly from a wall
polyptych	a series of paintings on several adjoining wooden panels, usually with ornate gilded frames
porta	gate
presepio	Christmas crib
putto	cherub
reliquary	a usually elaborate container for a saint's bones; sometimes they take the form of the relic – arm- and hand-shaped reliquaries are common
Renaissance	used to refer to art and architecture between (roughly) 1420 and the mid sixteenth century; the term was used during the Renaissance itself to refer to the rediscovery of ancient Roman theories and motifs
stucco	plaster used for decorative work
tessera	the individual piece of a mosaic
torre	tower
transept	the arms of a church running north–south
travertine	the most common stone in Rome – cream, now usually speckled with dirt
triptych	painting on three adjoining wooden panels
trompe-l'œil	illusionistic
tufa	a dull porous stone much used in ancient Rome

General

belvedere	viewpoint
corso	avenue
festa	holiday (or party)
fontana	fountain
parco	park
piazza	square
piazzale	large piazza
via	street
vicolo	alley

Whenever possible Italians pronounce acronyms as if they were words. IVA is eeva, DC is deeechee; while members of the PDS become Pidiessini.

DC	Democrazia Cristiani (Christian Democrat Party)
EPT	Ente Provinciale di Turismo (Tourist Board)
IVA	VAT (Imposta Valore Aggiunto)
MSI	Movimento Sociale Italiano (Fascist Party)
PDS	Partito Democratico della Sinistra (former Communist Party)
PSI	Partito Socialista Italiano (Socialist Party)
RAI	Italian state broadcasting company
SIP	Italian state phone company

GLOSSARY

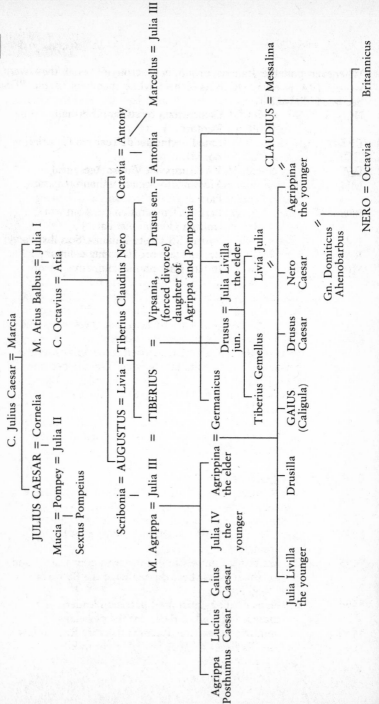

THE JULIAN HOUSE

* = Traditional Date

*8C BC	Rhea Silvia is raped by Mars. Romulus and Remus are thrown into the Tiber, then rescued and brought up by a she-wolf or prostitute.
*753 BC	Romulus kills Remus and founds Rome on the Palatine.
*750	Rape of the Sabine Women.
*747	Tarpeia opens Rome's gates to the Sabines. The Romans and Sabines fight until the women stop the battle. Peace is made, and the Romans and Sabines unite.
*715	King Numa Pompilius.
*673	King Tullius Hostilius. Celian Hill annexed to Rome.
*641	King Ancus Marcius. Aventine Hill annexed to Rome.
*616	The Etruscan Tarquin Priscus is elected king. Forum is drained and the Circus Maximus laid out.
*579	Tarquin is assassinated on the orders of Ancus's sons. His widow, Tanaquil, persuades the people to accept her son-in-law, Servius Tullius as king. Servius extends Rome and introduces the class system.
*534	Servius's daughter Tullia, married to Tarquin's son, persuades him to eliminate Servius. Tarquin becomes King Tarquin the Proud. Seats are installed in the Circus Maximus and the main drain, the Cloaca Maxima, is excavated.
*509	Tarquin's brother Sextus rapes Lucretia. She commits suicide and the Romans, led by her husband's friend Brutus, oust the Tarquins.

End of the Kingdom of Rome

*507	The Roman Republic is founded. Brutus and Lucretia's husband Collatinus are the first Consuls.
*506	Tarquins and Latins declare war on Rome. Cloelia taken hostage on the Janiculum and escapes by swimming across the Tiber.
*499	Thanks to the intervention of the twin gods Castor and Pollux, the Romans beat the Latins at the Battle of Lake Regillus.
*494	Plebeians revolt against their patrician leaders. A tribunate is founded to represent the plebeians.
*450	A committee of ten (the decemvirs) codify Roman law into the Twelve Tables. A father's right to kill a daughter for drinking or committing adultery is

enshrined and, because of a woman's *propter levitatem animi* (frivolity of the spirit), when her father dies she passes under the guardianship of a tutor.

*449	Verginia is stabbed to death by her father to keep her from the amorous clutches of the Decemvir Appius Claudius. The decemvirs are overthrown.
434	War against the Etruscans.
390	Gauls sack Rome. Women, children and armed men take refuge in the Capitol. Old people are left in the city.
264–241	First Punic War (against Carthage).
238	Rome annexes Sardinia and Corsica.
219–216	Second Punic War. Hannibal crosses the Alps. The Romans are heavily defeated at the Battle of Cannae and two Vestal Virgins, accused of taking lovers, are blamed and put to death.
212	Rome conquers Sicily.
202	Rome, under Scipio Africanus, conquers Carthage.
200–168	Conquest of Greece. Greek gods are introduced to Rome.
186	A thousand men and women are executed for immoral act during the Bacchanalia.
167	Booty and foreign slaves flood into Rome. Roman citizens no longer have to pay taxes, but many poor men and women are unemployed as their jobs are taken over by slaves.
149–146	Third Punic War. Carthage is razed to the ground.
133–121	Influenced by their mother, Cornelia, the Gracchus brothers attempt to introduce land reform and give citizenship to virtually all Italians. The aristocrats are furious, and the brothers and their followers are murdered.
112–104	North African War against Jugurtha. Jugurtha surrenders to the plebeian general Marius, creator of Rome's first professional army.
106	Birth of Cicero.
100	Birth of Julius Caesar.
92–89	The 'Social Wars' against former Italian allies who want independence. Rivalry develops between plebeian Marius and conservative Sulla.
86	Marius dies insane.
82–78	Sulla becomes dictator, passing laws to please the reactionary aristocrats and destroying the power of the people's tribune. An ugly, pocked, worm-ridden womaniser who was married five times, he dies in 78.

84	Birth of Catullus.
73	Revolt of Spartacus, leader of captive Gauls and Thracians. He is joined by slaves, herdsmen and shepherds, and they defeat the Romans four times. Pompey, helped by Crassus, eventually slaughters them on the Appian Way.
70	Pompey and Crassus are elected consuls. Virgil is born.
65	Julius Caesar is appointed aedile (in charge of entertainment).
63	Birth of Octavian (the future Augustus).
63	The Catiline Conspiracy. Cicero beats Catilina in the election for consuls. Catilina plans an insurrection and a coup, but conspirators are arrested and executed. Publius Clodius dresses as a woman and participates in the rites of Bona Dea, organised by Caesar's wife, Pompeiia. Caesar divorces Pompeiia and marries Calpurnia, whose father is soon to be Consul.
61	Clodia becomes Catullus's lover.
60–50	Caesar, Pompey and Crassus form the first triumvirate.
*59	Clodia chucks Catullus. Cicero accuses her of being a whore.
55	Caesar invades Britain.
53	Crassus defeated and killed by Parthians.
51	Caesar conquers Gaul.
50	Caesar crosses the Rubicon and seizes Rome.
48	Caesar defeats Pompey at Pharsalia and meets Cleopatra.
45	Caesar declared Imperator.
44	Caesar is assassinated by Brutus and Cassius.
43–32	Second triumvirate – Octavian, Mark Antony and Lepidus.
42	Battle of Philippi. Octavian defeats Brutus and Cassius, and they commit suicide.
39	Attempt to solve tension between Octavian and Mark Antony by marrying Antony to Octavian's sister, Octavia.
38	Augustus marries Livia.
36	Lepidus deposed.
32	Antony divorces Octavia.
31	Battle of Actium. Antony and Cleopatra commit suicide and Octavian becomes the sole ruler of the Empire. Octavia looks after Antony and Cleopatra's two children.
27	Octavian declared 'princeps' and changes his name to Augustus.

The Roman Empire

BACKGROUND

25	Augustus's daughter Julia marries Marcellus.
23	Marcellus dies.
21	Julia is married to Augustus's general, Agrippa.
*18	Morality laws introduced to stamp out adultery and increase the birth rate.
12	Agrippa dies.
11	Livia's son Tiberius is forced to divorce his wife Vipsania and marry Julia.
5	Julia is unfaithful. Tiberius, annoyed that Augustus intends to make one of her sons his successor, retires to Rhodes.
2	Julia is accused of making love on the Rostra, and banished to the island of Pandataria.

AD

2	Julia's son Lucius dies.
4	Julia's son Gaius dies. Tiberius is adopted as Augustus's successor.
14	Death of Augustus. Tiberius becomes emperor.
29	Death of Livia.
37	Tiberius dies. Caligula accedes to the throne. Commits incest with three sisters, and generally indulges in debaucheries and cruelty. Legalises the cult of Isis.
41	Caligula is assassinated. Claudius accedes. Two unsuccessful marriages are followed by a disastrous third – to Messalina. After she commits bigamy with a political enemy she is killed, and Claudius marries Agrippina the Younger. She persuades Claudius to adopt her son Nero as his heir.
54	Claudius dies after eating a plate of poisoned mushrooms – Agrippina was probably responsible. Nero becomes emperor, and eventually his mistress, Poppaea, persuades him to have Agrippina murdered. The first attempt – a collapsing boat designed to drown her – fails: she manages to swim to safety. But shortly afterwards she is stabbed.
64	Nero clears Rome's slums by setting fire to the city.
65	Nero begins the Golden House.
67	Saints Peter and Paul are martyred.
68	The Senate declare Nero a public enemy, and he kills himself. In the following year, there are four emperors. The last, Vespasian, remains on the throne.
70–76	The Colosseum is begun.
79	Vespasian dies and his son Titus becomes emperor.
81	Titus dies of fever. His brother Domitian becomes emperor, and begins to redesign the Palatine.

INDEX

Practical details such as opening hours, telephone numbers, transport details, prices, the standards in hotels and restaurants and popularity of certain bars and clubs are all liable to change. The guide will be constantly updated over the coming years, so please write in – we'll give free copies of this or any other Virago guide for the best letters. Address correspondence to:

Ros Belford
Virago Press Ltd
20–23 Mandela Street
Camden Town
London NW1 0HQ

Other Virago Woman's Travel Guides available:

PARIS

A city intent upon pleasure and revolution where spectacle has always reigned: George Sand, disguised as a man, roamed its *quartiers*; Colette wrote of its seductive charms, celebrated too in the lesbian salons and in the '*chanson realiste*' of Piaf. And in its intoxicating freedom Simone de Beauvoir electrified readers with *The Second Sex*.

NEW YORK

From the Statue of Liberty (from whose unveiling women were barred!) to seething go-go bars, from Red Emma Goldman to Guerrilla Girls and Lipstick Lesbians, from the hurly-burly of Broadway to Dorothy Parker's round table repartee at the Algonquin, the 'big apple' offers up its legendary contrasts of glamour and gaudiness.

Also of interest

ARE YOU TWO . . . TOGETHER?
A Gay and Lesbian Guide to Europe

Lindsy Van Gelder and Pamela Robin Brandt

'I hope Lindsy Van Gelder and Pamela Robin Brandt stay together
for eternity or at least long enough to cover the world'
– *Rita Mae Brown*

'I wish I'd travelled with Lindsy and Pam, who are funny, energetic,
cultured and curious' – *Edmund White*

Fourteen destinations, among them Amsterdam, Berlin,
Copenhagen, London, and Venice, of special interest to lesbians and
gay men, are engagingly and wittily explored in *Are You Two . . .
Together?* – a marvellous mix of historical detail, anecdote, practical
information, maps and recommendations of sights, hotels,
restaurants, bars and discos, and what to read.

You *won't* discover the opening times of the Louvre, but *will* get a
taste of the Paris salons of Gertrude Stein (tea the strongest drink)
and Natalie Barney (Mata Hari once rode in nude on a white horse),
the dream castles of Bavaria, and their creator King Ludwig,
defended against a charge of wickedness on the grounds that 'he
never even accompanied his soldiers, apart from on the piano'!

So either sit back and enjoy a bit of armchair travel or book your
tickets to Capri, the Loire, Wales, Sitges, Mykonos . . .